THE JOURNALS AND
LETTERS OF
FANNY BURNEY

CHARLES BURNEY, D.D.
From a portrait by Sir Thomas Lawrence

THE JOURNALS AND LETTERS OF

FANNY BURNEY

(MADAME D'ARBLAY)

❧❧

VOLUME III

GREAT BOOKHAM 1793–1797

LETTERS 122–250

❧❧

Edited by

JOYCE HEMLOW

with

PATRICIA BOUTILIER

and

ALTHEA DOUGLAS

OXFORD

AT THE CLARENDON PRESS

1973

Oxford University Press, Ely House, London W.1

GLASGOW NEW YORK TORONTO MELBOURNE WELLINGTON
CAPE TOWN IBADAN NAIROBI DAR ES SALAAM LUSAKA ADDIS ABABA
DELHI BOMBAY CALCUTTA MADRAS KARACHI LAHORE DACCA
KUALA LUMPUR SINGAPORE HONG KONG TOKYO

*Printed in Great Britain
at the University Press, Oxford
by Vivian Ridler
Printer to the University*

CONTENTS

LIST OF PLATES

JEAN-BAPTISTE-GABRIEL-BAZILLE (1745–1817)
Provisional genealogical table of his immediate family

BAZILLE
Jean-Baptiste-Gabriel
(1731 – 21 Jan. 1817)
conseiller du Roi
Maire nommé de Joigny
Député à l'Assemblie Constituante

m. 22 July 1766

Marie Edme Euphémie
DELAMARE
(bp. 20 Apr. 1745 – 21 Oct. 1803)

—Jean-Baptiste-Gabriel-Edme
  (23 June 1767 – 29 Sept. 1804)
  m. 16 Apr. 1793
  Marie-Julie RAGON DESFRINS
  (b. 1767 or 72 – Mar. 1840)

—Jean-Baptiste
  dit PRECOURT
  (bp. 18 Dec. 1768 – 23 Sept. 1808)
  commissaire des guerres

—Joseph-Baptiste Gabriel
  dit FRESNIERE
  (bp. 3 Jan. 1770 – d. 1795/6)
  m. 3 Mar. 1795 his cousin
  Magdelaine-Sophie BAZILLE du
  Villard
  (bp. 23 Aug. 1765 – 28 Aug. 1796)

—Edme
  (bp. 7 Mar. 1771)

—Marie-Euphémie-Claudine
  (bp. 8 Feb. 1772 – 12 Sept. 1833)
  m. 1794
  Pierre-Antoine MEIGNEN
  (d. 1827)
  wood merchant at Villevallier

—Pierre-Jean-Baptiste-Edme
  dit DELAMARE
  (bp. 12 Aug. 1775 – d. Mar. 1796)

Great Bookham,
30 August [1793]

To Doctor Burney

A.L.S. (rejected Diary MSS. 4864–[7], Barrett, Eg. 3690, ff. 49–50b),
30 Aug.
Double sheet 4to   4 pp.   *pmks* LEATHER / HEAD   4 SE 93   wafer
Addressed: Dr. Burney, / Chelsea College, / Midlesex.
Endorsed by CB: 1793
Edited by FBA, *retraced throughout, and* p. 1 (4864) *annotated and dated*: ·⊰·
1793 (6) Bookham—Lady Schaub—Miss Thrale   Gardening
Edited also by CFBt.

Bookham,
Augst 30th—

I have been longing to write to my dearest Father ever since I
last left Chelsea[1]—but I have wanted something for an opening
that he might not think a mere intrusion upon his time. Nothing,
however, will offer—I am tired of waiting—& must therefore
entreat my dearest Father to call to ⟨memory⟩ that former kind
patience which made him wish to ⌜hear from me whatever
dearth of matter robbed my letters of any other recommendation.⌝[2]

We did not get to our little Home[3]—after quitting you,—till
past Eleven o'clock, ⌜though we made no attempt to see dear
little Norbury,[4] & changed Horses at Epsom.⌝ You will perhaps
conclude we moved so slowly from our weight, & that M.
d'Arblay repented his '*Shakesperian eagerness*'—no such thing!
we had not got 20 yards, before he discovered that he could
admirably have brought my Toilette Table, which would have
stood before me *as a Desk*, on which *Boyer, Guthrie, your History,*

122. [1] The d'Arblays had gone *c.* 15 Aug. 1793 for a two-week visit to CB at
the Royal Hospital, Chelsea.
  [2] This letter, originally written in pale ink, was overwritten in later years
by FBA, with obliterations and editorial revisions. With the exception of a few
uncertain words the original has been deciphered as above. Her revised or overwritten version is given in the textual notes.
  [3] At the Hermitage (still so called) in Great Bookham.
  [4] Charles Norbury Phillips was attending his uncle's 'Academy' at Hammer-
smith.

Johnson's Lives,[5] ⌐& the favourite Books in my possession which he has heard me mention,¬ might most conveniently have been placed. Thus your plan of shewing Charles's cargoe proved rather an incentive than an intimation. He thinks Charles understands *packing up a Carriage* the best of ǀ any of the family.

You will have seen by the news papers that Mrs. Lock has lost her Mother.[6] ⌐This event hurried the Party from Cheltenham, & has confined them ever since their return.¬ Lady Shaub was 80—& had every tooth perfect, & white, & every faculty in full use; & died, finally, of a hurt she received from an accident!!——Mr. Lock thinks she would, else, certainly have lived to be 100.

We have not yet begun our *Maisonette* in Norbury Park: M. d'Arblay is his own Architect, & all his plans—which, literally, cannot be less than 100, from the time he first undertook drawing them—prove too expensive. He makes all possible retrenchments, but he cannot relinquish the little commodious *particularities* which make him desire to be his own Constructor; & these, our hum-drum surveyor,[7] who is affronted at being directed, assures him double the cost. How the matter will terminate I know not—but at present the contest is lively, & M. d'Arblay's want of language, & the man's want of ideas, render it, to me, extremely diverting.

⌐Our dearest Susanna has not been quite well ever since you saw her, but yesterday, when we dined with her, she looked abundantly better than I have seen her since she parted with her Norbury.¬

Mr. Cooke, our vicar, a very worthy man, & a goodish—though by ǀ no means a marvellously *rapid* Preacher—tells me he longs for nothing so much as a Conversation with Dr. Burney, upon the subject of Parish Psalm singing.—He com-

---

5 Probably Abel Boyer (see p. 150), *A French–English Dictionary* (1702) and ?William Guthrie, *A General History of England . . .* (4 vols., 1744–51), as well as Dr. Burney's *A General History of Music* (4 vols., 1776–89). For FB's presentation copies of *Prefaces to the Poets* (10 vols., 1779–81), see her letter of 16 Aug. 1780 (*DL* i. 443). Two of these volumes are preserved in the Hyde Collection.

6 *The Times* (30 Aug.) reported the death on 26 Aug. of Marguerite (de Ligonnier du Buisson) de Pesne (*c.* 1713–93), widow of Sir Luke Schaub (1690–1758), the diplomat. For a description of his career and his collection of paintings see Rudolf Massini, *Sir Luke Schaub* (Basel, 1953).

7 The local carpenter eventually engaged was Samuel Ockley or 'Oclee' (1749–1809), whose birth and death, as well as the births of his children, are recorded in the parish registers of Ashstead, Mickleham, and Dorking.

plains that the Methodists run away with the regular Congregations, from their superiority in Vocal devotion, & he wishes to remedy this evil by a little laudable emulation. ⌜He hopes extremely, he says, that when you come into Surry you will indulge him with a little advice & discourse.⌝ His Wife, Mrs. Cooke,[8] is a very sensible & benevolent woman, & excessively kind to me. All the Mickleham Neighbourhood are very civil; but I am desirous, for the present, to avoid any new acquaintance.

I have just had a very kind Letter from Miss Gomme,[9] which has given me great pleasure—but nothing amidst my congratulatory Letters,—has so much assailed me as the ready warmth of interest in my new situation which has been shewn me by *Miss Thrale*—whose general cold character seems, on this occasion, to have given way to one of the most zealous, & earnest affection—⌜with warmest offers to manifest it in any way I can point out[10]—⌝

M. d'Arblay has heard nothing of his Brother[11]—who is a determined Aristocrate,—which causes much dread for him. We see no News-paper—& though œconomy, not choice, keeps us thus stagnant of the World's Currents, we are probably much the happier for our ignorance,—all french intelligence depressing & rendering wretched whoever receives it—especially so severe a sufferer as M. d'Arblay.—He has just taken to *Gardening*,— | & with such violence of enthusiasm, that he could not believe himself susceptible of any fatigue, till the excessive exercise had almost demolished him. He had never had a spade in his Hand till yesterday—& I am sure he has worked harder in 5 or 6 Hours than any hired Labourer would have done in

---

[8] The Revd. Samuel Cooke (1741–1820), M.A. (Oxon., 1764), rector of Cotsford and vicar of the parish of St. Nicholas, Great Bookham (1769–1820), had married, 16 June 1768, Cassandra Leigh (1744–1826), daughter of Theophilus Leigh (1693–1785), Master of Balliol (1727 ff.). She was a first cousin of Jane Austen's mother Cassandra Leigh (1739–1827), who became, 26 Apr. 1764, the wife of the Revd. George Austen (1731–1805).

[9] This letter is missing.

[10] Preserved in a 'Scrapbook containing ms. material relating to Frances Burney d'Arblay and her family and friends' (Berg) is the A.L.S. from Hester Maria Thrale, dated Southampton, 12 Aug. 1793, offering her best wishes and those of her sisters. After deferring to FBA's judgement ('I have so long accustomed myself to think your Opinion on almost every Subject so invariably right . . .'), she referred to their friendship, requesting 'an Opportunity of proving mine to you'.

[11] François Piochard d'Arblay, Sʳ de Blécy (1756–95). It was not until August 1797 that M. d'A received news of his brother's death (see Ll. 245 and 246).

3 or 4 Days.—It is better, however, than incessant reading &
writing. He sat up till 1 or 2 o'clock in the Morning after our
return from Chelsea, to new arrange our Liliputian Library—
for which he has seized my Dining Table.—No great mischief!
for he can far better *cover* it than our Cook. Adieu, Dearest sir,—
will you forgive such a rustic Letter?—& indulge me, when you
have a moment to spare, with the sight of the least little line of
your beloved Hand?—no where—no where will—or *can* it be
more gratefully, more joyfully received than by your ever

dutiful & most affectionate
F. D'Arblay

M. d'Arblay begs his best Respects. We join in presenting
them to my Mother, ⌐who I hope continues in emended health
& when I can I will write to Mrs. Meeke.[12] James met us
yesterday at Susan's.⌐

[12] Mrs. Burney's daughter Elizabeth Allen (b. 1761), who, sent to Paris in 1775
to improve her education, had eloped to Ypres, where on 12 Oct. 1777 she
married Samuel Meeke (d. *c.* 1796), a native of London (see *HFB*, pp. 70–2, and
a certificate inserted in the parish registers of St. Margaret's, King's Lynn). Termed
by her family 'an adventurer', he may have been the 'Samuel Meeke of the Inner
Temple, Timber Merchant' who, having been sued by a member of the Allen
family, was involved in 1768–71 in a Chancery suit (PRO, C. 12/61/6). If so, it was
conjecturally the loss of the suit and consequent debts that forced him to live
abroad. 'Bessy', however, by all accounts blatantly unfaithful to her husband, often
turned up in England, and according to a letter from her sister Maria (Allen)
Rishton (Barrett, Eg. 3697, ff. 216–19b) to FBA, 12 [Aug. 1793], she was in King's
Lynn at this time: 'my Poor Unhappy Sister . . . has again Compleatly deceived us
. . . a tongue so inured to falsehood and a heart so Callous to the Agonising
Emotions she beheld in both my brother [the Revd. Stephen Allen] and my self
I could not have supposed a human being Capable of and yet I left her with my
heart quite at Ease that she was a sincere penitent'.

The most informative comment so far on record is that offered by the precocious
Norbury Phillips, aged 5, as he listened to the 'terrible stories of Mʳˢ Meeke'
related to his mother by Letty Brookes (SBP, Journal for 6 Mar. 1790, Berg) : '*What,*
did she go away from her husband with another *Gentleman!*—Why then I think She
was like *Queen Helen,* who was such a naughty Woman & *left Menelaus to go away
with Paris.*—'

By December 1796 'Bessy' had become a 'Mrs. Bruce', with an address, the
Post Office, Bristol; and here her skittish career seems to have come to an end. Mr.
Bruce, a widower, alleged to have married her for her money, kept her close,
depriving her of every comfort, until her death *c.* 1826. See *Catalogue* for A.L.S.
from SHB to her aunt Mrs. Young, 12 Dec. 1796; and A.L.S. from Cornelia Cambridge to CFBᵗ and CBFB, Oct. [1826].

123   Great Bookham, 16 September [1793]

To Doctor Burney
and Mrs. Burney

A.L.S. (rejected Diary MSS. 4870–[3], Berg), 16 Sept.
Double sheet 4to   4 pp.   *pmks* LEATHER / HEAD   19 SE 93   wafer
Addressed: Dr. Burney, / Chelsea College, / Midlesex.
Docketed by CB: 1793
Edited by FBA, p. 1 (4870), *annotated and dated*: ⋇ 1793 (7) Bookham
French affairs—Sir Lucas Pepys   Lady Rothes—

Monday, Sept. 16.
Bookham.

With what true happiness did I receive your Letter & most
kind parcel[1] my dearest dear Father!—We were fortunately at
Susan's when they arrived, yesterday Evening—I am sure your
whole Library from poor Mr. Hayes[2] gave you not HALF the
pleasure these 5 volumes gave *me*, *those* came with melancholy—
these, with every sensation that could most delight me. — — — I
am told, however, only to thank for *three* — — M. D'Arblay will
speak himself, he says, for his own property.—

How truly humane is the Plan for some further relief for the
voluntary Exiles & pious Martyrs of France![3]—Did ever any
Country, or any Time produce, in one & the same Nation,
before this period, contrasts so striking of consummate disinterested virtue, & attrocious, unheard of Guilt?—You must
never *Delvile*[4] occupation that has a tendency so good & kind as

123. [1] In a letter of 12 Sept. (Barrett, Eg. 3690, ff. 51–3), partly printed (*DL* v.
218–20), CB mentions sending an edition of Milton, a copy of *Rasselas*, and Philip
Miller, *A Gardener's Dictionary* (2 vols., 1731–9, but reprinted in nine or more
editions before 1793).
    [2] John Hayes (*c.* 1707–92) had bequeathed to CB 'all my Collection of Books
being in my Library in James Street aforesaid with the Book Cases therein and
likewise all my Manuscripts I also give unto him a Book of the prints of Houghton
Gallery and also such Medals and ancient Coin as shall be found in my said Library
at the time of my decease not otherwise by me disposed of' (P.C.C. Fountain 564,
proved 13 Nov. 1792). See also CB's will (Scholes, ii. 265).
    [3] CB had become honorary secretary to the Society of Ladies, which, led by Mrs.
Crewe and the Marchioness (later the Duchess) of Buckingham, was attempting
to raise additional moneys for the relief of the French Clergy (*Memoirs*, iii. 184–7).
For Mrs. Crewe's concern, see CB's letter (op. cit.).
    [4] CB sometimes punned on the name and ostentatiously 'busy' character of the
elder Delvile of FB's novel *Cecilia*. See his letter, op. cit.: 'this [*secretaryship* (above)]'

5

working for such Subjects. I hardly know how to wish you rest when such is your labour. What a truly good & benevolent Heart is Mrs. Crewe's! one would think it formed with the same partial perfection as her outside.

The plan is so simple I should never have suspected its author, though all the circumstances of its benignity would ¹ have led me to a fair surmize.—May every possible success attend it, & recompence your exertions, my beloved Father.

Our Gardening Hobby-Horse has given way, of late, to a literary Courser—how long that will run I know not;—but if the Race will continue thus alternately mental & corporal, I can have no wish, & no fear, each rectifying whatever in either may be excessive.

Lady Rothes & Sir Lucas Pepys have just settled themselves in the remainder of the Summer at Juniper Hall,⁵ where M. D'Arblay resided till the end of last July. Sir Lucas made us *his first visit in this neighbourhood*, with great kindness: & Lady Rothes came to me the next Day. Yesterday we returned them our thanks, & spent a very pleasant Hour with them. Sir Lucas tells me he has almost resided at Windsor wholly of late,—but not for the King, whom he never knew better. This was a true joy to me to hear, as I am sure his Mind must suffer eternal agitation, from his various parental fears, now for his people—now for his sons.⁶—O I am sure he must sometimes be torn to pieces! —I can never think either of him or of the Queen but with the deepest concern.—Unhappily, M. D'Arblay immediately, & with a Heart-felt sigh, declared he concurred in your sentiment 'that ¹ no Man alive, with a grain of Modesty, would venture to predict how, or when, the evils *of these times* may end!'—Yet he is much pleased with the affair of Toulon⁷—more from its example, than from any permanent good in itself.

has *Delviled* me not a little.' He had opened his letter with the 'parading' apologies which FB had given to the elder Delvile (*Cecilia*, bk. iii, chap. ii).

⁵ According to the Land Tax Assessments (Surrey County Record Office, Kingston upon Thames), Sir Lucas Pepys rented Juniper Hill from David Jenkinson in the years 1795–6 and in 1797 became the owner. Apparently he had first rented Juniper Hall.

⁶ Three of the King's sons, the Duke of York, Prince Ernest, and Prince Adolphus, were engaged in the wars on the continent.

⁷ The Royalists of Toulon, in rebellion against the Convention, had offered on 29 August to open the Port to the British Navy. Lord Hood's preliminary declaration, dated 23 Aug., had offered protection and assistance if among other conditions 'a candid and explicit declaration in favour of monarchy is made at Toulon and

Your care, & the *dear* DO Dr. James, my dearest Sir, I hope
has fully answered—I shall long for certain communication 'or
any other reason' for again delighting my Eyes with your most
loved Hand. I say nothing for Susanna, as she writes for herself.

I have had very kind words from M^e De La Fîte since my
last: Miss Planta,[8] in her second Letter, expresses warm hopes
M. D'Arblay will settle finally & wholly in England, & says—
'it is with the Wretches of France we are at War—nothing could
be more unjust than to extend our prejudices against their
victims.—' a sentiment that, *from* HER, & dated *Queen's Lodge*,
assures me my connection with a nobly suffering Loyalist is
rightly understood where most anxiously I should fear any
misapprehension. I am sorry for the difficulties of poor Mrs.
Char. Smith's Daughter[9]—I *must* spare room for my thanks to
my Mother or I should chat on—on—and on—Dearest—dear
—dear Sir Adieu! Most dutifully

& fervently your F. D'A. [1]

I beg my kindest Love to my dear Sarah—*horrours accumulate*
of Letter Writing alone keep me silent to her,—*till I hear again*—
& then I promise a very handsome Epistle.—She told Me, too,
she had something to amuse me—which I wait for.

I rejoice you have so much to do with Mr. Windham.

I forget if I told you, that after seizing my Dining Table,
for Books, Globes, Music Desk, Mandoline, & Writing implements,—& then re-placing it with another—M. D'Arblay has
now seized the *re-placement*?—& left me only the little Tea
Table?—Which however, lamentation apart, proves sufficiently

Marseilles, and the standard of royalty hoisted'. When Toulon complied with the
terms and proclaimed Louis XVII King, Lord Hood issued a second proclamation,
dated 28 Aug., agreeing to 'take possession of Toulon, and hold it in trust only for
Louis XVII until peace shall be re-established in France'. The documents are
printed in *AR* xxxv (1793), 'Chronicle', 171–3.

[8] See i, L. 23 n. 56; i, L. 3 n. 2. These letters are missing.

[9] Charlotte Smith's second daughter, Anna Augusta (1774–95), had married
on 12 Aug. 1793 in the parish church of Storrington, near Petworth, Sussex,
the French *émigré* Alexandre-Marc Constant de Faville, chevalier de St. Lazare
(born *c.* 1763). When the couple were unable to find a Catholic priest willing to
perform a second ceremony that would make the marriage 'binding according to
the Laws of France', Charlotte Smith addressed CB as the parent of a daughter who
had been married in the Chapel of the Sardinian Ambassador 'to beg . . . directions'
how the marriage of *her* daughter might likewise be 'a second time performed by
a Catholic Minister'. For the difficulties encountered, objections raised, etc., see
three letters 13 Aug., ⟨21⟩ Aug. *pmk* 22 AU, and 15 Oct. 1793 (Osborn) and CB's
reply to the first letter (Comyn), 19 Aug. 1793.

spacious! I did not tell you *We are a famous* Mandoline Player!
' '*PON my Word* !'—

Mrs. Lock's Mother, Lady Schaub, who is just Dead at 82
had all her Teeth perfect, & of the most brilliant Juvenile
whiteness!— [1]

[To] Mrs. Burney.

Your Letter was peculiarly kind, Dear Madam, in being
written after my dear Father's recovery from the attack he had
just mentioned—a circumstance to lighten all its other melancholy tydings, though by no means to make me read them unmoved. I am very sorry for Mrs. Styleman[10]—& I grieve to see
your fears for poor Mrs. Hoole.[11] I had heard from Mrs. Cooke,
here, who is acquainted with her, that she was better. I am truly
concerned at the mistake. I hope the next budget from India
will be kinder. I should like to write there, if I knew how. The
Sorcier [1] desires his best Respects. He studies English hard against
his next meeting: which we hope will be ere long at Mickleham.
I am sorry for poor little Bungay.[12] I fear my good old friend Mr.
Hutton imagines me *a mere poor miserable Dupe, taken in by an artful
French avanturier,* as he has not sent me one word of congratulation or good will.—If he thinks so, it is *he,*—Heaven be praised!
—is the Dupe!—which I bear with great philosophy, if one of
us must be Dupe. I am very sorry he is so indifferent—& his
worthy friend Mrs. Scott.[13] I had a letter from Mrs. ord[14]
t'other Day, who is well—adieu, Dear Madam,

most sincerely & respectfully yours
F D A

[10] Catharine Henley (*c.* 1724–93), the daughter of Henry Holt Henley (d. 1748)
of Leigh, Somersetshire, had married 9 June 1752 Nicolas Styleman (1721–88) of
Snettisham Hall, a Justice of the Peace, and in the year 1776, High Sheriff of
Norfolk. A great wastrel, his career is outlined in the MS. (County Record Office,
Norwich), 'Memories of Armine' (1909–10) by Jamesina Waller. Mrs. Styleman,
'relict of the late Nicolas Styleman, Esq', had died suddenly at Snettisham on 22
Aug. 1793 (*Norfolk Chronicle* . . ., 31 Aug. 1793). The M.I.'s are, of course, in the
parish church.

[11] Elizabeth Young (1768–94), Arthur Young's daughter and Mrs. Burney's
niece, had married in 1791 the Revd. Samuel Hoole (*c.* 1758–1839). She was to die
of consumption at Abinger, Surrey, 1 Aug. 1794 (*GM* lxiv. 769).

[12] Unidentified, though the family name appears in the parish registers of King's
Lynn as early as 1646.

[13] The younger sister of Mrs. Montagu, Sarah Robinson (1723–95), who had
married in 1751 George L. Scott (1708–80), from whom she separated permanently
in 1752. Lately in failing health, she was to die at Catton near Norwich on 3 Nov.
1795.   [14] See i, L. 1 n. 8.

124   [Great Bookham, 19 September] 1793

To Mrs. Waddington

A.L. signature cut out (Diary MSS. vi. 4808–[11], Berg), 1793
Double sheet 4to   4 pp.   *pmks* LEATHER / HEAD   19 [S]E 93   wafer
Addressed: Mrs. Waddington, / Lanover Court, / Abergavenny, / Monmouthshire.
Edited by CFBt *and the* Press.

1793

The account of your surprise, my sweet Friend,[1] was the last
thing to create mine: I was well aware of general astonishment,
—& of yours in particular.—My own, however, at my very
extraordinary fate is singly greater than that of all my Friends
united. I had never made any vow against Marriage, but I
had LONG—LONG been firmly persuaded it was—*for ME*—a state
of too much hazard, & too little promise, to draw me from my
individual plans & purposes. I remember, in playing at Questions & Commands, when I was thirteen, being asked *When I
intended to Marry?*— —& surprising my playmates by solemnly
replying 'When I think I shall be happier than I am in being
single.—' It is true, I imagined that time would never arrive; &
I have pertinaciously adhered to trying no experiment upon any
other hope—for many & mixed as are the ingredients which
form what is generally considered as happiness, I was always
fully convinced that Social Simpathy of character & taste could
alone have any chance with *me*. All else I *always* thought—&
now KNOW to be immaterial. I have only This peculiar—that
what many contentedly assert, or adopt, in Theory—I have
had the courage to be guided by in practice.
   We are now removed to a very small House[2] in the *suburbs* of

124. ¹ GMAPW's letters were returned to her in 1821.
   ² Later called 'The Hermitage', the messuage (a garden, small orchard, and
house, to which an ell was subsequently added) is at present the property of Mr.
Robert D. C. Emus of Great Bookham. Formerly part of the Manor of Eastwick
and called variously Fairfield Place, Fair Plot, or the Pound Piece Plot, it belonged
in the time of the d'Arblays to Catherine Bailey, *née* Shelley (*c.* 1741–1820), the
widow of John Bailey (d. 1790), a churchwarden in the 1770s at least and a considerable citizen of Great Bookham, as his widow continued to be. The Land Tax
Assessments (Surrey County Record Office, Kingston upon Thames) show the
widow Bailey to have been the owner of two dwelling houses, one of which (inherited from her family) she occupied; the house above she rented to various ten-
ants in the years 1791–1813, when it passed into other hands. The records for 1794

a very small village, called Bookham. We found it rather inconvenient to reside in another person's Dwelling, though our own Apartments were to ourselves. our views are not | so beautiful as from Phenice Farm,[3] but our situation is totally free from neighbours & intrusion. We are about a Mile & an half from Norbury Park, & 2 miles from Mickleham. I am become already so stout a Walker, by use, & with the help of a very able supporter, that I go to those places & return Home, on foot, without fatigue, when the Weather is kind.—At other times, I condescend to accept a Carriage from Mr. Lock; but it is always reluctantly, I so much prefer walking, where, as here, the Country & Prospects are inviting.

I thank you for your caution about building: we shall certainly undertake nothing but by contract: however, it would be truly mortifying to give up a House in Norbury Park; We defer the structure till the Spring, as it is to be so very slight, that Mr. Lock says it will be best to have it hardened in its first stage by the summer's sun. It will be *very* small,—merely an Habitation for Three people, but in a situation truly beautiful,[4] & within 5 minutes of either Mr. Lock or my Sister Phillips. It is to be placed just between those two loved Houses.

My dearest Father, whose fears & draw backs have been my sole subject of regret, begins now to see I have not judged rashly, or with romance, in seeing my own road to my own felicity. And his restored chearful concurrence in | my ⟨everlasting⟩ & *constant principles*, though new station, leaves me, for myself, without a wish. *L'Ennui*, which could alone infest our retreat, I have ever been a stranger to, except in tiresome company—& my Companion has every possible resource against either feeling or inspiring it.

As my Partner is a *French man*, I conclude the wonder raised by the connection may spread beyond my own private circle: but no wonder upon Earth can ever arrive near my own in having found such a Character from that Nation.—This is a prejudice certainly impertinent & very John Bullish, & very arrogant; but I only share it with all my Country men, &

are missing but 'Dalminee' appeared as occupier in 1795 and 'D'Aloninee' in 1796. It was probably in the latter part of August 1793, however, that the d'Arblays moved in from Phenice Farm (ii, L. 120 n. 6).

3 Ibid.

4 The habitation in West Humble was not built until 1796–7.

therefore—must needs forgive both them & myself!—I am convinced, however, from your tender solicitude for me in all ways, that you will be glad to hear that *The Queen & all the Royal Family* have deigned to send me wishes for my [hap]piness, through Mrs. Schwellenberg, who has written me *wha[t y]ou call* a very kind congratulation.[5]

I long much for news of your being recovered from that terrible sickly state, my dearest Marianne—Pray let me, if possible, hear a better account soon. Surely that cruel state cannot last[6]—You were quite right in conjecturing I *wrote*,[7]— certainly I could not have *spoken* to the Q[ueen]—on such a subject, had the person in question been of her own Court & first favour: however, ǀ before any engagement had passed between us—I had previously paved the way, by saying to her one M[orning] That I should cease to think Honour & integrity existed in the World, if ever I lost my opinion of their residing in M. D'Arblay.—This was too strong an assertion to be easily forgotten. I had already told his story & situation.

I find my excellent Friends the Locks met with Mr. Bernard Dewes & his lovely Daughter at Cheltenham.[8]—

Mrs. Lock & her fair Daughters charge me with their most kind Compliments—& my sister Phillips with hers—& her Love to boot, if you will accept it. Your Note was perfect in its kind & Mrs. Lock means to write in one of my Letters—This is too full, but the next I will keep in order.

Pray give my Comp^{ts} to Mr. Waddington. I have shewn your sweet little miniature[9] to M. d'Arblay, who is impatient to see

---

[5] The letter (in the hand of an amanuensis), dated Windsor, 3 Aug. 1793, is preserved in a grangerized edition of the *Diary and Letters*, v, pt. ii, 206 (NPG): 'Her Majesty and all the Royal Family wish you happiness, but none more so—than Madam / yours affectionately / E. Schwellenberg.'

[6] GMAPW was again pregnant (see L. 129).

[7] With respect to her engagement to d'Arblay.

[8] Bernard Dewes (*c.* 1743–1822), GMAPW's uncle, had married in 1777 as his first wife Anne De la Bere (d. 1780). Their daughter Anne would be about 15 years old.

[9] FBA had apparently possessed two miniatures of Mrs. Waddington. In 1840 FBA's niece and executrice Charlotte Barrett sent one of the miniatures to Mrs. Waddington's daughter Mrs. Bunsen. In extant letters of gratitude, dated 30 Mar. 1840 and 8 Sept. 1842 (Berg), Mrs. Bunsen states that the miniature of her mother (the one returned to her) was painted, as FBA later states, by Mrs. Delany. The second miniature, according to the above letters, was a gift to FBA from Mrs. Waddington's father John Port of Ilam (*c.* 1736–1807). Described (loc. cit.) as 'out of powder, in a blue gown, & more than a profile', it can be seen in the Berg Collection of the New York Public Library.

the original, & continually regrets having missed you that Evening at Mr. Lock's, when we drank Tea there together. He was in the very next Room,—much disordered by some adverse circumstances, which menaced a further procrastination of our Adventures than he could then see the end of, & he knew not who was the party so near him, & was too melancholy to join in any.—Shall you come to Town next Spring?—You MUST make Bookham a long Airing some Morning in that Case—We have no Beds, alas!—but open arms to my Marianne—ever & ever.

Pray kiss your lovely little ones in my Name—which I wi[ll] write *very* legibly in signing my self ⟨M⟩y Dear Marianne's

very & ev[er fai]thfully affectionate

Direct still the same,

the postman comes on hither.   [*signature cut away*]

125   [Great Bookham, *c.* 26 September 1793]

To M. d'Arblay

A.L.S. (Berg), *n.d.*
Single sheet 4to   2 pp.   (7·8 × 6·3″)
Edited by FBA, p. 1, *annotated and dated*: ✲   *Bookham* 1793   (I)   (1)
Written to the bravest, yet tenderest of Men on his project to join the Royal Army collecting at Toulon, a few months after our happy—happy marriage—

Do not be astonished at my consternation—nor attribute it wholly to weakness—I had deceived myself into a belief that the Profession of blood was wholly relinquished—I had understood you that you had satisfied yourself, & might now, with a safe conscience, retire from public life.—If this had been my belief before I belonged to you—before I had experienced that perfect felicity which I hardly thought mortal, but which you have given to my existence — — — Judge the bitterness of my disappointment at this juncture!—

I know—& acknowledge the force of what you urge, but the strength of your arguments, however they may carry conviction to the judgement,—offer no peace, no consolation to a stroke so unexpected—

Nevertheless—I cannot endure that the tenderness of your Nature should be at variance with the severe calls of your Honour—You have generously said you would take no step without my consent—My Tongue REFUSES to pronounce it— but my Pen shall write it—Take it then,—my sad—but full— CONSENT—which however reluctantly given I will never torment you with calling back —— *Do whatever you think right*—& only join in my prayer That Heaven may preserve to me the Husband of my Heart!—

F·A·D

F·A·D ^I

I promise you shall find me better when you come Home—but *pray* show this to nobody.—

126 Great Bookham, 29 September 1793

To Doctor Burney

L.S., 29 Sept. 1793, printed in *DL* (1842–6), vi. 5–8, *c.* 3 printed pages.

Bookham, September 29th, 1793.

When I received the last letter[1] of my dearest father, and for some hours after, I was the happiest of all human beings. I make no exception, for I think none possible: not a wish remained to me; not a thought of forming one.

This was just the period—is it not always so?—for a blow of sorrow to reverse the whole scene: accordingly, that evening M. d'Arblay communicated to me his desire of going to Toulon.

He had intended retiring from public life: his services and his sufferings in his severe and long career, repaid by exile and

126. [1] This is the A.L.S. (Osborn), 25–[6] Sept. 1793, that CB himself had termed 'a letter made up of crumbs from rich folks' table', that is, compliments and good wishes for the d'Arblays as excerpted from letters he had recently received from Mrs. Crewe, Burke and Mrs. Burke, among which was the A.L.S. (Comyn), Burke to CB, 15 Sept. 1793, subsequently printed in part in *Juniper Hall*, pp. 181–3. 'As they will be crumbs of some comfort to you, & perhaps not unpleasant to M. D'Arblay, I transcribe', said CB, 'with pleasure.' FBA so valued the excerpts as to print them in *Memoirs* (iii. 182–4), and the 'personal kindness' of the Burkes upon her marriage did much, she there recorded, to reconcile CB to it, 'new stringing his hopes, and lightening his anxieties'.

confiscation, and for ever embittered to his memory by the murder of his Sovereign, had justly satisfied the claims of his conscience and honour; and led him, without a single self-reproach, to seek a quiet retreat in domestic society: but the second declaration of Lord Hood[2] no sooner reached this little obscure dwelling,—no sooner had he read the words Louis XVII. and the Constitution to which he had sworn united, than his military ardour rekindled, his loyalty was all up in arms, and every sense of duty carried him back to wars and dangers.

I dare not speak of myself, except to say that I have forborne to oppose him with a single solicitation: all the felicity of this our chosen and loved retirement would effectually be annulled by the smallest suspicion that it was enjoyed at the expense of any duty; and therefore, since he is persuaded it is right to go, I acquiesce.

He is now writing an offer of his services, which I am to convey to Windsor, and which he means to convey himself to Mr. Pitt. As I am sure it will interest my dear father, I will copy it for him.[3]

This total break into all my tranquillity incapacitates me from attempting at this moment to compose any address for the poor suffering clergy;[4] but, as nothing could give me greater comfort than contributing the smallest mite in their favour, I beseech my dear father to let me know in what manner I should try—whether as a letter, and to whom; or how: besides, I know

[2] The first clause of the Declaration of Toulon (*c.* 25 Aug. 1793) expressed 'the unanimous wish of the inhabitants . . . to adopt a monarchic government, such as it was originally by the constituent assembly of 1789'. Lord Hood's second Proclamation (28 Aug. 1793) promised support of 'a monarchy . . . as accepted by their late sovereign in 1789'. See *AR* xxxv (1793), 'State Papers', 172–3; and L. 123 n. 7.

[3] This document is missing. In *Memoirs*, iii. 190, FBA stated that 'before the answer of Mr. Pitt to the memorial could be returned, the attempt at Toulon proved abortive'. The possibility of 'encouraging corps of emigrés to serve in the Vendée and other parts of France hostile to the National Convention' was debated in the House on second and third readings on 11 and 17 Apr. 1793. See also Secretary Dundas's letter to the King, 26 Oct. 1793, *Later Corr. Geo. III*, ii. 113.

[4] FBA was about to write *Brief | Reflections | relative to the | Emigrant French Clergy: | earnestly submitted | to the Humane Consideration | of the | Ladies of Great Britain.*

As CB reported in his letter of 25–[6] Sept. (Osborn), Mrs. Crewe had commissioned him to beg both Hannah More and FBA to write in support of her charitable plan. 'People only see the *coarse vulgar* side of *this business*—& some good female writer w^d do well to put out some short essays to throw good colouring on such a subject, & bring *precedents*, if possible, out of the age of chivalry.'

Hannah More donated to the cause the profits of her *Remarks on the Speech of M. Dupont* . . . (published 1 Apr. 1793; 2nd ed., 20 Apr.). The pamphlet, selling at 2*s.* 6*d.*, netted £250.

so little what has already been said,[5] that I am at a loss where to look, or where to shun; yet I would gladly make any experiment in my possible power, and M. d'Arblay particularly wishes it.

How flattering and kind Mrs. Crewe![6] and how delightful to me what is said by Mr. Burke! I entreat you to take the first opportunity to thank them warmly, and to assure them their kindness of remembrance is a true joy to me, and to return my most grateful thanks to the very amiable Mrs. Burke.

I have had congratulatory letters every day this week.

Miss Ellerker[7] has written, and begs to be introduced to M. d'Arblay. Are we not coming into high fashion?

Ah! if peace would come without, what could equal my peace within?

Let me not forget to say that even M. De Luc sends me his felicitations, in an ardent letter of friendly kindness written by his excellent wife,[8] and his joy for M. d'Arblay in the late affair of Toulon and acknowledgment of the Constitution.

My dearest father, before this tremendous project broke into our domestic economy, M. d'Arblay had been employed in a little composition, which, being all in his power, he destined to lay at your feet, as a mark of his pleasure in your attention to

[5] Previously printed were Burke's appeal entitled 'Case of the Suffering Clergy of France' (*The Times*, 18 Sept. 1792); and, prefaced to Hannah More's work of April 1793 (above), 'A Prefatory Address to the Ladies, &c. of Great Britain, in behalf of the French Emigrant Clergy'. In a laudatory poem *The Emigrants*, the dedication of which was dated 10 May 1793, Charlotte Smith depicted the landing of the French fugitives at Brighton.

Previously printed also were sermons on the subject by such preachers as James Chelsum (1738–1801), Walker King (*c.* 1752–1827), James Scott (1733–1814), Francis Wollaston (1731–1815), and George Henry Glasse (1761–1809), some of which had been delivered on 2 June 1793, the day appointed for the reading of His Majesty's Letter on behalf of a Collection for the French Clergy. In an Appendix to a Sermon preached on 26 Oct. 1793, Thomas Rennell (1754–1840), then Prebendary of Winchester, paid homage to the 600 'persecuted Martyrs' who were given shelter in the King's House at Winchester. Despite this encouragement 'A Village Curate' (*GM* lxiii (1793), 508–9) found cause to complain of the hostile and prejudiced reception given to his efforts to collect for Frenchmen and Roman Catholics.

[6] Though Mrs. Crewe praised Hannah More's 'right notion of . . . modesty' and her Preface as '*elegant & delicate*', she would nevertheless fix upon Madame d'Arblay 'for *such an address* as might please all the world ab^t the *female character*'. 'There! put that in your pocket', added CB (loc. cit.).

[7] Elizabeth Mainwaring Ellerker (1751–1831), eldest daughter of Eaton Mainwaring Ellerker (*c.* 1722–71) of Risby Park, Yorkshire and sister of Lady Leicester (iv, L. 337 n. 16). FB had known the Ellerker sisters since 1782 (*DL* ii. 114).

[8] Margaret Cooper (d. 1806) had married in 1785 Jean André de Luc (i, L. 3 n. 3). Her letter is missing.

his horticultural pursuit. He has just finished copying it for you, and to-morrow it goes by the stage.⁹

Your hint of a book from time to time enchanted him: it seems to me the only present he accepts entirely without pain. He has just requested me to return to Mrs. Lock herself a *cadeau* she had brought us. If it had been an old court-calendar, or an almanac, or anything in the shape of a brochure, he would have received it with his best bow and smile.

This Toulon business finally determines our deferring the maisonette till the spring. Heaven grant it may be deferred no longer! Mr. Lock says it will be nearly as soon ready as if begun in the autumn, for it will be better to have it aired and inhabited before the winter seizes it. If the *mémoire* which M. d'Arblay is now writing is finished in time, it shall accompany the little packet; if not, we will send it by the first opportunity.⁹

Meanwhile, M. d'Arblay makes a point of our indulging ourselves with the gratification of subscribing one guinea to your fund, and Mrs. Lock begs you will trust her and insert her subscription in your list, and Miss Lock and Miss Amelia Lock. Mr. Lock is charmed with your plan. M. d'Arblay means to obtain you Lady Burrel¹⁰ and Mrs. Benn.¹¹ If you think I can write to any purpose, tell me a little hint how and of what, dearest sir; for I am in the dark as to what may remain yet unsaid. Otherwise, heavy as is my heart just now, I could work for them and your plan.

Adieu, dearest, dearest sir: ever and ever most affectionately, most dutifully yours,

F. D'A.

⁹ As is indicated by CB's acknowledgement of the gift in his letter (Berg) of 4 Oct. 1793, the 'composition' was M. d'A's translation of FB's poem 'Willy' (i, L. 8 n. 5).

¹⁰ Sophia Raymond (1750–1802) married in 1773 William Burrell (1732–96), LL.D. (1760), 2nd baronet (1789). A poetess and dramatist, she published two volumes of amusing occasional verse (1793), *Telemachus* (1794), and *Theodora, or the Spanish Daughter; a Tragedy* (1800). The Burrells lived at Deepdene, Holmwood.

¹¹ Margaret Fowke (*c.* 1758–1836) had married in 1778 John Benn (1759–1825), who on 11 Apr. 1795 assumed by Royal License the name Benn-Walsh, cr. Baronet (1804). The Benns lived at Leatherhead.

127   [Great Bookham, 20 October 1793]

To Doctor Burney

A.L. (Diary MSS. vi. 4824–[5], Berg), *n.d.*
Single sheet 4to 2 pp.
Edited by FBA, p. 1 (4824), annotated and dated (probably from pmk on a cover since discarded): ⁝⁝⁝ 21 Oct. 1793 (9) F.d'A's. Tract for the Emigrant Priests Now written & preparing for the Press.
Edited also by CFBt and the Press.

Sunday Noon
[20 Oct. 1793]

My dearest Father will think I have been very long in doing the little I have done,—but my mind is so anxiously discomfitted by the continued suspence with regard to M. D'Arblay's proposition & wish—that it has not been easy to me to weigh completely all I could say—& the fear of repeating what has already been offered upon the subject, has much restrained me, for I have seen none of the Tracts that may have appeared.[1] However, it is a matter truly near my Heart, & though I have not done it rapidly, I have done it with my whole Mind, &— to own the truth, with a species of emotion, that has greatly affected me, for I could not deeply consider the situation of these venerable Men without feeling for them to the quick. If what I have written should have power to procure them *one more guinea*, I shall be paid.

I shall send the scrawl to you by the stage on *Tuesday*.[2] I have still to Copy it.,—& But I have the pleasure to give you another Subscriber, *Mrs. Hume*,[3] a Lady who has listened to the eloquence of Mrs. Lock, who never sees any one without producing the Plan. Mrs. Lock | begs you to trust her for the guinea. Mr. Lock enters into this business with the warmest approbation.

If you think what I have drawn up worth printing, I should suppose it might make a little 6ᵈ paper, to be sold for the same

127. [1] See L. 126 n. 5.   [2] On 22 Oct.
[3] Elizabeth Blaquier (d. 25 Aug. 1825), who had married in 1787 the Revd. Dr. Travers Hume (d. 18 July 1805), Dublin, rector (1785–1805) of Glassnevin and Ardee. A niece and heiress of Lord Macartney (1737–1806), Mrs. Hume was probably visiting Lady Macartney at Packhurst, Abinger Common.

purpose it is written.⁴ Or will it only do to be printed by the expence of the acting Ladies, & given Gratis? You must judge of this.

My duty & Love to my Mother & Sarah—I will now go & Copy with all my Might, as it must go to-morrow to Mickleham to be ready for the stage. We have here neither stage nor post.

Adieu, ever most & most dear Sir!—

M. D'Arblay charges me with his best Respects.

128   Great Bookham, 27 October [1793]

To Doctor Burney

A.L. (Diary MSS. vi. 4806–[7], Berg), 27 Oct.
Originally a double sheet 4to, of which FBA later discarded the second leaf   2 pp.
Edited by FBA, p. 1 (4806), *annotated and dated*: ⁜ 1793   (11) Barbarous Execution of the Queen of France Marie Antoinette
Edited also by CFBt *and the* Press.

Bookham,
Octʳ 27ᵗʰ

My most dear Father,

The terrible confirmation of this last act of savage hardness of Heart has wholly overset us again¹—M. D'Arblay had entirely discredited its probability, &, to the last moment, disbelieved the report: not from milder thoughts of the barbarous Rulers of his unhappy Country, but from seeing that the Death of the Queen could answer *no* purpose, helpless as she was to injure them, while her life *might* answer some, as an hostage with the Emperor. Cruelty, however, such as theirs, seems to require no incitement whatever; its own horrible exercise appears sufficient

⁴ FBA's pamphlet, eventually published by Thomas Cadell, in the Strand, on 19 Nov. 1793, comprised 27 pages in a blue paper wrapper and sold for 'one Shilling and Sixpence'. Inscribed on the *verso* of the title-page is the note: 'The profits of this Publication are to be wholly appropriated to the Relief of the EMIGRANT FRENCH CLERGY'. An 'APOLOGY' (pp. iii–v) was a justification on the grounds of benevolence for the entry of a female into public affairs.

128. ¹ The execution of Marie-Antoinette (1755–93) on 16 Oct. 1793.

both to prompt & to repay it. Good God! that that wretched Princess should so finish sufferings so unexampled!—

With difficulties almost incredible, Me de Stael has contrived, a second time, to save the lives of M. de Jaucourt & M. de Montmorenci,[2] who are just arrived in Swisserland, we know as yet none of the particulars; simply that they are saved is all: but they write in a style the most melancholy to M. de Narbonne, of the dreadful ¹ fanaticism of Licence, which they dare call Liberty, that still reigns, unsubdued, in France.[3] And they have preserved nothing but their persons!—of their vast properties they could secure no more than pocket money for travelling in the most penurious manner. They are therefore in a state the most deplorable. Swisserland is filled with Gentlemen & Ladies of the very first families & rank, who are all starving, but those who have had the *good fortune* to procure, by disguising their quality, some menial office!— —

No Answer comes from Mr. Pitt; & we now expect none till Sir Gilbert Elliot makes his report of the state of Toulon, & of the Toulonese;[4] till which, probably, no decision will be formed whether the Constitutionals in England will be employed or not. ⌐If *not*, certainly Lord Hood has given hopes & expectations that, having disappointed, will make all other Towns, *constitutionally* inclined, fear to trust any other engagement from any other admiral. In transactions so important & so delicate, there should be⌐

[the second leaf is missing]

² For Madame de Staël's rescue of her friends of the Constitutional party of 1791, see ii, Intro., xvi, and for the second rescue, the 'agents', and the methods, see Herold, p. 129.
³ These letters are missing but in a letter of 5 Oct. [1793] to the comte de Narbonne (printed in Solovieff, p. 301), Madame de Staël refers to 'nos pauvres amis Matthieu et François', 'Je les ai pêchés dans cet abîme d' horreur'.
⁴ Cf. L. 126 n. 3. Gilbert Elliot (1751–1814), 4th Bart. of Minto (1777), appointed on 25 Sept. 1793 (see *DNB*) Civil Commissioner to Toulon and Privy Counsellor. For a vivid description of his assignment and the muddled conditions at Toulon, see *Life*, ii. 161–210.

129   Great Bookham, 28 November 1793

To Mrs. Waddington

A.L.S. (Berg), 28 Nov. [17]93
Double sheet 4to   4 pp.   a sliver, line 14 (*recto*) and line 12 (*verso*), cut
out of the first leaf   *pmks* LEATHER / HEAD   30 [N]O 93   wafer
Addressed: Mrs. Waddington, / Lanover Court, / Abergavenny / Monmouthshire

> Bookham,
> Novr 28th 93

Ah, my sweet unfortunate Friend! how have I grieved at this
sad & unexpected stroke![1]—to write to you—to pity—& to pray
for you, are requests I am undeed most ready to fulfil, & I
would to God my true simpathy could afford you any comfort.
—I can see none for this blow, but in the very situation so lately
lamented, but which now affords the sole as well as best prospect
of future consolation. Take, therefore, the utmost care of your
dear & precious life, & of the life it promises to some soft little
filial soother of this calamity.[2]

I forget if my little Namesake had been innoculated before—
tell me, my dearest Marianne, & that she has had that terrific
disorder favourably, & is well, & that you suffer her innocent
pra[ttle] to [*line cut*] [in some de]gree the distress of your Mind.

I am sure Mr. Waddington must have been deeply afflicted;
I beg you to tell him I feel for him also—though never, I confess, in any degree for a Father as for a Mother in these early
losses: the maternal love is perhaps strongest at the time when
the paternal is only preparing for future affection. |

When is the time I must anxiously hope for a line from Mr.
Waddington, my dearest Marianne? Pray let me know.

M. D'Arblay interests himself much in your Name & proceedings, from the interest he so nearly witnesses their kindling
in his Companion: & he bids me say, that he so sincerely grieves
for your loss, that if we were within any moderate distance, he

129.   [1] The death of Mary Anne Waddington on 23 Nov. 1793, aged 1 year and
7 months from an inoculation for smallpox.
   [2] A child Emelia was to be born on 3 Feb. 1794. FBA's namesake had been born
on 4 Mar. 1791.

would make his first essay of a widower's life, in granting me a week's furlough to abide with my so much loved Marianne.—

Your Letter, before this melancholy event, began in a manner very affecting to me by its kindness, & retrospective comments — —[*part of line cut out*] completely *lovely* in innocence & youthful gracefulness— —Mrs. Agnew writes me word she hears a very bad account of Mr. Dewes senʳ³—I hope he is now recovered. I know no wants & failures with respect to yourself will prevent your earnest good & warm wishes on this occasion. ¹

We are now in a small House at Bookham,⁴ where I fancy we shall remain near a year—for M. D'Arblay has offered his services at Toulon, & therefore we shall defer all building, all schemes whatsoever, till we see what turn matters take there, & whether the Constitutionalists will be called forward. You may easily believe how little *I* wish such a Call! Would to God He were as well satisfied with being left out! but the dreadful state of his wretched Country, & his wish to assist in placing the Son of his murdered Sovereign on his Throne, make him consider himself as not yet perfectly a private man, except either Republicanism, or Arbitrary power should finally prevail. To neither of those will he ever lend his aid: to his *King* & a *limitted Monarchy* he would offer,— —O but too willingly—his services & his life.

I drive the reflections to which this leads from my Mind as much as I am able, for *nothing else* molests it. Our retirement is precisely what suits us both,—we ¹ mingle at our pleasure with the Locks & the Phillips, & our Books, & our writings, & our mutual instructions & studies in our several languages, offer us employments inexhaustible. The shortness of every Day is our sole lamentation. The Night constantly surprises us before we are aware of its approach. I should have a thousand kind condolances for you if my dear Friends knew I was writing, & knew the unhappy Cause of my expedition. But I will not lose a post. Yesterday we all met at Norbury Park, where we spent the Day. That delightful dwelling is just the half way House between my dearest sister Phillips & our Maisonette. Adieu, my loved & truly lovely & loveable Friend! Heaven comfort you!—write

³ Mrs. Agnew's letter is missing, but Court Dewes (*c.* 1741–93) had died on 11 Nov. See i, L. 9 n. 8.
⁴ See L. 124 n. 2.

to me as soon as you can—as long Letters—& as often.—God bless you! *Your*—*My* beloved & revered M[rs]. D[elany]'s sweet Sacharissa is now opposite me.[5]

F. d'A.

I have just been writing a little Tract for the poor fugitive starving French Priests—I pray it may do them any good— —

130   Great Bookham, 8 January 1794

To Charles Burney

A.L. (Osborn), 8 Jan. 1794
Double sheet 4to   4 pp.   *pmks* LEATHER / HEAD   10 JA 94   wafer
Addressed: Dr. Charles Burney, / Academy, / Greenwich
Docketed, p. 1: 1794

Bookham,
Surry.
Jany 8th —

So how do do this new year, My dearest Carlos? You have sent me your usual kind remembrance, which I *un*usually prized,[1] it was so long since any token of amity had passed between us—We have long since, however, agreed never to remonstrate nor worry about Letters & answers.

I shall be truly happy to hear from yourself that you are as well as I hear of your being by others. Pray let me know the veracious veracity with proper propriety with the speediest speed.

I have been ill & confined for 5 weeks, but am now well, & getting abroad again.

I hope Rosette is well? My kind Love & best wishes. And pray a word of her Health in your 3 or 4 lines. I ask no more this busy season. And I would *give* no more, fearing bad precedents, —but that I am ¹ commissioned by M. de Narbonne to inform you that a *learned Grecian, of French extraction* has heard of your Fame, & covets the erudition of your acquaintance. M. l'Abbè

---

⁵ See ii, L. 120 n. 7.
130.   ¹ The letter is missing.

Le Chevalier travelled with the Duc de Choiseul to Constantinople & to Greece—& *It was he* who discovered the Tomb of Achilles—[2]

I assured M. de Narbonne I thought such a discovery would be more precious to you than the Mines of Peru were to Pizarro.

He is also a perfectly amiable & worthy character, as well as thus curious & learned—And— —he has no view, nor wish, personal, but to travel more, & more, & more, & gain new knowledge of countries, antiquities, & national singularities. |

This Gentleman means to call upon you, for a little Greek *confab.*—I am sorry I can't be of the party. A little comfortable clack in that snug language would be very agreeable to me. However, you will indulge me, perhaps, with a few minutes of what passes,—I like original Dialogues of all things.

I think Norbury very much improved in all particulars, both of person & mind, & the dear little fellow is perfectly content with his school life, & speaks of every thing & every body with pleasure & affection.[3] I did not expect this so soon, his happiness & indulgence at home considered.

Pray give my kind Love to Carluccini.

L'Abbe Le Chevalier speaks English pretty well—but I suppose *that's a trifle*, as I conclude you will scorn to talk in the vulgar language. Indeed, writing to & of such a personage, I am surprised I have fallen into it myself. Pray excuse it. 'Twas an accident from haste. |

I have just had a Letter from my Mother,[4] with a *much* better account of our dear Father. I have been quite overset by some former Letters concerning him. Heaven grant him soon to be more fully recovered!—

M. d'Arblay desires me to present you his kind remembrance. He was *particularly* pleased with my dear Charles, & said his Countenance & figure announced *un brave homme.*

---

[2] Jean-Baptiste Le Chevalier (1752–1836), professor of philosophy and mathematics at Navarre and in 1784 secretary to Marie-Gabriel-Florent-Auguste de Choiseul (1752–1817), comte de Choiseul-Gouffier (1771), who was appointed in that year ambassador to Constantinople. At that time Choiseul explored several sites associated with Homeric legend and in 1791 (21, 28 Feb. and 21 Mar.) Le Chevalier, confounding his own studies with those of Choiseul, read papers on the subject before the Royal Society of Edinburgh, of which on 4 Jan. 1791 he had been elected a member. His 'Tableau de la plaine de Troye . . .' was published in the *Transactions* of that Society, iii (1794), pt. ii. 3–92.

[3] Norbury Phillips, aged 9, at this time placed in Charles Burney's school recently removed to Greenwich.   [4] This letter is missing.

Adieu, my ever dear Brother.

our Susanna is well.

The Captain called here 10 Minutes ago. He tells me I may direct to Greenwich.

131   Great Bookham, 8 January 1794

To Doctor Burney

A.L. (Barrett, Eg. 3690, ff. 56–61b), 8 Jan.

Two double sheets 4to   8 pp.   *pmks* LEATHER / HEAD   10 JA 94   wafer

Addressed: Dr. Burney / Chelsea College / Midlesex—

Endorsed by CB: Relation de M. Beaumey / 1794

Also a double sheet 4to, the continuation of the story of M. de Beaumetz, which may have been sent with the above or under a separate cover now lost. Paged 1–12, 12 pp. in all.

Edited by FBA, p. 1, *annotated and dated*: ⁂ ⁂ 8 Jany 1794   (1)
            M: DE BEAUMETZ

p. 5: ⁂—94 (1) *Continuation M. de Beaumets.*

p. 9: ⁂—94 (I.) ⌐continuation of M. de Beaumetz⌐

Bookham—

I had *invented*, as our Charlotte was wont to say, a long Letter to my beloved Father, just as I was taken too ill to write a short one: I am now again *capacitated*, but the accounts of his Health have taken up all my thoughts & all my interest. I have just written to my Mother,[1] whose kind frequency of accounts obliges me inexpressibly; & I will now prepare a Letter for sending off against I hear again, by return of the Carrier: for, having found out our dwelling, the *post courrier* will no longer leave our Letters at Mickleham.

I had proposed giving the little history which had exceedingly interested us all here, of the escape of M. Beaumey[2] the last

131.   [1] The letter is not extant.

[2] Bon-Albert Briois, chevalier de Beaumetz (b. 1759; d. 1801 or ?1809 in Calcutta), had been elected 30 Apr. 1789 as deputy of the Nobility of Arras (province of Artois) to the States General. President of the Constituent Assembly (26 May–8 June 1790) and later a member of the *Directoire du département du Pas-de-Calais*, he fled to England *post* 10 Aug. 1792, where he associated himself with Talleyrand, eventually accompanying him to the United States. According to Glenbervie (i. 27), Beaumetz had returned to France 'on account of his only

24

fugitive French Gentleman who has saved himself from the barbarous despoilers of his Country & Countrymen. I have now a less lively impression than before my illness of his relation; but such as I recollect I will give.

M. Beaumey was a Member of the first Assembly, & is esteemed one of the most able men, one of the most instructed, & one of the worthiest of France. The famous speech which perhaps you may remember reading under the name of M. de Salles,[3] in defence of the late King, after his forced return from Varennes, was composed & written by M. ᐦ Beaumey but as he was a known Friend of the King & Royal Family, he was certain it would produce no effect, perhaps scarcely be heard, if spoken by himself. He presented it, therefore, to M. de Salles, who read it, & with an applause that filled with hope & joy all the partisans of the unfortunate Louis.

He accompanied that lamented Prince to the *Legislative* Assembly, (of which he was not Member, but Enemy) with M. le Duc de la Rochefaucault,[4] with whom, & some others,) he was Member of the then department of Paris. He mentioned a circumstance to us that convinced him, he said, the people, in their Hearts, however wildly misled, were *instinctively* Royalists. The little Dauphin was near being crushed by the Crowd, & separated from the Queen & his family: a Grenadier, to save him from suffocation, took him up in his arms, & held him to their full extent,—the Man was Tall & well looking, & the Child infinitely beautiful & interesting—& the moment this spectacle was thus suddenly presented to the people, even in the midst of their ferocious pursuit of the whole Royal Race, there was a vehement—a universal burst of loud applause, from all mouths & all hands — — No Danton, no Robbespierre, no Barrere & no Dumont nor Lequinio had been aware of the incident, & hardened them against ᐦ its affecting surprise.[5]

daughter' and had only lately (Nov.–Dec. 1793) been able to make a second escape, this time 'disguised as a sutler'.

³ *The Times* (21 July 1791) had reported 'an excellent speech' made in the National Assembly on 15 July 1791 by Jean-Baptiste Salle (*c.* 1759–94), vindicating 'the purity of the King's intention'. CB could have read the published work *Déclaration de Salle . . . dans l'affaire du ci-devant Roi . . .* (1792), which the National Assembly had ordered to be printed and distributed (*Morning Chronicle*, 22 July 1791).

⁴ Louis-Alexandre de la Rochefoucauld, duc de la Rochefoucauld, who was brutally murdered on 4 Sept. 1792 (i, L. 33 n. 23).

⁵ Notorious for oratorical powers and hardness of heart were Georges-Jacques

After that fatal 10 of August, & the imprisonment of the King, & demolition of the Monarchy, M. Beaumey, in danger of immediate assassination, flew to England — — O that the excellent Duc de la Rochefaucault had flown hither also!

Here he remained, till he flattered himself the first heat of pursuit of all the Friends to the King & Constitution was over. He had left a Daughter, & a Mother[6] in France—& he soon expended the very little he had been able to bring with him; He therefore determined to risk a returning.

M. d'Arblay endeavoured to dissuade him,—& with words that he has repeated to us all, & says, occurred to him every Day during his stay in France,—'What!' cried he, with that frankness that so marks his character with his Friends, 'will you go again, at this time, to France?—'You must either be *un fou* or *un Coquin*, to keep your Head there upon your shoulders.'

To be less marked, he went by the Name of his Father,[7] instead of that of his *Terre*,—&, for some time, I believe, he lived pretty quietly, endeavouring to secure some property to bring over to England, with his Daughter, just 16, & his Mother. But latterly, when the cry against every Man of Family, & every ex-constituent, became outrageous, he was obliged to retreat from those dear Relations, not to involve them in his danger. A party then was formed,[8] consisting of ' Mad[e] de Laval, Mother to M. de Montmorenci who was at Juniper, M. de Jaucourt,

Danton (1759–94); Maximilien-François-Marie-Isodore-Joseph de Robespierre (1758–94); Bertrand Barère de Vieuzac (1755–1841), 'l'Anacréon de la guillotine'; André Dumont (1764–1836), who on his mission of July 1793 had terrorized the *départements du Nord*; and Joseph-Marie Lequinio (1740–1813), who was associated with cruelties in the Vendée (1793). '[Il a] fait manger les bourreaux à sa table' (Larousse).

6 Beaumetz's mother, *née* Marie-Albertine Palyart (*fl.* 1745–94), had married presumably *pre* 1759 François-Joseph Briois de Beaumetz (d. *pre* 1794). Available biographies of Beaumetz fail to record a youthful marriage, which, since his daughter is 16 years of age at this date, would probably have taken place *c.* 1776–7 when he was 17 or 18 years old.

In Philadelphia on 17 Jan. 1796 Beaumetz married Mrs. Sarah (Lyons) Flucker, sister-in-law to General Henry Knox, a widow of modest means with a grown family. For comments on the imprudence of the match, see Médéric-Louis-Elie Moreau de Saint-Méry (1750–1819), *Voyage aux États-Unis de l'Amérique, 1793–1798*, ed. Stewart L. Mims (New Haven, 1913). On 27 May 1796 Beaumetz and his wife embarked for Calcutta on the ship *Asia* arriving in the following November. His last known letter from India is dated March 1801.

7 That is, Briois.

8 For this group of Constitutionalists, see 'The Juniper Colony', ii, Intro., ix–xix. According to Madame de Staël (letters of July 1793, Solovieff, pp. 272–3; and Jasinski, *Lettres inédites à Louis de Narbonne*, pp. 147–50), the group had found refuge near Abbeville.

who was here also, M. J de Broglio, younger son of the Mare-chal,[9] himself, & some others, & they retired to a Chateau belonging to one of the party, in the North.

Here they were all much respected & loved by the Peasants, & lived in a retired & tolerably decent manner, known to be *ci dévants*, yet so good & amiable, that the peasants resisted making any information against them.

This tranquility was soon broken: Dumont,[10] the detestable Dumont, began a circular visit in those parts, as Commissary, i.e. Dictator, from the Convention. Informed of his approach, they all quitted the Chateau, & sought concealment where & how they could, as he vowed indiscrimiate vengeance against ALL PRIESTS & ALL NOBLES. But, when he had passed the im-mediate vicinity of their abode, gently & carefully they had agreed to return. M. de Laval & M. Beaumey were re-entering together: when they were informed, that Dumont had some where procured intelligence concerning M. de Jaucourt & M. J de Broglio: he had pursued them; but still the peasants refused to betray them—till, in a corn field, a little Boy, whom they had not dared to caution, espied M. de Broglio, hid amidst the Grain, & shouted to Dumont to follow him. He was instantly seized, & put to prison; Dumont exclaiming aloud 'See honest Peasants! See what are these Nobles!—they hide themselves in your Corn, to blight & destroy it, & cause a Famine! This is the work of Nobles & Priests!'

M. de Jaucourt was just by,—but found means to escape, & is now in Swisserland.

'But,' continued M. Beaumey, 'what astonished us most was the infatuated credulity & stupidity of the Peasants: when they related to us this incident, they added 'so good as they seemed, M. de Jaucourt & M. de Broglio! who could have thought they were so wicked as to want to starve us!'

'And thus,' he added, 'it is all over France!—they think the Convention infallible, & submit to their decrees as to decrees from Heaven, saying *The Law must be obeyed*—we *all live by the Law*!!—

---

[9] Auguste-Joseph de Broglie, styled prince de Revel (1762–95), Colonel of the English Regiment de Broglie (1794), died in Schwilnau, Westphalia, 26 Jan. 1795. He was the son of Victor-François de Broglie (1718–1804), 2nd duc de Broglie (1745), prince of the Holy Roman Empire (1759), maréchal de France (1762).
[10] See n. 5 above.

The rest of the party now found it necessary to separate & M. Beaumey determined to make an effort for coming again to England. He walked off alone, with nothing but what he could himself carry. The first Town where he was obliged to stop, for rest & refreshment, he was seized: though not known, yet suspected. A certificate was demanded, of his character, Name, &c—He ventured to send for one to a place where he had chiefly resided, & where his new name would be known, & where he believed himself beloved & respected. ^l Day after Day, however, pass'd, & no certificate arrived. He feared, not being understood, it had been refused. The Hour was fixed for his trial before some Court,—but on that very Morning, the Certificate from his faithful adherents was received. This affected him with every sort of pleasure a Man can feel. He was released, &, with this sort of passport, he journeyed on. News of the barbarous Commissary being in the neighbourhood, obliged him to again stop at another little Town. He prevailed upon 3 good women to give him a Lodging, up 3 pair of stairs, though he could not disguise he was fearful of being seen. They were very kind, & suffered him to remain some Days, till this alarm was over. But, just as he was quitting them, an order was issued for no person to appear in the Streets till all the Houses had been searched, as suspected persons were in the Town.

These 3 poor women, terrified to Death, besought him now to leave their abode, as their lives might pay the forfeiture of his being found in their apartments. He was obliged to comply; —but, by skill, & their help, he contrived to escape out of the Town before the terrible revolutionary Gang could surprise him.

He travelled on—but the next place of necessary rest was just threatened with a Commissioner. The general dread inspired by the visits of these bloody Dictators is not, he says, to be painted. He could find no ^l asylum, no refuge—& after various trials & expedients, he was driven to the resource of again imploring protection from the 3 women—the domiciliary visit of that spot was paid.—He knocked at the Door hastily—a woman from the first floor opened it—he durst not enquire for his friends, lest they should refuse him—but he hurried past, with a familiar sort of nod, as if entering upon some customary business. The woman let him pass—& he ran up 3 pair of stairs. He shut the Door of the Room when he entered it—&

began telling his persecutions: but the poor women, screaming & terrified, conjured him to begone. At this instant, some sound without announced another search—he supplicated for a place of concealment—they refused—they said they were lost for-ever —he assured them he would die a thousand deaths rather than betray their compassion, & that if he was found, he would persist that they were ignorant of his retreat. Still they durst not consent—but instant slaughter he knew would follow his being taken before any revolutionary tribunal: he knelt to them—he took an oath the most solemn to secure their own safety if he should be taken—but nothing prevailed, till he adjured them in the name of *Religion*, asking how they would answer for themselves hereafter the casting to unprovoked destruction an innocent man!—This voice touched them—they had heard no call in this strain long!—they instantly promised him their best aid. One of them conveyed him softly into a little spare old Garret, uninhabited, where she covered him with rubbish— prayed God for his protection—& left him. — — And here, in less than ¹ an Hour, he heard the horrible entry of the dreadful surveyors—One of the poor women ventured hastily up to him, while they searched below, beseeching him to keep quiet, praying him to remember not to betray him, weeping at his danger, & covering him almost to suffocation with fresh rubbish.—Here he remained a terrific but not *countable* interval,—&, as the Gang approached, higher & higher, nearer & nearer, he heard a woman exclaiming 'O, you'll find him—I am sure he's in the House—I let him in myself, & did not know he was a stranger.' He now found he was informed against by the woman on the Ground Floor: & his hopes diminished every step they advanced.—At length—his Garret Door was opened—a Peasant, as he heard by the dialect, entered first—& turning round, said 'O, here's nothing here!' — — & away they all went!—Imagine his astonished relief! He thinks the man was on a forced duty, & would not examine more closely: but he must have been less than mortal not to have rejoiced, in hearing the whole Gang, in their way down stairs, reviling the woman who had betrayed him as a false informer.— ¹

When all was clear, he had only time to pour his blessings upon the 3 good women, & to make off, lest this *Informer*, piqued to prove her words, should make a search by herself. But he thinks it was *fear*, & a desire to pay her Court to the wretches upon the watch, & not wickedness or cruelty that made her impeach him. Otherwise, the scrutiny would have been more severe. Such, however, is the Iron hand of Terror, (the constant order of the Day,) with which that wretched country is governed, that All obey what is called *The Law* indiscriminately, & even with the same infatuated alacrity, & credulity in its decrees, that—heretofore, belonged to their obedience to their Kings.

When M. Beaumey quitted his Protectresses, it was dark: he walked towards the high road,—but, at the corner of a narrow street, he heard himself followed, & soon was touched upon the arms: he turned—& saw one of his 3 friends, muffled up, & out of breath. He had paid them all for their services, not, he said, as they deserved, but as he was now able: they had accepted with an air of repugnance his offering, yet without disputing it:—this poor woman, however, now returned with it in her hand—'Take this back,' she cried,—'we are poor,—but we are safe— ¹ you may have much occasion for all you are worth— God grant it may save you!'

He was now obliged to change again his disguise, & make interest with a travelling Pedlar to let him accompany his travels & his toils. This man had a wife, & they both agreed to admit him of their party, provided he would carry neither arms, papers, nor Money.

With these people, selling all sort of small merchandise, he continued a considerable time, living as they lived, lodging where they lodged, & aiding their labours in what they had to bear about for sail. They did not know who he was, but were sure he was *ci-divant*;—yet were they such good hearted creatures, he felt secure they would not have betrayed him, unless from immediate fear for their own lives: not from hope of gain or reward.

A circumstance now happened the most affecting of his whole history: These people, in following their business, & without the least idea of his connections, travelled, with an Ass which carried the heavy part of their Goods, to the village where resided his beloved Daughter & Mother.—They stopt at a little Auberge, to feed the Ass:—during this little interval, he stole, unobserved, from his fellow-travellers, & went to the corner of a lane well known to him, whence he could see the Chimneys ¹ of that Chateau[11] which held all that was most dear to him. He did not attempt to describe what he felt in those moments—but the recollection interrupted the narration—& merely that he got safe, with little further impediment, to the frontier, & thence to England, finished his account.

He durst not—even for an instant—attempt to see these dear Relations:—he knew they would be directly imprisoned, even if he escaped, for having received him for half a Moment.

He arrived in London with just 4 Guineas in his pocket! — —

When he came to Mickleham,[12] at the invitation of M. de Narbonne, & Capt. Phillips, M. d'Arblay hastened to see him; —&, though his spirits at that moment were elated, from his safety after such Dangers, & his reception by his few friends in England, he was touched, even to Tears, at sight of M. d'Arblay —a sight, he said, truly touching, in times such as these, to see one Friend—one Countryman—who seemed happy!—

Immediately after, we all round met him at Mr. Lock's. There is an openness of countenance, a natural vivacity, & a most enlivening readiness upon all subjects, that directly catch whoever sees him. He has a strong personal likeness to our good & excellent King,—the Profile has an even striking resemblance —& this did not tend to prejudice me against him, you will believe, my dearest Father. ǀ

He insisted, afterwards, upon making us a visit—he wanted to see the *chaumiere of M. d'Arblay.*—I asked him if he had ever believed he could have lived in such a *Closet?*—he assured me he had seen nothing that appeared to him more respectable than such a retirement.

In talking over the present state of France, he said he saw but little hope of the reduction of its Tyranny except by *Famine.* The infatuation, or the terror, of the people was such, that they neither reasoned nor revolted from whatever was proposed, & he is sure they may raise armies after armies till all Europe is deluged in blood, while the word Liberty is the watch word, & while pillage is the constant pay! But *Famine* he thinks a very probable, however horrible, Friend to a better cause, & better Days.

[11] In Arras.
[12] Having escaped from France for the second time between November and December 1793, Beaumetz presumably visited Mickleham before the end of the year.

One thing, he says, frequently struck him, during his disguise, & familiar intercourse with the Peasants & common people: *they all expect a King*, he says,—& with an ignorance the most astonishing of all that is acting by their Tyrant Governors, for, in their own discoursing upon public matters, he has several times heard them ask of one another *But when the Republic is fixed*, & our wars are over, *who is to be King?*—He is firmly persuaded, that even to this Hour, the French at large are instinctively monarchical.

———

I spent the Day yesterday at Mrs Lock's, where I met Susanna, quite well. I am only not *strong* yet myself: but I have no complaint. M. d'Arblay desires his respectful Compliments. Thanks for the Print[13]—*Mr. William* speaks highly of the Design: M. d'Arblay is very fond of it.

*January 8*th. I have just received my Mother's most comforting Letter[14]—a thousand thanks for it—those ⟨2⟩ sheets being written I send them off, to beguile an half Hour. God grant my beloved Father may continue amending!—I will send the rest of this history if it interests enough to be worth postage.[15]

132   Great Bookham, 9 January 1794

To Esther (Burney) Burney

A.L. (Berg), 9 Jan. [17]94
Double sheet 4to   4 pp.   *pmks* LEATHER / HEAD 11 JA 94 wafer
Addressed: Mrs. Burney, / No 2 Upper Titchfield Street, / Portland Place, / London
Endorsed by EBB: Janry—94
Editorial marking, p. 4: Suppressed

13 Unidentified.   14 This letter is missing.
15 To this offer CB replied in his letter of 5 Feb. 1794 (Berg): 'A 1000 thanks for your pacquet of the wonderful escapes of M. Beaumey—But what will he & many others do in this unexpected order for quitting England? The times grow more & more tremendous every day. There will certainly be exceptions in this order, wᶜʰ [he adds pointedly] can never be intended to reach quiet folks remote from the Capital.'

9 January 1794

Bookham,
Jany 9th—94

Our Susanna encourages me, my dear Esther, to enter upon affairs & discussions the most interesting & most important—& yet, of a nature so delicate, that I am not quite at my ease in commencing such subjects, undesired by yourself. It is not that I think you, like some dear though too proud spirits to which you allude,[1] *impatient of counsel*—I have always known the contrary—but first, I know not what counsel to give—& secondly you have written to me, of late, my dear sister, totally without reference to any of your concerns.

Do not imagine this a reproach—I know so well the cause that I should be highly unjust if it affected Me any other way than by sorrow. I know, & have felt by the whole of your manner, that you have deemed my reserve & concealment on the most interesting event of my own life unkind & unfriendly.—

Yet, *all within*, never was I less either than during that whole agitating & distressed period of my existence.[2] I *longed* to confide in you, longed with a yearning that helped to add to my ¦ difficulties & anxieties.—If ever we so meet that I can relate the circumstances of my situation fully, you will conceive—& I think forgive my silence.——yet, through every obstacle, I went one Day to Titchfield street purposely to open my whole Heart into your bosom—. You were in the City—& I had no other opportunity, except by writing,—& why I used not that belongs to my full detail. I can now enter no further, or I shall have paper for nothing else.

How much—how deeply I am touched by the statement of affairs in T[itchfiel]d Street I can hardly say.[3] I had flattered myself all was prosperous—however, all may again become so, in the wonderful turnings & changes of this eventful Epoch,— & it is the Spring alone that decides effectually & positively upon Mr. B.'s business; for as *all the World* is Daily growing

132. [1] The allusions are lost with EBB's letter, to which this is the reply.
  [2] From March to July 1793.
  [3] Charles Rousseau Burney (1747–1819), a skilful harpsichordist, had difficulty in enlisting pupils in numbers sufficient to support his family, of whom there were surviving at this time one son and five daughters (all unmarried).

poorer, people come later & later to Town, to defer expences they can less & less incur. Nevertheless, I think you perfectly wise & right not to wait for that flattering, short, & delusory period, for forming plans, & arranging some system of conduct that may accord with the year *throughout*, & not fluctuate with I all its fluctuating seasons. Easily, too, can I conceive how hard will be all retrenchments—especially where the comforts to be diminished have all been so virtuously & so laboriously earned. This, however, is notorious, & therefore my dear Esther & her excellent Partner will have no censure to apprehend in any change they may find necessary—on the contrary, I am sure any such will be seen with respect & approbation. Your large family is so well known, & the universal encrease of all common expences, is so every where bewailed, that œconomy, even the most palpable & minute, far from letting you down, will render you, I am certain, still more estimable in the Eyes of all those whose good opinion you value. The great difficulty will be settling in *what*, & *how* to œconomize, for where the accommodations of life have never amounted to extravagance or luxury, it seems impossible to abridge, but by falling into absolute distress.—And yet, if something, however small, however *very VERY* small, is spared from every *Weekly* Bill & account, the sum total in the *year* will be considerable. *I* do not now preach from a Palace — — — our little Establishment is the *most* œconomick I can *any* way form; but *Town* & *Country*, a *Family* & only a SINGLE PAIR, are so different, & have such different claims, pursuits, & necessities, that I am well aware I we can suggest nothing to each other from our separate experience.

I am perfectly of Susanna's opinion to deliberate with our dear Father as to Mrs. Ogg[4]—& to deliberate very maturely, as so much of F[anny]'s future life may depend upon its first opening. one thing there is I *decidedly* wish—but I know it will be hard to your feelings—though I think it must lastingly meet with the

---

[4] Probably Susanna Thomas (*c.* 1734–1820), daughter of the Rt. Revd. John Thomas (*c.* 1696–1781), Bishop of Winchester (1761), and wife of the Revd. Newton Ogle (1726–1804), D.D. (1761), Dean of Winchester (1769). In earlier days the Dean, genial, musical, and something of a poet, 'so comical, so sensible, and sweet-temper'd, *eke* handsome!' was a welcome visitor at St. Martin's Street (*ED* ii. 94, 103 and n. 1; 111–19, 298–9). A close friend of EBB and of EBB's friend Mrs. Chapone, Mrs. Ogle had probably offered to take or to place EBB's second daughter Frances (1776–1828) as a companion or governess.

reward of *their* best approbation—& this is to spare your lovely
little Cecilia till she is sufficiently deep-rooted in the affections
of Mrs. — & of *Mr.* H[awkins] to be regarded, pecuniarily,
as their own.⁵ Perhaps you may feel this impossible—yet I hope
you will make an *effort*, during the present unfixed & wavering
state of things. I shall honour it with my whole Heart, knowing
your just fondness for that bewitching little darling, & her
instinctive love & gratitude.—adieu—my kind love to Mr.
B[urney]—God send you, my dearest Esther, better Days &
brighter prospects, &, above all, God preserve your precious
health,—prays most *fervently* your ever affecte & faithful

F. d'A—

our Susanna is, thank Heaven quite well. So am I, though yet
weakened, by what has passed. Before her own illness, that dear
Susan came to my Bedside through Mud, through Mire, with
shoes, stockings, & a Night Cap in her Pockets—she Slept by
me in M. d'Arblay's cane Bed—& Mrs. Lock lent us Bedding
for that Gentleman to sleep on the Floor in his own Room, after
being upholsterer for all the Party.

I intended saying much of Mrs. Chapone,⁶ but must defer it
till I write next—I have always loved as well as respected her.

M. d'A. sends you his kind Comp^ts. I hope his receipt will act
as a charm. [Than]k God My mother writes good news of my
dear Father.

Susanna, with kindest Love, bids me say every thing came
well & safe & *all that*—we met yesterday at Mr. Lock's.

⁵ EBB's fourth surviving daughter Cecilia Charlotte Esther (1788–1821) was
shortly to be in effect adopted (see 'Worcester Journal') by her father's sister Ann,
the wife of the Revd. John Hawkins (i, L. 7 n. 23), whose living was Halstead,
Essex. SBP had grown very fond of Cecilia when as an infant she had been placed
in the care of Letty Brookes (L. 150 n. 6) and nursed in a cottage in Mickleham
from 25 May 1789 to the end of that year and also from March until August of
1790. Mrs. Locke and SBP often called at the cottage, and the child became a great
favourite with both women: 'We c^d scarce get away from her . . . I wish she may
be another dear Etty!' 'The little Baby is a very interesting Child—& I *think*—
promises to be more like her dear Mother than any of her other Children—I hope
she will be a good Girl & not disappoint me' (see SBP's Journals, Barrett, Eg. 3692,
ff. 33b, 153b; and cf. Mrs. Locke, Barrett, Eg. 3697, f. 179). And a typical passage
in SBP's Journals, Mar.–Aug. (Berg): 'We had the little Cecilia who is a delightful
Child—I have seen many more beautiful, but few equally interesting—I feel at
this time that I c^d with pleasure adopt her—'

The 'Worcester Journal' also has long accounts of Cecilia.

⁶ In frequent letters to EBB (see *Catalogue*), Mrs. Chapone (i, L. 9 n. 3) regularly
included kind messages for FBA; and unlike some of FBA's former friends, she
included M. d'A in her best wishes and invitations.

133   Great Bookham, [27 January 1794]

To Doctor Burney

A.L.S. with PS. by M. d'A (Barrett, Eg. 3690, ff. 70–1b), *n.d.*
Double sheet 4to   4 pp.   *pmks* EPSOM ⟨2⟩7 JA 94   wafer
Addressed: Dr. Burney, / Chelsea College, / Midlesex.
Endorsed by CB: 1794
Edited by FBA, p. 1, *annotated and dated*: ⁕ 5 1794   (5) Emigrant Priests
Miss Thrale.

Bookham,

My dear—dear—dear—Father What very—very great
pleasure your beloved Hand has just given me![1]—I could hardly
believe my Eyes at first, when I saw the direction—so beautifully written, too, — — how good, how kind to thus set my
Heart at rest, after so long & fearful an anxiety! — — M.
d'Arblay is this moment gone to make his toilette for carrying
the welcome tydings & bulletin to our dearest Susanna, ᵀ&
/ thence / My thanks to the Post.

M. d'Arblay, with his *best respects*, accepts your kind offer,[2]
and will be much obliged by the loan of Tom Jones—which he
has only read in French.[3] Perhaps you may entrust it to Susan,
when she has the happiness to spend a little time with you, which
I know she is delighting herself with projecting—We will return
by her the ⟨Prints⟩ & News papers.

Andᵀ I will send you Miss Thrale's Letters on the subject of
the respectable Priests.[4] How sincerely I congratulate you upon

---

133.   [1] CB's letter of 25 Jan. 1794 (Berg) announcing that he was so far recovered
from an attack of rheumatism as to be able to write and to leave his bedroom. The
crippling of his hands is evident in his writing, especially in the address, penned as
best he could with sore and stiffened fingers, in large sloping legal script.

[2] CB, having learned that M. d'A was studying English, had offered 'any particular authors in our language in my possession wᶜʰ he most wishes to read'. 'I hope
he will not spare the Chelsea circulating library' (op. cit.).

[3] Possibly in the translation (1750) by Pierre-Antoine de la Place (1707–93). In
a letter of 5 Feb. 1794 (op. cit.), CB mentions having 'borrowed Sall's every-day
Tom Jones for M. D'arblay: as mine, bequeathed to me in the 8ᵛᵒ Edit. of all
Fielding's works is in a splendid aristocratic birthday suit, unfit to travel in: being
bound in red Morocco with gilt leaves & the Lord knows what finery—If it shᵈ
have happened to be "brushed by the hands of rough mischance", en route, it wᵈ
have vexed you & M. D'arblay perhaps more than me'.

[4] 'I have told [Mrs. Crewe]', CB had written in his letter of 25 Jan. (op. cit.),
'how admirably Miss Thrale *had* taken up the cause of the poor *Grey beards*'. Miss

the noble success your indefatigable Measures & cares in their favour has produced. I did not know Dean Marley was ¦ *Bishopised*, I am very glad to hear it at the same moment that I hear of his beneficence.[5] M. d'Arblay has had a charming Letter from Comte Lally upon the *brochure*[6]—I intend also to enclose that, & dear Mr. Twining's,[7] for your perusal, by Susanna.

I rejoice very much that Mrs. Crewe is in Town, & her spirited kindness in her *menaced* visit at your Bed Side reconciles me completely to the bold deed of appearing before her en Robe de Chambre et en pantoufles. She is a most sweet & invaluable Friend, & Loves my dear Father as he merits.

We had yesterday a visit from Mr. Lock almost purposely to tell us the great Majority,[8] for We have lost a Friend at Leatherhead of M. d'Arblay's, Mr. Benn, who used to send us the Papers, but who is gone to winter in London. I laughed to see you use the same term *'frantic'* for Lord Stanhope[9] that Mr. Lock had used yesterday: but I have seen none of the debates: Monsieur promises to bring me the whole cargo from Norbury Park on his return.

I should really have thought the gentle arrest of M. Tho[s]

Thrale's letters, sent to him by FBA, he thought 'natural, affectionate, & humane—I love her & her sisters better than ever' (5 Feb., op. cit.).

[5] In his letter of 25 Jan. (Berg) CB had told of the success of his 'ladies' in raising subscriptions in Ireland and how Richard Marlay (*c.* 1728–1802), M.A. (1752), Dean of Fern (1769), Bishop of Clonfert (1787), of Waterford (1795), had 'collected & sent to Mʳˢ Crewe £200'.

[6] M. de Lally's letter to M. d'A, dated 9 with *pmk* 11 DE 93, is preserved in the Scrapbook (Berg) 'Fanny d'Arblay and friends. England. 1759–1799', p. 92. It was later annotated by FBA, '. . . upon the address to British Females for the French Emigrant Priests. by F d'A.'

[7] The Revd. Thomas Twining (1734–1804), B.A. (1760), M.A. (1763), Vicar of Fordham (1764–1804), Rector of St. Mary's, Colchester (1788–1804), the well-known translator of Aristotle's *Poetics* (1789). Perhaps, apart from Samuel Crisp (*HFB, passim*), the most beloved of the family friends of the Burneys, he appears engagingly in the early diaries (e.g. *ED* ii. 6, 13 n., 20–4, 35–9). See also in Lonsdale and Scholes (indexes). His letter is missing.

[8] In a division in the House of Lords on 21 Jan. 1794 an amendment advocating peace with France (as against war) was defeated by a majority of 97 to 12 (*The Times*, 22 Jan.). 'What a wicked gang', commented CB in his letter of 25 Jan. (op. cit.), 'it is who oppose it [the war]!—& what a frantic fellow is Lᵈ Stanhope, with his eloge of the Jacobins, atheists, & anarchists!' 'I had not felt myself so well & alert for a long time, as the great & unexpected Majority . . . made me.'

[9] Charles Stanhope (1753–1816), styled Viscount Mahon, 3rd Earl (1786), referred to in *The Times* (of 13 July 1791) as 'President of the Revolutionary Society', moved on 23 Jan. 1794 ' "an humble Address . . . praying that his Majesty would be graciously pleased to acknowledge the FRENCH REPUBLICAN CONSTITUTION" '. *The Times* (24 Jan.) reported that the House, quite tired of the 'unbounded eulogium' of the French Constitution, 'loudly called for the Question', which put, was 'negatived by the WHOLE HOUSE, the MOVER excepted'.

Payne[10] | & of the great orator of the Human Race, M. Cloots,[11] might have sickened even Lord S[tanhope] of this unexampled Convention. I always think of the words that so long impressed M. Beaumez, 'il faut être ou *Coquin*, ou *fou*,' to have any thing to do with them: it is charity, therefore, to *write* Lord Stanhope *down an ass*. I long to see the speeches. I hope Mr. Windham has done himself justice—in other words, has spoken.[12]

⌐M. d'Arblay intends asking *something else* besides Tom Jones. —But I shall ⟨beg that till⟩ the next opportunity, as I believe he rather wishes it to be a *gift* than a *loan*.—[*tear*] & ⟨certainly⟩ *I* say it is quite *indecent* of us to be without 2 *books* of my Father's[13]—⌐

I am almost ashamed to use the word *fortunate* in speaking of Toulon[14]—yet Good Heaven ! — — what an escape from how useless a sacrifice must I ever look back to Mr. Pitt's not accepting M. d'Arblay's services!—for *I* never could buoy myself up with those sanguine expectations of the constitutional spirit of all the South of France that made M. d'Arblay believe the risk, be whatever the personal event, well worth running for his unhappy Country. — — |

Susanna & little Fanny trudged to see me, with *shoes in their Pockets*, & Norbury for an Esquire, on Wednesday Morning[15]—

[10] Thomas Paine (1737–1809), arrested in Paris on 28 Dec. 1793, deprived of his acquired French citizenship, and imprisoned as an Englishman for about ten months, was released (4 Nov.) when his claim to American citizenship was confirmed by James Monroe (1758–1831), then recently appointed minister to France.

[11] Jean-Baptiste Clootz (1755–94), Baron von Gnadenthal, German-born Utopian philosopher and self-styled citizen of the world, was arrested in Paris on 28 Dec. 1793 and guillotined in March 1794.

[12] Windham spoke on 21 Jan. 1794 (*The Times*, 22 Jan.) in support of the war with France, taking issue, in particular, with Sheridan, who had argued that the wars that France was forced to wage without its borders gave cause to some of the bloody measures employed within.

[13] CB interpreted this hint as a request for his works *The Present State of Music in France and Italy* (1771) and *The Present State of Music in Germany, the Netherlands, and the United Provinces* (1773). A copy of the last he agreed to send; the Italian Tour he had need to 'ferret . . . out somewhere' (5 Feb., op. cit.).

[14] Toulon capitulated to the forces of the Convention under Napoleon *c*. 17, 18 Dec. 1793, and the English evacuated the town and set sail by 19 Dec. (*The Times*, 16 Jan. 1794). The failure was attributed partly to a republican counter-revolution and partly to a general state of insurrection and anarchy within the port. See also Sir Gilbert Elliot, *Life*, ii. 202–8. Thus CB, writing to FBA on 25 Jan. (Berg): 'How fortunate it was that M. D'Arblay & his friends did not go to Toulon! I expected that place, while in the hands of Royalists, wᵈ have been a rallying point for all the Friends of *Monarchy*, limited or otherwise, in that part of the World—but republicanism, anarchy, & terror, are *evil spirits* too powerful in that Quarter to be cast out or subdued but by self destruction and Massacre.'

[15] 22 Jan.

but she suffered with her Teeth the next Day for the expedition: on Tuesday we met for the Day at Norbury Park.

⌐My kind love to my Mother, I shall send her Richard's[16] letter by Susan. She will be sorry to hear Mrs. Waddington has lost the little beautiful Child, the youngest, that she brought to see me at Chelsea.[17] Poor Mrs. Waddington is broken Hearted by this blow. 'Tis the second out of only 3 she has already had to lament.⌐

Adieu, Dearest dear Sir—with a thousand & a thousand thanks for your 'Heart-dear' Letter—ever most affectionately your dutiful

F. d'A.

Think of our horticultural shock last week, when Mrs. Bailey,[18] our Landlady, 'entreated Mr. d'Arblay not to spoil her Fruit Trees!' — — Trees he had been pruning with his utmost skill & strength! — — However, he has consulted your Miller[19] *thereupon,* & finds out she is *very ignorant*—which he has gently intimated to her.

Love to Sarah

[M. d'Arblay added a postscript at the top of the first page]

La lettre de *notre Fanny* est si remplie que je n'ai que ce moyen de vous presenter mes hommages Je vous remercie de l'offre toute aimable que vous nous faites et vous remercie bien davantage encore de la lettre que vous avez ecrite à ma femme et qui fera plus pour sa santé que tous les remedes de la faculté. N'allez pas croire cependant qu'elle soit malade. Non: mais elle etait inquiete et ne le sera plus.

[16] See i, Intro., lxxiii   [17] Mary Anne (L. 129 n. 1).
[18] See L. 124 n. 2.   [19] See L. 123 n. 1.

134 [Great Bookham, 8 February 1794]

To Doctor Burney

A.L.S. (Barrett, Eg. 3690, f. 62–b), *n.d.*
Originally a double sheet 4to, of which FBA later discarded the first leaf.
2 pp.   *pmk* DARKING   wafer
Addressed: Dr. Burney, / Chelsea College, / Midlesex.
Endorsed by CB: 1794
Edited by FBA, p. 1, *annotated and dated*: ·⁑· Bookham, 8th Feby 1794.   (2)
Bookham Gardening. Mr. CANNING's *debut*

[*the first leaf is missing*]

The Times are indeed, as my dearest Father says, tremendous,[1]—& reconcile this retirement Daily more & more to my
Chevalier—Chevalier every way, by Birth, by his order, & by
his Character, for to Day he has been making his first use of a
restoration to his Garden, in gathering Snow drops for his fair
Dulcinea—you know I must say *fair*, to finish the phrase with
any effect.

⌐I feel very sensible of the gratitude I owe to the graci⟨ous⟩
silence of the Critical Review[2]—¬

I am very sorry for the sorrow I am sure Mr. Burke will feel
for the loss of his Brother,[3] announced in Mr. Cooke's paper

134.   [1] The phrase is quoted from a letter of 5 Feb. (Berg) from CB, who, in speaking of Beaumetz and the deportation of Frenchmen suspected of political intriguing,
hoped that exceptions would be made for 'quiet folks remote from the Capital'. It
is probably out of respect to her father's warnings and in an attempt to quiet his
fears that FBA stresses M. d'A's horticultural pursuits, giving full explanations of
such journeys as he made to London.
   [2] *Brief Reflections relative to the Emigrant French Clergy* had been favourably reviewed,
however, in the *Monthly Review*, xii (Dec. 1793), 455, and in the *British Critic*, ii
(Dec. 1793), 450; and was to have a three-page spread in the *Critical Review*, x (Mar.
1794), 318–21; and favourable mention in the *European Magazine*, xxv (Jan. 1794),
32, for its 'elegance of style, acuteness of observation, and spirit of philanthrophy'.
The first reviewer, like those to follow, well remembered Fanny Burney, *Evelina*,
and *Cecilia*; and the Charity Sermon, it was thought, did 'much honour to the head
and heart of the writer'. The *Critical* reviewer rejoiced to have 'found our favourite
again'. Though he noted a 'degree of stiffness in the manner' and some loss in 'the
easy play of the pen' and though, as to argument, he cavilled somewhat at the
political innocence of the French Clergy, 'still—she writes again, and by continuing
to write we are sure she will again delight and again instruct us'. And he concluded
with two words only of advice to 'the amiable author'—'*Write on*'.
   [3] The obituary appears in *The Times* (7 Feb. 1794): 'Yesterday morning, suddenly, Mr. [Richard] Burke, the Recorder of Bristol, and brother to the Right Hon.
Edmund Burke, Esq. after an illness of about five minutes, at his chambers in
Lincoln's-inn.'

yesterday. Besides, he was a comic, good humoured, entertaining man,—though not bashful.

⌐Our Susanna has been very much disappointed indeed at not seeing you with her charming Boy. The Captain called upon me yesterday on his way to Kingston, & gave a good account of Chelsea & London but the Letter to day was worth 50 such accounts.⌐

My excellent & most friendly neighbour, Mrs. Cooke, is much disturbed at present by the Stage exhibition of a Relation of her family, *the Hon. Mrs. Twisleton*.[4] This latter is Daughter in Law to the queer whirligig Lady Say & Sele[5] I met formerly at Mrs. Paradise's,[6] or, as Mr. Seward called her, Mrs. Purgatory. I had a kind remembrance ⌐ from that latter gentleman the other Day —*or week*—through Mr. William Lock, with whom he corresponds occasionally.

What an excellent opening Mr. Canning has made at last?[7] *Entre-nous soit dit*, I remember, when at W[indsor]—that I was told Mr. Fox came to Eton *purposely* to engage to himself that young man, from the already great promise of his rising abilities, & he made Dinners for him & his nephew, Lord Holland,[8] to teach them political lessons.—It must have had an

---

[4] Charlotte Ann Frances Wattell (*fl.* 1788–98) had married on 26 Sept. 1788 the Hon. Revd. Thomas James Twistleton (1770–1824), D.D. (1819). 'A very pretty woman' and 'by no means a stranger to Provincial Theatres', she had made her first London appearance at Covent Garden on 1 Feb. 1794, when she played Belvidera in *Venice Preserved* (*The Times*, 3 Feb.), her style being 'highly SIDDONIAN'. In that winter she played various roles in London and in the following season made appearances (on 26 Dec. 1794; 12, 19, 28 Feb., 28 Mar., and 21 Apr. 1795, see Genest; and the *Bath Journal*, 23, 30 Mar.) at the Theatre in Bath, later playing in Dublin and Edinburgh. In *Thraliana* (ii, 915 and n. 6) there is a record of the 'Honourable' Mrs. Twistleton being turned out of the Bath Assembly 'because she had acted on the stage'.
Her husband secured a Deed of Separation (17 June 1794) and later (26 May 1798) a divorce (*LJ*, xli. 520–1, 540–2, 608).
[5] Elizabeth Turner (1741–1816), who had married in 1767 Thomas Twistleton (*c.* 1735–88), *de jure* (1763) and *de facto* (1781) Lord Saye and Sele, 10th Baron, was the daughter of Sir Edward Turner, Bart., of Ambrosden, Oxon., and his wife Cassandra *née* Leigh, a second cousin of Cassandra (Leigh) Cooke. Lady Saye and Sele is depicted in lively fashion in *DL* ii. 59–66.
[6] Lucy Ludwell (1751–1814) of Williamsburg, Virginia, who had married in 1769 John Paradise (1743–95), D.C.L. (Oxon., 1776). A lively friend of the Burneys in their early years, she appears in *ED* ii. 313–16. See also Archibald Bolling Shepperson, *John Paradise and Lucy Ludwell of London and Williamsburg* (Richmond, 1942).
[7] George Canning (1770–1827) had delivered his maiden speech on 31 Jan. 1794, the timing, manner, subject, and success of which are assessed at length by Dorothy Marshall, *The Rise of George Canning* (1938), pp. 47–62.
[8] Henry Richard Fox (1773–1840), later Vassall-Fox, 3rd Baron Holland (1774), also educated at Eton and Oxford (matric. 19 Oct. 1790). On the deaths of his

41

odd effect upon him, I think, to hear such a speech from his Disciple! Mr. Lock now sends us the Papers for the Debates every 2 or 3 Days: he cannot quicker, as his own household Readers are so numerous. I see almost nothing of Mr. windham in them, which vexes me: but I see *Mr. Windham* in *Mr. Canning*. I hope you return Mrs. Crewe's sweetness tenfold, now you are again, thank God, abroad? Count Lally & Mr. Twining are ready for the next jaunt of the Captain.⁹ M. d'Arblay has not yet been out, except upon his own *Rheumatic* walk. He is now about a new Grammatical work, for the study of English.

> Adieu most dear of dear Fathers,
> affectely & dutifully yours
> F d'A

I beg my kind Love to my Mother: I have made Saratina handsome amends as far as quantity can count.

I have just heard from Mrs. Rishton of Miss Ann Coke's inte⟨nded⟩ marriage with Mr. Anson,¹⁰—is he Bro⟨ther of⟩ our Miss Anson?¹¹

135   Great Bookham, 2 March 1794

To Doctor Burney

A.L. (Barrett, Eg. 3690, f. 63–b), 2 Mar. [17]94
Originally a double sheet 4to, of which FBA later discarded the second leaf   2 pp.
Edited by FBA, p. 1, *annotated*: ⋇ (3)
Gardening—Mandoline   gay content!

> March 2ᵈ—94
> Bookham.

How kind, my dearly beloved Father, how excessively kind this more than compliance with my wish & M. d'Arblay's

parents in 1774 and 1778 (see *DNB*) he was brought up by his maternal grand-father and his uncle Charles James Fox.
    ⁹ Captain Phillips, who will either deliver the letters or place them in the penny post.
    ¹⁰ In a letter of 3 Feb. [1794] (Barrett, Eg. 3697, ff. 225–6b) Maria Rishton had reported the 'Approaching Marriage' of the 2nd daughter of Thomas William Coke (1754–1842), cr. 1837 1st Earl of Leicester of Holkham. Anne Margaret Coke (1779–1843), was to marry on 15 Sept. 1794 Thomas Anson (1767–1818), cr. 1806 Viscount Anson.
    ¹¹ Thomas Anson's sisters were Mary (1763–1837), Anne (1768–1822), and Catherine-Juliana (1780–1843).

request! We have not yet got the dear Print,¹ nor have I seen it, but M. d'A. says he thinks it a much better impression than that in the *Company Boudoir* at the Captain's.² This idea I have begged him to keep to himself!—The Captain I find has received your most kind directions, not to deliver it till it is framed. When we have got it, & placed it in its post of honour, I mean to say 'Pray will you please to accept a description of our Drawing Room?—' If I add to it that of the whole MANSION perhaps two or 3 pacquets might contain the detail—even if our out-houses & Grounds are included.

⌐I am not quite without hope of giving my dear Father my verbal thanks—a regale for which I long! next May when we have thoughts of taking a week's *Londoning* at dear Charlotte's. It is not yet certainly arranged, but it is the Castle in Spain at the moment in the air,—& it is, at least, very pretty to look at.⌐ ¦

M. d'Arblay is quite recovered, & my winter walk is nearly finished: but he is now about another grand operation, the name of which, this cold Weather, may perhaps make you shiver. He found it very unamusing to have a Walk without any *but*, & be always obliged to turn short back from one end to the other end,—& he was deterred from carrying it round the little field, because Our Landlady does not care to have her fruit Trees dug up! — — So what does he do, but resolve to make a *But* of his own,—which is neither more nor less than *an Arbour*. And, for this purpose, he has been transplanting lilacs, Honeysuckles & Jessamines, root, mould & branch, till he has been obliged, in the coldest Days, to as completely new attire as Richard may be at Calcutta upon one of the hottest. As we are not yet possessed of a wheel-barrow, he is forced to carry all upon his back: but perhaps you will suspect he means, hereafter, to lessen his manual labours by some Orphean Magnetism, when I tell you he has lately *composed an Air*, to a song of his own writing, which he plays upon his Mandoline, — — & plays in defiance of the poor [Instrument's wanting two capital strings.]³

[the second leaf is missing]

135. ¹ Apparently the engraving (1784) by Bartolozzi of Reynolds's portrait of CB (see frontispiece, Lonsdale, and also Scholes).
² At Mickleham, among works by Edward Francesco Burney, William Locke, Jr. and others highly prized by Phillips and SBP.
³ The words in brackets FBA had (in her editorial capacity) transferred to the lower margin of p. 2, presumably from the top line of p. 3 before destroying it.

136   Great Bookham, 22 March 1794

To Doctor Burney

> A.L.S. (Barrett, Eg. 3690, ff. 66–9b), 22 Mar. [17]94
> Two double sheets 4to   8 pp.   *paged 1–8*
> *Edited by* FBA, p. 1, *annotated*: ❊ ❊   (4)
> French affairs. Dauntless Openness yet noble forbearance of M. d'Arblay—
> Gardening—M. de La Fayette
>   *Annotated*, p. 5: ❊ ❊ (4) in continuation   Gardening—
>   *Edited also by* CFBt.

Bookham,
March 22ᵈ—94

My most dear Father,

I am this moment returned from reading your most welcome
& kind Letter at our Susanna's,¹ ⌐whither I strolled this Morning
for the first time since the long showery weather. M. d'Arblay,
who defies the elements, has brought & carried *bulletins* in the
meanwhile, but our own personal separation has never been of
such length till now, since my residence in the neighbourhood—
And we have now lost our half way House, where we constantly
visited on the same Days — — I found there dear Susan looking
very well, & her blooming little Fanny, & her merry little
William in perfect health. She charged me to give her best
thanks for the charming Letter which she had received yesterday, but as I told her I should write immediately, she *reserves
herself* for a few days hence.⌐

The account of your better health² gives me a pleasure
beyond all words,—& it is the more essential to my perfect
contentment, on account of your opinion of our Retreat. I
doubt not, my dearest Father, but you judge completely right,
& I may ¹ nearly say we are BOTH equally disposed to pay the
most implicit respect to your counsel.³ We give up, therefore,

---

136. ¹ The A.L. of 19 Mar. 1794 (Barrett, Eg. 3690, ff. 64–5b) from CB to FBA,
with a note (signed E.B.) from Mrs. Burney, shows no signs of having been posted
but was probably carried to Mickleham by Captain Phillips. CB's letter to SBP is
missing.

² CB had reported (op. cit.) having 'for more than a fortnight enjoyed more
exemption from bodily pain than for many months before'.

³ CB had prefixed the counsel he meant to give (op. cit.) by an anecdote of his
meeting with John Crewe, M.P., who had asked—' "Was M. D'arblay in the
House (of Commons) yesterday?" ' 'He probably supposed', CB opined, 'that the

all thoughts of our London excursion for the present, & I shall write to that effect to our good intended Hostess very speedily.[4]

I can easily conceive far more than you enlarge upon in this counsel: & indeed I have not myself been wholly free from apprehensions of possible *embarrass* should we, at this period, visit London; for though M. d'A. not only could *stand*, but would *court* all personal scrutiny, whether retrospective or actual, I see daily the extreme susceptibility which attends his very nice notions of Honour, & how quickly & deeply his spirit is wounded by whatever he regards as injustice. Incapable, too, of the least *trimming* or disguise, he could not, at a time such as this, be in London, without *suffering*, or *risking*, perhaps Hourly something unpleasant — — — — *Here* we are tranquil, undisturbed, & undisturbing — Can Life, he often says, be more innocent than ours? or happiness more inoffensive? — he works in his Garden, or studies English or Mathematicks, while I write, — when I work at my needle he reads to me, & we enjoy the beautiful Country around us, in long & romantic strolls, during which he carries ¹ under his arm a portable walking Chair, lent us by Mr. Lock, that I may rest as I proceed. He is extremely fond, too, of writing himself, & makes from time to time memorandums of such Memoirs, poems, & anecdotes as he recollects, & I wish to have preserved. These resources for sedentary life are certainly the first blessings that can be given to Man, for they enable him to be happy in the extremest obscurity, even after tasting the dangerous draughts of glory & ambition.

The business of M. de la Fayette[5] has been indeed extremely

Motion in favour of M. de la Fayette's enlargement from prison (wch you will see, wth the debates on the subject in all the papers) w^d have brought M. D'A. to Town.' But, CB continued, whatever interest M. d'A 'may feel for the fate of his *ci-devant* commander, unless [he] was determined on again resuming a military life, I cannot help expressing my humble opinion of his being right, (in the present state of things, during the narrow & illiberal manner wth wch foreigners, particularly are watched) to remain as quietly as possible in his retreat'.

With further remarks on the Alien Bill, the support given by the English Jacobins to Lafayette, affairs in France, and the 'imminent danger of religion, morals, liberty, property, & life', CB begged FBA to present his 'Compliments to M. D'Arblay, & to remind him of Candide's last injunction.—viz. *Qu'il faut cultiver notre jardin*. & with this new axiom I finish & give you my benediction'.

⁴ Charlotte Ann (Burney) Francis.

⁵ The 'business' was the long debate in the House on 17 Mar. 1794 respecting the detention in prison of Lafayette, M. de Latour-Maubourg, and a few other Constitutionalists (see ii, Intro., xvii) by the King of Prussia. The motion that ' "his Majesty would . . . interfere in such a manner as . . . to effect the release of those Gentlemen" ' was defeated by 153 to 46 (*The Times*, 18 Mar.).

bitter to him. It required the utmost force he could put upon himself not to take some public part in it. He drew up a short, but most energetic defence of that unfortunate General, in a Letter he meant to print, & send to the Editor of a paper which had traduced him,[6] with his name at full length. But after two nights' sleepless deliberation, the hopelessness of serving him, with a horrour & disdain of being mistaken as one who would lend any arms to weaken Government at this crisis, made him consent to repress it. I was dreadfully uneasy during the conflict, knowing far better than I can make him conceive the mischiefs that might follow any interference, at this ǀ moment, in matters brought before the Nation, from a Foreigner. But, conscious of his own integrity, I plainly see he must either wholly retire, or come forward to encounter whatever he thinks wrong. Ah— better let him accept your Motto, & *cultiver son jardin*![3] he is now in it, notwithstanding our long walk, & working hard & fast, to finish some self-set task that to-morrow, Sunday, must else impede.

⌐What you say of our *Neighbour* is most just,⌐—But could you help smiling at Mrs. Cooke's fey neighbour's *kind wishes* for the visitors of the poor *rustical Brethren*? they would have had plenty of time, had such a breeze as she desired taken place, to give one another the fraternal salutation!

I am much obliged to Lady Lucan & think it indispensable to tell her so, in common decency.[8] I shall write a little note,

---

6 What had outraged d'Arblay, however, was an article (*The Times*, 14 Mar. 1794, p. 3) accusing Lafayette of 'treachery towards the unfortunate ROYAL FAMILY OF FRANCE'. 'A second JUDAS', it was alleged, while pretending to contrive the King's flight, the secret of which had been entrusted to him, 'he sent an express to *Drouet*, the postmaster at Varennes, . . . with orders to stop [the royal] progress by alarming the country'.

M. d'Arblay's reply, dated 15 Mar. 1794, a draft of which is extant (Osborn), took issue with the particulars of the charge: it would have been impossible to find couriers to send in time; Lafayette had not been entrusted with the secret; Drouet was the postmaster not of Varennes but of Ste-Menehould. As for Lafayette's friends the Constitutionalists, they were 'dévoués à cet infortuné Monarque— Ennemis egalement du Despotisme et de l'Anarchie, ils ont été constament les deffenseurs de l'ordre'.

7 CB's comment, possibly in his letter to SBP, is missing.

8 Margaret Smith (d. 27 Feb. 1814) had married 1760 Sir Charles Bingham (1730–99), 7th Baronet (1751), cr. Baron Lucan (1776), Earl of Lucan (1795). CB had recounted (op. cit.) having been 'twice to Lady Lucan's *blue* conversazioni's'. The 'invitation to the 2ᵈ *blue* party' he had sent to FBA, as she was included in it.

which you will have the kindness to let Sam drop for me by any opportunity.

We have not yet received the Print, But the knowledge it is destined for us gives us pleasure.[7]

I doubt not but Mrs. Thrale will make an excellent work of the Synonime Anglois,[9] Though I think, with you, something of l delicacy in *les nuances* might be better given. I am glad she is about a work which may mentally amuse her—Alas!—alas!—

I am glad you meet Lord Spencer[10] at Lady Lucan's,—what an acquisition a Man of his Character to Government!—M. d'Arblay sometimes says—*I cannot conceive how there can be two minds amongst honest men as to this War!*—though God knows, as to its *causes* he can conceive but too well a thousand!

As I have interested you a little for the very amiable M. Beaumetz, I have borrowed the Letter he wrote to M. d'Arblay upon quitting England.[11] *You* will pardon his civilities about

[9] At Lady Bank's conversazione CB had learned (loc. cit.) of Mrs. Piozzi's forthcoming *British Synonymy; or, an Attempt at Regulating the Choice of Words in Familiar Conversation*, which was to appear in two volumes early in April 1794.

CB had 'long wished such a work to be undertaken by one equally learned in books & acquainted with the *Ton de la bonne conversation*—I know few women more likely to succeed in so difficult an enterprise than Mrs T.—her book will be enlivened, at least, with illustrations, allusions, & wit, however nice discriminations may elude her research' (op. cit.). Cf. Walpole (xii. 92–3, 174): 'Dame Piozzi . . . mistakes vulgarisms for synonymous to elegancies.'

[10] George John Spencer (1758–1834), styled Viscount Althorp (1765), 2nd Earl Spencer (1783), who 'as a peer . . . adhered to Fox until 1794 when he went over to Pitt with the Portland Whigs' (Namier and *DNB*).

[11] The Alien Bill of 8 Jan. 1793 had placed the French refugees under police supervision and gave authorities the necessary power to deport them. In a letter of [31 Jan. 1794], preserved in the Scrapbook (Berg) 'Fanny d'Arblay and Friends. France. 1679–1820', the comte de Narbonne informed SBP that Talleyrand had received by that date orders to quit England within five days.

Beaumetz and Talleyrand, finally complying with some such order, boarded a ship bound for Philadelphia *c*. 1–3 March. Impeded by delays in the Thames and a storm in the Channel, the *déportés* sailed finally from Falmouth *c*. 21 Mar. 1794, arriving at Philadelphia on 28 April. Beaumetz's farewell to d'Arblay, dated 'Londres, 1 mars. 1794', is preserved in the Scrapbook (Berg) 'Fanny d'Arblay and friends. England. 1759–1799': 'Adieu donc, Mon cher D'Arblai, mon cher compagnon de révolution, de guerre, et d'émigration . . . nous voilà donc séparés.'

With respect to *Evelina* and *Cecilia*, copies of which had been given him by SBP to read on the voyage: 'Je vais les apprendre par coeur, les traduire en français, les recomposer en Anglais, et corriger tous mes *blunders* par l'étude de ces charmantes modèles.'

Thus CB in his letter (Osborn) of 14 Apr.: 'But poor M. Beaumetz! How was it possible for him to write so tranquil & good humoured a letter in such circumstances as those in wch he left this country, after such treatment in his own! Nothing but the native gaieté du Coeur of a true old-fashioned Frenchman c^{d} have reconciled him to such a fate. I always loved & admired the natural cheerfulness & hilarity of the people of France . . .'.

two little Books,[12] &, for the rest, the good humour & softness with which he writes, at so bitter a period, when absolute want of subsistence drives him so far from all communication & intelligence with a Child & a Mother[13] so dear to him, will, I think, shew you the philanthropy & philosophy of Character by which he so immediately made all here his friends.

M. d'Arblay, to my infinite satisfaction, gives up all thoughts of building in the present awful state of public affairs: I to shew you, however, how much he is '*of your advoice*', as to *son jardin*, he has been drawing a plan for it, as he means to lay it out, when we can go to work. The Ground has long been made over to him by Mr. Lock,[14] & will be at his service whenever he pleases. It is near the River Mole, & just at an equal distance from Norbury House & Susan House. I intend to beg—or borrow—or steal—(all one) the little Plan, to give you some idea how seriously he studies to make his manual labours of some real utility. ⌐You will be so kind as to return it by the next opportunity. Mr. Lock's Cart comes to Norbury any Friday.¬

This sort of work, however, is so totally new to him, that he receives every now & then some of poor Merlin's *disagreable Compliments*,[15]—for when Mr. Lock's or the Captain's Gardeners *favour our Grounds* with a visit, they commonly make known that all has been done wrong! Seeds are sewing in some parts, when plants ought to be reaping, & Plants are running to seed, while they are thought not yet at maturity. I our Garden, therefore, is not yet quite the most profitable thing in the World; but M. [d'A] assures me it *is* to be the staff of our Table & existence.

A little, too, he has been unfortunate; for, after immense toil in planting & transplanting Strawberries round our Hedge, he has just been informed they will bear *no Fruit the first year*—: & the *Second*, we may be *up the Hill & far away*!—

[12] Beaumetz's civilities were repeated by Talleyrand himself in a letter (NPG) to M. d'A, dated Philadelphia, 9 mai [1794]: 'Cecilia a été lu par tous nos passagers, et même par notre capitaine qui s'est fort aisément accoutumé aux moeurs gentlemen; le matin il lisoit Evelina et Cecilia, et le soir au lieu de manger du boeuf salé il nous démandoit du sirop de groseilles / vinaigre / de M^{de} Lock—.'

[13] See L. 131 n. 6.

[14] Although both a deed of gift and a 99-year lease were proposed by Mr. Locke and discussed, no legal document was ever signed, and the house and land were subject to a forced sale when in 1814 William Locke, Jr. made plans to sell Norbury Park. The fatal delay in signing the documents is explained by M. d'A in a draft Memorial (Barrett, Eg. 3700B, ff. 88–9b) of date *c*. 1814.

[15] Quotation from Joseph Merlin (i, L. 3 n. 118), 'a great favourite at our house' (*ED* ii. 58, 242, 300). See also Scholes, ii. 203–9.

Another time, too, with great labour, he cleared a consider-able compartment of *Weeds*—& when it looked clean & well, & he shewed his work to the Gardener, the Man said he had de-molished an asparagrass Bed! M. [d'A] protested, however, nothing could look more like *des mauvaises herbes*.

His greatest passion is for transplanting. Every thing we possess he moves from one end of the Garden to another, to produce better effects; Roses take place of Jessamines, Jessa-mines of Honey suckles, & Honey suckles of lilacs, till they have all danced round as far as the space allows: but whether the *effect* may not be a general mortality, summer alone can deter-mine.

Such is our Horticultural history. But I must not omit that we have had for one week Cabbages from our own cultivation—every Day! — — ' O, you have no idea how sweet they tasted! we agreed they had a freshness & a goût we had never met with before. We had them for too short a time to grow tired of them, because,—as I have already hinted, they were beginning to run to Seed before we knew they were eatable.

We mean, during Mr. Lock's sejour in Town, to send back Tom Jones, & to beg something else in exchange, *pr Cart*.

I had proposed myself, I own, infinite pleasure in seeing my dearest Father, & all the family, this spring,—yet, all things considered, I feel no repining to give up what might be bought too dangerously: I do, however, most earnestly hope my beloved Father will make his Mickleham visit this Summer,—& I shall then see him Daily while he stays,—& he will yet more endear to me my *little possession* by once or twice breathing in it: & it will give a satisfaction to his kind thoughts in our separation, to see personally, that though very small, it is very comfortable.

I must leave this bit for what my Gardener will dictate, & only now add myself my dearest dear Father's most dutiful
& most truly affectionate
F: d'A.—

137   Great Bookham, [*post* 14] April 1794

To Doctor Burney

A.L. (Barrett, Eg. 3690, f. 74–b), Apr. [17]94
Originally a double sheet 4to, of which FBA later discarded the second
leaf   2 pp.
    Edited by FBA, p. 1, *annotated*: ❖ (7) on Dr. Burney's re-meeting Mrs.
Thrale Piozzi.

Bookham, April
— 94

Why what an exquisite Letter,[1] my dearest Father!—how full
of interesting anecdote, & enlivening detail!—The meeting with
our once so very dear Mrs. T[hrale]—so surrounded by her
family, made me breathless,—& while you were conversing
with the Seignor, & left me in doubt whether you advanced to
her or not, I almost gasped with my impatience & revived old
feelings, which presently you re-animated to almost all their
original energy. How like my dearest Father to find all his kindness rekindled, when her ready Hand once more invited it! —
— I *heard* her voice in '*Why here's D*ʳ *B. as young as ever*' & my dear
Father's in his parrying answers. No scene could have been
related to me more interesting or more welcome. *My* Heart &
Hand, I am sure, would have met her in *the* same manner. The
friendship, miserably as it has been broken, was too pleasant in
its first stage, & too strong in its texture, to be *ever* obliterated,
though it has been tarnished & clouded till scarce visible.[2]

137. [1] 'Who among many others shᵈ I have met wᵗʰ at Salomon's Concert' [Monday
7 Apr.], wrote CB in his letter of 14 Apr. 1794 (Osborn), 'but Mʳ & Mʳˢ Piozzi and
all the Miss Thrales? The Ladies all on the same sopha, & la mere in the middle!
... I hastened towards it, & met her Eyes with their usual fire & good humour—she
held out her hand & mine met it with great eagerness & pleasure—"Why here's
Dʳ B. as young as ever"—"Oh I am but just made up, quo[th] I—indeed but just
got up, from a bed of sickness" —&c &c well, we talked, & laughed as usual, and
I never saw her more lively, good humoured & pleasant in my life. My old affection
for her all returned, & I wᵈ have done anything possible to have shewn it with the
same impressement as in the best of Johnsonian, Thraliana & Streatham times.'
See also *Memoirs*, iii. 198–9.
    [2] FBA, reading over her letter in later years, interpolated after her original
comment on Mrs. Piozzi: 'I wish few things more earnestly than again to meet her.'
    To explain the word Protegés and to soften her comments about Miss Thrale's
cold manner, she later interpolated interlinearly: '—The Emigrant Priests. What
Pity that her manner is not more Demonstrative.—for she often chills where she
would be glad to thaw:'.

Miss ⏌ Thrale, whether her cold manner allowed her to shew it or not, must, I am sure, have been much gratified by what you said to her of her reverend Protegés.[2] — —

⌐But is not this a most extraordinary step of M. l'Eveque de Troyes? When M. d'Arblay instantly *offered* his translation to the use of the Society, & promised it to the Public,[3] is it conceivable that one of that body could undertake another without acquainting him, or letting him, except by accident, know of such intentions? M. d'Arblay began it instantly upon my Dear Father's intimating a desire he held to see it with the utmost pleasure & alacrity. Nor did he ever repine at his trouble, though it was declined by the united voices of M. de St. Pol, M. Wilmot, & M. Cadell,[4] upon your applying to them—but he always meant to print it, some time or other, for *himself*, if it should never be reclaimed by those for whom it was performed—but certainly, to suffer it to come forth by any other Translation,⌐

[*top margin*, p. 1]

P.S. I send you a taste of asparagrass, most fortunately overlooked by my Weeder.

[*the second leaf is missing*]

[3] Advertisements like that in the *London Chronicle* (21–3 Nov. 1793) as well as the final page of *Brief Reflections* gave notice that a translation of the tract was '*preparing for the press by* M. D'ARBLAY'. As with FBA's work, the proceeds were to go, presumably, to the Ladies' Society, of which CB was the secretary (L. 123 n. 3).

In the meantime Louis-Mathias Barral (1746–1816), évêque de Troyes (1788), de Meaux (1802), archevêque de Tours (1804), comte de Barral (1808), in England since 1791, had undertaken, as had M. d'Arblay, a French translation of FBA's *Brief Reflections . . .* (19 Nov. 1793). In an explanatory letter (Berg) of 6 mai 1794, he informed M. d'A that it was his plan to publish his translation abroad (L. 143 n. 2). Arrangements for publication in the Netherlands were, however, to prove nugatory, as see his letter (Berg) of 4 mars 1796: 'Les événemens qui ont mis en fuite le dépositaire de mon manuscript, ont pendant plusieurs mois empeché l'impression; plus tard elle eut été inutile et oubliée . . . De sorte que mon manuscript a le même sort que le votre par des raisons sembables.' Both letters are preserved in the Scrapbook (Berg) 'Fanny d'Arblay and Friends. France. 1679–1820'. See also a letter (Osborn) from CB to Mrs. Crewe, 5 Aug. 1794.

As far as the editors have been able to determine, no translation of *Brief Reflections* was printed.

[4] For the publication of M. d'A's translation, CB had solicited the interest of Jean-François de La Marche, évêque et comte de St.-Pol-de-Léon (i. L. 5 n. 19), who, in London since 1791, was active in the relief of French emigrants; that of John Wilmot (1750–1815), organizer of the Freemasons' Hall Committee for the relief of the refugees (1790); and of Thomas Cadell, the elder (1742–1802), the publisher of FBA's tract.

138   [Great Bookham, April 1794]

To Doctor Burney

A.L.S. (The University Library, Newcastle upon Tyne, G63466, MSS. Misc. 56), *n.d.*
Originally a double sheet 4to, of which the first leaf is cut away and missing   2 pp.   wafer
Addressed: Dr. Burney, / Chelsea College.
Edited by FBA, p. 1, *annotated*: William Phillips
Docketed in pencil: MSS. Misc. 56

. . . ⌈for any ⟨such⟩ deed against what they call their Government!⌉—Brissot[1]—Carra, Gorsas, Clootz, Manuel, Roland-Lacroix—Danton—how little could they imagine, when with such savage insult they erected the scaffold of Murder in the Place de la Revolution, in full sight of his own Palace, for the unhappy King, they were building the structure whence their own heads, as prematurely though not as innocently, were to be brought to the block!—

I am called off to a sweeter contemplation,—little Willy,[2] whom you will love very much, is just arrived. I have been playing with him till I am breathless, & [I have] now made him over to M. d'A. who, most opportunely, has lately treated himself with a Wheelbarrow,—& upon this he has placed a certain blue Coat lined with fur, made for a winter journey in keen cold, & a Pillow at the head, & the little man is there seated, with an exulting delight that no future pleasure can ever succeed, if equal. M. d'Arblay is his Coachman, & his little face is bright with joy, while his voice shouts its full contentment. You must not expect to see him like Norbury, for he is not handsome; but he is good humoured, gay, ¦ honest, very sensible, & very good. Pray when you see his Mama tell her he complains she is gone to *London & Dorking, upon a postchaise,* & his sister Fanny but *upon a Cabolay.* How glad I am you were able to be at Esther's

138. [1] Jean-Jacques-Pierre Brissot de Warville (1754–93), Jean-Louis Carra (1742–93), Antoine-Joseph Gorsas (1751–93), Jean-Baptiste Clootz (1755–94), Pierre-Louis Manuel (1751–93), Jean-Marie Roland de la Platière (1734–93), Jean-Paul de Lacroix (1754–94), and Georges-Jacques Danton (1759–94), all elected at one time or another to the National Convention and all now, with the exception of Roland, who committed suicide, guillotined.
[2] John William James Phillips, now nearly 3 years old.

on Saturday Evening! what a pleasure for Susanna!—I am very glad, too, you have renewed some acquaintance with M. de Narbonne, who is so amiable, as well as cultivated & high bred, that he has almost only to be known in order to be loved. My dear Mrs. Lock writes me word that Mr. Lock told her he & you *most minutely* agreed in your opinions upon the little brochure sur les prêtres—so she leaves me to imagine how it was abused! Adieu, my ever dearest Sir, — I beg my love & Duty to my Mother & Sarah,—& am ever & aye

Your most affectionate & dutiful
F.d'A.

139   Great Bookham, 25–7 April 1794

To James Burney

A.L.S. (PML, Autog. Cor. bound), 25–7 Apr. 1794
Double sheet 4to   4 pp   trimmed   *pmk* ⟨28⟩ A⟨ ⟩ 94   wafer
Addressed: Captain Burney, / James Street, / Westminster.

Bookham,
April 25th—94.

A thousand thanks, my ever kind Brother, for your affection-ate invitation, which I should accept with equal speed & pleasure, if I consulted only the desire it awakened of shaking hands with you; but I am under a very long promise to make my first Town residence with Charlotte, — — &, indeed, before I enumerate 99 reasons for declining your offer, I may as well mention the 100th—viz — — we have, for the present, entirely relinquished all thoughts of leaving Bookham.[1] Our motives

---

139. [1] In acquiescence to the fears of CB, who in his letter of 14 Apr. (Osborn) had reiterated his warnings 'à propos to coming to Town': 'I really think that M. D'A. determined very prudently not to come while things are in such a ferment, & People are so narrowly watched. . . . It is very natural & amiable in M. D'A. to love his friend & commander M. de la Fayette, & to wish to prove him to have been well-intentioned & faithful to his poor King; but it w^d be difficult now to convince the friends of our present Governm^t or even that of the late Lord North, that he was a friend to England during the American War. And his cause now being taken up by our most violent Jacobins, who wish so well to the Jacobins of France w^d render the task still more difficult.'

are purely prudential, for we are seized with no spirit of misanthropy—on the contrary, we are in perfect charity with our own lot, & *consequently* with all mankind,—for nothing so surely inspires good humour with the World, as good humour ǀ with our own fireside.—& it would be hard if we quarrelled with ours at this moment—having got none!

I thank Mrs. B[urney] very sincerely for her obliging participation in your proposition: & when times & seasons permit our junction, peradventure we may make a division of our favours, & M. d'Arblay may seek to sustain—*at*tain rather—the character of a French husband, by accepting an apartment in one House, while I betake me to another. You know the French custom—& I would not have such a Cavalier pass, in the Metropolis, for a Goth & Barbarian, however he may content himself to be no more refined in the Country.

But really, my dear James, I must tell you—Compliments being over—I am amazed at your effrontery ǀ in assuming to yourself a merit of writing so very rarely! — — I confess to you, however, in private, *I* should not have much cause to repine if such omissions of indolence or neglect were to be reckoned praise worthy,—for few people, then, need hold their heads higher for similar accomplishments than your *fair sister.*

Your *thinking* of coming from Chesington was very kind,—pray thank Mrs. B[urney] for her concurrence in the idea: but I shall thank you much more heartily, I trust, some time this Summer.—Yet it is grievous that we have no accommodation! We can give you nothing but *Chaste Embraces!*—very meagre fare after such a journey! You will conclude me a very fit Partner for a POOR HALF STARVED MONNSEER FRENCH!—However, I'll tell you what we will do—we will Walk with you from hence to Mickleham, *& give you a very good Dinner at the Captain's!* ǀ So you see, we have some hospitality about us.—

How sorry I am I shall see poor Mr. Sleepe no more![2]—I had a Letter from my Aunts[3] yesterday, who, poor souls, have been scarce alive, they say, till lately.

I hear you have formed some scheme about our internal

---

[2] A relative of FBA's mother, James Sleepe (i, L. 7 n. 7) was buried at St. Luke's, Chelsea on 3 Feb. 1794.

[3] CB's sisters Rebecca (1724–1809) and Ann (1722–94), who since 1791 were living in Richmond. The parish register records the burial of the latter on 23 Aug. 1794. Their letter to FBA is missing.

defence,[4] & we both wish much to see it—for I forgot to mention our Philanthropy extends not to the National Convention of France—to *Robertspierre*,[5] rather, for he alone has all power there. So if you have any pretty plan for '*a very pretty murder*', or two, as poor Dick[6] used to say, in case of a visit here, nobody will give it a better reception. My kind Love to Mrs. B[urney] & make Martin submit to a *baiser* in my name. Adieu, my dear Brother, ever your most affect.[e]

F. d'A.

M. d'A. greets you most sincerely & cordially, & loves you very much by constant remembrance of your not only Fraternal —but Paternal kind offices: & he kisses the Hands of you[r dear] lady very affectionately.

Ap. 27th I have just got your new little dear bit,[7] my dearest James—how can you make such horrid tempting propositions, to allure to indiscretion & frolic?—Give my Love to all that around you, in your next family batch, & tell them I have a very constant & affectionate Memory in absence.

140   Great Bookham, 27 April 1794

To Doctor Burney

A.L.S. (Barrett, Eg. 3690, ff. 72–3b), 27 Apr. [17]94
Double sheet 4to   4 pp.   *pmks* LEATHER HEAD   A⟨P⟩94   wafer
Addressed: Dr. Burney, / Chelsea College, / Midlesex.
Endorsed by CB: 1794
Edited by FBA, p. 1, *annotated*: ⁜ ⁜ ⁜   (6) on the Translating F. d'A's Essay for the Emigrant Priests—& on M. d'Arblay—his life—conduct— character—exquisite Disposition—

Bookham,
April 27th—94

M. d'Arblay, my dearest Father, is vext you do not use his full powers in the full sense he has made them over to you.[1]

---

[4] James Burney's *PLAN | of | DEFENCE against INVASION* appeared only in 1797 (L. 236 n. 2), when invasion seemed imminent.
[5] For this spelling and its derivations, see *Thraliana*, ii. 874, and n. 4.
[6] Richard Thomas Burney (i, Intro., lxxiii), FBA's half-brother.
[7] Not extant.

140. [1] M. d'A's letter and CB's letter, to which this is the reply, are missing.

He thinks that not to produce the translation with his Letter to l'Eveque,[2] would now appear as if the offer had been a mere gasconade—he begs you, therefore, without hesitation to forward it, if this is also your opinion.

For *me*, I confess myself amazed & disturbed by this proceeding in *both* the Bishops. Had *any* Frenchman *translated* the little work, after M. d'Arblay's public engagement, I should have thought it ungentlemanlike; but in any of that respectable body, for whom it was written, & to whom his own translation was offered, it was a part proceeding the last I could have expected, without previous application to *you*, *him*, or *me*.

The matter, however, being so, & M. de Narbonne being strongly of opinion that any contest upon it would be beneath his friend, whom he thinks could receive no *credit* from *any* translation, — — I shall now dwell upon it no more. And M. d'Arblay himself tells me he *works off all black humours* in his Garden. What, indeed, to *him* is a *disagrèment*, after his many deep misfortunes & disappointments?

How often—O how often do I regret that my beloved & dearest Father cannot, for some time *de suite*, see the sun rise & set with a character so formed to become every way dear to him! — — so replete with every resource for chearful solitude, & happy retirement!—so *very* like himself in disposition, humour, & taste, that the Day never passes in which I do not, in its course, exclaim *How you remind me of my Father*! — —

Is not this news from the Continent, as well as from the West Indies, *very* excellent?[3] We wanted to make ourselves Tower & Park Guns, for a little rejoicing. However, not having Cannon or Powder, M. d'A. has contented himself with only making me another new walk, in our Orchard, which must serve instead.

I forgot to mention in my late Letters [that] I have seen good Mr. Hoole.[4] I heard he had visited our worthy neighbours, the

---

[2] See Ll. 127 n. 4, 137 n. 3.

[3] FBA could have read the report of the Duke of York's victories at Landrecy and Cambray in *The Times* (24 Apr. 1794); and in *The Times* (23 Apr.) the report of the capture by 21 Mar. of the islands of Martinique, Ste. Lucie, and Guadeloupe.

[4] John Hoole (1727–1803), translator of Ariosto, Tasso, and Metastasio, who often visited his son, the Revd. Samuel Hoole (*c.* 1758–1839), curate at this time of Abinger-Wotton, Surrey.

Parson & his wife, & Mrs. Cooke meant to oblige me by discouraging him from calling. I desired her to rectify that mistake, if he came again, for my resolute declining of all new acquaintance, to avoid dress, &c is very remote from involving seclusion from old friends. He accordingly presented himself soon after, & I was very glad to see him. As he spoke French with as much difficulty as M. d'A. speaks English, M. d'A, on hearing he had translated ¹ Ariosto & Tasso, attacked him in Italian—but was much surprised to find he was not even understood! how very different to know, & to speak a Language!—M. d'A. is himself an instance, for he hesitates in pronouncing *How do do?* & he wants no assistance in reading Hume, or even a *News paper*, which is far more difficult, because more diffuse, & subject to local cant.

I see *your Name*, my dearest Father, with *generals, statesmen, Monarchs, & Charles Fox*: in a collection of *bon mots*!⁵ I am dying for the work. If you have it, I beseech a peep at it by some opportunity. I will carefully return it. O—& have you, dear sir, the words of the Cunning Man? M. d'Arblay accompanies himself on his Mandoline, by Ear, in all the songs of the Devin du Village,⁶ & he thinks to take them so in English, would be a good lesson of English Metre.

adieu, my ever dearest sir, my Love & Duty to my Mother & Sarah ever most

affec^{ly} & dut^y

F D'A

Susanna writes me word she had a delicious full Family day at Chelsea on Wednesday. Willy liked his Wheelbarrow so well, he came again Yesterday, & asked for his *Cabolay*.

---

⁵ FBA could have seen the advertisements in *The Times* (2 and 3 Apr. 1794): 'This day is published, in two Vols. price 8s. / A new Edition, being the 3d, much enlarged, of / ELEGANT ANECDOTES, BON MOTS, and / CHARACTERISTIC TRAITS, of the greatest Princes, / Politicians, Philosophers, Poets, Orators, and Wits of modern / Times; such as the Emperor Charles V. King of Prussia, Peter / the Great, Henry IV. Charles XII. Louis XIV. Voltaire, Swift, / Garrick, Dr. Johnson, Des Cartes, Sir R. Steele, Addison, Ho- / garth, Dryden, Metastasio, Charles I. Oliver Cromwell, Dr. Bur- / ney, Richardson, Mr. Fox, Mr. Erskine, &c. &c. / By the Rev. JOHN ADAMS, M.A. [?1750–1814].' The first edition had appeared in 1790.

⁶ Rousseau's *Devin du Village* (1752), adapted by CB in 1765 for the English stage as *The Cunning Man*, was first presented on 21 Nov. 1766 at Drury Lane, where in the season 1766–7 it was performed fourteen times and in February 1768, twice (MacMillan, p. 228). Published in 1766, it ran to two editions in November (Scholes, i. 107–17; Lonsdale, pp. 70–3). A third edition, appearing on 4 Dec. 1766, contained both the French and English text (*London Chronicle*, 2–4 Dec.).

141   Great Bookham, [*c.* 27 April 1794]

Conjointly with M. d'Arblay
To Mrs. Phillips

A.L. & A.L. (Berg), *n.d.*
Originally a double sheet 4to, of which FBA later discarded the second
leaf   1 p. torn in two but mended, as see Textual Notes
   Edited by FBA, p. 1, *annotated and dated*: ❖ *1794.* Je crois (No I) (2)
A: & F:d'A. to Mʳˢ Phillips. / Kept for the sweet Kindness to *la Compagne
heureuse!* on the other side.—Written at four / not many / Months after their
happy union.—

[*By Madame d'Arblay*]

   Unluckily, my Susan, we were out upon one of our long
strolls, with dear Mr. Lock's dear Chair,[1] when Jenny[2] arrived;
& so I must but sign & send, in conscience—
   & beg my best loving love to my dearest Charlotte—& the
little group around you both—I *long for long* ⟨details upon all
man⟩ner of subjects—I hope to get to Norbury P⟨ark⟩ for a
[xxxxx *3 or 4 words*][3] Fri[day][4] Eve, & to you on Saturday for a
ditto—but I cannot venture on to Mickleham so late as I understand the Travelling will end—God bless & bless you All—
   Your dear Willy has had a bowel complaint, on Thursday, &
yr. Maid: had the sense to carry him to Mr. Ansell[5] on Friday,
& on Saturday he was here, in *his Cabiolet*, digging & hoeing,
gay, well & good as possible. Jeny[2] says he is perfectly hearty
to Day.

[*By M. d'Arblay*]

   J'espère, ma bien aimée Soeur, que vous aurez bien voulu
être mon interprète auprès de toute notre famille à qui vous
aurez dit, sans doute, combien je regrette de ne pouvoir lui
rendre mes devoirs cette année. Ce n'est pas la privation la
moins cruelle dont j'aye à accuser le malheur des circonstances
fâcheuses que l'esprit public est venu agraver: mais si j'ai à

---

141.   [1] A folding chair (L. 136, p. 45).
   [2] SBP's servant.
   [3] The words have been obliterated by the glue used to repair a torn page (see
Textual Notes).
   [4] On 2 May.   [5] An apothecary from Dorking (i, L. 6 n. 4).

gemir sur les fleaux qui ont presque totalement detruit ma malheureuse Patrie, Je benis à chaque instant l'aimable compagne qui m'en a donné une nouvelle, en m'attachant à une famille que j'honnore et respecte autant que je l'aime.

Vous arrivez, donc enfin, Vendredy et le Capitaine aussi j'espere. d'aprés votre lettre Je me flatte aussi de revoir M^r de N[arbonne] dites lui je vous prie que je vous attens tous trois avec impatience:—Mais puisque vous avez prévu le jour de votre arrivé et

[*the second leaf is missing*]

142 Great Bookham, 2 May 1794

To Esther (Burney) Burney

A.L.S. (Berg), 2 May [17]94
Double sheet 4to   4 pp.   *pmks* LEATH[ER] / HEAD   6 MA 94   wafer
Addressed: Mrs. Burney, / Upper Titchfield Street, / Portland Place—
Endorsed by EBB: 1794
Arithmetical scribbling, right fold, p. 4.

Bookham,
May 2^d—94

A little word I must send to my dearest Etty, to tell her again & again how truly all her Letters interest, & many of them affect me. Would to God I could manifest my constant warm affection better than by its declaration!—your troubles & fears & harrassing cares,[1] my dear Esther, go to my Heart,—but what amazes me in the midst of them is your incessant Engagements. I cannot comprehend how you find time or strength for what overwhelmed *me* both in leisure & health, without any family toils, or any mind-wearing difficulties, when I lived in Town. I cannot, also, but most seriously apprehend for your health, delicate as it is, from hot rooms & cold exits, joined to the great fatigue attending Dress & preparations for all Evening visits. I have always thought you risked yourself considerably too much, for the gratification of your *acquaintance*,—your *friends* must all love you too sincerely ever to be hurt at a negative that

142. [1] Cf. L. 132 and n. 3.

is given only from personal discretion. I won't say *forgive* me for this exhortation, because it arises from feelings you cannot be angry at. I only wish to impress you with a little reflexion upon your own *inestimable* value to your whole House, that it may excite sufficient courage to counterbalance the too great facility which makes you think it impossible to resist solicitation where you can be of service *out* of it. The motive is amiable, but it does not amount to a duty, like the preservation of a health so essential to the well doing ⏐ of your family. And when I read your touching details of the sleepless nights occasioned you by nursing, & by perplexing conflicts, I know too much of the drudgery of the Toilette & late Hours & courteous exertions, to frames much stronger than *yours*, to doubt for a moment the undermining mischief you may owe to them.

I compassionate & admire at once the parting with your loveliest Cecilia:[2] & her sweet little affectionate speeches, & the *Eyes* you describe of her last Morning, moved me extremely. She will never forget you, my Hetty, nor grow indifferent to you —& I MUST hope that you will be amply paid, ultimately, for the painful separation. My beloved Mrs. Lock, & her beautiful Amelia, both unite in declaring her the most interesting & lovely little Creature they ever saw. Mrs. Lock, too, pretends *you 'look sweetly'* but that I know you will only scout.—I grieve at your last hints about my dear & good namesake[3]—I easily conceive her feelings,—& *your's,* ⏐ O could I as easily relieve as participate! — — Marianne will I am sure prove a comfort to you, & what Mrs. H[awkins] said concerning her,[4] &c makes the comfort double, in obviating any hard & rending plans of parting with her. I earnestly hope she & the excellent Sophy will contrive between them, to manage your Amelà—for I am *sick* when I think of *your* passing such nights, while so weak & unhardy. The two dear Girls are far fitter for such work, though it is severe to *any* one: but if they think of it in the light of saving

² See L. 132 n. 5.

³ Frances Burney (1776–1828), soon to take a post as governess with the family of Algernon Percy (1750–1830), 2nd Baron Lovaine of Alnwick (1786), cr. Earl of Beverley (1790). See also a letter (Berg) SBP to FBA, 24 June 1795, and L. 242 n. 16).

⁴ Lost with EBB's letter are Mrs. Hawkins's assurances or advice concerning the eldest daughter Hannah Maria or Marianne (1772–1856), but evidently she was to remain at home for the present and with her sister Sophia Elizabeth (1777–1856) help to rear the youngest child Amelia Maria (1792–1868).

you, they will see it as *their own* first good. Does Mr. B[urney] keep well himself? My kind love to him. We have given up our London journey for the present, which is a deed of more prudence than pleasure, as I had delighted in the prospect of seeing my dear Father—Sisters—Brothers—& a few elect this spring. However, the Time may come, when my patience may be recompenced. Mean while, I have, indeed, no other trial for it. Adieu, my every dear Esther. Yrs ever

F. d'A

I meant a WORD—& here is a long HANDSOME Letter! — — My Love to [all a]round. ǀ

N.B. I began this for susanna to carry—but missing her, I cannot refuse myself this vacancy in *her* Letters, to send it off, as a little remembrance individual. My Love to that dearest dear when you next embrace her—& to my dear Bessy⁵—& Marianne —& Fanny—Sophy, and *Mr. Edwardus*.

---

143   Great Bookham, 9 May [1794]

To Doctor Burney

A.L.S. (Barrett, Eg. 3690, ff. 75–6b), 9 May
Double sheet 4to   4 pp.   wafer
Addressed: Dr. Burney, / Chelsea College, / Midlesex.
Edited by FBA, p. 1, *annotated and dated*: ⁖ –94   (8)
on the Eveque de Troyes translation of the Essay for the Priests.
Edited also by CFBt.

Bookham,
May 9th·

How kind is my dearest Father, & how strait to my Heart comes his kindness! The *Chanterelles* have vibrated to that of M. d'Arblay. The Cunning Man he is reading with great pleasure, &, from its simplicity, & his remembrance of the French, with as much facility as prose. It will be an exceeding good lesson with his Mandoline. We shall expect Hawkesworth[1] with

⁵ Elizabeth Warren Burney (or 'Blue').

143. [1] John Hawkesworth (*c.* 1715–73), *An Account of the Voyages undertaken by the order of his present Majesty for making discoveries in the Southern Hemisphere* (3 vols., 1773). CB, who in 1771 had recommended Hawkesworth to John Montagu (1718–92),

impatience, & take the utmost care of it, as I know it to be an *offering binding* from the good & grateful Author.

━━━━━▸

M. d'Arblay has just had a Letter from the Eveque de Troyes.[2] He protests he is very sorry to have *done that thing*, like Dick, but he does not make any proposition whatever to relinquish it ⌐& casts all the blame on the misinformation of the Eveque who belied him. He has sent a page of his *Preface*, which you have seen, but we will enclose you the Letter ¦ for your perusal by the first pacquet or opportunity.⌐

I confess myself considerably hurt by this business. What in the World can the public think of it? My philosophic Gardener, however, made his first chagrin his last, & read this final sentence with perfect *sang froid*, telling me I should be at least a little consoled that there were finer things said of me in the Preface than in decency, he could have said himself.

⌐I must write an explanation of the affair, as well as I may, when it is advertised, to Mrs. Schwellenberg, from whom I have just had the satisfaction of a kind message through my dear Mrs. Lock.⌐

We were anxious Mr. Lock should have an interview with her, as M. d'Arblay had been informed, that the King had been told he *had served in America against England, as Secretary to M. de la Fayette.* Who could have invented such a complete falsehood?— M. d'Arblay ¦ begged Mr. Lock simply & roundly to make known—First, that he never was in America: Secondly, That he had never any connexion with M. de la Fayette but as his *Equal*, except with respect alone to *Military* precedence: & thirdly, that, having been an officer in the Royal Artillery from

---

4th Earl of Sandwich, First Lord of the Admiralty (1748–51, 1763, 1771–82), as a suitable editor for the papers bearing on Cook's voyages, evidently possessed a presentation copy of the work (see Lonsdale, pp. 111–12).

    [2] See L. 137 n. 3 for the Bishop's letter of 6 mai 1794. Stating that but for l'évêque de Léon he would, on hearing of M. d'A's plan, have abandoned his own translation, the Bishop de Troyes went on to justify his work on the grounds that it was not to be published in England but 'en Suisse ou dans les Pays-bas, tandis que l'annonce de la votre [*sic*] était relative uniquement à l'Angleterre'. He added that the notice of M. d'A's translation (appended to FBA's work), 'supposait un très [*sic*] prompte publication' and since six months had passed by, he thought the enterprise might have been abandoned. He enclosed the Preface to his work, with its praise of FBA, asserting that the pamphlet was the most brilliant of several pieces that would 'faire connaître hors de l'Angleterre, les efforts généreux de la Nation Anglaise en faveur du clergé emigrant [*sic*] français'.

12 years of age, (by particular interest,) he had never served any man whatever (officially) but his King.[3]

⌐For the *Royal* murderers summarily rewarded in kind,[4] I find myself always rejoicing—but M. de Malesherbes cost me dear.[5] What a shameless Massacre is his!—72—& so respectable a man! Again the widow & Dsse of the Noblesse aged 62—& 63,[6] Good God—We have lately seen the papers very irregularly, Mr. Lock's not having arrived, & Mrs. Cooke having made a change; but the few that have come into our way have made our Hearts ache—[7]

How much pleasanter to me to think of your evening *Literley* —I am very glad for Mrs. Radcliffe & her £500[8] & I *act* 'think of That, Master Brooke!' if *so*[9]—I have not yet seen my dear Susan, for it has rained almost all day long, but I have had a note delivered, & sent —— Mr. Cooke this moment ᶦ calls in to tell me Lᵈ S[tanhope], his Brother Mr. S[tanhope] & more have been ordered before the Privy Counsel on suspicion of Treason—what can this mean?[10] —— thanks to my Mother for

---

[3] See M. d'A, ii, Intro., x–xi.

[4] Danton, for instance, and Camille Desmoulins (1760–94), both of whom voted for the death of the King, were themselves executed on 5 Apr. 1794.

[5] Malesherbes (ii, L. 49 n. 11; L. 68 nn. 9, 10) was guillotined on 22 Apr. The *St. James's Chronicle* (8 May 1794) recalled his benevolence and energy of mind, and as well, his frank and homely appearance (his neat black coat, formal wig, squat round figure, drollery and gaiety), attributes that excited merely ridicule in 'frivolous Courtiers . . . only capable of judging of a Minister of State by the elegance of his person'. 'He was loved and sought after by Louis XVI; he was ridiculed by the corrupt courtiers; and he was guillotined by a sanguinary faction.'

[6] Guillotined on this same day (22 Apr.) were Diane-Adélaïde de Rochechouart (*c.* 1732–94), who had married in 1751 Louis-Marie-Florent, comte (afterwards duc) du Châtelet (1727–94); and Béatrix de Choiseul-Stainville (1730–94), who had married in 1759 Antoine-Antonin, duc de Grammont (1722–99). The *London Chronicle* (3–6 May) gave the ages of the Duchesses (above) as 62 and 64 respectively; and in spite of the error FBA made in recalling the age of the latter, this was the list she must have seen.

[7] To M. d'A, who must have known, or known of, many of those lately guillotined, Robespierre's purges and the lurid events of his Reign of Terror must have been painful indeed, to say nothing of the decrees of the National Convention militating against Royalists, Constitutionalists, and *émigrés*.

[8] CB, in a letter now missing, had evidently referred to Ann Radcliffe's *The Mysteries of Udolpho* (4 vols.), which had been advertised in *The Times* (2 and 8 May 1794) to appear within a few days and for which the publishers G. G. and J. Robinson of Paternoster-row had paid £500 (*DNB*).

[9] Cf. *The Merry Wives of Windsor*, III. v.

[10] The rumour was incorrectly attached to Charles, 3rd Earl Stanhope. It was rather his domestic tutor and secretary, Jeremiah Joyce (1763–1816), a member of

Two letters in which I shall soon be her debtor incontinently. Not a word from that lazy Sarah. Mrs. Rishton acquaints me she is to have the pleasure of visiting you ere long at Chelsea. I hope she will be able to give me a glimpse of her while she is at Shere which is not more than nine or ten miles off.[10]

The other Day, M. d'Arblay picked up a Critical Review at Mr. Cooke's, with an article on the *Reflexions*: so I find I am too Aristocratic for them[11]—however, it seems done by some one who has a sort of *personal* kindness for me, as so much praise & encouragement is mixt with an evident dissatisfaction with the little work itself.

M. d'Arblay is at this moment rectifying his Mandoline with your Chanterelles, which delight him. Adieu, my dearest dear sir—I shall consult you soon upon a *secret plan*—not *plot*!—

> ever—ever most affect[ly] &
> dutiful yr.
> F. d'A.

Sunday morn. The Books arrived last night, & Charles, when a little Boy, never more delighted in opening a pacquet than M. d'A.—a thousand thanks. Susan is here, & Fanny, & send millions of Loves & duties.

P.S. We flatter ourselves the Capt. will have brought us the Print[12]—To-morrow we are all to meet, if it is fine.

the Society for Constitutional Information and of the highly suspect London Corresponding Society, who was arrested on 4 May 1794 at Lord Stanhope's residence at Chevening, Kent, on a charge of 'treasonable practices' (*DNB*) and brought before the Privy Council. Thomas Hardy (1752–1832), founder of and secretary to the London Corresponding Society, was arrested on 12 May; Horne Tooke, on 16 May. These radicals, with a few others (see *AR* xxxvi (1794), 263–80), were brought before the Privy Council for questioning, were imprisoned, tried, but eventually freed (*DNB*).

[11] A long and favourable review in the *Critical Review*, x (March 1794), 318–21, pointed out a few faults in *Brief Reflections* (see L. 134 n. 2), but as to politics remarked only that FBA had 'decidedly chosen hers'.

[12] See L. 135 n. 1.

144   Great Bookham, 6 June [1794]

To Mrs. Waddington

A.L. (Berg), 6 June
Double sheet 4to   1 p.   lower right corner of the second leaf torn away
and replaced   *pmks* DARKING   ⟨1⟩3 ⟨J⟩U 94   wafer
Addressed: Mrs. Waddington, / Lanover Court / Abergavenny—
Scribbling in Italian, p. 4.
Docketed in ink, p. 1: 1794

Bookham,
June 6th

What is become of my dear Marianne? & her Emily?[1]
what, of the more chearing lines I was bid hope should succeed
the last few melancholy ones? God forbid any new distress!—I
have been far from well myself during this interval,—a bilious
attack, which without coming to any crisis, has robbed me of
appetite & strength, seized me suddenly at that period, & hangs
upon me with tormenting constancy still. I cannot, however,
wait longer without news of my sweet Marianne, for whom I
am continually anxious & unquiet. may the news be better &
more congenial to my wishes!

Mr. B. Dewes has lately, in a manner the most welcome to all
my feelings, sent me the dear Chimney Piece[2] of our MOST
revered's last workmanship. What an invaluable gift to me!—It
will be my dearest ornament in my new Parlour, whenever that
is built—& I shall suspend over it the miniature dearest to its
loved author.[3] God bless you always my dearest *Mary*!—

144. [1] See L. 129 n. 2.
   [2] Mrs. Delany made 'numberless mantel-pieces with Etruscan and other
designs in cut paper laid upon wood, which had the effect of inlaying' (Delany,
2nd s., iii. 502).
   [3] See L. 124 n. 9.

145 [London, 16 June 1794]

M. d'Arblay
To Madame d'Arblay

A.L. (Berg), *n.d.*
Originally a double sheet 4to, of which FBA later discarded the second
leaf   2 pp.
Edited by FBA, p. 1, *top margin, dated and annotated*: July—1794   I
Written on quitting me at Bookham,— / to accompany his darling friend, /
M. de Narbonne, afterwards God Father / to Alexander, in his leaving
England / to emigrate nearer to re-admission / into his unhappy country.

Ce Lundy matin

Ce matin, ma bonne amie, je suis moins malheureux, et
j'espere que c'est un presentiment que tout va mieux. j'ai bien
besoin de le penser pour soutenir plus longtems la cruelle situation dans la quelle je me trouve. Je vais cependant essayer de te
rendre compte de tout ce qui s'est passé depuis notre separation.
Tu sais dejà, je crois, que nous n'avons pu prendre le chemin le
plus court, ce qui nous etait absolument egal. Je ne crois pas
que l'on ait jamais vu deux figures plus tristes.[1] j'aurais desiré
rendre à mon ami ce voyage moins desagreable: mais tous les
efforts que je faisais pour paraitre moins absorbé par mon inquietude, n'etaient que de vraies grimaces. Cependant mon ami
etait loin de se douter du sacrifice que je lui fesais! lui, même
paraissait occupé bien douloureusement à recapituler tout ce
qu'il a eprouvé de fâcheux depuis cinq ans, et son depart ǀ parait
avoir rouvert toutes les plaies que les soins tendres qu'il a reçus
en ce pays avaient comme cicatrisées. Arrivés à Tottenham,
nous sommes descendus chez la Princesse,[2] qui a été toute

145. [1] The comte de Narbonne, having been interviewed by Pitt, had received,
according to Adrien Arcelin, 'Réponse . . .', *Annales de l'Académie de Macon*, 2nd
ser., vii (1890), 33–45, 'l'vis impératif de quitter l'Angleterre'. The comte, accompanied by d'Arblay, had apparently left Mickleham or West Humble on Sunday,
15 June, intending to sail from Dover on 17 June (see also Jasinski, *Lettres inédites à
Louis de Narbonne*, p. 289).
   It was at this time that a packet of Madame de Staël's letters was 'trusted confidentially' to d'Arblay, see Jasinski, op. cit.; and also Charlotte Barrett, in a letter
to Henry Barrett [Jan. 1840] (Eg. 3702A, ff. 108–9): 'they are beautiful—just like
Corinna—mais—not possible to print'. These are the letters that, deposited with
the larger part of the d'Arblay archive in the Berg Collection, NYPL, were published in 1960 by Georges Solovieff and 1960 by Béatrice W. Jasinski.
   [2] The princesse d'Hénin and the comte de Lally-Tolendal had moved from

aimable, ainsi que Lally. Tous deux m'ont demandé tes nouvelles avec beaucoup d'interest, et m'ont parus bien reconnaissans du souvenir que l'on conserve d'eux dans le canton que nous habitons. Lally surtout s'est montré trés affecté de ta maladie: car ma profonde tristesse ne lui ayant point echappé, il a bien fallu que je lui disse que le depart de mon ami n'en etait pas l'unique cause. J'ai trouvé chez la Princesse M^de la C^esse de Monthron,³ mon amie de plus de 18 ans, et celle de M^de la M^ise de germigney⁴ depuis leur enfance. J'ai su par elle que cette femme interessante etait à Boulogne, ou même elle la croit encore. Ses cheveaux etaient attelés pour rentrer en france lors du decret sur les Emigrés, ⌐un decret qui m'a echappé.⌐ ⌐

[*the second leaf is missing*]

146   Great Bookham, 16 June 1794

To M. d'Arblay

A.L. (Berg), 16 June [17]94
Double sheet 12mo   3 pp.   wafer
Addressed: Pour / Monsieur d'Arblay—

Bookham—
June 16.—94¹

I have just received a Letter too dear to let me wait till to-morrow to thank for it—I have had no severe returns of spasms,

London to Richmond late in 1793. Cf. Walpole, xii. 30 (letter of 15 Oct. 1793): 'she talks of letting her house here' [in Richmond].

³ Angélique-Marie d'Arlus du Tailly (*c.* 1745–1827), who had married *c.* 1767 Claude-Philibert, comte de Mouret et de Montrond (*fl.*1767–92). A biography of her son Casimir (1769–1843) by Henri Malo, *Le Beau Montrond* (1926), gives the chief events of her life: her education and marriage, her friendships with la princesse de Poix and la princesse d'Hénin, her emigration at the close of 1790 to Neufchâtel and later with her youngest child to England, where she remained until 1799. Having lost her husband and a large part of her fortune by these emigrations, she resided for the remainder of her life at Besançon.

⁴ Denise-Victoire Chastelier du Mesnil (*fl.* 1750–1813) became the wife of Jacques-François de Germigney, marquis de Germigney (d. 1790).

146. ¹ Though the second sheet of M. d'A's letter of [15 June 1794], the *verso* of which normally would have carried address and postmarks, was torn away, the letter would presumably have been posted late Sunday evening or early enough on Monday morning to reach Bookham in time for FBA to write a reply on the same day.

& think they will pass over—be tranquil, mon meilleur Ami—
I feel as if I should get quite well when I see you again.—

My beloved nurse[2] salutes you cordially. I have been forced
to see Dr. Moore,[3] | who came whether I would or not — — he
gave no opinion, but says he will prescribe for me.

How I rejoice you have had news of M^e la M^sse de G[ermig-
ney]!—

My dear nurse will not leave me till she consigns me to mon
chef.—

If you see my dearest Father, with my tenderest duty, tell
him I have now the best advice, as well as | care.—that I can
have in your absence—

I have written a few [lines] to M. de N[arbonne].[4]—I have
done nothing but by recollection of what mon ami said he
should wish.

Mon amina[5] is here, assisting me to demolish your superb
present of strawberries. He calls for you continually to come &
dig with him—& drive his wheelbarrow.

147   Great Bookham, 5 July 1794

To Mrs. Waddington

A.L. (Berg), 5 July [17]94
Single sheet 4to   1 p.
Scribbling, p. 2.

Bookham, July 5th—94

Ever since my last Letter to my dearest *Mary* I have been in
a most suffering state, till within these last 3 Days—& only by
proxy of M. d'A. or my sister Phillips have I written even to my
dear Father—but I am now *much better*, though it will not be
immediately I shall be wholly recruited from so long an assault.
—I was quite relieved by the sight at last of your hand—though
I am very little satisfied with the account of your poor Emily, &
touched to the Heart by what you say of her dear Mother—

---

[2] FBA's sister, SBP.   [3] See ii, L. 68 n. 41.
[4] Not extant, though the comte de Narbonne mentions in a letter (Berg) to
M. d'A, 21 Aug. 1794, having received a letter from SBP.
[5] John William James Phillips, aged 3.

Endeavour to arm yourself with more strength, my sweet Marianne, & victory may be nearer than you apprehend, for MUCH MUCH is our self-power, when exerted with earnestness, & with *ALL OUR MIGHT*—This is but my 3ᵈ little billet since I have resumed the use of a Pen—it must not therefore be longer than to beg a *better account* of my ever dear Friend with all the speed Truth will admit,—& to say God bless her!—

I knew nothing of the Death of poor Mr. Dewes till your last Letter[1]—Pray tell me something of his affairs & Will, & particularly how *YOU* fare, & who has his Papers & Letters—I wish much to recover my own.

148   Great Bookham, 16–21 July 1794

To Mrs. Francis (*later* Broome)

A.L.S. (Barrett, Eg. 3693, ff. 55–6b), 16–21 July [17]94
Double sheet 4to   4 pp.   *pmks* EPSOM   22 JY 94   green wafer
Addressed: Mrs. Francis, / Margate. / to the care of Dr. Charles Burney,
Endorsed by CBF: Sister d'Arblay July 21. / ans. — — Augᵗ 1794
Edited by CFBt.

Read This First

July 21ˢᵗ I lost by various causes 3 posts since this was begun—& in the mean time I have received a *business answer* from our dear Carlos—pray thank him *in confidence*, & *say noting* in public of any Letter, as we are upon a little Secret transaction.[1] He will find an answer on his return home.

147. [1] See L. 129 n. 3. In a will (P.C.C. Dodwell, 588), made 6 Nov. 1780 and probated (with six codicils) on 2 Dec. 1793, Court Dewes provided his sister Mary (Dewes) Port with an annuity of £100 for life, desiring 'that her husband may have nothing to do with it'. 'To all and each of her younger Children' he bequeathed £500, adding variously to the bequests in a codicil of 9 June 1793. To the eldest son John Port, 'already sufficiently provided for', he left a legacy of £50. Of his sister's family, Mrs. Waddington alone he fails to mention by name; and he made no disposition of 'Papers & Letters'.

148. [1] CB Jr.'s letter is missing but the business in hand was the production of one of FB's blank-verse tragedies, the manuscripts of which, described by the editor in 'Fanny Burney: Playwright', *UTQ* xix (Jan. 1950), 170–89, are the possession of the Berg Collection, the NYPL. It was not until late September or early October, however, when FBA was at Chelsea, that CB Jr. sent for a manuscript, as see his undated note among holograph scraps relating to *Edwy and Elgiva* (Berg): 'I shall

Bookham,
July 16th—94

How long it is since I have written to my dearest Charlotte!
& how kindly she has bestowed upon me three Letters in the
*interim*²—I have been, indeed, in a very suffering state, & Letter
writing has been next to impossible to me: but I am now gaining
strength daily, & I flatter myself I shall have no further relapse.³

How truly shall I rejoice in seeing my ever beloved Charlotte
again! & in seeing her with her lovely little family, & for so long
a period, & in a way in which we may so perpetually meet! The
period will, however, seem very short when it approaches to its
end, though after talking of a week, & after so entire a separation, its prospect & promise seems so full & capacious. M.
d'Arblay will not fail looking about, & Susanna will take the
other side for the same; & there is a fair hope of a small house
at Mickleham that will just suit you & the little tribe, ¹ now
ocupied, but expected to be vacated in a week or two.⁴

I think you perfectly right to leave London at this Season of
the Year, & I hope you bathe all round; there is nothing so
bracing & healthy. I attribute my recovery from the tedious
languor into which pain had thrown me, almost entirely to a
sort of shower bath I have invented for my own use, consisting
of only a Washing Tub, in which I stand, without any capital
Drapery, & a bason of water which I throw over my shoulders.

bring some tragedy home with me, for our consideration, & perusal—' Of the two
tragedies 'Hubert De Vere' and *Edwy and Elgiva*, FBA may have first sent the
former, though it was evidently the latter that CB Jr. submitted to Sheridan *c.*
15 Dec. 1794 (L. 163 n. 4). The production of the play on 21 Mar. 1795 and its
failure are reflected in FBA's Ll. 161 and 163 and notes, and Appendix A. See also
Edwy and Elgiva, ed. Miriam J. Benkovitz, (1957), Intro.

² These letters are missing.

³ FBA's illnesses, the result of her pregnancy, continued, and the plans for
CBF's visit to Bookham failed.

⁴ After some weeks at Margate CBF visited SBP and from Mickleham on
24 Sept. 1794 she wrote to the d'Arblays, then at Chelsea College. CBF's letter
(extant, Berg) reflects the news of FBA's health that she had recently received from
M. d'A: 'Je révoyois Notre Fanny—à moitié habillée, comme vous me la réprésentez
—le teint et les yeux encor animés tellement "que l'on ne diroit pas qu'elle a été,
et qu'elle est malade" . . . puis je songe toujours qu'elle a vous—qu'elle a mon Pere
—et qu'ainsi elle est entre les mains de tout ce qu'elle a de plus cher au monde—'
To FBA she wrote of her disappointment in the Surrey visits planned. 'The only
comfort our dear Susan & myself can derive is, that this sad illness has happened
where there can be the best advice procured—pray give my kind love to my dear
Brother d'Arblay, & tell him we shall depend upon his writing to us every day 'till
you are quite recovered—I am greatly disappointed in losing this opportunity of
making more acquaintance with him—.'

I have a little dark Closet in my Bed Chamber that is admirably adapted to this cooling & refreshing purpose.

I was more sorry for the awkward appearance to Mrs. M:[5] than surprised at the awkward feel which made you relinquish the visit upon second thoughts. Yet I hope you called & made Friends before you left Town? Pray tell me.

Pray enquire of Charles in *a business like manner*, if he has received at Margate a Letter upon mere business from me? I earnestly hope he is now stout & well, but it is very necessary I he should not forget too soon that he has been ill. urge him all you can to cool rooms & cool diet. I shall hope for some account of your proceedings, & if you make any pleasant acquaintances & excursions.

We live here what all the World would call a most romantic life, for we are devoted to each other, in always seeking the same amusements & employments, in enjoying equally the Country, Walking, reading, writing, & conversing. We always seem to have much time before us, yet every Day cheats us of half we meant to do in it, & we are ready to quarrel with it, when it is over, that it won't begin all again. How rare is the lot, how precious are the minutes, where this is the case! I am not an Ingrate to my fair Planet,[6]—I have known too much of life to want admonition to gratitude for such a Catastrophe to my history.

I assure you M. d'A. partakes sincerely in my promised pleasure in the sight & society of my dearest Charlotte. You are to teach him a great deal of English, he says, by making him talk it to you very frequently: & your Children are I to help: & little Charlotte is to pay back the lessons she receives from her dancing Maitresse, to a certain gay & gallant Gentleman, who proposes Kissing her little hand.

Poor Susanna & all her three Children have had the swine's Pox,[7] & the House is still under its infection, so that We dare not meet, & have been separated some time. How fortunate for me it was not while I was ill;—for she came to me & nursed

[5] Conjecturally Marianne (Popple) Mathias (1724–99), who had married in 1752 Vincent Mathias (*c.* 1716–82). Their daughter Albinia Skerrett (i, L. 28 n. 2) and their sons Thomas James (*c.* 1754–1835) and George Augustus Vincent (*c.* 1763–1848) were early and life-long friends and favourites of CBF.

[6] FB was born on 13 June. Gemini was the sign of the zodiac; and Mercury, her planet.

[7] Today called chicken-pox.

with that alacrity & tenderness you can need no description of
to understand. It is too like your own proceeding, my own
charlotte, to the same Person. The sweet Mrs. Lock also ceases
not contributing all in her power—& I have a constant overseer
who never tires of his office. He was very sorry he could not see
you when he accompanied M. de Narbonne to Town,[8] but he
never left that parting friend one moment till he hurried back,
after watching with him all Night, to Bookham, where he had
left me under the care of dearest Susan, & so ill, that no consideration would have taken him away but that of seeing the last
of his dearest Friend upon Earth. Adieu, my beloved Charlotte,
Remember me MOST affectionately to my dear Charles, & give
my Love to Rosette, & Compts. to Mrs. Bicknel: & *Kiss a me*
Charlotte, & Marianne & clement, & their little Cousin Charles.
Pray let us hear at what time you shall be ready for your rural
abode. God bless you ever & ever.

F. d'Arblay.

149   Great Bookham, [10] August [1794]

To Doctor Burney

A.L.S. (Barrett, Eg. 3690, ff. 80–1b), Aug.
Double sheet 4to   4 pp.   *pmks* EPSOM   11 AU 94   wafer
Addressed: Dr. Burney, / Chelsea College, / Midlesex
Endorsed by CB: 1794
Edited by FBA, p. 1, *annotated and dated*: ⁂ ⁑ –94 (9)
After the First Visit—& by surprize—of Dr. Burney to the Hermitage of
M. d'Arblay & F. d'A. at Bookham.

Bookham,
August

It is just a Week since I had the greatest gratification, the
most complete, the most exquisite joy I ever, I think, experienced[1]—no—there was never so dear a thing done—so kind
a thought—so sweet an execution—my dearest dear Father! how

---

[8] On 15 June 1794.

149. [1] In concern for FBA's health and in compunction conceivably for having
prevented the visits of the d'Arblays to London, CB had unexpectedly appeared
in Bookham.

softly & soothingly it has rested upon my mind ever since!—
Abdolonime[2] has no regret but that his Garden was not in better
order,—he was a little *piqué* he confesses that you said it was not
very neat—& *to be shor*!—but his passion is to do great Works,—
he undertakes with pleasure, pursues with energy, & finishes
with spirit — — but then, all is over! he thinks the business *once*
done, *always* done, & to repair, & amend, & weed, & cleanse—
O, these are drudgeries insupportable to him!

However, you should have seen the place before he began his
operations, to do him justice: there was then *nothing else* but
mauvaises herbes, *now*, you must at least, allow, there is a *mixture*
of flowers & grain! I wish you had seen him, yesterday, mowing
down our Hedge—with his *Sabre*!—& with an air, & attitude
so military, that if he had been hewing down ¹ other legions
than those he encountered — — i:e: of spiders—he could
hardly have had a mien more tremendous, or have demanded
an Arm more mighty. God knows—I am 'the most' *contentte
personne* in the World' to see his Sabre so employed!

You spirited me on in all ways, for this week past I have taken
tightly to the *grand ouvrage*.[3] If I go on so a little longer, I doubt
not but M. d'Arblay will begin settling where to have a new
shelf for arranging it!—which is already in his rumination for
Metastasio,[4]—he says he cannot possibly excuse you the *smallest
tract*, much less memoirs of an author he so highly admires. — —
I imagine you now seriously resuming that work. I hope to see
further sample ere long.

We think with *very* great pleasure of accepting yours & my
Mother's kind invitation for a few Days. I hope, & mean, if
possible, to bring with *me* also a littel sample of something less
in the dolourous style than what always causes your poor
Shoulders a little Shrug.[5]

---

² The simple gardener in Fontenelle's *Abdolonime, Roi de Sidon* (1725), who turns
out to be a descendant of kings. FB's translation of another work of Fontenelle is
extant (Berg); see also *HFB*, p. 16.

³ Unimpressed by FB's tragedies and always uneasy at the risks of stage production, CB had urged his daughter to continue with her third novel.

⁴ CB's *Memoirs of the Life and Writings of the Abate Metastasio* was to be advertised
by the *Morning Herald* (24, 26 Feb. 1796), by *The Times* (10, 28 Mar., 1, 2, 4 Apr.),
and by the *London Chronicle* (1, 3 Mar.) as 'this day published'.

⁵ It was FB's practice to sketch characters in abstract terms and to write preliminary dialogues that were only later incorporated in plays and novels (see *HFB*,
p. 164). The 'sample' may have been a bit of lively dialogue for the novel eventually
to be called *Camilla*.

Apropos—(*did not you hear a Gun go off?*) Mr. Lock, to whom I had delivered my historic dismality[6] to read at Mr. Angerstein's,[7] & thence forward to Greenwich, as I told you, is sanguine about ⌐ it beyond my most daring hopes, & equally to those of my far more intrepid Companion. He has made but one critique, & that upon a point indifferent to me, & which I shall yield *without a pang*. He pronounces peremtorily upon its success—however, I am prepared for its failure, knowing the extreme uncertainty of all public acts. ⌐I have heard no word from Charles & indeed—he & Mr. K[emble] have not yet had the *Doloric*.⌐

Mr. & Mrs. Lock were very sorry to have missed you. Mr. Lock was gratified—even *affected* by my account of the excessive happiness you have given me. He says from the time of our inhabiting this Maisonette, *one of his first wishes* has solemnly been that you should see us in it: as no possible description or narration could so decidedly point out its *competence*: *he*, he says, who knew the uncommon character which was to be its Master, expected all that has followed of its sufficiency, but he can easily conceive the anxiety of all who had not had so near a view of it, upon an experiment so great. How thankfully did I look back the 28th of last month[8] upon a year that has not been blemished with one repentant moment! —— Ah, dearest sir,—our Susanna had not spirits to begin upon the subject I have hinted to you,—she is still, & always, in hopes it may blow over—& would not sully, she says, so *infinitely* sweet a visit by a topic to *her* a true Tragedy!—⌐God grant the Boy not taken but as companion for papa[9]—& nothing more ⌐ has come to my knowledge about it, in any way, since I wrote last.

Sunday ⟨*eve*⟩ I have just had a letter from Susanna, that yesterday she heard the Capt. was ill, at James Street & she

6 Possibly 'Hubert de Vere', as is suggested by Benkovitz, op. cit.

7 See i, Ll. 9 n. 5; 16 n. 9.

8 The date of FB's marriage in the parish church of Mickleham (ii, L. 120 n. 3): 'Ah, my dearest!' SBP wrote on the anniversary date 28 July 1794 (Berg): 'I have but to wish that this second year may produce an aggregate of happiness equal to the portion which has been granted you during that now closed upon us—You have experienced some sorrows—of late Alas! much suffering *au physique*, Yet I feel it would be too unreasonable to hope, or even ask from Heaven another year of enjoyment more uninterrupted & perfect—.'

9 The plans being formed by Molesworth Phillips to return *with his family* to his estates, the farmlands of Belcotton, County Louth, Ireland. He had removed his son from CB Jr.'s school at Greenwich with the determination, as it later turned out, to place him under a tutor in Dublin.

instantly set off for London. You will probably know it before this. I long for some tydings what is the matter.

What a harrowing picture is that of M. de Montgaillard,[10] both of past & to come!—But⌐ how truly grieved was I to hear, from Mr. Locke, of the Death of young Mr. Burke![11] What a dreadful blow upon his Father & Mother! to come at the instant of the Son's highest & most honourable advancement & of the Father's retreat to the bosom of his Family from public life!—His Brother, too, gone so lately!—I am most sincerely sorry, indeed,—& quite *shocked*, as there seemed so little suspicion of such an event's approach, by your account of the joy caused by Lord FitzWilliam's kindness.[12] Pray tell me if you hear how poor Mr. Burke & his most amiable wife endure this calamity, & how they are. I beg my Love to my Mother & to Sarah. ⌐Mr. & Mrs. Locke charged me to present you their very *respectful* compliments.⌐

Abdolonime has been hard at work ever since you came, in *hopes* of such another Surprise. adieu, my dearest—dearest Father—Pray always be glad of the kind this Day Week for the sake of your most affectionate & dutiful

F. d'A.

150   Great Bookham, 2 September [1794]

To Doctor Burney

A.L. (Barrett, Eg. 3690, ff. 84–5b), 2 Sept.
Double sheet 4to   4 pp.   *pmks* DARKING   4 SE 94   wafer
Addressed: Dr. Burney, / Chelsea College, / Midlesex.
Endorsed by CB: 1794
Edited by FBA, p. 1, *annotated and dated*: ⁂ –94   (10)

Answer to a most entertaining account of Dᵣ Burney's meeting Lord Erskine *amicably* at Mrs. Crewe's.

[10] FBA had apparently been reading *Etat de la France au mois de mai, 1794* (London, 1794) by Jean-Gabriel-Maurice Rocques, comte de Montgaillard (1761–1841).

[11] Burke's son Richard (b. 1758) had died on 2 Aug. 1794.

[12] Burke's patron and friend, William FitzWilliam (1748–1833), after 1807, Wentworth-FitzWilliam, styled Viscount Milton, 2nd Earl FitzWilliam (1756). On the elder statesman's decision to leave the House of Commons, Lord FitzWilliam offered the borough of Malton to Richard, Jr. and in July 1794 Burke and his son journeyed to Yorkshire for the election. For this 'one of the happiest and proudest moments of Burke's life' and the quick reversal in the death of his son from pulmonary tuberculosis, see Carl B. Cone, *Burke and the Nature of Politics: The Age of the French Revolution* (Lexington, Ky., 1964), pp. 145–6, 443–5.

Bookham,
Septr 2^d

What very sweet Letters[1] does my dearest dear Father write!
—he cannot, I am sure, want to be told with what avidity they
are read. I long prodigiously to know something of the '*other
Irons*'[2]— that impede Metastasio. M. d'A.—though, to say the
truth, he had not waited your injunction to prepare place for
the 2 octavos[3]—received it with extreme pleasure, & promises
it shall certainly be ready.

⌐I have just been made very happy by a Letter from Esther
that assures of the safety of her little darling,[4] though it speaks
most touchingly of its sufferings, & what they have cost its poor
Mother. My poor Aunt too, I find, has been very unwell, though
she is now reviving.[5] Letty Brooks[6] is now a most solid comfort
to her, & consequently, to us all.—I feel very uneasy for poor
little Martin[7]—my dear Charlotte whom I met & dined with at
Mickleham on Monday, says he is terribly fallen away, & was
by no means in a good or right way. His Father is so wrapt up
in him, that I really doubt if he will ever know another happy
Day should any fatal calamity deprive him of the poor little
fellow. I have had, however, no later news, & therefore hope
he may be recovering. |

Our half Mourning will begin on Monday s'night—after
which we will be gladly in wait for orders—but I shall immediately write to my Mother upon this subject.⌐

The meeting with Mr. Erskine amused me extremely. I
thought him exactly all you say when I saw him at Mrs. Crewe's.[8]

But your parting exclamation, of concern at his present
undertaking, is inimitable[9]—'Tis surely no bad sign that he took

150. [1] Eg., CB's letter, *pmk* 28 A⟨U⟩ 94 (Barrett, Eg. 3690, ff. 82–3b), much of
which FBA later obliterated.

[2] See Lonsdale, pp. 370–9.

[3] The '2 thick 8vo Vols' eventually ran to 3 vols. 8vo.

[4] Amelia Maria had had the smallpox. EBB's letter, like most of her correspondence, is missing.

[5] CB's sister Rebecca Burney (1724–1809) of Richmond, who is recovering from
the loss of her sister Ann or Nancy who had died in August.

[6] Lettitia Brookes (b. *pre* 1767–d. *post* 1811, see 'Worcester Journal'), the
daughter of CB's half-sister Mary (b. 1712), had helped nurse EBB's children in
1789 and was now to be a companion for life to Rebecca (above). CB mentioned
her in his will (Scholes, ii. 263) as 'my Niece, LETITIA BROOKE' and provided her
with an annuity.

[7] JB's son. (See L. 151 n. 1.)   [8] In June 1792 (i, L. 24 n. 44).

[9] At a dinner at Hampstead of a week or so earlier CB had 'hit it off so well' with

it so quietly. It certainly was not want of words, nor want of wit, that made it swallowed in peace. I *stopt* at it,—expecting a Volley of democracy 'to make my Hair all stand on end'— imagine, then, if I did not smile to find nothing! You know I told you, when you were here, that the Democrats *have a mind to you*,—in no less than 3 of their Books this Summer have you had a good word.—However, as I am all for conciliatory measures, in these perilous times, I confess my laugh was de bon coeur, not of spleen, to see your name celebrated even by Courtney,[10] Williams,[11] & the Foxiana editor.[12]—If it were not for a lift from that confirmed Aristocrate, our old friend Mrs. P[iozzi],[13] I know not what posterity could conclude.

the Erskines as to be invited to a 'rebound dinner' given by them at Serjeants' Inn. See CB to FBA, *pmk* 28 A⟨U⟩ 1794 (op. cit.). At the first dinner a 'long dish of Politics' was 'muffled in temper and prudence' and at the second, Erskine presented CB with one of his 'printed speeches, with a wish to see me as often as possible—There's your works!'

'Well, though [a] great Egotist & Coxcomb, he has a wonderful flow of Ideas & readiness of words. He repeated several of his speeches on extraordinary trials, wch were really ingenious & entertaining. . . . But he's a terrible abettor of faction, & seems to think himself obliged to defend every seditious rascal that wants him. He is retained for Horne Tooke—I c^d not help telling him as we were parting great friends, that I was sorry he had pledged himself to so toilsome, mischievous an employment, & it seemed to make some impression.'

[10] John Courtenay (1738–1816), M.P. (1780–1807, 1812), author of pamphlets on the French Revolution, one of Pitt's opponents, and a lively but indecorous debater in the House (*DNB*). In *The Present State of the Manners, Arts, and Politics, of France and Italy; in a series of poetical epistles, from Paris, Rome, and Naples, in 1792 and 1793* (1794), he had eulogized CB in the lines (p. 92): 'Give me BURNEY's sweet style, give his Genius and Art, / That appeals to the judgement, yet touches the heart; / And I'll tell you, why music cures frenzy and spleen—'

[11] Probably David Williams (1738–1816), a well-known radical and Founder of the Literary Fund (*DNB*), though in his numerous works on politics, religion, and education, no reference to Dr. Burney has as yet been located.

[12] Though the epithet may suggest a collection of Charles James Fox's *bons mots* along with the witticisms of CB and others, no such work has been found.

In the years 1794–5 CB was preening himself on the approval of a succession of radical writers who, since 1789, despite difference in politics, had cited his works (see above; also *Memoirs*, iii. 195; and a letter (Berg) of 9 June 1795 to FBA).

It is possible, therefore, that FBA meant by the 'Foxiana editor' one of these radical writers or editors there named, and that in this case she was referring specifically to William Godwin (1756–1836), who in 1785 had been appointed to write the historical article regularly included in the *New Annual Register* and who in the section 'Biographical Anecdotes and Characters', pp. [91–5] of the *Register* (1789) had reprinted in its entirety CB's 'Essay on Musical Criticism' as excerpted from his *General History of Music*, iii. v–xl, adding in the section 'Domestic Literature', pp. [254–5], a laudatory review of the third and fourth volumes of CB's *History*.

[13] Mrs. Piozzi, in her study of the synonyms, 'Melody, Harmony, Music', *British Synonymy*, ii. 21–9, took occasion to quote Plato, and in support of him, Rousseau, to the effect that 'if any considerable alteration' were to take place 'in the MUSICK of a country, he should, from that single circumstance, predict innovation in the laws, a change of customs, and subversion of the government'. Burney, she went on to observe, had formerly noted the 'steady perseverance and constancy' of

We are wholly ignorant now of public news, ᵀ& probably are the better off! Mr. Lock & all his family have been gone for more than a week to Lincolnshire, where they will spend a Month with Mrs. Boucherette, whom you may remember, when Miss Crockett,¹⁴— ¦ Also our good Rector & his wife have been absent 〈 〉 several weeksᵀ [xxxxx *3 lines heavily inked over but apparently explaining that because of the absence of the Cookes as well as the Lockes, the d'Arblays have not seen the usual bundles of newspapers*], so we shall arrive at Chelsea like two people dropt from the Moon, begging to know *what party means.*

I am really much concerned at your hint about Mr. W[ind-ham].—I feel perfectly discontented to have a Man of such a Mind & such a character employed in mechanical drudgery.¹⁵ Besides—it cannot last. He has too much spirit & independence to lend his name without his influence, or to have his influence *presumed,* where in fact it has no play. And I should be very sorry indeed to have him break with administration at such a period. I hope Mr. P[itt] will better know his value than to carry sole command high enough to irritate a defection.

———

So you have got Mr. E[rskine]'s speeches?¹⁶—certainly they were not a present likely to be *de trop* from any duplicate in your Library! I divert myself with the thought of seeing you running them over, with that sort of toleration which recent eating & drinking with a man always breeds, even in causes the most ungenial. 'What passion cannot Woman wake or quell?—If the invitation had not been given by a fair female, I have a notion your Seat at the Dinner Table must have sought another proprietor. However, I *am glad of it*—I love no branch so much as the Olive branch, & never more delight than in seeing all parties willing, nay anxious, to do justice to my dear Father. ¦

Frenchmen 'to one particular taste in this art' and had lived to see the French 'along with a change in the mode of receiving pleasure' from music, 'murder their own monarch, set fire to their own cities . . . a wonder to fools, a beacon to wise men'.

¹⁴ Emilia Crokatt (*c.* 1761–1837), stepdaughter of John Julius Angerstein (i, L. 16 n. 9), married in 1789 Ayscoghe Boucherett (1755–1815) of Willingham, Lincs., M.P. (1796–1803).

¹⁵ On Windham's coming over with the Portland Whigs to Pitt in early July 1794, it was at first proposed that he be Secretary of State. On 11 July 1794 he became Secretary of War with a seat in the Cabinet.   ¹⁶ See n. 9, above.

˹Our Susanna & her Fanny were with us two Days ago, looking in good health. The Capt. is getting well. What I have communicated seems now *not so certain*, & I have strong hope may blow over.[17] With any but so excentric a Character, I should have concluded the contrary, but still it is *hovering*, though in forms so frequently contradictory that it is impossible to fully fix any stable judgement, either upon the real intent, or the internal causes. Sometimes the aspect is that of a terrible break up, at others the wilfulness of a restless mind that loves to spread confusion, cause wonder, & displace tranquility. Your little anecdote of '*foolishly*' inquiring after his health, is characteristic of all the rest. We all met to a Dinner at Norbury, before the Lincolnshire journey, & he then looked well, & seemed out of his Ague toils.˺

I never think of Mr. & Mrs. Burke without grief for them.

To be sure you won't meet Ld. Macartney when he returns, at Mrs. Crewe's?—I anticipate the pleasure that will give you.[18] We shall bring back Hawkesworth, which M. d'A. has just finished. He delights in the idea of being *let loose* in your Library & study, to make minutes of successors, to be petitioned for in rotation. He is now immensely slaving as abdolomine, in rearing a seat in the midde of a Tree, which he calls the Belvedere. Won't you mount it next year? There will be a Branch to hold by, by which my Mother herself may ascend.

Adieu, most dear Sir—I hope now very soon to *exchange Irons*. I shall bring such of mine as are portable. I am surprisingly well, & strong. I have walked twice to & from Norbury park, refusing all carriages: & once to Mickleham.

M˓ Jerningham has just given me his Tragedy[19]—with a very pretty letter We have [received kind] offers & words from M˓ K[emble][20] with the Comp˓˓˹ [*tear*]

[17] Phillips's plan to move his family to Ireland was to materialize in 1796.

[18] In August 1792 Lord Macartney, preparing for his Embassy to China, did CB 'the honour to consult me in procuring a Military band, bespeaking a barrel Organ . . . to give the Chinese an idea of our mechanics, and to bespeak such music as was most likely to be wanted by such a band as w˓ be in his excellencies suite'. In gratitude for this aid, Macartney had presented CB with a 'magnificent silver ink-stand with a most flattering Latin inscription' ('Memoirs', Berg; also *Memoirs*, iii. 217–19). For other mechanisms taken to China, see i. L. 24 nn. 30, 65.

[19] *The Siege of Berwick* by Edward Jerningham (1737–1812), first played on 13 Nov. 1793, had undergone alterations as described by Walpole (xii. 62, 69, 83, etc.). Publication was advertised in *The Times* (24, 25 Dec. 1793). See also L. 153.

[20] John Philip Kemble (1757–1823), actor, and at this time manager of Drury Lane Theatre.

151   Great Bookham, 6 September [1794]

M. d'Arblay
To James Burney

L.S. & A.N. in hand of FBA (PML, Autog. Cor. bound), 6 Sept.
Double sheet 4to   1 p.   wafer
Addressed: Captain Burney, / ⌈Margate, / Kent.⌉
Readdressed: James—Street / Westminster
Postdated incorrectly in pencil, p. 1 : 1795

Bookham,
Septr 6th

I feel so sincerely anxious for some intelligence of poor Martin,[1] that I cannot forbear entreating you my dear Brother, to write me a couple of lines with news of him. We have heard nothing whatever since your Letter to Susanna, so long ago, & every post brings only disappointment. Do, conquer your repugnance to writing so far as to say *where you are*, & *how you* are. Give my love to Mrs. B[urney] with the most affectionate & warmest wishes of

Yours most truly
A: d'Arblay.

[Madame d'Arblay added]

M. d'A. interests himself in this request very earnestly. The Capt. is quite well again.

We dined at Mickleham last week, to meet Charlotte & her babes.[2]

We shall go ere long to Chelsea for a few Days.

Esther's little Amelia has caught the small pox, & had it miserably ill, but is now recovering. I hear but melancholy accounts of poor Aunt Becky, who must now feel very forlorn. Letty Brooks stays with her,—probably for life.

I Shall be *very sorry* if you should not be in Town when we are at Chelsea.

151. [1] Martin Charles (1788–1852), who was suffering from a 'paralytic affection of one side of his face' (Manwaring, pp. 206–7). CB reported in a letter (Berg) of 17 Nov. 1794: 'Martin gets well & more riotous & noisy than ever.'
[2] On Monday 1 Sept.

152   Great Bookham, 12 October [1794]

To Doctor Burney

A.L.S. (Barrett, Eg. 3690, ff. 86–7b), 12 Oct.
Double sheet 4to   4 pp.   *pmk* 14 OC 94   wafer
Addressed: Dr. Burney, / Chelsea College, / Midlesex.
Endorsed by CB: Octr 12. 94
Edited by FBA, p. 1, *annotated and dated*: ⋇ –94   (11)
on returning from a Chelsea visit about 2 months before the Birth of
Alexander Charles Louis.—

Bookham,
Octr 12.

I had purposed, in quitting my dearest Father,[1] to have
recommended to his blessing a little Being that — — if, like
Lord Townshend's[2]—it resembles *either* its Father *or* its Grandfather cannot but deserve it—the subject, however, & its
object, were too tenderly interesting to me for the moment of
separation—& my voice failed—& my fullness of meaning lost
me all power of expression.—I must not, however, give up my
recommendation—since your Race, my dearest Father, seems
destined to extend itself by every branch, so must your kindness,
your goodness, your affection — — & whether or not I live to
so blest a moment as to present you myself my little Infant, you
must see it—love it—give it your benediction, & a prayer for
its well doing.—

This is very serious—but I have now done with it—& will
go to other & less touching subjects. ⌐

⌐I have a great deal to say to my Mother which I will communicate in a Letter *all to herself* on a Post Day & mean while,
I only desire my love & compts to her, & my hearty thanks for
her kindness.

152. [1] The d'Arblays had made a visit of about a month (*c.* 8 Sept.–10 Oct.) to
Chelsea College (see L. 154 and CBF's letter of 24 Sept., Berg).
[2] A friend of CB from 'his Lynn days' (Scholes, ii. 260), George Townshend
(1723/4–1807) of Raynham Park, Norfolk, 4th Viscount (1764), cr. Marquis (1787),
Lord Lieutenant and Vice-Admiral of Norfolk (1792), Governor of Chelsea Hospital (1795), Field Marshal (1796). CB could also have known the 3rd Viscount
(1738), Charles Townshend (1700–64) of Lynn Regis. CB or his wife, who was
formerly an Allen of King's Lynn, could well have judged, therefore, the likeness
of the 4th Viscount's youngest son, James Nugent Boyle Bernardo (b. 1785), to his
father or grandfather.

Sarah is such a tremendous Mænad about my epistolary misdemeanours, that I know not if she will accept any thing short of a folio Letter,—let me try her, however, in the mean while, with begging her not to reject my cordial love thus *third handed*, but first hearted.⁜

M. d'Arblay has begun an entire new arrangement of our Maisonnette, in which every thing is to be reversed. He finds it a change perfectly indispensable,—*for* it offers a delicious opportunity to use all his new tools. It is really fortunate that it occurs to solid advantage, for the effect would be too seducing to resist seeking a Cause, if none presented itself. He finds them more & more agreeable every Hour. ⎮ And for Me, I am delighted in the hope that when the Snow falls next Winter, instead of courting the lumbago by working in the Garden, he will discover various necessities in the House, which will turn him to mechanics, & save my flannel.

The Garden he has found much out of order—none of ses *Gens*³ having once entered it since we departed. Our Susanna came to me the morning after my arrival,—accompanied by James & Mrs. B[urney]. Martin gets strength daily, I hear. I have not yet ventured beyond our orchard. This morning our little Parlour was laughably crowded: Mr. & Mrs. Lock, my Susanna, Miss Lock, Mr. William, Mr. Charles, Mr. George, & *ourselves at westminster*,⁴ formed a Group that could only have been enlarged, by the expulsion of our Tables, or their adoption for sofas.

⎾Mr. Locke tells us that the people in the North, whence he is just returned, experienced precisely the same ⎮ alarm that was felt in London upon the reopening the Parliament of the year before last.⁵ I think it no bad thing, for it may make them doubtful, & hold the Loyal Loyal, & he says they are stout as ever

---

³ A tag, referring, in the private language of the Burneys, to delinquent, missing, or non-existent lackeys or servants. The phrase originated with the duc de Guignes (1735–1806). See *ED* ii. 113–14; *Memoirs*, ii. 64–5.

⁴ 'Witness ourself at Westminster' is part of the formula used in Royal signatures to warrants, Royal Commissions, and the like, as was pointed out to the editor by Professor S. E. Sprott of Dalhousie University.

⁵ The Lockes had paid a long visit (*c.* 25 Aug.–*c.* 11 Oct.) to the Boucheretts (L. 150 n. 14) at Willingham, Lincs.

For the purpose of calling up the militia as an aid in quelling 'seditious practices' and 'acts of riot and insurrection', the King had called a special session of Parliament for 13 Dec. 1792. See his Proclamation and Speech, *AR* xxxiv (1792), 166–9.

I know you see the excellent & most kind Mr. Farquhar,[6] I beg to be remembered to him in the best possible manner— I felt much fatigue & lassitude 2 days after my coming, but all to day I have been alive & most alert.

May I beg you to give my love to Esther, & entreat her to bring with her my watch which I left by my bedside, & a loose dressing Gown, which I had bespoke at Thom's,[7] when, which I trust will be soon, she travels this way.

Also—my love to Charlotte, & an entreaty she will order the Glass Man to forward my miracle Machine[8] with all expedition.

You know not how you delighted my Monsieur by the little ⟨tune⟩ & the change of the commemoration just at last. He has told me of them with extreme pleasure repeatedly. He is preparing work for to morrow, sorting tools, & too vehemently engaged for any thing beyond sending you his most affectionate respects. & ditto to *your Boy*, who he says upon the whole, is a very good one indeed, & did the honours *'very well'*. I have not room now for his message for Sally. Adieu, most kind Sir—Accept my best thanks *for all*—& forgive [my] most involuntary reversement of a time so precious.—

Your F.d'A.⫟

153   Great Bookham, 13 October [1794]

To Edward Jerningham

A.L.S. (The Henry E. Huntington Library), 13 Oct.
Double sheet 8vo   1 p.   lower right corner of second leaf torn off   seal
Addressed: Edward Jerningham Esqr—
Annotated in pencil, p. 1: D Burney / Madame D'Arblay

Mr. Jerningham would have received long ere now my best acknowledgements for his elegant Tragedy,[1] & kind remembrance, had not a most ungrateful indisposition forcibly seized

---

6 Sir Walter Farquhar. See i, L. 23 n. 82.
7 Alexander Thom, Scotch factor, appears in London commercial directories from 1769–95, with an address in 1794–5, 'Blossoms-inn, Lawrence-lane, Jewry'.
8 A pair of spectacles.
153. 1 *The Siege of Berwick* (L. 150 n. 19). FB had met Edward Jerningham in May 1780 at Bath (*DL* i. 350). 'He seems a mighty delicate gentleman; looks to be painted, and is all daintification in manner, speech, and dress.'

me & my faculties almost on the very Day that they reached me. I entreat him to accept now my sincere, however tardy thanks, in full conviction that nothing less than insensibility to the merit of the one, or the kindness of the other, has so long kept silent his

obliged h^e serv^t

F: d'Arblay.

Bookham, Surry,
Octr 13th

154   Great Bookham, 16 October 1794

To Mrs. Waddington

A.L. (Berg), 16 Oct. [17]94
Single sheet 4to 1 p.

Bookham
near Leatherhead, Surry,
Octr 16—94.

How long it is since I have heard from my dear Marianne, or written to her!—yet her last Letter was reviving, by a better account of her health—but I have been at Chelsea—where I spent a Month,—& I have been very ill—I was seized in the middle of the night, while there, & obliged to call up all the House, & send for a Physician: & I was under his care, (Mr. Farquhar) the whole time I remained. We returned to our beloved little habitation, after a visit in all ways but this unfortunate illness, the most comfortable, gay, & affectionate ever made—last week.—I can now assure my ever tender Friend I am well again — — But — — — how shall I be about Christmas? — — — ah! I did not want self experience to make me feel for what so often you have described of *your* feelings & *your* sufferings!—

My Partner, however, who daily encreases the debt I owe him of my life's happiness, rejoices—& I must be a wretch of ingratitude & insensibility to regret whatever he can wish.— Adieu, my sweet Mary—I am sure of your kindest prayers & sympathy. God bless you—*Kiss me* your Fanny & Emily—

Best Comp^{ts} to Mr. W.

155   Great Bookham, 21 October 1794

To Doctor Burney

A.L.S. (Barrett, Eg. 3690, f. 89–b), 21 Oct. [17]94
Single sheet 4to   2 pp.   *pmk* 22 OC 94   wafer
Addressed: Dr. Burney, / Chelsea College, / Midlesex.
Endorsed by CB: Oct^r / 1794.
Edited by FBA, p. 1, *annotated*: ·⁕· (13)
about Two months before the Birth of Alexander
Edited also by CFBt.

Bookham,
oct. 21.—94

How infinitely sweet & soothing is my dearest Father's
Letter!—yet there is one paragraph in it I was long in getting
through!—I began—& stopt—& re-began—again, again &
again, — — — the Picture it presented me is so touching—yet,
to *me*, so beautiful!—my dearest Father fondling the little
Bookhamite!¹ — — The charming Stanza, too, which so kindly
you call a Portrait,² drew tears of pleasure into more Eyes than
mine—though *poetical licence* has made its Answerer, since,
dispute the exactness. Every play of words upon the Tools is a
badinage delightful³—& M. d'A. thinks it the *best English* he ever
read. He says he should soon be at his ease in the language if it
were always as well handled! I am very glad you go on so
ardently with Metastasio. ⌐The part you are now at is as
amusing to yourself as it will be hereafter to your readers⁴—
I am quite sorry and mortified to have been so checked in my

---

155. ¹ In his letter of 18 Oct. 1794 (Berg) CB had drawn a picture of himself as a
'*great old grand-father*, who you know is quite a child with children; who loves to
romp & be foolish with them; & who hopes to live to have many a roll & a tumble
on the floor with the Bookham Brattikin whatever it may be. Therefore keep up
your spirits & do *your* business well, & *lette me do*—Never fear mine.'
  ² The 'Portrait', as a compliment to the ideal life at Bookham, Surrey, was CB's
translation of the closing verses of Metastasio's Pastoral in *il Re Pastore* (loc. cit.).

Our simple narrow mansion / Will suit our station well, /
There's room for heart expansion, / And peace & joy to dwell. /

  ³ An elaborate play of words on seven or eight tools of the carpenter's tool-box,
including the hammer, which will 'knock in the head the foul fiend politics' and
the *Vice*, which need not be put into practice (loc. cit.).
  ⁴ To illustrate 'the moral view wch the bard had in writing each piece', CB
determined to make verse translations of scenes from Metastasio's plays (Lonsdale,
p. 374).

course[5] of all that preceded this initialy in making a fanciful & interesting imitation.

I have continued amazingly well since I last wrote—Mrs. Lock will be enchanted to form this species of *loving friendship*— she has long had a real reverence for your talents & character, though I have never known from what particular Channel the *latter* has seemed so familiar to her.

Our Susanna has been relieved from a great anxiety by this same man that has won my dear Father,[6] & sweet Mrs. Lock has been making her *personal thanks* in the most eloquent manner upon their meeting under our tent t'other morning. Lady North[7] has given me a warm recommendation of a *garde malade*; but I dread a person who has served a Countess. Susanna & Mrs Lock have conceived an excellent idea upon this subject, which I shall explain *at large* upon my next *smale Letter*, to be explained to *you*, *in brief*. M. d'Arblay would have written to *Sarah* to Day, but we thought it more discreet to send another Letter 4 or 5 Days hence, as I think my dear Father & all my dear Circle of B's will pass on intelligence from time to time & neglect now, & dearth afterwards. My kindest Remembrances, & M. d'A's to my Mother, &, if you see them, to my Brothers, & all my sisters. Your Tool Box was the happiest kindness you could do *me*, for my monsieur works harder with it than any Carpenter[7] or Joiner in the Kingdom. 'Tis at present perfectly his rage.

Martin goes on quite well.

adieu ever dearest Sir!—Kindest & most beloved!—

Fd'A.—

Pray tell my Mother I have tried to imitate her soup twice with no success—I see M. d'A. thinks me as [a] bad Boy! that way.— But—how long should the Pot [set on the] Fire?

P.S. I open my letter to say the pacquet is just arrived from Mickleham ⟨to day⟩ thanks to my Mother—our Monsieur cannot wait to *write*.

---

[5] In the writing of *Camilla*.
[6] Sir Walter Farquhar (i, L. 23 n. 82).
[7] Anne Speke (d. 17 Jan. 1797), widow of Frederick North, 2nd Earl of Guilford (1790), Prime Minister (1770–82) and better known as Lord North (i, L. 23 n. 16).

156   [Great Bookham, *post* 17 November, 1794]

To Doctor Burney

A.L. (Barrett, Eg. 3690, f. 88–b), *n.d.*
Originally a double sheet 4to, of which FBA later discarded the second
leaf.   2 pp.
Edited by FBA, p. 1, *annotated and dated*: ⁘ Oct^r / je crois / 1794   (12)
Edited also by CFBt.

My dearest beloved Father,
    What a beautiful little Poem![1]—'tis almost a history of
Practical Music, while 'tis a *philosophic badinage* upon the various
tastes of various nations.—We have read it again & again &
always with fresh delight. The Picture of France in its singing &
dancing Days is sweet & touching—'*Comparison*' there, indeed,
that points out *preference of good from bad*! my Gardener was much
pleased with the horticultural allusions—but the *conclusion*—ah!
I may say, as well as think what I will of the rest, 'tis the *conclusion* that comes most home—that I read with tears of pleasure
to myself first, & tried vainly for voice to read it in *any* way this
Morning to Susan & Mrs. Lock—Susan, who loves M. d'A. as
if his *born* Sister, could not resist the infection—& the soft Eyes
of Mrs. Lock were glistening with simpathy —— yet we all fall
into rages at the unjust epithet given to '*lines*' at the end.
    I wish, Yesterday Morning, when I put it into M. d'A.'s hands,

156. [1] In response to M. d'A's '*amiable badinage*' and by way of 'apology for my ill
treatment of *French Music*, wch he says I have done—*bien à tort*!', CB had composed
a poem of 176 dimeters and included it in his letter of 17 Nov. (Berg). 'Et voilà ma
Palinodie.' Though largely political in content, it had praise for 'the *kingdom* of
France' / 'When the heart used to dance / And keep time with the Feet / In coincidence sweet!' The close, all things considered, FBA had some cause to find
moving:

> So adieu *mon cher Fils!*
> May your love never cease
> For the Wife of your breast—
> And as for the rest,
> Dear Sir, you are sure
> While life shall endure
> Of regard and affection
> Confirm'd by reflexion
> From him who now signs
> These pitiful lines.
>
>   Chas Burney

without a previous word, & who read the first page with composed satisfaction, you could have peeped at the sudden brightening of his Countenance, when he turned over the leaf—it was quite dramatic in its effect. |

But I am extremely sorry, indeed, for my poor Mother, & this new past attack, & most severe languor.[2] I am ashamed myself Daily for not writing to her, & thanking her for her kind letter & commissions executed, &c, but I have literally not had a pen in my hand since I wrote to you last but for two Minutes to beg *dear Etty* to excuse me to her, & to all others—for Working is the only thing I find ⟨quite⟩ incommodious—& I have been so slack in arrangements of various sorts, that I have never had so little time for combatting distaste to that employment. I beg you to present her my best respects, & sincere ⟨wishes⟩ for her Speedy re-establishment.

Roscius is entirely silent[3]—all ways I persevere. K[emble] it seems is already engaged. The piece he accepted & with the most flattering expressions—but the *time* is not mentioned, & I know Emilia Gal[otti] was 5 *years accepted* before it was performed.[4] So I wait with great philosophy because little repine

[*the second leaf is missing*]

[2] 'Your mother', CB had reported in the letter above, 'had a return of her frightful Hemorrhage, more violent than ever—was blooded 2ce in 24 Hours—It has abated, & I hope will again entirely subside; but it has left her extremely weak and languid—.'
[3] Possibly a reference to Sheridan, at this time patentee and chief proprietor of Drury Lane Theatre, who was eventually to read FBA's play (L. 163). Kemble had already been persuaded by CB Jr., see Herschel Baker, *John Philip Kemble. The Actor in His Theatre* (Cambridge, Mass., 1942), pp. 193–4: 'As the great and good drinking companion of Fanny's brother, the celebrated classical scholar, the Rev. Charles Burney, Kemble had the grace to accept it, though with private qualms.'
[4] An English translation of Lessing's play had been produced at the Theatre Royal in Drury Lane on 28 and 30 Oct. and on 1 and 4 Nov. 1794. For studies on the possible translators and on the delays in production, see Edward Dvoretzky, 'The Eighteenth-Century English Translations of *Emilia Galotti*', *Rice University Studies*, lii, no. 3 (Summer 1966), 1–24; Kemble's Memorandum Book 28 Oct. 1794 (BM Add. MSS. 31,972); and W. C. Oulton, *History of the Theatres of London* (2 vols., 1796), ii. 167.

157   [Great Bookham, 8 December 1794]

Conjointly with M. d'Arblay
To Mrs. Francis (*later* Broome)

A.L.S. & A.L.S. (Berg),   *n.d.*
Double sheet small 4to   4 pp.   *pmk* 8 DE 94   2 wafers
Addressed: Mrs. Francis, / Downing Street, / *near Mr. Pitt's*, / Westminster.
Endorsed by CBF: Sister d'arblay / Nov — — — 1794 / ans: Nov — —

[*By M. d'Arblay*]
Dear Sister

I love you with all my heart, i.e. as well as possible. and your Fanny's health is as Strong as is my friendship towards you. But that's not all. You know there are seven planets, seven Cardinal virtues, seven mortal vices, seven grecian Wises, seven Sacraments, seven worldly wonders &c. Do'nt be astonished If I dare entreat you to do for us Seven commissions.

1th Will you be so good to send us, in a Deal box two feet and four inches long, six inches high, and ten inches broad, the bank-notes you have exchanged. If a box of another size and of second hand can be more easily procured, I am not very eager to have it with the fore mentioned exact dimensions—

2th As the said banknotes will not *fulfil* the purpose to *fil* up the fore said deal box, which I intend to put upon my window with some flowers, be pleased to inclose my garden's *under coats.*

3th Perhaps you will find place enough for the attorney's letter that Mr Edward[1] who is, I hope, in better health, has been so good to have drawn up.

4th Perhaps too we may receive in the same box six pounds of wax candles. I should prefer to have them *unnew,*—i.e. as the doctor has them for his Study.[2]

5th Our Brother Charles, in his friendly visit, promised us to give you the best direction for some wine we want. A second deal box of the same size, and with equal destination should be sufficient to contain it.

157. [1] Edward Francesco Burney, to whom the d'Arblays entrusted such funds as they wished to invest. He would have needed the power of attorney.
[2] That is, six pounds of wax candle-ends.

6th Be so good to pay for the gown M^{rs} DAy. had from Mrs Ham's shop.³

7th The same favour is wanted for a hat which has been bought by our dear lazy sister Sarah who may give you the direction of the inn where are to be sent all these commissions to arrive safely here.

Now, my dear Sister, if you would favour us with your | god-mothership for the little *inconnu* so eagerly expected, as you have been so good to offer it to M^{rs} D'Ay. it would give her particular pleasure, in which I should participate most cordially. Then dear sister God bless you, my dear little mistress,⁴ & all! and believe [me] truly and for ever Your most obedient Servant

A. d'Arblay

[By Madame d'Arblay]

My dear, dear Charlotte—How miserably I have ill merited your kind Letters, as far as appearances speak for me—but writing is the only thing in which I have quite failed, & which I find a repugnance to unconquerable *You* will forgive it, my tender Charlotte—& pray do not let me by that means lose hearing from you—the sight of your hand is a regale & a joy to me.

M. d'A: had mistaken, as you will gather by the above, about the Godmothership. I believe there is some *RELIGIOUS* scruple in the way.—your most kind offer about commissions I gratefully accept, my dearest Charlotte—but I must entreat to know how the account stands since last settled, to this time, after the purchases to be added—& the 5th of January | another 25 will be due from Mr. Mathias⁵—How I laughed at his '*NONSENSE*'!⁶

---

³ Both SBP and FBA regularly dealt with a firm of Hams, probably Thomas Ham, Linen-Draper, whose shop in the years 1792–1801 was at 19 St. James's Street, Covent Garden, and in the years 1789–91, at 231 The Strand. A 'mantua-maker' by the name of Ham also emerges in the London directories, and one of her compeers, advertising in *The Times* (24 Dec. 1796), supplies current prices: 'Callicoe Morning Dresses, from 5s. to 6s. Fashionable jackets and Coats 7s. Plain Gowns 3s. 6d. Corsets from 15s. to 18s.'

⁴ Charlotte Francis, now about 8 years old.

⁵ The quarterly payment of FBA's pension of £100 per annum.

⁶ Thomas James Mathias (*c.* 1754–1835), succeeding his father Vincent (*c.* 1716–82) in the Royal service, became successively Treasurer's Clerk, Vice-Treasurer, and Treasurer of the Accounts of the Queen's Household. For CBF's records of the jokes of the Mathias brothers (L. 148 n. 5), see *ED* ii. 302–12; parts of her Journal for 1795 (Berg); and scrap of a Journal (Barrett, Eg. 3706B, f. 5b). E.g., the refusal of a servant to feed 'a pet hedgehog'; 'Indeed ma'am . . . I am not used to wait on no such inferior trumpery.'

—I beg you to remember me *most best* to my dear Father—& to Esther—Charles—James—Sarah—Edward—All as you see them—for I write not to any one now. I have just got a most admirable Nurse—one would make you laugh heartily by her orders & manner & comic simplicity & understanding united— I am shocked at *your Caps*, my dear love, which I only want *opportunity* & *thought* to join for returning—They have never been on my Tête a single moment since I left Holcomb⁷— I know how your most fervent wishes will attend me in this advancing critical time—I thank God my courage rises to meet my fate Daily, be it as it may—Life could never be more precious to me nevertheless—I remember your kind and dear promise, which I now accept for the *christening*, if feasible to yourself to then fold & be folded in the arms of

your most affec^{te}   F d'A

158   [Great Bookham, 16 December 1794]

To M. d'Arblay

A.L. incomplete (Berg), *n.d.*, with an editorial note (p. 3) by FBA addressed to AA, 8 May 1825

Double sheet small 4to   4 pp.

Edited by FBA, p. 1, *annotated and dated*: ⚹ *For M. d'Arblay Bookham*—16 Decr 1794 (N° 6.)

NB. a day & half previous to the Birth of Alexander

Docketed, p. 4 *by* FBA: an unfinished address to my best Friend, written 2 days before the Birth of our Alexander, in case I had not survived.

On 8 May 1825, *annotated and dated*, p. 3, *by* FBA: To my dear Alexander / I leave this little Memorial of the Happiness & blessed lot of his Mother before she became such—

After that epoch—he witnessed it— —& kindly & feelingly partook of its bereavement— — / *8. May. 1825.*

The moment of danger now fast approaching—presses upon probability to end in Death—If so—O Husband of my Heart, read some consolation for the loss of Her who so truly knew to appreciate you, in this last Farewell—which, solemnly as in the

---

⁷ On a visit to Maria Rishton at Thornham in Nov. 1792 (see i, L. 38) FB had apparently called on the Cokes of Holkham.

awful epoch of life's final dissolution, announces her tenderness to have sprung first from just admiration of your noble Character,—& to have lived encreasing to her latest breath from the softest gratitude for your invariable kindness, & goodness, united with the warmest delight in the dear & constant view of the chaste, the innocent, the exemplary tenour of your conduct, & the integrity, the disinterestedness, the unaffected nobleness of your principles & sentiments.—Heaven bless you, my d'Arblay! here & hereafter! here, with the continuance of the same worth that alone gives true superiority, ¦ & hereafter— with the recompence of eternal life & bliss!—& with—O may be such the bounty of God!—with a re-union with Her who fondly sees herself the Wife of your bosom!—beloved as she loves!—

I leave you no injunctions—I ever held Death-Bed requests cruel from short-sighted Mortals, who ill can judge what events & circumstances may render them impracticable—improper— & even baneful—.

And why recommend to you what will become at once the first care & first joy of your life, our Child?[1]—Ah! Merciful Heaven! if

[*end of fragment*]

159   **[Great Bookham, 9 January 1795]**

To Doctor Burney

A.L. (Barrett, Eg. 3690, f. 90), *n.d.*

Single sheet 4to 1 p.

Edited by FBA, p. 1, *dated* (*possibly from the postmark on a cover now lost*) *and annotated*: ⁂ 9. Jan^y —95 (1)

on the receipt of a most generous Baptismal Present for the Christening of Alexander.

158. ¹ According to the baptismal records of the parish church of St. Nicholas, Great Bookham, 'Alexander Charles Louis, son of Alexandre Gabriel Pieuchard D'Arblay and Frances his wife [was] born December 18ᵗʰ 1794 and baptised April 11ᵗʰ 1795'.

 M. d'A (with SBP), writing to JB (PML), announced the arrival of Martin's '*walk-fellow* cousin, already two hours old'. 'The Mother and her Child are quite well.'

Could I tell my beloved Father half—half—half the pene-
tratingly soft sensations—with very strong emotion—he has
given me, I think that consciousness of happiness would be the
best payment for a testimony of kindness[1] not greater than truly
unexpected—*I*, my most dear Father, have never been amongst
the *Credules* of your amazing riches—far, far from it—& heard
the fabrication with extreme indignation—but this encreases
my gratitude & my surprise at once at this most generously
paternal action—& it seems so to mark a sweetness towards my
Baby—*that* melts me—sooths me—doubles, trebles, the exquisite happiness with which I fold the little darling to my
bosom—I have whispered him what a grandfather he may
boast—Indeed it is a very interesting little Creature, already,
& has a thousand little promises of original intelligence—I am
forbid turning over—& this, my first Pen since my Maternity,
was now put into my hand by the Chief Nurse who till now
has strictly withheld from me all such instruments.—Heaven
bless my beloved & most tenderly kind Father! I write so ill
only from writing on my Hand for I am wonderfully well. My
best respects to my mother & Love to Sarah. We are impatiently
expecting *advices from Bath.*[2] |

159. [1] The dimensions of the gift (probably money) are lost with missing letters.
[2] From CB Jr., who was at Bath at this time, as is indicated by the forwarding
to him there of a letter (Oxford, All Souls), dated 17 Jan., from Dr. Parr. CB Jr.
had sent *Edwy and Elgiva* (see L. 163 n. 4) *c.* 15 Dec. to Sheridan, whose decision he
might now be expected to have; and on 2 Feb. he reported in lively doggerel
having carried a copy of the play *via* Miss Schwellenberg to the Queen (Scrapbook
(Berg), 'Fanny Burney and family. 1653–1890', p. 62):

> To the Queen's House I went, when I'd powder'd my hair,
>   And had put on my very best coat;
> That Coat, which so oft made the Bath Belles declare,
>   That I look'd like a person of note!
> High Ho! the dear Schwell—'twas for sweet little Schwell!

By this time Charles had seen 'at the bottom of some of the Bills of Drury Lane
"*a new Tragedy called E. & E.* is in rehearsal". Several of the papers mentioned it, &
in terms very flattering, though not in the puft way.'

160   [Great Bookham, 7 March 17c5]

To Mrs. Waddington

A.L.S. (Berg), *n.d.*
Double sheet 4to of which the second leaf is nearly all torn away   1 p.
pmk   7 MR 95   wafer
Docketed in ink, p. 1 : March 1795

Ah my Marianne! — — What an age since I have written!—
what delight—& what torture has filled up the interval—my Baby
is all I can wish—my opening recovery was the most rapid I ever
witnessed or heard of—but in a fortnight the poor thing had the
Thrush—communicated it to my Breast—& in short — — after
torment upon torment, a Milk fever ensued—an abscess in the
Breast followed—& till that broke, 4 Days ago, I suffered so as
to make life—even My happy life—scarce my wish to preserve!
—need I say more—

I am now fast recovering once more—living on Bark—Porter
& raw Eggs—incessantly poured down—much reduced, you
may believe—but free from pain & fever—Therefore in a fair
way—

But — — they have made me wean my Child!—O my
Marianne! you who are so tender a Mother can need no words
to say what that has cost me! But God be praised my Babe is
well, & feeds, while he pines—adieu—& Heaven bless you! I
grieve sincerely for your cruel loss[1]—my poor dear unfortunate
young Friend!—may your children bless & repay all! prays yr[s]
                                                        F d'A

160. [1] GMAPW's favourite brother George Rowe Port (*c.* 1774–94), second lieutenant on board H.M.S. *The Reprisal*, had died of yellow fever at Antigua on 20
June 1794. Dubbed by Mrs. Delany, because of his beauty and grace during childhood, the 'little Vandyke', he appears in her *Autobiography*, 2nd s., iii, 5, 312, 384,
388–9, 448.

e

PLATE I

Theatre Royal, Drury-Lane.

This present SATURDAY, March 21, 1795,

Their Majesties Servants will act a new Tragedy called

EDWY and ELGIVA.

THE CHARACTERS BY

Mr. Kemble, Mr. Aikin, Mr. Palmer, Mr Barrymore, Mr. Caulfield,
Mr. Whitfield, Mr. Bensley, Mr. Benson, Mr. C. Kemble,
Mr. Trueman, Mr Packer, Mr. Banks, Mr Maddocks, Mr. Phillimore,
Mrs. Siddons, Mrs. Powell.

The Prologue to be spoken by Mr. Barrymore.
And the Epilogue by Mrs. Siddons.

To which will be added, (for the 22d Time) in three parts,

A Grand Heroic Pantomime, composed by Mr. J D'EGVILLE, called

ALEXANDER the GREAT;

Or, The CONQUEST of PERSIA.

The MUSICK composed by Mr. KRAZINSKY MILLER,
The Scenes, Machinery, Dresses and Decorations are entirely New.

MACEDONIANS.

Alexander, Mr. J. D'EGVILLE,
Hepheftion, Mr. C. Kemble, Clytus, Mr. Dubois,
Perdiccas, Mr. Fairbrother, Parmenio, Mr. Phillimore, Ptolemy, Mr. Caulfield,
Attalus. Mr. Benfon, Eumenes, Mr. Bland, Philip, Mr. G. D'Egville.

AMAZONS.

Thaleftris, Mrs. FIALON,
Mifs Collins, Mifs Heard, Mifs D'Egville, Mifs Redhead, Mifs Stageldoir,
Mifs Stuart, Mifs Tidfwell, Mrs Bramwell.

PERSIANS.

Darius, Mr. FIALON,
Son of Darius, Mafter Menage, Oxathres, Mr. Boimaifon, Memnon, Mr. Webb,
Arfites, Mr. Maddocks, Spithridates, Mr. Banks, Ræfaces, Mr. Lyons,
Syfigambis, Mrs. Cuyler, Parifatis, Mrs. Hedges, Artemifia, Mrs. Butler,
Statira, Mifs J. HILLISBERG,
High Prieft of the Sun, Mr. Roffey.

Attendant Females.

Mifs Brooker, Mifs Phillips, Mifs Daniel, Mrs. Harris, Mrs. Hafkey, Mifs Chatterley,
Mrs. Briggs, Mifs Granger, Mrs. Jones, Mifs Menage, Mifs D'Egville, Mifs Wheatley.

The Piece will conclude with

The ENTRY of ALEXANDER into BABYLON,

And his MARRIAGE with STATIRA.

The Scenery designed and executed by Mr. MARINARI, and his Affiftants.
The Machinery defigned by Mr. CABANEL, and executed by him and Mr. JACOBS.
And the Dreffes and Decorations by Mr. JOHNSTON, and Mifs REIN.

NO MONEY TO BE RETURNED.

Printed by C. LOWNDES, next the Stage-Door. Vivant Rex et Regina!

On Monday (8th, night) the WHEEL of FORTUNE, with (23d time)
ALEXANDER the GREAT, On Thurfday (9th night) the WHEEL of
FORTUNE, with (24th time) ALEXANDER the GREAT. (Being the laft
time, but one, of Performing till the Hollidays.

The Grand Heroic Pantomime of ALEXANDER the GREAT; or, the Conqueft of Perfia will be performed every night till farther notice.

A new Opera in three acts, called JACK of NEWBURY is in Rehearfal

A playbill for the only performance of Madame d'Arblay's tragedy

From an original in the British Museum

161 [Greenwich, 22 March 1795][1]

M. d'Arblay
and Madame d'Arblay
To James Burney

A.L.S. & PS. (PML, Autog. Cor. bound), *n.d.*
Double sheet 4to 1 p. red seal
Addressed: Capt Burney / James, Street N° 26 / Westminster.
Postdated in pencil, p. 1: early 1795

Your Sister, my dear James, would be very obliged to you if you may copy for her what is said in the news papers concerning her Tragedy.[2] She receives from all parts the intelligence that all the papers have acquainted the Public with her *Secret*. We See three Papers, in which nothing upon that Subject is to be found, and I am sure that Heaven is silent upon this topic, since I have in vain read over the Sun & the Star.

I send you back your Banknote with a thousand thanks & as many loves.

Your friend & brother
A. d'Arblay

Your sister & the baby are well, but very angry against this dreadful weather which retards their going on quickly— Remember us to Mrs Burney & Martin—

———————

[PS. by Madame d'Arblay]

I am dying to see these paragraphs *Pray, pray* copy them—

161. [1] After the *première* of *Edwy and Elgiva* at Drury Lane Theatre on Saturday night, 21 March, CB Jr. had taken the d'Arblays to Greenwich, where they were to remain for a visit of three weeks.

In Letter 163 FBA will herself give an account of the calamitous night when in a house 'crowded throughout, and the Boxes chiefly with persons of distinction' the play met the sad but risible fate described in the reviews (Appendix A, p. 366–7).For the comments of Mrs. Siddons, Mrs. Piozzi, and others, see *HFB*, pp. 246–7, Benkovitz (op. cit.), and Baker (op. cit.).

[2] The letter is undated but Sunday 22 March must have been the last day on which the playwright could have cherished any hopes of anonymity. On Sunday and Monday (22 and 23 Mar. 1795) no less than sixteen newspapers, as may be seen from the marked copies in the Burney Collection of Newspapers (BM 885), expressed in varying degrees their concern and amazement that the authoress of *Evelina* could have written the ludicrous lines of a tragedy that kept the house in laughter for much of the evening of 21 Mar. See further, Appendix A, pp. 366–7.

162   [Greenwich, *c.* 22 March 1795]

M. d'Arblay
To Madame d'Arblay

A.L. (Berg), *n.d.*
Single sheet large 4to   2 pp   The upper right corner conjecturally
bearing the name of the recipient has been torn away
Edited by FBA, p. 1, *top margin, annotated*: (2)
Written after the miserable representation of Edwy & Elgiva, in April,, —95.

Supplement à la note remise à

En y reflechissant davantage, je me confirme de plus en plus
dans l'opinion que toi seule as vu la chose dans son vrai jour. En
effet quelles sont les raisons qui ont fait changer d'avis tes amis
qui dabord etaient si portés à en demander l'impression—?[1]

Quelqu'un dont les conseils sur ces sortes de matiere sont d'un
très grand poids a dit: 'La prevention aiguisera les traits de la
Critique qu'il ne faut pas accoutumer à exercer son talent
destructeur contre l'auteur d'Evelina et de Cecilia parceque sa
reputation dans les siecles à venir peut essuyer quelque echec
dans un combat que la malignité naturalle des spectateurs
aimera à prolonger—Premierement, n'en est il pas de la
reputation litteraire comme de tout ce qui a sa source dans
l'opinion,—et n'arrive-t'il pas toujours qu'on est bientôt porté
à renverser entierement l'idole qu'on a pu un moment envisager
sans eprouver cette sorte de respect qui enchaine les serpens
de l'Envie—? Une fois en liberté est il natural de croire qu'ils
changeront de nature?—Non: et le seul moyen de rendre inutile
et impuissante la rage qu'a excité dans eux le tort qu'a eu Miss
B[urney] F[anny] de faire Evelina et ¹ [*tear*] d'agraver ce tort en
continuant à ecrire, et en fesant s'il se peut, mieux encore, sans
s'embarasser de critiques qui s'eclipseront devant les ouvrages
qui les auront produites — — Veut on dire que ces critiques
seront dirigées même contre les deux Romans si connus de Miss

162. ¹ A plan for printing *Edwy and Elgiva*, probably arranged by CB Jr. with some
publisher here unnamed, seems to have been summarily revoked. CB had evidently
opposed the plans, see his letter to FBA (Berg), *pmk* 2 AP 95: 'My earnestness for
not printing was brought on by the general opinion of others who wish you well, &
of whose judgment I think highly.'

B F.? soit: et je suppose pour un moment que toute une nation a été à ce sujet dans un long aveuglement—en ce cas n'y aurait il pas de la folie à se refuser à convenir qu'il est impossible qu'un peu plutôt, ou un peu plus tard, on verrait ces ouvrages dans leur vrai jour? mais ce n'a pu être l'intention ni de Mr Windham de Mr de Narbonne Ils ont donc uniquement voulu parler des travaux litteraires qu'on attend encore de M^de d'Ar[blay]—Eh bien, je dis que la grace est rompue, et qu'il faut qu'elle s'endurcisse d'avance contre les epines d'une carriere qu'elle a jusqu'à present trouvée semèe de roses—Longtems l'Envie la voyant si jeune, a mis sur le compte de l'indulgence des succès qu'elle n'a pu voir sanctionner de plus en plus par la renomée—

une autre raison doit, dit on; nous faire renoncer à l'impression de la Tragedie, une piece bien reçue du Public n'ayant rapporté à son auteur que 40 guinées,—mais il s'agit bien ici d'un tel calcul!

bon soir!

163   Great Bookham, 15 April 1795

To Mrs. Waddington

A.L. (Diary MSS. vi, not numbered, Berg), 15 Apr. 1795
Double sheet 4to   4 pp.   *pmks* EPSOM   22 AP 95   22 AP 95   wafer torn
Addressed: Mrs. Waddington, / Lanover Court, / Abergavenny—Monmouth—
Edited by CFBt.

Bookham
April 15th—95.

So dry a reproof from so dear a Friend? —— And do you, then, measure my regard of Heart by my remissness of Hand?— Let me give you the short History of my Tragedy fairly & frankly.[1]

I wrote it not, as your Acquaintance imagined, *for the Stage*, nor yet *for the Press*—I began it at Kew Palace—at the very time our beloved mutual tie, your revered A[unt] D[elany] was

163. [1] It is to GMAPW's request that we are indebted to the only running account of the writing and production of *Edwy and Elgiva*.

there on a visit to Mr. Smelt:[2] &, at odd Moments, I finished it at Windsor; *without* the least idea of any species of publication.

Since I left the Royal Household, I ventured to let it be read by my Father, Mr. & Mrs. Lock, my Sister Phillips, & —— of course, M. d'Arblay: & not another human Being. — Their opinions led to what followed—& my Brother Dr. Charles shewed it to Mr. Kemble while I was on my visit to my Father last October.[3] He instantly & warmly pronounced for its acceptance, but I knew not when Mr. Sheridan would see it, & had not the smallest expectation of its appearing this year. However—just 3 Days before my beloved little Infant came into the World, an Express arrived from My Brother, that Mr. Kemble wanted the Tragedy immediately, in order to shew it to Mr. Sheridan, who had ǀ just heard of it, & had spoken in the most flattering terms of his good will for its reception.[4]

Still, however, I was in doubt of its actual acceptance, till 3 Weeks after my confinement, when I had a visit from my Brother, who told me he was the next Morning to read the Piece in the Green Room.

This was a precipitance for which I was every way unprepared, as I had never made but one Copy of the Play, & had intended divers corrections & alterations:—absorbed, however, by my new charge, & then growing ill, I had a sort of indifference about the matter, which, in fact, has lasted ever since.

The moment I was then able to hold a pen, I wrote two short Letters to acknowledge the state of the affair to my Sisters[5]—& to one of these, I had an immediate laughing answer—informing me *my confidence* was somewhat of the latest, as the Subject of

[2] Mrs. Delany's visit of two weeks in October or November of 1786 to Kew, when as a guest of the Royal Family she was billeted with Mr. and Mrs. Smelt (i, L. 12 n. 18; and Delany, 2nd s., iii. 427–8) supplies the beginning dates for the composition of the play.

[3] See L. 148 n. 1; and for Kemble's misgivings, L. 156 n. 3.

[4] It was shortly after 15 Dec. 1794, then, that the play was sent to Sheridan. On [9 Jan. 1795] FBA was 'impatiently expecting' the decision (L. 159 and n. 2), of which she must have been apprised a few days later.

[5] These letters, presumably to EBB and CBF, are missing; but from 6 to 21 March advertisements announcing 'a new tragedy called EDWY and ELGIVA' had appeared intermittently in *The Times, Star, Sun, Morning Herald, Morning Chronicle,* etc. Though at no time was the author's name printed or any hint given of her identity, the reviews of 22 and 23 Mar. abundantly show that the 'secret' was well blown abroad, probably by the managers.

The Drury Lane Playbills of 7, 9, 10, 12, 14, 16, 17, 19 Mar. (preserved in the Burney Theatre Collection, the BM, 937 c.13) regularly carried the announcement, and on Saturday 21 Mar. *Edwy and Elgiva* had a full billing (see Plate II).

it *was already in all the News-papers*!—I was extremely chagrined at this intelligence—but, from that time, thought it all too late to be the herald of my own Designs. And this, added to my natural & incurable dislike to enter upon these egoistical details unasked, has caused my silence to my dear Marianne— & to every ¹ Friend I possess. Indeed, speedily after, I had an illness so severe & so dangerous, that for full 7 Weeks the Tragedy was neither named nor thought of by M. d'A. or myself—

It was not my *Health enabled me to go to Town*—I was too much indisposed to make a single visit there, even to my sisters— I merely went, ONE NIGHT, to alight at the Theatre, where I was met by my Sister Phillips,⁶ with whom, & M. d'A. & my Brother Dr. C[harles] I sat, snug & retired & wrapt up in a Bonnet & immense Pelice, in Mr. Sheridan's Box to see Mrs. Siddons & Mr. Kemble⁷ in *Edwy & Elgiva*. And except this once, & for this purpose, I entered not London. I could not risk my Babe there, & I would not leave him, thus early, for a single Night upon any consideration, except eminent danger to a dear friend. I spent near 3 Weeks in the pure air of Greenwich,⁸ at my Brothers, with M. d'A. & our little inseparable, & there my family visited me, & Mr. & Mrs. Lock, but I was too much an Invalide to receive *any others*.

The Piece was represented to the utmost disadvantage, save only Mrs. Siddons & Mr. Kemble,—for it was not written with any idea of the stage, & my illness & weakness & constant *absorbment* in the time of its preparation, occasioned it to appear with so many *undramatic* [ef]fects, from my inexperience of Theatrical requisites & demands, that when I saw it, I perceived myself a thousand things I wished to *change* The Performers, too, were cruelly imperfect,⁹ & made blunders I blush

---

⁶ In a letter (Berg) of [20 Mar. 1795] SBP had completed the arrangements: 'Heaven bless you my love, & our sweet little Boy—Try to be *stout*— . . . It is a sad pity we can only meet at the Theatre— . . . I shall send my Fanny wᵗʰ Sally to join the Titchfield Street party—Pray let yʳ directions be clear & explicit as to the Box I must ask for . . .'

⁷ They took the title roles (Plate II).   ⁸ From 21 Mar. to 11 Apr.

⁹ 'The Acting was disgraceful to the Company, and shamefully injurious to the Author', asserted the *Morning Advertiser* (23 Mar.). 'The Prompter was heard unremittingly all over the House. If the Piece was *accepted*, it should have been *played*. There is no palliation for imperfect study in a Theatre of the Metropolis.' Other reviews, for example, that in the *Morning Post and Fashionable World* (23 Mar.), made the same complaint: 'the Prompter was heard, in many instances, before the actors.'

to have ˡ pass for mine,—added to what belong to me—the most important Character, after the Hero & Heroine, had *but 2 lines* of his part by Heart![10] he made all the rest at random—& such nonsense as put all the other actors out as much as himself—so that a more wretched performance, except Mrs. S[iddons], Mr. K[emble] & Mr. Bensley,[11] could not be exhibited in a Barn. All this concurred to make it very desirable to *withdraw the Piece for alterations*—which I have done.

And now you have the whole history—& now—are you appeased?

I [g]rieve you have still those cruel Head achs—but I rejoice your little ones are well. I am now without the smallest Complaint, but still not *my own man* for strength. I live continually in the air of our little Garden, however, & shall soon be *robust* again. Have you heard poor *General* Goldsworthy[12] fell from his Horse in an apoplexy? He is well again, nevertheless, & I have had a Letter Franked by him since. My charming Friends the Locks are all in Town still.

Adieu, Naughty Girl!—
ever yours

When you write to Mrs. M[atthew] M[ontagu][13]pray mention the anecdote of my being *Merely* & *Wholly* at Greenwich, except those *few Hours* one Evening—for I find it was thought I was in Town—as Mrs. Montagu Senʳ *made me a visit* at Mrs. Lock's, where she concluded me to be.

---

[10] This was John Palmer (*c.* 1742–98), who played the part of Aldhelm. 'Usually correct', he was 'extremely imperfect', the *Public Ledger* (23 Mar.) noted; and the *Oracle, Public Advertiser* (23 Mar.) expressed its 'ASTONISHMENT . . . that any ACTOR can dare stand before the MANAGER, who engages his services, and *receive* EVERY WORD of his PRINCIPAL SCENE from the *mouth* of the Prompter!' 'Duty demands *not* his CENSURE [of the play], but his PERFORMANCE.'

[11] Robert Bensley (*c.* 1738– *c.* 1817) played Dunstan. Many of the reviewers praised the principals. 'It was kindness in Mrs. SIDDONS to lend her person and voice to character undiscriminated, and dialogue unimpassioned' (*Oracle*, op. cit.).

[12] See i, L. 5 n. 10.

[13] See i, L. 5 n. 14.

Great Bookham, 1 May 1795

To Mrs. Francis (*later* Broome)

A.L.S. (Barrett, Eg. 3693, ff. 57–8b), 1 May [17]95
Double sheet 4to   4 pp.   *pmks*   EPSOM   2 MA 95   green wafer
Addressed: Mrs. Francis, / N° 9, / Downing Street, / Westminster.
Endorsed by CBF: Sister d'arblay / 1795.

cher little Bookham,
May 1st—95.

How many thanks I owe my kind Charlotte for her admirable
Stewardship, & very entertaining Letter. I return, with my best
thanks, & *best hand*, the receipt, & pray give my Comp^{ts} from
time to time—that is, *once a quarter*, to Mr. Mathias. I am glad
he is so much of your parties, for I think him particularly
agreeable & pleasant, as well as cultivated & sensible.

But—what parties you have, my Charlotte![1]—Why you are
quite a *bas bleu*!—well, let those laugh that win! let no laughs
make you relinquish a mode of happiness, & a species of society,
equally honourable, instructive, & entertaining. I am quite
delighted at your progress in this *bluism*; it was always to your
taste, & it is now in your power to prove what that taste is better
than by mere assertion.

What Mr. Cumberland said of Mrs. Ord is very severe
indeed[2]—yet not wholly without foundation, I fear, with regard
to her stoicism, as I find Esther was also much *struck*—with her
extreme composure.[3] I thank you much for the *bon mots* you

164. [1] Parts of CBF's Journal describing the social evenings, 3, 8, 11, and 15 Mar.,
are preserved in the Scrapbook 'Fanny Burney and family. 1653–1890' (Berg),
p. 64.
   Between 3 and 11 Mar. CBF had entertained her brothers Charles and James
and their wives, Boswell and his daughters, Mr. and Mrs. Skerrett (i, L. 28 n. 2),
and on both occasions the clever and comical Mathias brothers, who 'kept us on
the broad grin the whole Evening—'. The second evening was very 'merry & jovial',
the gentlemen having discovered an extra dozen of wine. 'Boswell indisputably
drunk . . . attempting to make love to me, but . . . happily the love fit wore off.'
   On 8 and 15 March CBF had dined with the Mathiases in Scotland Yard.
   [2] CB's letter (Berg) of 7 May 1795 tells of his having dined with Charlotte where
he met the Hooles, the Mathiases, and Richard Cumberland, but the comments
and *bons mots* of the latter are lost with the letter in which CBF had apparently
recorded them.
   [3] Mrs. Ord had already lost five of her children (i, L. 9 n. 1) and recently (on
Monday 16 Feb.) her daughter Charlotte (b. 1753) had died of burns in the

indulge me with of Mr. C.—& those of Mr. Bozzy.[4] Pray let me at least partake of your parties by *Letters*. I think you should afford me an Epistle—not a LACOONIC EPESSTLE, upon every of these recreations. You shall have the account again, when you are an old lady, & will be glad to revise your gayer scenes: & meanwhile, you will give me great ⏐ pleasure, & of the sort I have not spared *you* in former days.[5]

We can arrange nothing immediately about quitting our dear little Hermitage,—I tremble about the small pox when I think of London. Yet we shall be extremely happy to pay a visit of so long promised pleasure to my dearest Charlotte—

M. d'A. has been Gardening incessantly since our return. You would not know the place again, so much he has performed.

Our domestics go on much as usual in most points, though in the capital ones of cleanliness & neatness, I have had the satisfaction to work a thorough reform. The House is as changed as the Garden. *Miss Slip* continues her old tricks,—I wish she could get a lesson from Capt. Mirvan,[6] to cure her of her fondness for being so slippery!—but with *us* she is incorrigible: nevertheless, I now so delight to keep my Bambino myself, that I bear her *gliding qualities* better than most people would do,— & in other respects, she has much to recommend her. She is clean, & keeps the Babe most perfectly & delicately nice & healthy & pure. The nights are still the worst; I dare not trust her,—but I doubt if I could trust any body, so precious is my nocturnal Charge—& the dear Infant sleeps sweetly the greatest part of the night at present, & disturbs me as little as is possible. ⏐

lamentable circumstances described, for example, by the *St. James's Chronicle* (19 Feb.) and copied by the *Reading Mercury*, *Oxford Gazette* (23 Feb.): 'As Miss Ord [of Queen-Ann Street] was standing with her back to the fire, her sash caught fire, which soon communicated to her head-dress. She rang the bell, but the servant who attended, had not the presence of mind to roll her in a carpet, but conducted her into the hall; opened the street-door, and called for assistance. Some persons coming by, got the lady into the street, and attempted to roll her into the snow; but it was the Coachman of Lady Somers who put out the flames effectually, by wrapping his great coat round her. She was so terribly burnt, that she died on Monday.'

4 In the Journal (above) CBF had recounted Boswell's retelling of Seward's joke about the poll tax recently imposed on 'all the heads th[at] wear powder' and on 'the *stock* of wine in the merchants' hands': ' "Pitt has now taxed us *Stock & Block*" —meaning s^d Boswell, that when the Stock mounts into the Block it is *stock & block*.'

5 In earlier journals like the 'Tingmouth Journal' of 1773 (*ED* i. 228–62) or the 'Streatham Journals' of 1778 (*DL* i. 53–149).

6 A character in *Evelina*. 'The Captain says he won't stay here to be *smoked with filth* any longer' (i. 12).

He continues to be Tall & Thin—he knows that was always my taste for my Heros!—

I entreat you to let me have the Sum total now standing of my Account with you, my dear Steward. Pray do not forget it.

Mrs. James Burney gave me a flourishing relation of your Ball[7]—I am quite enchanted at your present plan of life. It is precisely what I should recommend for you. Your shaken nerves & worn spirits require the recruit of all the gaiety & life you can rationally & with propriety obtain. And I have no fears for my dear Charlotte that she will ever exceed their bounds. She has a natural discretion, & a native modesty of Character, that will always guard her. Who is *Dr. Crighton?*[8] you must make me acquainted with your new acquaintances. I dare believe the good Mr. & Mrs. Hoole have passed their time very happily with you. Every body Speaks well & honourably of Miss Day.[9] How enchanted must my dear little Charlotte have been with the Dance!—Do you keep up *your French* with her?

Our dearest Susan looks still very ill!—& I have been able to see her but twice!—the roads are so indifferent, & we are *both* so *unrobustified* as yet. Nevertheless, I am so stout & so free from every species of malady, that I am—the WORLD'S WONDER—in imitation of my Babe, who is pronounced THE IDOL OF THE WORLD—& by | Whom?—the best of all Judges—His own Father & Mother!—So his fame, & his name, are made for-ever more.

Distribute for me duties & Loves & Compliments to Mankind —I like to speak in a large & comprehensive manner.

Adieu, my ever dear Charlotte—I am *truly* happy in hoping your Health considerably better. Observe your present mode, & my past injunctions—which I think exactly coincide, upon this very interesting subject. Yours ever & ever & ever most affectionately

F d'A

M. d'A. sends you all kindness—& his best devoirs to his fair little Mistress. Remember me to her with a chaste embrace—

---

[7] Still another party given by CBF, of which no other account is extant.

[8] Possibly Alexander Crighton (1763–1856), M.D. (Leyden), whom CBF mentioned (loc. cit.) having met at the Mathias's on 15 March and indeed 'partout'.

[9] Probably Ann Day (*c.* 1762–1821), governess to CBF's children.

& bid her *kiss me* Marianne & clement.[10] I hear from all that Clement is quite a beautiful Boy. Tell him to continue me his Letters. I shall answer *in kind* with great punctuality.

165   [Great Bookham,] 13 May 1795

To M. d'Arblay

A.N.S. (Berg), 13 May 1795
Single sheet half 4to 1 p.
Edited by FBA, p. 1, *annotated*: (3) +The Birth Day,!—of my incomparable Husband—

To

Monsieur d'Arblay.

———————

May 13ᵗʰ 1795.+

———————

I have nothing appropriate for my beloved Friend upon this dear Day,—My only Manual & visual homage must be a Rose enrolled in two juvenile burlesque poems,[1] which I present for his diversion: — — he will not think This my only homage— while my Heart beats—all other can but be symbolic & secondary. — —

Frances d'Arblay.

——————————

[10] Clement Robert Francis, now about 2½ years old.
165. [1] Not identified.

166   Great Bookham, 13 May [1795]

To Doctor Burney

A.L.S. (Diary MSS. vi, not numbered, Berg), 13 May
Double sheet 4to   4 pp.   *pmk* 16 MA 95   wafer
Addressed: Dr. Burney, / Chelsea College, / Middlesex.
Edited by FBA, p. 1, *annotated and postdated by* FBA: ⌗ ⁑ ⁑ —95   (2)
Baby Alex—Mr. Cumberland on Edwy & Elgiva. Bookham happy
Hermitage—
Edited also by CFBt.

Hermitage,
Bookham, May 13.

You have not one Letter to translate, my most dear Father,
from your adored Metastasio, more gayly sweet, more kindly
amiable than this last original you have bestowed upon me.[1]—
Mr. Cumberland is curious, & surprising[2]—Mrs. Paradise, *the
very Woman*,[3]—Mr. Twi[ning]'s abstract is delicious,[4]—Mr.
Hastings, reviving,[5]—Lady Spencer, just what I could expect,[6]
—*Fox & Windham* good dramatic encountering,[7] — & — —

166. [1] In a letter of 7 May 1795 (Berg) to FBA, CB gives the usual accounts of his
social and literary engagements, taking care to relay the condolences of his and
FBA's friends on the failure of *Edwy and Elgiva*. Most of his letter was copied by
CFBt and printed in *DL* v. 252–5.
  [2] Cumberland had offered (op. cit.) to read a revision of *Edwy* or any new play
that FBA could write, and from his experience he would 'risk his life on its
success—'.
  [3] Mrs. Paradise (L. 134 n. 6), having 'fastened on' CB, had held him 'tight' with
accounts of her husband's illnesses and her own.
  [4] In his letter of 7 May (op. cit.) CB had copied a full page of Thomas Twining's
letter of sympathy on the 'sad catastrophe' of 21 March. From the dramatic scenes
of *Evelina* and *Cecilia* he would have expected FBA to succeed in Tragedy and he
regrets with CB that she should have ventured out of her own genre. 'I hope Mʳˢ
Dʼ. is not *much* mortified by this untoward business. There is really no *reason*, au
fond, why she should. Her excellence in the *Prose Epic* is undisputed. Is it any
reflection upon Genius of the *highest* class, that it is not calculated to excel alike in
every way?' And he continued with an amusing critique of the Gothic novel (its
forests, castles, and trap doors with iron rings) and a comforting comparison of
them with FB's works.
  [5] For the proceedings at Westminster Hall, 'As much crowded as on the first
day', see *AR* xxxvii (1795), 'Appendix to the Chronicle', 111–16. Warren Hastings
(i, L. 17 n. 3) was acquitted on 23 Apr. CB had 'visited him the next morning, &
we cordially shook hands' (op. cit.).
  [6] For the hospitality of the Spencer family and CB's praise of them, see *DL* v.
253–4.
  [7] An unscheduled meeting of political foes at the Literary Club (*DL* v. 254).

Warton!—O, the *very Man!*[8]—But the best of all is the story of resuscitation, & the happy effect of bustle & exertion. My dearest Father is so made for society—*that* is the truth & moral of the fable—& society is always disposed to be so just towards him, that it is impossible, when he is shaken back to it, he should not—like the Man of Sicily[9]—find himself *put to rights.*— For bustle & exertion—*like tobacco hic*—(Lord! how learned & grand I am in my illustrations!)—*if you are well, may,* by over-draughting, *make you sick,*—but, after a short repose, & a little discipline to boot,[10]—*if you are sick,* they are just the things to *make you well.* The Mind wants pulling out a little, to recognize its own elastascity.

Horticulture prospers beyond all former even *ideas* of prosperity. How—HOW I do wish you could come & take an Hour's work here!—it would mingle so well with Metastasio!—the employment—the fragrant surrounding Air—the sweet refreshing Landscape— | & your partner in labour, all would be congenial, with Metastasio, &, consequently, with You—for you know, when we were all to chuse who we would be if not our dear identical & always all-preferable selves,—*You* fixed upon Metastasio—And, indeed, in many, nay most respects, it would hardly be a change.

To be sure, as you say, 'tis pity Monsr d'A. & his Rib should have conceived such an antipathy to the petit Monsieur!—O if you could see him now!—*My Mother* would be satisfied, for his little cheeks are beginning to favour of the Trumpeter's: &

[8] For the badinage on the unities and Joseph Warton's playful acceptance of CB's judgement of the dramatic merit of Metastasio, see *DL* v. 254.

[9] The protagonist of an anonymous work *An Agreeable | CRITICISM, | of the | City of Paris and the* French; | *Giving an ACCOUNT of their | Present* State *and* Condition. . . . | Being a *Translation* of an *Italian* LETTER, written lately from | *Paris,* by a *Sicilian,* to a Friend of his at *Amsterdam.* . . . *By a* French *Gentleman* (1704). This comic satire, probably long known to the Burneys, has an introductory chapter, 'The Author's Way of Living at Paris'. His programme includes waking with the sun, writing or reading, then, 'Having finish't the Study of the Morning, which is the *Motion of the Mind,* [to] begin the Motion of the Body'. The Man of Sicily then walks out and fills up the day and the evening with social life, going to bed as late as he can.

[10] See John Ray, *A Collection of English Proverbs* (Cambridge, 1678), p. 296; and Francis Grose, *A Classical Dictionary of the Vulgar Tongue* (1785). The well-known rhyme, reflecting the estimation in which tobacco was at first held as a medicine, must go back almost to the discovery of the plant:

> Tobacco hic
> Will make you well if you be sick.
> Tobacco hic
> If you be well will make you sick.

Esther would be satisfied, for he eats like an Embryo Alderman.
He enters into all we think, say, mean, & wish! his Eyes are sure
to sympathise in all our affairs, & all our feelings. We find some
kind *reason* for every smile he bestows upon us, & some generous
& disinterested *motive* for every grave look. If he wants to be
danced, we see he has discovered that his gaiety is exhilarating
to us; if he refuses to be moved, we take notice that he fears to
fatigue us. If he will not be quieted without singing, we delight
in his early goût for les beaux arts. If he is immoveable to all we
can devise to divert him, we are edified by the *grand serieux* of his
dignity & philosophy; if he makes the House ring with loud
acclaim because his victuals, at first call, does not come ready
warm into his mouth—we hold up our hands with admiration
at his vivacity. |

The Conversation with Mr. C[umberland] astonished me. I
certainly think his experience of stage effect, & his interest with
players, so important, as almost instantly to wish putting his
sincerity to the proof. How has he got these two Characters, one
of Sir *Fretful Plaigery*,[11] detesting all works but those he owns, &
all authors but himself,—the other, of a Man too perfect even
to know or conceive the vices of the World, such as he is painted
by Goldsmith in Retaliation?—And which of these Characters
is true? I am not at all without thoughts of a future revise of
Edwy & Elgiva, for which I formed a plan on the first Night,
from what occurred by the repr[esen]tation: but then—I want
Mr. Palmer[12] to be so obliging as to leave the Stage!—Though
every body agrees he would not dare, after what has already
passed, play the same part a second time. Let me own to you,
when you commend *my bearing so well a theatrical drubbing*,[13] I am
by no means enabled to boast I bear it with conviction of my

[11] Which character of Cumberland is nearer the original, that painted by
Sheridan in the envious Sir Fretful in *The Critic* (1779) or that delineated by Goldsmith in *Retaliation: a Poem* (1774)? In the triumphal days of *Evelina*, FB had found
Cumberland very much the former (*DL* i. 288–92). Now the triumphs were his,
and '3 successful new plays in one Season' as compared with the dismal failure of
Edwy seems to have softened his feelings towards FBA. Cf. *The Times* (23 Mar.):
'The "WHEEL OF FORTUNE," was stopped in its attractive round, on Saturday
evening, by a Tragedy . . .' See also A.L. (Berg) CB to FBA, 9 June 1795.
[12] See L. 163 nn. 9, 10.
[13] A reference to CB's sympathetic letter, *pmk* 2 AP 95 (Berg), on the universal
condemnation of *Edwy*: 'I honour your heroism. I always Feared pelting, & more
for you than myself: as you used to be more hurt at news-paper praise than others
at abuse. . . . But you have gulped the bitter— . . . and the less one talks of sickening
things the better. It is but one chapter of our ill-luck the more. . . .'

utter failure: the Piece was certainly not heard, & therefore not really judged. The Audience *finished* with an *UNMIXED* clap on hearing it was Withdrawn *for ALTERATIONS*,[14] & I have constantly considered myself in the *PUBLICLY ACCEPTED* situation of having at my own option to let the Piece die, or attempt its resuscitation,—its *reform*, as Mr. Cumberland calls it. And should this be my ultimate act, it will be worth thinking of that he has made such a proposition. However, I have not given one moment to the matter since my return to the Hermitage. ⌐

⌐I have not, however, neglected equally the other,[15] & less have done because you so strongly recommended to me. but that will be a great work—I mean in bulk—& very long in hand— Pray save me Proof sheets of the Estratto dell arte poetica[16] for you say I must not write on the play without reading it—a word to the wise. — —⌐

My dearest Susan spent yesterday here, &, too tired to walk back, slept upon our warm soft sofa, with a fire, & Curtains contrived by *My Upholsterer*—who lives in the House with me,— as well as My Gardener, & the rest of *Mes Gens*.[17] ⌐Tell my Mother not to *make signs at her nose*, for *mes Gens* are very fragrant! —I am very sorry she has been so ill, I beg my love & Respects to her, & I hope ⟨Summer time⟩ will set her right. I say nothing in detail of Sarah, for she [managed] to write to Day herself.⌐

The Letter You enclosed me I meant to Copy for you,—& will when I next commit *a few pleasing words* to paper. It is anonymous again,—but not from *Mrs. Felix*![18] it is from some *ENRAGÉ* at what he calls the *inhuman crush* of Edwy & Elgiva. How glad I am you carried your felicitations to Mr. Hastings! Our excellent neighbours the Cooks know him & are overjoyed —[xxxxx *1 line*]   Dear—dear—dear Sir, Adieu!

F d'A

⌐M. d'Arblay's ⟨journey to London concerned business left in his charge⟩. He is gone to aid sweet Susan Home. My kind love to Sall. our Norbury friends are detained in Town by the illness of the lovely Amelia, but we hope only a Day or two—⌐

[14] According to the newspapers, the applause expressed approval of the announced withdrawal rather than the prospect of re-playing.

[15] *Camilla*.

[16] CB's translation of parts of Metastasio's *Estratto* on Aristotle's *Poetics* (Lonsdale, p. 375).

[17] See L. 152 n. 3.   [18] These letters are missing.

167   Great Bookham, 15 May 1795

To James Burney

A.L.S. & PS. signed by M.d'A (PML, Autog. Cor. bound), 15 May [17]95
Double sheet 8vo 1 p. *pmks* EPSOM 16 MA 95 wafer
Addressed: Captn Burney, / James Street, / Westminster—

                                Bookham Hermitage
                                    May 15—95
It has just been whispered in my Ear that there is a glimpse
of an idea that you—& Mrs. B[urney]—& Martin may—just
possibly—come & reside at Mickleham for a year or two[1]—O
my dear Brother! What a delicious society, with our retained
Susan, will that make us!—we desire & wish NOTHING so much
in this World— *We*, I say, for ardently M. d'Arblay sympathises
in the full warmth of my earnest wish.—
    And so—
    I hope heartily your House in Town will go off.
                        AND
That your House at Mickleham will *Stick a hand*!—
                                    That's All.
                                Signed—F. d'Arblay—
with all my heart A. d'Arblay

168   Great Bookham, 10 June 1795

To Charles Burney

A.L. (Osborn), 10 June 1795
Double sheet 4to 3 pp. *pmks* LEATHER / HEAD 10 JU 95 wafer
Addressed: Dr. Charles Burney, / Academy, / Greenwich, / Kent.

                                    June 10—
Dearest Charles,   1795
How are you? How are yours?—
I am well. So are ours.
        167. ¹ These plans apparently came to nothing.

I begin with dignity, because I am going to write upon business.
But — — — 'What's the Play to Night?'
  Edwy & Elgiva?—
  No!—'Tis out of sight! — —
  Well!—let that pass!
     and
  'Write me down an Ass!'
  Be sure don't fail, Mr. Sheridan!—
  Answer. No, upon my Honour!—

So now to new matter.
I have had an extraordinary message from Mr. Cumberland;[1]
—that he *knew* the play would fail, by what he gathered from
the players before performance; but that so well *he* thinks of it,
that — — if I will either *reform* it for the stage, or write a new
one with my best powers, & submit it to his inspection before
representation, he will risk his life upon its success.—!
What think you of this? Give us your notion. He said it to my
Father, & bid him forward it to me. [1]
Now to something else.

I have had a long & warm & fervent exhortation from the
good & wise seer Cambridge,[2] to print the Tragedy by subscription. He is sure the Names, &c, would be splendid, etc also
the consequence—which shall be nameless, being rather vulgar
where the Muses are in question.
     And
I have had a Message to the same effect, with the same
advice, in form & ceremony, sent me, openly & with great
kindness, from Mrs. Montagu.[2]
     And—
I have had a spirited anonymous Letter urging ditto forcibly.[2]

So Much for That.

168. [1] See L. 166 n. 2.
 [2] Richard Owen Cambridge (i, L. 1 n. 6) and Elizabeth Montagu (i, L. 3 n. 82).
These letters are missing.

Now—to *The* business.

All things considered,—& weighty are some of them! — — have just come to a resolution to print my Grand Work,[3] of which you have never yet heard,—by subscription.

But

As in some points it is very disagreeable to us both to take such a measure—And as in all points, it is a thing to be done but ONCE in a Life, we wish to do it to MOST advantage. |

It is not finished.

And I don't know how long it will be.

But I fancy in 6 Volumes such as Cecilia, or in 4 Oct^{vo}

Now what ought to be the subscription?

Pray give me your idea.

And know you in the least what the expence of the printing will be?[4] Good paper & Letter, though not the *superlative*.

We think to have Subscriptions received by Messrs Payne, Cadell, & Robinson.[5] Advise upon this subject, I pray.

Must we have *proposals* printed?[6]

or will newspaper *advertisements* suffice?[7]

We mean to open with all the speed we can arrange.

---

[3] A new novel *Camilla*.

[4] 'The Cash accompt books of William Strahan' (6 vols., 1777–1829, BM Add. MSS. 48, 828–33), printer, show under the date 28 Dec. 1797 (vol. i) that for the printing of *Camilla* (5 vols.) the publishers were charged £183. 6s.

[5] The choice of publishers had become a matter of family disputation, JB favouring his brother-in-law Thomas Payne (1752–1831), successor (1790) to the bookseller 'old Tom Payne' (1719–99) of Castle Street, near the Mews-gate. CB also approved the son of his old friend of the popular old bookshop and now a family connection; if, however, the novel was to be published by a *group* of booksellers, he thought it far from prudent to omit his own highly reputable, not to say influential, publisher G. G. & J. Robinson of Paternoster-row. An index to FB's literary reputation is provided by the rivalry of the publishers for her new work, and Robinson, incensed at his eventual exclusion from the final arrangements, was, as CB feared, to turn inimical to *Camilla* '& her mother' (see Ll. 178 n. 1, 204 n. 3).

At the top or near the top of the trade was Thomas Cadell 'the elder' (1742–1802), who with T. Payne & Son had published FB's *Cecilia* in 1782, paying £250 for the copyright (see receipt, Berg). And on 30 June 1795 Thomas 'the younger' (1773–1836), having succeeded his father in the firm of T. Cadell Jun. & W. Davies in the Strand, solicited CB Jr.'s 'Influence towards obtaining for them jointly with Mr Payne, the first Offer of the Copyright' of FBA's new work (see his letter, preserved in the Scrapbook (Berg) 'Fanny d'Arblay and friends. England. 1759–1799', p. 104).

Eventually (*pre* Mar. 1796) the d'Arblays were to sell the copyright to T. Payne, the younger (see Ll. 190, 213), for £1,000.

[6] SBP in the course of her letter of 17 Oct. (Berg) to FBA mentions the Proposals, which, printed on separate sheets, were supplied, for example, to the ladies taking subscriptions for the work.

[7] Eventually the novel was to be advertised in columns of two running inches, but of this, much, later.

Give us your Counsel, my dear & ever kind Brother & Agent. My kind Love to Rosette—& Carlino, & kind remembrance to Mrs. Bicknell. M. d'A. subscribes largely to the above. ᛁ

169   Great Bookham, 13 June 1795

To Doctor Burney

A.L. (Diary MSS. vi, not numbered, Berg), 13 June [17]95
Double sheet 4to, (9·3 × 7·5″) 4 pp. the second leaf of which is cut down to 6″
Addressed: Dr. Burney, / Chelsea College, / Middlesex.
Endorsed by CB: June 13ᵗʰ / Nº 4
Edited by FBA, p. 1, *annotated*: ⌗ ✳ (3)
On the proposed Subscription for Printing Camilla,
Edited also by CFBt.

Bookham,
June 13.—95.

My beloved Father,

How I rejoice my business Letter¹ did not arrive an Hour or two sooner! it might have so turned your thoughts to itself as to have robbed me of *'FORE GEORGE! a more excellent Song than t'other!'*² I would not have lost it—I had almost said for ALL my subscription—& I should quite have said it, if I listened more to impulse than to interest.—How I should have enjoyed being with *'that Rogue'*, as you call her [Mʳˢ Crewe], & Lady B[ucking-ha]m, peering at you & Mr. Erskine, confabbing so lovingly!³ The Democrats court you so violently,⁴ that Monsʳ d'Arblay

169. ¹ A letter, now missing, but obviously written *c.* 8 June by FBA to CB on the same subject as that broached in her letter of 10 June to CB Jr. It had evidently crossed with CB's letter of 9 June *pmk* 10 JU 95 (Berg; and *DL* v. 258–61).
² A tag often used by CB and FBA, its obvious source, Cassio's comment (*Othello*, II. iii.): ' 'Fore God, this is a more exquisite song than the other.'
³ The 'song 'that FBA had so much enjoyed was CB's letter of 9 June (op. cit.) with its account of Mrs. Crewe's *dejeuner*, at which, when strolling with the 'fashion-ables' and 'peripatetico-politicians' in the garden, he had been stopped by Erskine, who with 'infinite volubility' detained him on the subject of 'the *Reform of Parlia-ment*'. 'All this while he had hold of my arm,—& people stared at our intimacy—while that rogue Mʳˢ Crewe and the Marchioness of Buckingham were upstairs sitting at a window, wondering and laughing at our conjoberation!—'
⁴ CB prided himself on the many democrats or radicals, who, his 'aristocracy' notwithstanding, had mentioned him favourably in their publications. In addition

insists they have *found you out!* & that your Aristocracy is a feint.
— — — but I must fly from all this intellectual sport, & from
our Garden, & our Bambino, to write FIRST upon the business,—
or this, & those, will presently swallow all my paper, from
dearer, more congenial attraction.

How infinitely kind—how beyond all species of expectation,
—to write so speedily such another long Letter![5]—Dearest Sir!
how shall I thank you?—May but the Work do it, by affording
you similar relaxation for your leisure with its predecessors!—

All our deliberations made, even after your *discouraging* calculations, we still mean to hazard the subscription, as we *cannot*
follow your hint to settle a *round sum* now received on our little
Nonpareil—we shall require immediate service from whatever
is the interest money—we only desire or mean to guard him the
principal. I am sure you will feel this answer to be ǀ as equitable
& satisfactory as it is sincere. We are obliged to keep a servant
for him, which so much enlarges our expences, that an increase
of our income, is become absolutely indispensable. And, indeed,
for such casualities, I had previously determined, when I
changed my state, to set aside all my innate & original abhorrences,
& regard & use as resources MYSELF, what had always been
considered as such by others.[6] Without this idea, & this resolution, our Hermitage must have been madness. With them,—
I only wish my dear & kind Father could come & work at it,
with Abdolomine, to cure his lumbago,—as Abdolomine says it
would surely do,—& he would then see its comforts, its peace,
its harmony,—& its little *'Perrenial Plant'*[7]—& see many a view

to John Courtenay and William Godwin (L. 150 nn. 10, 12), there was William
Hayley (1745–1820), who in referring to Milton's father and his knowledge of
music had cited Dr. Burney, 'the accomplished historian of that captivating art',
see *The Poetical Works of John Milton* (3 vols., 1794), I. vi. In 'Musical Notes on the
Hindus', *Works* (13 vols., 1807), iv. 176, 195, Sir William Jones, 'a decided republican', had praised CB for his perspicuity and for the dignity he lent to 'the character
of a modern musician by uniting it with that of a scholar and philosopher'. In
Essays, Historical and Critical, in English Church Music (York, 1795), William Mason
(1724–97), though taking issue with CB on the subject of parochial psalmody
(p. 197), found that for many facts and definitions he could not rest upon a better
authority than Dr. Burney.
  [5] Letters written by CB on the publishing business and other pecuniary matter
FBA probably destroyed.
  [6] 'To increase her income by her pen' was a possibility long considered. See a
letter (Berg) from SBP to FB, 1–2 June 1793; and 12 June 1793 (Barrett, Eg. 3692,
ff. 190–1b). Also ii, Ll. 83, 101, and 104. See also ii, p. 148.
  [7] In his letter of 9 June (Berg) CB had combined his remarks on 'little Sandy'
with complimentary verses addressed to M. d'A on 'His flow'ry Arbors, & his

of retired life which he may have read as romantic, yet felt as desireable, realised. M. d'A. has arranged himself a Study in our little Parlour, that would be after your Heart's content, for literary chaoticism. — — but here I am running away from this same business again.—

I am extremely glad you mean to communicate with Mrs. Crewe—Her former great kindness, in voluntary propositions of exertion, upon a similar plan, I have never forgotten, &, consequently, never ceased to be grateful for, though my then shyness, & peculiarly strung nerves, made its prospect terrific, not alluring to me.[8] Now—when I look at my dear Baby, | & see its dimpling smiles, & feel its elastic springs—I think how small is the sacrifice of such feelings, for such a blessing.—You enchant me by desiring more Infantine biography.[9] With what delight I shall obey such a call, & report progress of his wonders from Letter to Letter!—I hope he will begin to speak soon. He gives several promising symptoms already, by most uncommon equivocal noises, that serve, as I believe, to try his own Ears as imitations — — — ⌐but others non success!

I have written to James this morning to beg his enquiries of the Paynes. I spoke to him briefly, yesterday, but my Heart was so full at *Mickleham*—where I dined for the last time[10]— that I could but make a short & scarcely clear harangue. I am sure he will do all he can. Poor Mickleham! if of that I began talking, *business* could indeed never be resumed—Heaven send her better! I rejoice she will pass a Month with you, you will interest her in Metastasio, & give her Music, as she has dear etty,—& I

[*a segment* (3 × 7·6″) *cut away from the bottom of the leaf*]

alleys green'. 'But there's not a flower in all your Eden half so sweet & lovely . . . He's not an Ephemeral, or an annual flower; but a perennial—an ever green.'

[8] The offer to solicit and receive subscriptions. See L. 171 and n. 8, Ll. 173, 175.

[9] CB had praised (loc. cit.) the Alexandriana included in FBA's L. 166: 'You never wrote a more lively letter than your last'. 'The beauties & virtues wch you have already discovered in this delightful plant, are nothing, to what you *will* discover, with a clear maternal magnifier. Pray continue to communicate to me all your discoveries in the pleasant *narratory* style of your last letter. . . . Pray be a faithful & minute biographer. You know I love infantine events & attempts at mental expansion. . . . Poor Boswell is gone! But his method of recording the colloquial wisdom of a *great man* is a good one—Try it upon a little one, who promises to be great.'

[10] On Friday 12 June just before the Phillipses had dismantled their house in Mickleham.

then shall print the proposals,[11] & promissory notes[12] can you, when some of his Devils visit you, enquire a little as to the cost of that & how many should be printed? I suppose not less than 2000. I intend, if possible, to draw up something for your examination, to send by my dear Susan. Certainly I think no time should be lost, & Mrs. Montagu & Miss Cambridge are vehemently of that opinion.

I thank you very much for your hint of *speedily*, other than naming a time till I am far enough advanced to keep it. The work *is* in *great*

[*a segment, as stated, cut away*]

My Gardener's every kindness possible. He is sure you would cure the Lumbago by coming to work with him.⊓

170   [Great Bookham, 18 June 1795]

To James Burney

A.N.S. (PML, Autog. Cor. bound), *n.d.*
Single sheet 8vo 2 pp. cut down to (3·8 × 4·75"). A large part of the right margin has been torn away

For My Brother James

———————

Thanks, my ever zealously Kind Brother [*tear*]
information. I confess the expence of printing[1] [*tear*]
⟨   ⟩lating, & all the minor expences not to be [*tear*]
the blow is struck, & must be followed up. [*tear*]
received by Messrs Payne, Robson,[2] Robinson, [*tear*]
& I beg you to present my Compts to Mr. Pa[yne] [*tear*]

11 See L. 168 n. 6.
12 Receipts to be given to the subscribers acknowledging payment for the novel were signed and sent from Bookham.

170. 1 £183. 6s. (L. 168 n. 4), nearly twice the d'Arblays' income per annum.
2 James Robson (1733–1806) of New Bond Street; for others see L. 168 n. 5.

proposals will be put, I believe, in all the ne[wspapers &]
be Printed separately for dispersing.³ I shall be [*tear*]
of Messrs Cadell & Robson, my Father will spea[k] [*tear*]
discussion about risks, profits, &c &c—we think t[hat] ¹
of course, the 10 p^r Cent will be adhered to.

If any objection, or observation occurs to you, you will have
the kindness to convey it me with speed.

The little *Idol of the World* is this Day half a year Old—&
more brilliant in beauty, more waggish in Wit, & more numerous in Noises than ever. In short, if I had not given him his
label before, I could this Day have chosen no other.—I am sure
my beloved sister will find every consolation for her lost home
& habitation⁴ under your Roof that affection & true kindness
can give.—My Love to Mrs. B. & Martinus.—In which M. d'A.
sincerely joins

your Most affec^te sister

F. d'A—

pray, Enquire — —

How must I place the Booksellers after
Mr Payne,⁵ who I think comes first?

171   Great Bookham, 18 June 1795

To Doctor Burney

A.L. (Diary MSS. vi, not numbered, Berg), 18 June [17]95
Double sheet 4to   4 pp.   *pmks* LEATHER / HEAD   20 JU 95   wafer
Addressed: Dr. Burney / Chelsea College, / Middlesex.
Endorsed by CB: June 18th / N° 5   Proposals & / *original titles*
Edited by FBA, p. 1, *annotated*:   (4) on Camilla subscription.
Edited also by CFBt.

³ Cf. Ll. 172 n. 1, 168 n. 6.
⁴ Writing from James Street on 17 June (Berg), SBP rejoiced that FBA 'was
spared the seeing our sad departure on Monday' [15 June 1795]. '. . . I followed
[M. d'A] into the Park—for I could not resist the desire I felt of treading once more
the path that leads to— — — to how many beloved spots!—to Bookham—to
Norbury!—'
⁵ Payne was placed first in all advertisements and announcements of the novel.

Bookham,
June 18th—95

My most Kind Father,

I am quite penetrated by such a quick Letter.¹ I answer immediately, ⌐because I see the affair with respect to the Proposals must be followed up instantly.

M. d'Arblay gives completely into the idea of Mrs. Crewe that the scrip. must be but a *Guinea* & prefers both worse paper, & acknowledgement & certainty of the Work, to making it more.

James has sent me a most exact compendium of the printing expence,² which amuses us both—they will swallow so much, that, at first, we were near drawing back from the project. Upon further reflexion, we still see, that if the success resembles that of its predecessors, it will answer well in the course of a few years, though it will be so short of a *Bookseller's bargain* at the beginning, unless, indeed, there is such a subscription as my Mother seems to augur.⌐

I like well the idea of giving *no name at all*,—Why should not I have my mystery, as well as Udolpho?³—but — — *now don't fly Dr. Burney!*—I own I do not like calling it a *Novel*:⁴ it gives so simply the notion of a mere love story, that I recoil a little from it. I mean it to be *sketches of Characters & morals, put in action,* not a Romance. I remember the Word ǀ *Novel* was long in the way of Cecilia, as I was told, at the Queen's House. And it was not permitted to be read by the Princesses, till it was sanctioned by a Bishop's recommendation,—the late Dr. Ross⁵ of Exeter. Will you, then, suffer *mon amour propre* to be saved by the proposal's

171. ¹ CB's advice on the subject of *Camilla* is missing and probably destroyed, but from SBP's letter (Berg) of 24 June one learns that the question under debate was the price to be charged for the novel. 'Mrs Crewe is for *a Guinea* subscription *in all*— but to be p^d at once—My Father—mother—James &c think the subscription at a Guinea w^d fill infinitely quicker than at a guinea & half—for my part, I confess I think the same, tho' I shall *begrudge* your *six* volumes at this price excessively.'

² See L. 168 n. 4.
³ See L. 143 n. 8.
⁴ SBP (loc. cit.) found 'all around me of my opinion' that in the proposals the new work should be described as a *Novel*. '. . . a *Novel* w^d be more unexceptionable & more certain to attract than *a new work*—' FBA's eventual acquiescence is reflected in the advertisements in the newspapers when the original caption 'a NEW WORK . . . by the author of Evelina & Cecilia' (see, e.g., *The Times*, 20 July, 5 Aug. 1795) was changed in 1796 to 'a NEW NOVEL' by etc.

⁵ John Ross or Rosse (1719–92), Chaplain to the King (1757), Bishop of Exeter (1778).

running thus—⌐as we both gain in thinking your objection to
the title may be well founded—⌐

──────

Proposals
for Printing by Subscription,
In Six Volumes duodecime
A NEW WORK
By
The Authour of Evelina & Cecilia.

The subscription will be one Guinea, to be paid at the time
of subscribing. &c[6]

──────

⌐omit, since you think it useless, the promise of signing.—⌐

To tell you the truth, My Mother's augury makes some
impression upon me not very painful,—she is, in general, rather
a *Cassandra*,—when I find her, therefore, a prophetess of success,
it gives courage the more abundant.

And so — — if you please, we will risk a *betweenity*, as Lord
orford calls the *demi-saison*, of proposals, i e—3000.

⌐I am very glad you concur with Mr. Lock against wire paper
& Hot presses.[7] Yet surely paper & type should be good & clear
& *respectable*.

I must write directly to Charles to speak to Mr. Cadell, & to
James, to Mr. Payne, to settle about raising subscriptions, as
the Proposals cannot be printed till that is settled. And in truth
the case is already ⟨far⟩ too far advanced for wasting time [½ *line
lost in obliteration and damaged margin*] I suppose my Mother will
question Robinson. I hear the Bookseller's profits for the
subscription are ⟨10⟩ per cent, to this of course, we agree.⌐

Mrs. Crewe does the Work & its Authour much honour by
offering to take a Book,—indeed I am sensibly flattered by her
kindness. Mrs. Lock — — will keep one, of course; &, Miss

---

6 See L. 172 n. 1.

7 Cf. Thomas James Mathias, *The Pursuits of Literature, a satirical poem in Four
Dialogues* (1794–7), Dialogue I: 'Shall I new anecdotes from darkness draw, / That
Strawberry-Horace on the Hill ne'er saw, / With *wire-wove hot-press'd* paper's glossy
glare / Blind all the wise, and make the stupid stare?' / '*All* books of *all* kinds', the
satiric note goes on to explain, 'are now advertised to be printed on a *wire-woven
paper* and *hot pressed*, with *cuts*. . . . Surely this *foolery* must soon cease.' And the more
fool still, the author who 'publishes *his own* works on a *wire-wove* paper, *glazed* and
hot-pressed'.

Cambridge answers for Mrs. Boscawen. Mrs. Montagu, I fancy, may also be counted.[8] To such characters I shall be happy to owe obligation — — & can more be said by *Hermits*, who would prefer all difficulties, to a debt of gratitude not highly seasoned with esteem & regard?

⌐Certainly I will not write so fast as to require 3 presses a Day. I should wish to correct the press more scrupulously than either Eyes or [*tear*] could be commanded for in such hard duty. Should I have the same number, or less, of promissory notes printed?[9]

As soon as ever the proposals are finally adjusted I must get them conveyed to all the capital newspapers, as the prelude for disseminating them. I wish this to be done the moment the Booksellers are settled, if you think my name still may stand.⌐

I am rejoiced you approve of Miss Ogilvie;[10] our Friends are enchanted with her. I am very glad you had so opportune & seasonable a discourse with the Duchess,[11] who, I hear, is a charming woman, & who is quite bewitched with Mrs. Lock. Your character of Lady Spencer is very piquant.[12] I remember Charles dined with her once at Althrop,[13] & was so much pleased with her, that | he said he *should patronize her*. M. d'A. is

---

[8] That is, to solicit subscriptions, receive money, and keep a ledger of the transactions. In a letter to Hannah More, dated Rosedale, 5 Aug. 1795, Mrs. Boscawen explains her involvement and that of others in the business (see Aspinall-Oglander, *Admiral's Widow* (1943), p. 165):

> My friends Mrs. Montagu and (still more earnestly) Miss Cambridge having *entreated* me to keep a book and receive subscriptions for Mmme. d'Arblay who advertises a novel for *next July*—a long time for me to look to.
>
> However, the task is undertaken, and the book already contains a most respectable large list, to which Miss Cambridge and Mr. Seward as Aides de Camp send frequent recruits. My own dear Duchess, too, has been very active *parmi les Grands*. Mrs. Crewe (La Belle) also keeps a book, and what is still better Mr. Hastings *même* another. And Mrs. Montagu . . . before her departure for Sandleford, left me 10 guineas for the book, while only desiring one copy.

[9] See L. 169 n. 12.

[10] Cecilia Margaret Ogilvie (1775–1824), daughter of William Ogilvie (*c.* 1740–1832) and the Duchess of Leinster (below).

[11] Amelia Mary Lennox (1731–1814), who married (1) 1747 James Fitzgerald (1722–73), 1st Duke of Leinster (1766), and (2) in 1774 her son's tutor William Ogilvie (above).

[12] This 'character' is lost but on 7 May (Berg) CB had described Lady Spencer as 'a pleasant, lively, & comical creature, with more talents & discernmᵗ than is expected from a character *si folatre*'.

[13] In future times CB Jr. was often to be in Lord Spencer's famous library at Althorp.

glad you met the Cte de Coigny,[14] whom he knows particularly
well, & who, he says, has *beaucoup d'Esprit*. I should be very glad
to hear good news of the revival of poor Mr. Burke. Have you
ever seen him since this fatality in his family? I am glad, nevertheless, with all my Heart, of Mr. Hastings honourable acquital.
Did you see, in the Papers, the history of *Mrs. Benn's* most
generously sharing a bequested £4000 per ann. with a disinherited Brother?[15]—The fact is true—& has lost us the only
friends M. d'A. has made a point of my receiving at Bookham.
She & her Husband came to take leave of us t'other day, as they
go to reside at the House of the Uncle who left the £4000, upon
Windsor Forest. They were till now Inhabitants of Leatherhead.
They have bequeathed my Gardener all their Carnations, 24
pots,—& 4 American plants, newly naturalized.—⌜What you
have heard of Miss Ogilvie's drawing is most true. Mr. Lock
showed us, last Sunday, a really wonderful Landscape of her
own composition as well as execution. She had made a present
of it to Mr. William.⌝ If you see M^r. Seward[16] before I write my
thanks, pray have the goodness to give them for his anecdotes,
which he has sent me. I must write a *Baby Letter* by its own self.
I have just heard from My dearest Susan[17]—I could not go to
see her depart—'twould have been trifling with our mutual
feelings too severely, because uselessly—

Adieu, Dearest dear Sir

---

[14] Augustin-Gabriel de Franquetot, comte de Coigny (1740–1817), maréchal de
camp (1780), in London since 23 Nov. 1793, if not earlier.

[15] John Walsh (*c.* 1727–9 Mar. 1795), by the terms of a will (P.C.C. Newcastle
228) dated 24 Nov. 1792 and probated 26 Mar. 1795, disinherited his nephew
Joseph Fowke (*fl.* 1792–5) in favour of his niece Margaret Fowke (*c.* 1758–1836),
who in 1778 had married John Benn (1759–1825). In compliance with the will
(above) John Benn had assumed on 11 Apr. 1795 the name Benn-Walsh, cr.
Baronet (1804). The Benn-Walshes were now to move from Leatherhead to
Warfield Park, Berkshire.

The newspapers, for example the *Reading Mercury, Oxford Gazette* (30 Mar.
1795), made much of Mrs. Benn-Walsh's concern for her brother, who by his uncle's
will had received only £1,000. 'A trait of generosity, deserving the highest en-
comiums, has happened within these few days—The late John Walsh, esq:
who died about a fortnight ago, left an estate of 4000l a year to his niece, Mrs.
Benn, and totally overlooked his nephew, Mr. Fowke. With a magnificence almost
unprecedented, Mrs. Benn said, that she had already fortune sufficient for her
wants, and reserving only a small villa in this county, rendered dear to her by early
habits, she made a present of 4000l a year to Mr. Fowke.'

[16] William Seward (1747–99), *Anecdotes of some distinguished persons, chiefly of the
present and two preceding centuries* . . . (5 vols., 1795–7). On 8 July 1795 (L. 177) FBA
mentions having received the first two volumes but not the third. The fourth
volume was advertised in *The Times* on the dates 9–10, 17–18, 24, and 27 June 1796.

[17] This is the letter of 17 June (see L. 170 n. 4).

⌐I beg you to take no notice *to the World* of what I say of abridging the work[18] lest it should be thought I mean to *gobble the subscription* — — whereas, I have en[deavo]ured, like Dr. Johnson, *to do my best* bound in *honour* to return them by [*tear*] thus circumstanced.⌐

The Bambino is half a year old—This Day.—
NB. I have not heard the Park or Tower Guns. I imagine the Wind did not sit right.

172   Great Bookham, 18 June 1795

To Charles Burney

A.L. (Osborn), 18 June 1795
Single sheet 4to 2 pp. *pmks* LEATHER / HEAD 19 JU 95 wafer
Addressed: Dʳ Charles Burney, / Academy, / Greenwich, / Kent.

Bookham,
June 18.—95

Half year's Birth Day of The Idol
of the World.
Drink his Health at
your next dinner.

My dearest Carlucci,
I know you to be now so busy, that I shall write merely & closely to '*the point & purpose*,'—
After much advising & deliberation, SEE HERE what we mean to put in the News papers—& distribute in separate papers

---

[18] FBA had at first intended to write six volumes, but with the price fixed at a guinea (rather than a guinea and a half) she decided on four, in the end writing five. In the advertisements in the newspapers the number vacillated between 4 (July and Aug. 1795), 4 or 5 (Feb. and Mar. 1796), and after 6 April settled down to five.

Proposals
For Printing by Subscription,
In Six Volumes Duodecimo
A NEW WORK
By the Authour of
EVELINA and CECILIA.[1]

The Subscription will be one Guinea, to be paid at the time of subscribing.

The Work will be speedily ready for the Press.

Subscriptions are received, & Receipts delivered, by Mes^{rs} Payne, Cadell, Robson and Robinson.

Now, my dear Charles, I beg you to Herald me the above names according to Etiquette, if I have placed them improperly.

And—to enquire, if possible, immediately, of Mr. Cadell if he chuses to be named thus. My Father will make the same enquiry of Robinson, &, I think, of Robson, & James of Mr. Payne. All according to the customary allowance, which, I hear, is 10 p^r c^t

I hear you thought of 2 Guineas for the scrip,—but we fear the times will not allow it,—& therefore must moderate our profits, if any, & skip wove paper, Hot Press, & all extravagance of elegance, for mere neatness & propriety.

My Father undertakes getting me the proposals & Receipts printed.

I am sorry to plague you till you are more at leisure, my dear Carlos, but every body says the Town is even *Hourly* emptying, & that the proposals should be printed & dispersed without delay. My Love to Rose & Carlini—& always kind remembrance to Mrs. Bicknel—ditto to all 4 from M. d'Arblay.

Truly, truly yours,
Dearest Charles !

I hope Mr. Sheridan is well? Many & Many thanks from M. d'A. for the Newspapers—

---

172. [1] It was not until 7 July 1795 that the *Morning Chronicle* printed:
This day is published,
PROPOSALS for Printing by Subscription, a NEW WORK, in Four Volumes. 12mo. By the AUTHOR of EVELINA and CECILIA: To be delivered on or before the 1st day of July, 1796. The Subscription will be One Guinea; to be paid at the time of Subscribing. Subscriptions will be received by T. Payne, at the Mews-gate; J. Edwards, Pall-mall; J. Robson, Bond-street; Cadell and Davies, in the Strand; and Robinsons, Paternoster-row.

173 Great Bookham, 19 June 1795

To Mrs. Waddington

A.L. (Berg), 19 June [17]95
Double sheet 4to 4 pp. *pmks* LEATHER / HEAD 20 JU 95 wafer
Addressed: Mrs. Waddington, / ⌜Lanover, / Abergavenny, / Monmouthshire⌝ / if from Home, / to be forwarded immediately. / June 19.
Readdressed: Clifton / Bristol
Edited by CFBt.

Bookham,
June 19.—95.

No, my dear Marianne, No—this 'poor intercourse' shall never cease, while the hand that writes the assurance can hold a Pen!—I have been very much touched with your Letter—its affection & its — — every thing. —Do not for the World suffer this our only communication to 'dwindle away'—for me, though the least punctual of all correspondents, I am, perhaps, the most faithful of all friends, for my regard once excited, keeps equal energy in absence as in presence, & an equal fond & *minute* interest in those for whom I cherish it, when I see them but at a distance of years, or with every Days sun. *Sun* it is, even in Winter, that shines upon sights so sweet as of persons beloved.—My dear & darling sister Phillips will now once more experience this truth,—for last Monday she left Mickleham[1]—Norbury Park—Bookham—every spot most dear to her, to go & live in London! — — will she, think you, for that, be ever absent from my Mind?—will my new ties—dear almost to adoration as they are to me—ever obliterate my former ones? No, my dear Marianne,—all those whom | I best love, have something, more or less, of resemblance—one to another, each, therefore, rather helps than mars my affection for the rest. I love *NOBODY FOR NOTHING*, my dearest Mary—I am not so tindery!—Therefore there must be change in the object before there can be any in me.

I have much to say to you, & shall order this Letter to follow you, if you are gone to Clifton—but nothing that so much

173. [1] On Monday 15 June. SBP's farewell note from Mickleham is extant (Berg): 'Ah my Fanny—I can but write one sad word—*Farewell*, & Heaven continue its dear blessings to you—I will write you very very soon—& be careful of y^r letters—'

presses as my earnest & fervant wishes for the success of your experiment, in the cure of your dreadful Head-achs,—which I *must* hope are not 'incurable.'—

And now I must tell you, that the beautiful Drawing, executed for you by the very first Genius,[2] I believe, of the Age, is, at length, engraved; & Mr. Lock desired me, when I next wrote, to give you his best Compliments, & entreat your acceptance of one of the first & best impressions; & that you will indicate how it can be conveyed to you most safely.

Mrs. Lock, at the same time, charged me with her kindest remembrance—& indeed all that incomparable family enquire about you continually, & take a true interest in your welfare.

Next, let me acquaint you that Mr. Charles Lock is on the point of Marriage with Miss Ogilvie,[3] Daughter of Mr. Ogilvie & the Dutchess of Leinster. A very accomplished & most amiable young lady, with considerable expectations, as well as splendid connexions. They are all very happy in the union. And Mrs. Lock said she was sure you would be glad to hear of what made them so. Do you think I told her [*tear*] mistaken?—

And lastly,—let me hasten to tell you something of myself, that I shall be very sorry you should hear from any other, as your but too susceptible Mind would be hurt again—& that would grieve me quite to the Heart.

I have a long Work which a long time has been in hand, that I mean to publish soon—in about a year.—Should it succeed like Evelina & Cecilia, it may be a little portion to our Bambino —we wish, therefore, to print it for ourselves, in this hope: but the expences of the Press are *so* enormous,[4] so raised by these late Acts to be tremendous, that it is out ǀ of all question for us to afford it. We have therefore been led, by degrees, to listen to counsel of some friends, & to print it by subscription. This is in many—MANY ways unpleasant & unpalatable to us both—

---

[2] See i, L. 35 n. 2. William Locke, Jr. was often praised highly in his time, cf. William Parsons's sonnet, 'To WILLIAM LOCKE, Esq. Junior, on his PICTURE of the DEATH of CARDINAL WOLSEY', *New Annual Register* (1791), [173]. In Bartolozzi's busy rooms the delay in engraving the drawing extended from *pre* October 1792 to July 1795 (L. 177).

[3] Cecilia Margaret Ogilvie (L. 171 n. 10) was a niece of the 3rd Duke of Richmond. For her wedding, see p. 134, n. 4.

[4] 'An Act for granting to His Majesty, several additional Duties on stamped Vellum, Parchment, and Paper . . .' had been passed in the House of Lords on 23 Apr. 1795 (*LJ* xl. 377, 389). The printing costs were eventually £183. 6s. (L. 168 n. 4).

but the real chance of real use & benefit to our little darling overcomes all scruples, & therefore—to work we go! —— You will feel, I dare believe, all I could write on this subject,—I once *rejected* such a plan, formed for me by Mr. Burke,[5] where Books were to be kept for me by Ladies, not Booksellers,—the Duchess of Devonshire, Mrs. Boscawen, & Mrs. Crewe—but I was an Individual then, & had no cares of *Times to come*—now,—THANK HEAVEN! this is not the case,—&, when I look at my little Boy— who is very sweet—I assure you *seriously*!— when I look at his dear innocent, yet intelligent Face, I defy any pursuit to be painful that may lead to his good.—He was half a year old yesterday. Adieu, my ever dear Friend—*ever*—

Pray make my Comp[ts. to] Mr. W[addington]—& send me a little accoun[t of] the success of your experiment, & of Clifto[n.][6]

174   [Great Bookham], 5 July 1795

To Charles Burney

A.L. (Osborn), 1 July 1795
Double sheet 4to   3 pp.   *pmks*   LEATHER / HEAD   1 JY 95   wafer
Addressed: Dr. Charles Burney, / Greenwich, / Kent.
Docketed, p. 4: M^rs D'Arblay

July 1.
1795

I entreat you, my dear Carlos, not to enrage,—I could not withstand the united voices that chorussed against your counsel;[1] but I shall try to reduce my plan, which will answer the same purpose as augmenting my conditions.

[5] In *Memoirs*, iii. 206, FBA asserted that the 'mode of subscription' was 'suggested for her by Mr. Burke to Doctor Burney'.

[6] It was probably after the receipt of this letter that Mrs. Waddington undertook to canvass her relatives and neighbours for subscriptions. Besides about ten members of the Waddington, Port, Dewes, and Granville families, the County Archivist W. H. Baker was able to identify some twelve of the subscribers (listed in *Camilla*, i) as possible residents of Monmouthshire at the time.

174. [1] CB Jr. had evidently favoured the price of a guinea and a half. The opinions of CB, CB Jr., and JB on matters relating to *Camilla* were reported by SBP, see *FB & the Burneys*, pp. 204–13. Cf. L. 171 n. 1.

I have received already *Something like* a proposal from Mr. Robinson,[2] to deliver 1500 *or* 2000 (ie, *2000*) copies, free of all expence, to the subscribers, for the Copy right afterwards.

And from Mr. Payne, an *actual* proposal, to deliver 1500 Copies, *clear*, to subscribers, & to allow at 10 shillings the set all subscriptions above 1500. That is, a clear gain of Eleven shillings the sett for all after the cited 1500.

Now I wish Mr. Robinson to be explicit,—&, if his offer is *within* Mr. Payne's, to treat with Mr. Payne; if *without* it, still to give Mr. Payne the refusal, as our connexion, & his acquaintance & character, all make but just, as well as pleasant. But if Mr. R[obinson] is highest, & Mr. P[ayne] flags,—then to close with Mr. Robinson.

Now upon all this I claim your | counsel, assistance, & promised *Jewish callousness.*

I beg you by the first opportunity to call & discuss the affair with my Father, & see good & kind James also first, if possible, as *he* is agent of Mr. Payne: & then to *go to work like a Man,* as you say '*Peas,*' with Mr. Robinson.

25 setts I shall demand, beyond subscriptions, if I part with the Copy right,—& I hereby insist & demand that not one of my Brothers or sisters play me the cruel trick of slyly subscribing. Deny me not the pleasure to present you my little work, my dear Charles,—I promise to accept *yours*, when you will but write in a less *outlandish lingo*[3]

Please to remark—& advise upon what follows — — viz.

I am now going to work, very reluctantly, to *curtail my* plan, & obviate threats of loss, or small profit — — I wish to know whether, if I part with the Copy right, it would not be rather an *advantage* to the Publisher to have 5 volumes instead of *4*, or else 4 large as Udolpho,[4] as *he* may then raise to non-subscribers. | Pray enquire this, if any treaty is entered upon.

Adieu, Dearest Carlos,—Loves to all around.

I shall beg no answers may be given till you have confabbed with my dear Father & Jemibus.

---

[2] The letters of the publishers are missing, as are most of CB Jr.'s letters.

[3] CB Jr.'s '*Appendix ad Lexicon Græco-Latinum, a Joanne Scapula constructum, et ad alia Lexica Græca, e codice manuscripto, olim Askeviano, in lucem nunc primum vindicata*' was published in 1789; his *Remarks on Greek Verses of Milton* was printed separately (1790) and appended to Warton's second edition of Milton's *Poems upon several occasions* in 1791.

[4] The four volumes 8vo of *Udolpho* (L. 143 n. 8) totalled 1,797 pages, each volume having from 428 to 478 pages.

I am in a prodgious twitter at all this! — —

Mr. Burke, formaly, *set me down* at between 2 & 3000 profit if I would print anything by subscription.

I believe the scrip will be very splendid.

Honble Mrs. Boscawen, Mrs. Crewe, & Mrs. Lock are to be my Lady Bookkeepers.

Adieu, Adieu.

175   [Norbury Park, 6 July 1795]

To Doctor Burney

A.L. (Berg), *n.d.*
Single sheet 4to 2 pp. *pmks* EPSOM 6 JY 95   red seal
Addressed: Dr Burney, / Chelsea College, / Middlesex.—
Endorsed by CB: Nature of the work declared, / N° 9 July 6th
Edited by FBA, p. 1, *annotated and dated*: ⁂ 6 July 1795   (5)
on Camilla publication &. subscription.

I cannot refrain sending my dearest Father Mrs. Boscawen's Letter,[1] which I beg to have returned by the first opportunity.

How kind is your Letter, your considerations, calculations, advices, & permission of adopting your counsel at pleasure— but I am quite grieved that offers so splendid & flattering should occasion *any thing* but satisfaction to my own nearest friends! I am yet fearful respecting the announced ⟨*First listing of*⟩ Mr. Payne. I am sure my interests in it he would all surely study, though the desire to regulate the whole himself makes it factious & unacceptable.[2] It is indescribably difficult what to decide,⌐ though 'tis laughable to have already such an *embarras de richesses*. But the epoch is critical—it will return no more, & it is our permanent dependance. ⌐Charles has not written yet.

175. [1] Now missing, as is CB's letter.
    [2] By this time FBA would have received SBP's letter dated James Street, Friday 3 July (Berg), a copy of which (Armagh) is printed in *FB & the Burneys*, pp. 209–13. While at James Street SBP, much under the influence of JB and his wife (*née* Sarah Payne, sister of the publisher), put in the plea: 'Mr Payne's proposal seems . . . really a liberal one—he is a particularly honest, fair dealing Man—if any agreement is entered into with him there is a greater certainty both from his general character & from his connection with our Family of its being unequivocally & honourably fulfilled than can be expected from any other Bookseller, & at least to give him no dissatisfaction is highly to be desired—'

I am glad it is not necessary to decide quite immediately, yet[n] I feel strongly with you what a peaceable tranquilising will *come over me* when I have nothing more to arrange of pecuniary matters. Could I tell how to avoid imposition, I should not hesitate to wish to guard the Copy entire: for these offers shew more & more what may be expected from the Current Sale.

The form of the *ladies Books*, Dear Sir, is simply a *morocco* memorandum Book,—I will copy Mrs. Lock's first page, which she has just shewn me.

[Sub]scriptions rec^d for a New Work by the Author of Evelina & Cecilia.

Duchess of Leinster[3]	— ⌐pd⌐
Lord Henry FitzGerald	— ⌐pd⌐
Lady Henry FitzGerald	— ⌐pd⌐
Lady Lucy FitzGerald	— ⌐pd⌐
Lady Sophia FitzGerald	— ⌐pd⌐
Mr. Ogilvie[3]	— ⌐pd⌐
Countess Talbot[4]	— ⌐pd⌐
Mrs. Fielding[5]	— ⌐pd⌐
Lady Burrel[6]	— ⌐pd⌐

Then, at the other end of the Book, she inserts Persons desiring to be set down, not yet paid

Mrs. Hartley — — — &c[7]

Can you, dear Sir, prepare one similar for Mrs. Crewe,[8] whose Name is one of my very *estest* in all ways, for preference, for use, for Honour, & for pleasure.

Now as to the NEW WORK—my dearest Father, I am most happy to let you into my secret, for I see it will be a *concord*; it *is* of the same species as Evelina & Cecilia: new *modified*, in being

---

3 The Duchess of Leinster, her second husband William Ogilvie (L. 171 n. 11), and three of her children by her first marriage: Lady Lucy Anne Fitzgerald (*c.* 1771–1851); Lady Sophia Sarah Mary (1762–1845); and Lord Henry (1761–1829), who had married in 1791 Charlotte Boyle (1769–1831), later Boyle-Walsingham, *suo jure* Baroness Ros (1806).

4 Charlotte Hill (1754–1804), who had married in 1776 John Chetwynd Talbot (*c.* 1749–92), 1st Earl Talbot.

5 Almost certainly Sophia Finch (*fl.* 1746–1815), who had married in 1772 Charles Feilding (d. 11 Jan. 1783), Commodore R.N. She was the daughter of Lady Charlotte (Fermor) Finch (1725–1813), governess (1762–92) to the royal children. FBA would have known her at Court.

6 Sir William and Lady Burrell of Deepdene, Holmwood (L. 126 n. 10).

7 Mary Hartley of Bath (i, L. 3 n. 99).   8 See Ll. 169, 171 and n. 8.

more multifarious in the Characters it brings into action,—but all *wove* into *one*, with a one *Heroine* shining conspicuous through the Group, & that in what Mr. Twining so flatteringly calls *the prose Epic Style*,[9] for so far is the Work from consisting of detached stories, that there is not, literally, one Episode in the whole plan,[10] ⌐my Dear Sir, which you may now make as public as you please, though I would rather you would keep to yourself all you can of detail. Should you like to see anymore mss before it is finished? If so, I will prepare against Susan's return from ⟨our⟩ 1/2 first Book—& 2 half Books [*corner torn*] ⌐

James proposes your *signing for me*,[11] to avoid dangers of travelling. I like the notion much, if you consent to it & would take such trouble, it would obviate every difficulty & *certainly* I would not for the world send an extra 2d receipt by the Lady Bookkeepers. They will have pleasure in demanding more when wanted. Mrs. Lock has done it to Day. The first 40 I took out were between her & Mrs. Boscawen—nothing is to be so indelicate as to force them upon them.[12]⌐

I will make my Work the best I can, my dearest Father. I will neither be indolent, nor negligent, nor avaricious. I can never half answer the expectations that seem excited! I must try to forget them, or I shall be in a continual quivering. Adieu most dear, dear Sir! I finish at Norbury Park, whence Mr. & Mrs. Lock send you kindest compts.

Why I am as '*reprobate*' as *you*, Dear Sir, with your Erskine's &c—for the Duchess of Leinster says *Charles Fox* will be most eager to subscribe — — Bambino is so well!—so sprightly, so

---

[9] See L. 166 n. 4.

[10] Relayed by SBP in her letter of Friday 3 July (op. cit.) was CB's advice on the structure of the new novel: 'My dʳ Father charged me to urge you to weave into one story of interest & length what you had yet to write—he thinks yʳ book consists of *detached stories*, and that the Public are all longing for & the booksellers depending on another Evelina or Cecilia.'

[11] CB declined this suggestion; but later the booksellers, JB, and others concerned seem to have been empowered to sign receipts (*FB & the Burneys*, pp. 204, 209–13).

If, in addition, the book keepers could be supplied with receipts already signed, they would not then have to secure and post them at a later time to the subscribers, who would have the extra expense of 2d. postage being collected in these years from the recipients.

[12] 'I have already', reported SBP on 3 July (op. cit.), 'been to Mʳ Payne with 260 receipts, which he desired to keep, they are in 3 papers from *Nº 41 to 100, fᵐ 101 to 200*, & fᵐ 201 to 300—the following 40 numbers my Father has kept for himself & Mʳˢ Crewe . . . the first 40 were not in the parcel you sent us & I suppose were taken out by Mʳˢ Lock before they came to us—in all we received 360. . . .'

smiling—he is already fit for your promised *Game of Romps* on the Carpet. ⌐Pray who has *Mrs. Ord* found to sign her Subscription?¹³ Such ⟨deceit⟩ has rather surprised me but I am very glad she will not be disappointed. My work *ought* to be in six volumes, after all, which is a grievous thing as I cannot accommodate that with the company *de quoi*!¹⁴⌐ I am gratified & frightened in turn every other Hour by this application of Booksellers—it shews such expectation!

176   Great Bookham, 7 July 1795

Conjointly with M. d'Arblay
To Charles Burney

A.L. & A.L.S. (Osborn), 7 July 1795
Double sheet 4to   4 pp.   *pmks* LEATHER / HEAD   10 JY 95   wafer
Addressed: Dr Charles Burney, / Margate—

[By Madame d'Arblay]

How completely unfortunate, my dearest Charles, that you were too much hurried to *undertake me* when I addressed you, which was when *all* was open for counsel & assistance!—yours came so late, we were fearful to disoblige All that had preceded —& now—that you are so kindly willing to *auctioneer* for us, we receive Letters to assure us such a step will breed absolute *family dissention*!¹—This is hard, & strange!—I thought my *Brain* work as much fair & individual property, as any other possession in either art or nature: but we cannot resolve upon offending the

¹³ Mrs. Ord had refused to be reconciled to FBA's marriage to a Frenchman, a Catholic, and a Constitutionalist but had nevertheless subscribed to the novel.
¹⁴ See L. 171 n. 18.

176. ¹ SBP's letter of 3 July (op. cit.) had included a report of a conclave at James Street in which CB Jr. had much offended James's wife (*née* Sarah Payne) by suggesting that the novel go to the *'highest bidder'*. 'Now he may be *too* sanguine in the matter', SBP commented, '& if he is trusted, he may perhaps affront the persons in question.' Payne, Robinson, and Cadell, she understood, had agreed to go together in the business and if this proposal were accepted it would have precluded CB Jr.'s plan of setting one against the other. 'Mr Payne . . . stands foremost amongst yr Booksellers, & is willing to take on himself any trouble that may result from it.'

Paynes—upon hurting James—upon bringing discomfort upon our darling & already so unhappy Suzanna!—I need say no more to your affectionate & brotherly Heart—We prefer all disadvantages to this danger.

Were it *not* so, those who first offered now coalesce, to *prevent* competition! ! !—but were it *not* so, I would entreat you to *make a round* of enquiry, before you struck your Hammer, that might render the coalition immaterial.

We are terribly chagrined—but must do the matter with the best grace we can assume, since our objects & rewards are 2 persons so dear to us, & the avoiding risking their peace with their connexions.—I beg ˡ earnestly you will write immediately, to say you have received this. My Father prefers our closing with Mr. P[ayne].

God bless you my dear Brother. We shall always repine this business was not in your Hands exclusively from the beginning. Loves to Rosette—Carlini—Mʳˢ B[icknell] if with you. I shall be uneasy for a line. M. d'A. is *truly yours*.

Bookham,
July 7.—95.

P.S. My dearest Charles don't let our *sensations* thus frankly avowed be further spread than to yourself, or the sacrifice we make will answer no purpose.

[*By M. d'Arblay*]

We shall expect your answer before we close any bargain, I hope I trust you will be so kind to pity and pardon us for the unpleasing affair in which your zeal for us has engaged you—

When Pope made an undertaking of the same kind as ours, his conditions with his bookseller were that he should have all the Sets for the subscribers & friends free of every expence, and besides that two hundred pounds for every volume.[2] But Pope — — yes I understand. I answer that in the present case we speak of an original work by an author very popular and of a sort of composition which is within the reading of a greater number of persons. Thus my comparison is not so *lame*.

---

[2] M. d'A's acquaintance with Pope's practices was doubtless derived from Dr. Johnson's 'Preface' to Pope, a bound copy of the proof sheets of which the Doctor had presented to FB in 1780. See *Memoirs*, ii. 178–82. See also *The Letters of Samuel Johnson*, ed. R. W. Chapman (3 vols., 1952), ii. 390. The bound sheets are now one of the treasures of the Hyde Collection. For terms offered FBA see L. 174.

James when he made his proposition for Mr Payne says
'*You can take your own time to consider these matters. If you do treat, the best offer is of course the properest to accept. But if the offers are equal, I hope you will think the preference may be given to Mr Payne.*' |

Now I ask how preference is to be given when all competition is spoken of as a personal offence.

To be sure the best of all means to make the offers *equal* was the coalition of the competitors. but how if the proposal of Mr Payne is so advantageous to us, has he been so eager to lessen his profits by a coalition when he had our promise that we should give him the refusal? I thank god I knew before this transaction all the transactors. I can say from the bottom of my heart, it will not at all lessen my setled *opinion* of their excellent character, but on the other side it will strengthen my *opinion* of human frailty—

Peace is above all! Thus our intention is to accept with that only condition that we shall be assured that, of the sets agreed upon, if some were left in our hands by a weak subscription, the bookseller or booksellers is or are to take them and sell them for our ow[n] account before they sell for their own If that condition is refused, we shall, decidely keep the Copy.

I will add to you that it is impossible in the present state of the business to retard a conclusion, your sister being almost spent by fear and sorrow since she heard, of those offences which we never intended to give to anybody, much less to those we respect and love If that anxiety is not to give way very soon, she will lose her best powers and become unable to compleat her undertaking.— |

You know my Dear Charles the offer of Mr Payne is to give us 1500 sets of the new work free of all expences, and to deliver the other sets above that number at the rate of ten schellings for each set.

I will propose *id est* ask 2,000 sets free of all expences, and to pay him twelve schellings instead of ten for the rest.

I have calculated that if we had, by chance, 4,000 subscribers he will have the copy right for 30^£ after his proposals and for 40^£ according mine. the maximum in the first case is 480^£.
in the 2° — 640^£.

axiom: of the Book's Trade

In the entertainment's line a book published by subscription, and well received, so generally, & so well appreciated, that its sale becomes, almost instantly, quick & general.

God bless you my dearest friend—my sincere compliments To Mrs Burney & Mrs Bicknel; & don't forget to remember me kindly to dear Charles— |

I am and I will allways be your grateful friend and brother,

A. d'Arb^l.

177   Great Bookham, 8 July 1795

To Mrs. Waddington

A.L. (Berg), 8 July [17]95
Double sheet 4to   1 p.   *pmks*   LEATHER / HEAD   10 JY 95   wafer
Addressed: Mrs. Waddington, / N° 13. / Princes' Buildings, / Clifton, / Bristol.

Bookham,
July 8.—95.

I earnestly hope to hear speedily that my dear Marianne has been strengthened & amended by her new experiments, & the pure & salubrious air of the Clifton. *change of air* I should rather say, for Wales is as famous for purity & salubrity as Clifton.

The beautiful Print will be sent you this Week, according to your directions; but I do not know on what day. You will find it very inferior, indeed, to the Drawing, though executed by Bartolozzi.[1] I think very much with you as to the figure of Memory,—which I have seen at Norbury Park, but do not yet possess; Mr. Seward has sent me the two first volumes of his very entertaining Collection,[2] but the third has not yet reached me: for that I think it, though not *interesting*.

The die is cast, as to the subscription — —

177. [1] See L. 173 n. 2; i, L. 35 n. 2.   [2] L. 171 n. 16.

The *Booksellers* you will see in some news-paper:[3] but my own best & favourite Bookkeepers are 3 ladies,—Mrs. Boscawen, Mrs. Crewe, & Mrs. Lock. And it is my own particular wish that those friends who chuse to *enter the lists* will subscribe to one of them. It is at once their gratification & my pride to have my business go through their hands.

All the beloved Lock Family are gone to London to the Wedding—Mr. William with the rest.[4] Tell me, my dearest Marianne, if you are *peculiarly,* or *locally* unwell? or only *generally?* & tell me, if possible, you are better, & in a fair way to profit from your journey, & Dr. Beddoes.[5]

178   Great Bookham, 15 July 1795

Conjointly with M. d'Arblay
To Charles Burney

A.L.S. & A.L.S. (Osborn), 15 July 1795
Double sheet 4to   4 pp.   *pmks*   LEATHER / HEAD   18 JY 95   wafer
Addressed: Dr. Charles Burney, / Margate.
Scribbling in pencil, p. 4: Trochaic / —cs / Iambic / c—

[*By M. d'Arblay*]

Bookham, July 15.—95.

CARTE BLANCHE! to our dear Don Quichote with many

³ The booksellers who had agreed to receive subscriptions were named in the advertisement in the *Morning Chronicle*, 7 July 1795 (L. 172 n. 1). J. Cawthorne, British Library, Strand, was added to the group of booksellers (see, for example, the *Star*, 15 Feb. 1796).

⁴ The marriage of Charles Locke (1769–1804) to Cecilia Margaret Ogilvie (L. 171 n. 10) took place at Marylebone Church on 9 July 1795, on which day, SBP and CB, driving into town, were overtaken by the wedding party, first, by 'Mʳ Lock in the phaeton wᵗʰ Amelia & Miss Emily Ogilvie' then by Mr. Locke's coach. 'Aaron's bright face, & large white Cockade caught my eye, & down flew the glass, for I hoped to have had a glimpse of something yet more interesting [probably the Duchess of Leinster, Mrs. Locke, & William] but the green silk blinds of the carriage were drawn down, to disappoint inquisitive persons—' Then came 'Mʳ Charles on horseback—Miss Lock wᵗʰ Mʳ Ogilvie in his curricle &c &c,' while Mr. Ogilvie's coach 'contained the Bride between her two brothers, & Lʸ Lucy & Lʸ Sophia Fitzgerald' (see SBP, 10 July (op. cit.), and also the *Locks of Norbury*, chaps. ix, x, xi).

⁵ Thomas Beddoes (1760–1808), M.D. (1788), who established at Clifton a 'Pneumatic Institute' for the treatment of diseases by inhalation (*DNB*). See also Bunsen, i. 40–1.

many thanks for his chevalresque and adventurous enterprise[1]
—A. d'Arblay

[*By Madame d'Arblay*]

CARTE BLANCHE! I repeat—there is no other possible
answer to such a Letter as your last, my dear, good, bold, kind,
generous Carlos! — — F. d'Arblay.

In full assurance of his future grateful concurrence, I here
sign for The Idol of the World, your Godson—

Alexander Charles Louis d'Arblay.

X

178. [1] Details of the business are missing but apparently CB Jr. was soon to strike
an advantageous agreement with T. Payne, at the Mews-Gate, and Cadell and
Davies, in the Strand, a partnership excluding, however, G. G. & J. Robinson of
Paternoster-row, CB's friend and publisher.

As proved to be the case, Robinson was 'piqued' and resentful at being left out,
and his 'ire', CB feared, might be productive of much mischief if it should be
expressed by his reviewers. See CB's letters (Bodleian) to CB Jr., 8 Apr and 3 Aug.
1796. See Appendix B, p. 368.

And SBP, now at Chelsea College, trembled to see her father's advice rejected.
'I wish from the bottom of my heart he may prove to have been mistaken, since
your ideas & plan of acting are so different from those he w^d pursue—' (SBP to the
d'Arblays, 10–11 July 1795, Berg).

But CB Jr., with his usual dauntless cheerfulness and activity, carried all before
him. His letter dated Margate, 12 July, obviously a reply to the d'Arblay letter of
7 July (L.176), is fortunately extant (Berg). Annotated by FBA in later years 'What
warmth of Zeal!', it is printed here in full.

I rec^d your letters yesterday: I read them: I took twenty four hours to deliberate on their contents.—In consequence, I now write most seriously to claim
the execution of the solemn promise, made so many years ago, and repeated so
frequently: 'that you would never part with any future Work, without making
me your Agent!'

I have written to my Father & to James to inform them, that I have urged
this claim; and in such a manner, that it is not very possible, that they can be
offended, even with *me*; but with *you* certainly not.—I have openly offered to
take all the odium on myself; & I will do it, my dear D arblays, in the face of my
father, my Brother, & all the Booksellers in the world.—

Now, do not disappoint me. I make a serious claim to a promise solemnly
given, and many a time & oft repeated.— — Remember!

Always your affect^te Brother
& zealous friend,
C Burney.

PS.—Sad weather—We are all pretty well. How is the Idol?—I long to see him.—
In my old age, he shall fight battles for me, as I am now waging war for him.

July 12—
24. Church Fields.
Margate.—

15 July 1795

P.S.

We have written to my Father & to James, to proclaim Your irresistability & deprecate all wrath.

I must now Answer your queries about the Work itself.

It is to all intents & purposes a Novel,—but I annex so merely to that title, in a general sense, a staring Love Story, that I hate so to call it.—However, the words at the opening of this Page leave YOU to do as you will. The Name of my Heroine is ARIELLA.[2] I had meant to burst it forth upon the Public in a blaze at the end,—but here, also,—as above.

If you will give a Title, I should chuse, YOUTH, or Ariella.

This is no more *un*straighway than the two *ors* to Cecilia, & Evelina, of *or* Memoirs of an Heiress, & OR A young lady's Entrance into life. |

I think it also expedient to hint—for consideration private— that Johnson[3] of St· Paul's Church Yard, whom I never saw, or before heard of, sent me word, some time ago, that he would take any thing I should produce, at ANY price that could be demanded. This came to me through Mrs. Lock, from Fuseli, the famous Painter.

And perhaps, as I now hear Robinson, Payne & Cadell *coalesce*,[4] it may be necessary to see some other, in order to *form* a competition. For, if we do not, as we meant, to oblige James, give the work to Mr. Payne at his own statement,—I see no medium between that, & doing positively the *best* with it.—*all this, as above.*

But you will not forget, my dear Knight Errant, that Mr. Payne, after all, is really promised the *Refusal*.

Perhaps, therefore, you should See him *last*, for his *upshot*.

But all now *as above.*—

I entreat, with whomsoever you deal, you will enquire whether it will be *better* or *worse* to curtail the Work. If we print ultimately for ourselves, according to our original plan, we

---

[2] Formerly Betulia (ii, L. 104 n. 5), it was finally changed to Camilla. FBA kept the sub-title: *or, a Picture of Youth.*

[3] Henry Fuseli (i, L. 24 n. 8) and his publisher Joseph Johnson (1738–1809) were on 'terms of intimacy and of the strictest friendship . . . for nearly forty years'. See John Knowles, *The Life and Writings of Henry Fuseli, Esq., M.A.R.A.* (3 vols., 1831), i. 299.

[4] It was SBP who in a letter of 3 July (*FB & the Burneys*, p. 212) had reported that 'Payne, Robinson and Cadell have agreed to go together in the business'.

always meant to make 4 *Udolphoish* volumes,[5] & reprint the Edition that succeeds the subscription in 6 volumes duod^{mo} common, for a raised price.

The *Work* will be better for *not* being lopped, as it's materials are fertile, & I must otherwise cut off short some purposes now very principal in my perspective. |

Mrs. Cooke, the Clergyman's Sposa, has just told me that she has a Message for me from Dr. Barrow[6] of Oxford, entreating me, with his Comp^{ts} not to be again, as he hears I have hitherto been, the dupe of Booksellers.

She also says, that a Relation of hers,[7] who was some way engaged with Robson of Bond Street, assured her he had heard Mr. Robson affirm that Payne & Cadell made 1500 *clear* the first year.!—This is such a public business now, that there would be a *Cry* against me for any ignorant folly of loss. — — James's Letter is just come; we thank you heartily. I see my dear James as I love to see him in it, fair, candid, good humoured, & kind.

This communication must all be ENTRE NOUS,—as *we delight to say at Paris*—Whatever you do must be from the *wholesale* Carte blanche—not the *details* here hinted, which might offend others of my advisers & Counsellers, to whom we have not bent. I think, with you, the association a device to stop your proceedings; but as it is not over delicate in fairness, I see, also, no reason why you may not make a competition from other quarters, if it appear desirable. I have certainly *NO* tie—& owe *no* gratitude—It was James alone I feared offending—but as he is so reasonable,[8] I see nothing more essential but the *Refusal* to Mr. Payne, who then can have no possible complaint to make of any of us. *All as above.*!—Think, however, how to guard against my Father's fears for the subscription being injured by the negociation.

[5] See L. 174 n. 4.
[6] William Barrow (1759–1836), D.C.L. (1785), archdeacon of Nottingham (1830–2).
[7] Possibly, though no near relation to Cassandra (Leigh) Cooke, William Leigh (1752–1809), LL.B. (1778), Rector of Little Plumstead (1779–1808), Dean of Hereford (1808), whose sermons, preached in Bath in 1792–3, were distributed, if not published, by J. Robson (among other booksellers).
[8] Cf. SBP's note on JB in her letter of 10–11 July (op. cit.): He spoke now 'very perfectly reasonably concerning you, y^r affairs, right of deliberating, & judging for yourself, &c, &c—& wth every mark of tender, brotherly love—tears even occasionally starting in his eyes—'

[*By M. d'Arblay*]

1° I do'nt know where the Subscription is advertised;[9] But I am sure People are almost everywhere quite ignorant of it. Do'nt you think that silence will injure our interests.

2° Do'nt you think too that the Public must be informed that the intended new work is or will be of the same kind as its two predecessors?

3° Mr Robinson estimated the new work ought to be of sixty sheets—viz—fifteen sheets for a volume. But, by an exact calculation of the MS. (at first, word by word, & afterwards line by line with a full page of Cecilia's impression, every volume must contain about 17 ^sheets $\frac{1}{2}$, that is for the whole 70 sheets. If we keep the Copy-right, we do'nt hesitate to make this sacrifice[10] as much as the work being divided in 12 books, 3 in each volume, it could be of 6—Vol. of 2 books each for the subscribers who should pay it 24 shellings in boards.[11] If we come upon terms with a bookseller, I think they must be contented with that speculation because the advantage to have 6. Vol. for which he will receive 24 Shellings. I.e. 3^sch more than one guinea will be a pretty good compensation for the augmentation of the ten sheets more, according the estimation of Mr Robinson. This augmentation of ten sheets, will be for us ten times 3^£· 15^sch according the price sent to us by James who has had it from Mr Payne himself. For the bookseller it should be certainly a little less. We give not 6. Vol. because we should be obliged to pay for the *Stitching* of two more. Is it possible that this stitching is of 3^pence by volume? That is the price we have been told by Susanna. To be sure as we are decided to make the foresaid sacrifice, it is a very *foolishness* to deprive ourselves of the benefit of it, by not publishing it? Do'nt you think so?

Our expence are 3^£ 15^sch for each sheet. about 10^£ 10^sch· for advertisements, but my opinion is that it should be better for our interests to make that last Sum double 10 per 100 of the receipt for the bookseller, and 3^pence by volume for the Sewing & Stitching. That is all. I estimate that our Bookkeepers Ladies

[9] The subscription was to be advertised in the *Morning Chronicle* on 7 July (L. 172 n. 1).

[10] Whether or not to sell the copyright was another matter of family disagreement: JB, *against*; CB, *for*, in order to save troublesome and expensive transactions (*FB & the Burneys*, pp. 204, 211, etc.; also L. 168 n. 5).

[11] Twelve books afforded a parallel with the Epic. As first planned, *Camilla* was to run to six volumes of two books each.

& their deputies will save us $\frac{1}{10}$ of the ten per cent. Thus we shall pay every set about eight shellings, for which the Bookseller will not disburse 6. shellings if we come upon terms.

A Subscription diminishes very much the price of the Copy right of a Science's book. That is not the case with an entertainment's book. Mr Didot a famous french bookseller says it is quite the contrary because when the work is well received, it is so generally appreciated everywhere that its sale becomes almost instantly as quick as general.[12] besides that we have in five family only 35 subscriptions where 5 or six sets only would be bought.

Forgive me, my dear Charles, this long letter. I repeat to you *CARTE BLANCHE.* Thus do'nt mind what I have written if it is not coincident with your thoughts.

my loves to you & yours.
A.A. |

We receive, just now, two very kind letters from St James Street & Chelsea. If all was wrong, Now all is right, and every one seems content with your Don Quichoting. Thus go on with *my good wishes* of which I hope you do'nt doubt.

---

179   Great Bookham, 15 July 1795

To Doctor Burney

A.L. (Berg), 15 July 1795
Double sheet 4to 4 pp. *pmks* LEATHER / HEAD   15 JY 95   wafer
Addressed: Dr Burney, / Chelsea College, / Middlesex.
Endorsed by CB: Powers to Chas—July 15th—95.
Edited by FBA, p. 1, *annotated*: ※ (6)
Zealous kindness of my dear Brother Charles for the Camilla publication.

Bookham,
July 15.—95.

My dearest Father,

Charles absolutely refuses to refund his powers, given so long ago, by *me*, & *confirmed* since by M. d'Arblay.[1] He is firmly

[12] François-Ambrose Didot (1730–1804), of a 'célèbre famille d'imprimeurs français', was the inventor of 'une presse à un coup'. He edited a series of books for the Dauphin and was noted in general for his 'belles éditions sur papier dit vélin' (Larousse).

179. 1 See L. 178 n. 1.

persuaded he can do better for us than the present offers promise—& his ardour & sanguine zeal are too kind to be received with coldness. I know, from the Birth of my little Bambino, he has desired to consider himself to him as a sort of second Father,[2]—& in his Letter this moment arrived, he *pleads his cause* to *us*, as if *we* wanted pleaders!—

'What Evelina, he says, does now for the Son of Lowndes,[3] & what Cecilia does for the Son of payne, let your third work do for the Son of its Authour.[4] — ' —

Can we resist such a call?—Is it in Nature?—

You, he says, are too delicate, & James too ignorant of *this* sort of business, to be able to act with the intrepidity he will do himself. ⌐He is as earnestly against us keeping the *Copy Right* as you are, though *that* is, & has been from the first, our own favourite intention & desire.

M. d'Arblay was all prepared for opening his own negociation with Mr. Payne, who refuses to accept us as infinitely too ignorant of any business to have any hand in it but Charles's— | but He carries all before Him.⌐

You will not, I am persuaded, be angry, my dearest Father,— the tender, darling tie by which he calls upon us dissolves, while it conquers us.—He seems to cherish a willing fondness for the little Infant that comes close—close to our Hearts. *Can* we repress it?—can we chill so kindly a warmth?—so dearly consoling to us, in the case of any fatal calamity to ourselves?

James has, I am sure, too honestly & truly our real interest at heart, to be offended, after the first few moments of *dépit*, that we give back to Charles an agency so long ago vested in him, from his voluntary offers.

Mrs. Cooke has just told me, that a person connected with her family,[5] was positively told, by Mr. Robson of Bond Street, that Cecilia *cleared* 1500 pounds the *first Year*!—

Dr. Barrow,[6] of Oxford, has just sent me a message, also,

[2] Preserved in the Scrapbook (Berg) 'Fanny Burney and family. 1653–1890', p. 62, is CB Jr.'s request of 27 Dec. 1794 that he be accepted as one of the godfathers to FBA's first-born. Having set his heart 'so very seriously and earnestly' on it, he had to that end driven to Chelsea to ask CB to relinquish a prior claim.

[3] William Lowndes (*fl.* 1784–1821), whose bookshop, according to London Directories, was located in the years 1805–21 at 38 Bedford Street, Strand.

[4] The letter containing this quotation cannot be found but see his letter (Berg), dated Margate 12 July [1795] (L. 178 n. 1).

[5] See L. 178 n. 7.   [6] See L. 178 n. 6.

through Mrs. Leigh, Mrs. Cooke's sister,[7] entreating me not to be, as he is credibly informed I have hitherto been, the dupe of Booksellers.—

Adieu, most dear Sir,—Our Susanna will, I hope, be empowered to write us word that you do not blame us, thus singularly pressed, for giving way.⌐

⌐There can certainly be but one wish in all my Family, though its attainment may appear to require different roads.

I rejoice to hear of your visit intended to Beaconsfield,[8] & I shall long for some intelligence how poor Mr. & Mrs. Burke are, & how you were received, son & Brother gone, since we all dined together at Mrs. Crewe's last.

M. d'Arblay has now ample employment—with his Translation, his spade, & his Calculations.⌐

The orchard has just been Mowed, & looks very *farrently*. The Garden is laboured at incessantly, [&] flourishes very gayly,— only — — we get nothing from it for the Table!—Things are always too soon, or too late,—they won't come up,—or they run to seed!—What apprenticeships are demanded for all species of undertakings!—However, he has made a new bridal seat, for Mrs. Charles Lock, which he surrounds with savoys & Carrots, though he bestows, a little ⟨usine⟩ upon it, a new small parterre —of Flowers—

⌐We are frightened here about Bread—Yesterday our Baker, from Fetcham, wholly failed us, in the morning, for want of Flour, which he could not get, for ready, or for *any* money!—& our loaves are 1st—& they fear they will with difficulty be had *at all* next week! how terrible & alarming!⌐ — — Adieu,⌐ adieu, most dear Sir!— ⌐

⌐Mr. Seward has carried 7 loafs to Miss Cambridge for his ⟨reception⟩.

A Friend of M. d'A—from Dorking,[10] a French Priest, has

[7] Mary Leigh (1731–97) had married *c.* 1763 her cousin the Revd. Thomas Leigh (*c.* 1734–1813), Rector of Adlestrop, Glos. (1763–1813).

[8] SBP had mentioned CB's plans in a letter (Berg) to FBA, 10–11 July 1795: 'On Sunday [12 July] . . . my Father goes to Beaconsfield wth Mrs Crewe'.

[9] The Corn Laws of 1791, placing a tariff on imports, together with poor domestic harvests from 1791 to 1794, caused a shortage of grain. *AR* xxxvii (1795), 'Appendix to the Chronicle', 133, shows a rise in the price of wheat (Jan.–July) from 7s. to 10s. 6d.

[10] Later (iv, L. 292) identified as a M. Daniel and probably the M. Daniel described by Louis-François, baron de Wimpfen (1732–1800), in an inquiry, dated London 2 July [1793] and addressed to the Treasury Office (PRO, H.O. 1/1): 'Un

just called upon him, & told him that Yesterday, for 24 Hours, *no bread* was to be got at Dorking, for any money! They talk of fearing an insurrection in London for Food.

. I *must* find time ⟨coûte qui coûte⟩ for a Baby letter—I have no want de quoi—⊓

180   Great Bookham, 21 July 1795

To Doctor Burney

> A.L.S. (Diary MSS. vi, not numbered, Berg), 21 July [17]95
> Double sheet 4to 4 pp. *pmks* LEATHER / HEAD 22 JY 95   wafer
> *Addressed*: Dr Burney, / Chelsea College, / Middlesex.
> *Endorsed by* CB: July 21. Mrs Boscawin's wish of a / visit—Name—Mr Hastings—1795
> *Edited by* FBA, p. 1, *annotated*:   (7)
> Camilla. Susanna Mr Hastings, Mr. Burke.
> *Edited also by* CFBt *and the* Press.

Bookham,
July 21st—95

My dearest Father,

I am in the uttermost amazement at no news of our Susanna, whom we expected all yesterday, *as we conceived*, by appointment.[1] I hope to God no accident has interfered, to prevent either her coming, or writing?—

⊓I have just received a message from Mrs. Boscawen, that she has now more cash in her House[2] belonging to me than she chuses to keep there in these bad times!—£60!—Is it not interesting?

But,—she declares she will deliver her Cash & her List only *to Dr. Burney*! — —

prêtre français . . . curé de St Barthelemy près du Havre de Grace . . . un fort honnête homme, mais un homme très indiscrèt et très inconséquent.' The Baron, disquieted by Daniel's activities as an alleged British agent and by his disclosure of some of the missions with which he was entrusted, had undertaken an investigation.

180. [1] In a letter of 10–11 July (op. cit.) SBP had promised to come to Bookham on 'Monday sen'night' (i.e., Monday 20 July) but in a letter *pmk* 25 JY 95 (Berg) she explains that she had meant to write and thought she had written 'Monday fortnight' (i.e., Monday 27 July).

[2] In June 1787, according to Aspinall-Oglander, op. cit., chap. xix, Mrs. Boscawen acquired Rosedale, facing the Deer Park, midway between Richmond and Kew. Her letter of this date is missing, but for another, see L. 189 n. 3.

So, my dearest Father, I hope as that is a challenge not very unflattering to *insist* on a visit from you, you will not be cruel. Pray let us know what I must say?⁊

I had heard of such uncommon exertions from her, & of her principal Agent, Miss Cambridge,[3] that I had written to beseech not to have my Book a *burthen*, & that the *name*, & honour of such a Bookkeeper, ⎮ was all I desired. Miss Cambridge writ me for answer—

'Mrs. Boscawen laughs at the notion of *her* & *I* sitting with our hands before us upon such a business.—she says she will not *accept* such a sinecure, though you so graciously offer it.'— Indeed, she has proved her words.

The Daughter, the Duchess of Beaufort, has just sent her in a list of Nine Dukes & Duchesses![4]—where in the World can she have ferretted out nine such who would subscribe? ⊓But, ⟨can we not⟩ learn of the advertisement in any newspaper? It seems only known where spread by ⟨our⟩ *Booksellers*.⊓[5]

How grieved I am you do not like my Name![6]—the *prettiest in Nature*! I remember how many people did not like Evelina, & called it *affected & Missish*, till they read the Book,—& then they got accustomed in a few pages, & afterwards it was much approved. I must leave it for the present untouched, for the force of the name attached by the idea of the Character, in the author's ⎮ mind, is such, that I should not know how to sustain it by any other for a long while. In Cecilia & Evelina 'twas the same: the Names of all the personages annexed with me all the ideas I put in motion with them. The Work is so far advanced, that the personages are all, to Me, as so many actual acquaintances, whose memoirs & opinions I am committing to *paper*.

[3] Charlotte (i, L. 1 n. 6), daughter of Richard Owen Cambridge of Twickenham. This letter is missing. For others, see *Catalogue*.

[4] Mrs. Boscawen's daughter Elizabeth (1747–1828) had married in 1766 Henry Somerset (1744–1803), 5th Duke of Beaufort (1756). Of the sixteen subscribers of ducal rank appearing in the printed list (*Camilla*, i), the Duchess of Devonshire probably needed no solicitation (see L. 191); Mrs. Locke would have secured the Duchess and Dowager Duchess of Leinster; Mrs. Crewe, the Duchess of Buccleugh and the Duke and Duchess of Marlborough; and Mrs. Burney, the Duchess of Newcastle (see CB to FBA, 6 Feb. 1796, Berg). The remaining nine were enlisted, then, by the Duchess of Beaufort.

[5] An advertisement had, however, appeared in the *Morning Chronicle* on 7 July (L. 172 n. 1).

[6] Camilla. See L. 178 and n. 2.

Mrs. Cooke, my excellent neighbour, came in with me from Church on Sunday morning, to read me a paragraph of a Letter from Mrs. Leigh of oxfordshire, her sister, — — after much of civility about the new work, & its author, it finishes thus—'Mr. Hastings I saw just now; I told him what was going forward, he gave a great jump,—& exclaimed "Well, then, now I can serve her, thank God! & I *will!*—I will write to Anderson to *engage Scotland*,[7]—& I will attack the East Indies myself!—"

⌐Yet with all this encouragement, if *the Public* does not come forth, *Friends* alone, with the utmost efforts & zeal, can only amount to a few Hundreds. We are anxious about the Advertisements appearing in the news papers. ⌐

I cannot keep off some uneasiness about Susanne—she is so punctual & comfortable in general. There must be some great mistake, but I *hope* to morrow's post will set us at ⟨ease⟩, or to-morrow's Day bring her. We have taken all the care in our power for Bread, & have now a *Housefull.*⌐

I am glad to understand from Susanna that Mr. Burke had still sometimes *gleams* of himself.[8] How he would have interested himself in this new work while his son & Brother lived, with whom he 4 times read aloud Cecilia![9] Probably the name of this will now but make him sad—

My love & duty to my Mother—Sally I have disinherited. Our dearest Susan will certainly come or write immediately! ⌐When she hears of our sure hope of a visit. God grant she is well⌐

Adieu, most dear Sir, ever yr dutiful Affecte
F d'A.

Bambino is quite well.

The Gardener says I must insert mille choses aimables de sa part & says he has not forgot he was promised some gooseberries—i e—the proofs of Metastasio.

---

[7] David Anderson (1751–1825), 'one of Hasting's most intimate and trusted friends' (Burke, *Corr.*, v. 312 n. 1), who after his return from Bengal (*c.* 1785) lived on his estate (St. Germains) near Edinburgh.

[8] SBP's account of CB's visit to Beaconsfield on [12 July] is unfortunately missing.

[9] Burke subscribed for five sets of *Camilla* in memory of his brother; five in memory of his son; five for Mrs. Burke; and five for himself (twenty sets in all), of which according to his suggestion (L. 191 n. 1) he probably took in one set.

181　　　　Great Bookham, 24 & 25 July 1795

Conjointly with Mrs. Locke
To Mrs. Waddington

A.L.S. & A.L.S. (Berg), 24–5 July 1795
Double sheet 4to 3 pp. *pmks* WHITECHAPEL BRISTOL
2⟨7⟩ JY 95　wafer
Addressed in hand of Mrs. Locke: Mrs Waddington / ⌐N° 2 Mall. /
Clifton / Bristol.⌐
Readdressed: Abergavenny
Docketed in ink, p. 1: 1795

[*By Mrs. Locke*]

I was extremely gratified, my dear Madam by hearing from
you in so kind a manner, altho very much concerned at the state
of your health—accept our united best wishes that it may be
speedily restored.—

How good you are to promise me an addition of subscribers[1]
to that which so warmly interests me,—I know you feel with me
precisely on that subject, & I wish you cou'd have the delight
which I enjoy of seeing that precious friend in the most perfect
health & happiness, with the sweetest & most thriving baby—
I hope she will add a few lines to this: but shou'd she not be able,
she charged me with her kindest love & ⏐ to entreat that you
wou'd not think of writing to her while it is so hurtful to you—
Mr Lock^e, my daughters, & all mine join in best thanks & kind
remembrances—I wish I cou'd present my new & very sweet
daughter to you, for I may venture to say that you wou'd like
her.[2] This renews my regret at the distance which deprives us of
your society—believe me my dear Madam with great regard
　　　　　　　　　Your obliged & affec^te humble Ser^t
　　　　　　　　　　　　　　　F Locke

July 24^h 1795
Norbury Park
Leatherhead
　Surrey⏐

181. [1] See L. 173 n. 6.　　　[2] Mrs. Charles Locke.

[*By Madame d'Arblay*]

Bookham Hermitage.
July 25.—95

Mrs. Lock & her two charming Daughters have just been here—I cannot let this go out of my hands without saying how I grieve for my dearest Marianne's sufferings,—certainly do not write till you are able to give a better account of yourself—but should that not be soon, make interest for me with some kind Hand to give me information; for, after a certain period, *no* news becomes frightful.

The enclosed will explain something of the manner of this business,—which I hear you are already employed in—my intelligence is from Miss Cambridge, who is chief Agent of Mrs. Boscawen, for whom she keeps an *under* Book—She says— 'I wanted to have an *agent of my own* at Cheltenham—but I am written word *Mrs. Waddington* is before hand with me there. They tell me, too, she is busy at the Hot wells.'—

Do you remember *Ariana*?³ that *impossible* name? as Gen¹ G[oldsworthy]⁴ called it?—Well, *she* keeps a second Book as Agent for Mrs. Crewe. Mrs. Lock will much like to call *you her's*, if you wish it. But do nothing that requires exertion, beyond what may animate & interest so as a little to amuse you from your pain, by the pleasure I know you will reap from any power of shewing your zeal. Adieu, my dear Friend,—Heaven recover, restore, *revive* & preserve you!—

F d'A

182   Great Bookham, 4 August 1795

Conjointly with Mrs. Phillips
To Esther (Burney) Burney

A.L.S. & A.N.S. (Berg), 4 Aug. [17]95
Double sheet 4to 4pp. *pmks* LEATHER / HEAD 5 AU 95 wafer
Addressed: Mrs. Burney, / Nᵒ 2. Hill Street / Richmond / Surry.
Endorsed by EBB: August 1795

³ The Hon. Ariana Margaret Egerton (i, L. 13 n. 16).
⁴ See i, L. 5 n. 10.

[By Madame d'Arblay]

Bookham Hermitage
Aug^st 4th—95

The account of your 'imbecillity,'[1] my dearest Etty, has much the same effect upon me as similar complaints which are made by Mr. Lock, who, whenever he forgets a name (that nobody, perhaps, would remember,) exclaims 'My Memory is totally gone!—' & when he does not catch every word in a cross conversation, sighs out 'I have wholly lost my hearing!'—I know you to be a little of the tant pis order for yourself,—but your paragraph of failing intellect is not written so as to make prosylites to your opinion.

I remember, in old times, my dear Esther, when a violent Cold had inflamed your Eyes, & swelled your nose, you declared, in utter despair, you were altered for life, that you were frightful to behold, & looked upon yourself as an ugly old woman already,—and, indeed, it must be owned with some reason, as, added to your personal odiousness, you were then just nineteen.—

I wish you could pass some time, you, Mr. Burney, & Marianne, at least, in some little habitation at Bookham;—I am sure you would like the strolls surrounding us,—they are sweetly rural, & wholly retired, ᛁ & how should Susanna[2] & I rejoice in your sight & society!—Don't tell my poor Aunt Beckey I say this, lest she should think it an underhand plot, to deprive her of her greatest comfort.[3]—I would not do that; I would wish only to take such time as would else be dedicated to *London*.

I am both surprised & pleased at this kind remembrance in Mr. R[ichard] Twining,[4] which I could so little expect. Pray write him my thanks, & tell him, since he has friends involved in his scheme, I should wish, if it is neither inconvenient nor disagreeable to him, he would take the trouble to keep his list for me till next January, as various of my friends & Agents are

182. [1] Not extant.

[2] SBP had apparently arrived for the promised visit beginning Monday 27 July (cf. L. 180 n. 1).

[3] EBB, with her daughters Marianne and Amelia, had departed on 10 July for her usual summer vacation at Richmond. See SBP's letter of 10–11 July (op. cit.).

[4] Richard Twining (1749–1824), a director of the East India Company (1793–1816) and head of the well-known tea company on the Strand, had with other members of the Twining family (including the Revd. Thomas) subscribed for seven sets of *Camilla*.

doing; for I shall not desire to collect the lists, & know the *State of the case*, till that period. His coming forward in this manner is very *Twiningish*,—but ask him if his Colchester Brother will ever forgive such voluntary zeal in a Burnean Cause? I have no fear, myself, but of a fraternal breach. Should he not scruple giving Mr. T[homas] T[wining] this mortal blow, I will convey the *all how & about it*, in a paper of the proposals, to his ¦ House in Town, and with some signed receipts to be delivered to those who form his list, & subscribe to him.

The names will certainly be printed.

Your accounts of Fanny are most delightful. Indeed I shall truly be glad to see the Letters. I am sorry, for her sake, at Lady Charlotte's Marriage.[5] The last Lady St. Asaph was a lovely young woman, Grand Daughter to the Duchess Dowager of Portland, the bosom friend of Mrs. Delany, at whose House I have often seen her. She had two or three Children.[6] Are they alive? Mrs. Lock is just now gone to spend a few Days with Lord Henry FitzGerald, Brother to Mrs. Charles.[7] I will give her your welcome news with pleasure upon her return. she both loves & admires You most affectionately as well as sincerely, & speaks of *your* regard for *her* with the warmest pleasure upon every occasion.

My Bambino is not yet grown horrid,—he is not yet *nineteen*, though!—but his teeth—that is, his *no* teeth, plague & torture him cruelly. And so his dear little fat Cousin[8] is still in that same barbarous situation? Pray tell me when she spoke her first word. I am collecting by all opportunities MATERIALS for expectation of that grand event from my Bamb.

We are delighted here with our Cottage full,—every little Closet,—commonly called Room, by courtesie,—is amply peopled, with sweetness, chearfulness, confidence & serenity. I was myself never in better health,—rarely in any degree as well. His rustic, simple, Gardening life agrees perfectly with M.

5 Lady Charlotte Percy (1776–1862), eldest daughter of Algernon Percy, 1st Earl of Beverley (L. 142 n. 3), in whose household Fanny Burney was employed as governess. On 25 July 1795 Lady Charlotte had become the second wife of George Ashburnham (1760–1830), styled Viscount St. Asaph, 3rd Earl of Ashburnham (1812).

6 The first wife of the Viscount St. Asaph (above) was Sophia Thynne (1763–91), whose maternal grandmother was the Dowager Duchess of Portland (1715–85). The three children of this marriage were: George (1785–1813); John (1789–1810); and Elizabeth Sophia (1786–1879).

7 Half-brother (see L. 175 n. 3).   8 Amelia Burney, b. 5 Aug. 1792.

d'Arblay, & our little one would never utter a cry,—if we could but bring him up TOOTHLESS.—I wish you could help to Nurse him. He is now of the Age when I know Babies to be irresistible to you.—Our darling Susan does not very much shock me by any marked antipathy to him—therefore I am not VERY much afflicted to have her with me—Dearest Soul! she chears what she can for us all. |

Adieu, my dear sister,—my love to Mr. Burney, & Marianne, & Sophy—& pray remember me tenderly to my Aunt Beckey, & tell her I design her a copy of my little work amongst the first. *you*, my dearest Esther, will receive yours hot from the Press, Susan I trust, has told you my insistance upon that subject for all my Brothers & sisters. Indeed, *we* could not forgive any underhand dealing in that particular. And I must here beg you to present my very affectionate remembrance to Edward, & tell him he must allow me the pleasure, upon this, ocasion, to include him as a Brother. I am sure he will not mortify me by any step that will thwart this wish. I know nothing either of service or pleasure he has yet refused me. — — Do you think I shall not a little tremble when the Day of appearance approaches? I am obliged to drive it from my head, or I should never be ready for it. Adieu—Dearest Etty—

yours ever & ever more
F. d'A.

Pray remember me to Miss Brooks.[9]
M. d'Ar. sends his kindest Compliments.

[By Susannah Phillips]

The letter is brought me to finish at the moment that the postman is come to fetch it my Esther, but I rejoice nevertheless in an opportunity of signing my name, & thanking my sweet sister for my part in her dear letter—I don't like the acc^t of y^r head my Esther—I know it is an *exaggeration*—but it is but a tragi comedy, & one does not laugh de bon coeur at y^r lamentable acc^t of *the State of y^r Intellects*—my kindest kindest love to dear Aunt Beckey—& to our Marianne & Sophy if wth [you]— & 100 kisses to the dear Bab[y]—most lovingly—

S. E: P.

pray remember me to Miss Brookes.

[9] See L. 150 n. 6.

183   Great Bookham, [19] November [1795]

To Mrs. Waddington

A.L. (Berg), Nov.
Double sheet small 4to   4 pp.   *pmk*   21 NO 95   wafer
Addressed: Mrs. Waddington, / Lanover Court, / Abergavenny.
Docketed in ink, p. 1: 1795

Bookham, Nov^r

How touched have I just felt myself with a mark of the fond early partiality of my ever dear Marianne which M. d'Arblay has this moment met with, by accident, in Boyer's french Dictionary![1]—& which I never recollect seeing before. I suppose my dear Miss Port there glided it, unseen, between the Leaves—which I have never happened to open at that place since. 'Tis a very pretty figure of a young Girl carrying a Basket of Flowers,[2] —'tis the first essay in Water Colours, as a dear line on the other side of the Drawing mentions. It must have been executed, & thus, unknown, presented, at Windsor—Dear GMP—or GMW —! how ever kindly, & ever partially, has your Heart stood my inalterable Friend!— —Your *last* exertions, however, have by no means given me equal pleasure, for I see with concern they have been difficult & troublesome to yourself. Money matters, besides,—essential as they are, carry never, to me, the same charm as one such little affecting trait from the Heart's original instinct as I have just met with. My beloved Mrs. Lock, however, more anxious for me upon this subject than I am for myself, is extremely pleased by your List,[3] & has inserted it in her Book with your Name to it. You talk of *further efforts*—these I absolutely require, by the love you bear me, & by the regard you have for all I value so much higher than interest, may be set aside. I have besought of all my ǀ Friends to accept but Volunteers. I am hurt to have the Work become a burthen to those I love. You have fully indulged your zeal—which nothing, perhaps, could *satisfy*,—but you must now indulge my humour.

I am obliged to preach thus again & again, to all my but too active Bookkeepers, whom I charge to remember my *peculiarities*

183. [1] See L. 122 n. 5.   [2] This watercolour is missing.
[3] See L. 173 n. 5.

as well as my interest. Let me he[ar] as soon as possible how you are, & a confirmation of your amendment. Is your sister[4] with you still? Is she amiable? is she like my dear Mary Ann?—is she a comfort & pleasure to you? Does my little name sake continue her love of study? & does Emily grow up to resemble her Mother?—Entreat for me your sister to have the kindness to write again, if your Eyes are still too weak. And remember me to Mr. Wadington. |

My Bambino was Eleven Months old yesterday, & he walks with one hand tolerably well, though always prepared for a tumble. His Eyes—you will wonder to hear—are much the colour of yours!—Do you think I can bear to look at them?

Certainly all the subscribers must send for their own Books. They will be delivered by the five Publishers named in the proposals.[5] The List is already singularly respectable, but I much question whether, ultimately, it will be numerous.

Gen. Goldsworthy[6] has had another dreadful fit—but is again recovered. What a Tax upon high living!. Adieu, my sweet Friend. *Pray* let me hear you are better.

The sweet Locks always love—always take a very tender & sincere interest in your Health & welfare. I never produce your Letters—but I always carry News of you—when I have it myself!—!!

[4] Probably Louisa Port (1778–1817). See v, L. 540 n. 2.

[5] See L. 172 n. 1. In due course (12–14 July 1796) the *London Chronicle* directed subscribers 'to apply for their copies to the respective Booksellers to whom they paid their subscriptions—Those who subscribed to the ladies who kept Books, may receive their copies on application to the Publishers.' For the addition of J. Cawthorne, see L. 177 n. 3.

[6] The object of GMAPW's early and lasting infatuation (i, L. 5 n. 10), news of whom FBA obligingly accorded.

184   Great Bookham, 26 December 1795

To Louis, comte de Narbonne-Lara

L.S. copy in hand of M. d'A (Berg), 26 Dec. 1795
Single sheet 4to   2 pp.
Edited by FBA, p. 1, *annotated*: ⁑ N° 15
To M. de Narbonne, (God Father of Alexandre), during his revolutionary
embarrassments, — — copied *for* & *by* the most partial of Husbands. N.B.
This was written in answer *to a Letter of bitter disappointment* from repeated
losses.

Bookham 26. X^{bre} 1795

What a letter to terminate so long & painful a silence![1] It has
penetrated us with sorrowing & indignant feelings. Unknown to
M^r d'Arblay, whose grief, & horrour are upon the point of
making him quite ill, I venture this Address to his most beloved
Friend, & before I Seal it, I will give him the option to burn or
underwrite it.

I shall be brief in what I have to propose; sincerity need not
be loquacious, & M. de N[arbonne] is too kind to demand
phrases for ceremony.

Should your present laudable, but melancholy plan fail,[2] &
should nothing better offer,—or till something can be arranged,
Will you, Dear Sir!, condescend to share the poverty of our
Hermitage? Will you take ǀ a little cell under our rustic Roof, &
fare as we fare? What to us—two *athanases*—is chearful & happy
will to you, indeed, be miserable; but it will be some solace to
the goodness of your Heart to witness our contentment;,—to dig
with M^r d'A. in the Garden will be of service to your health; to
nurse sometimes with me in the Parlour will be a relaxation to
your mind. You will not blush to own your little Godson—Come
then & give him your blessing; relieve the wounded feelings of
his Father—oblige his mother—& turn hermit at Bookham till
brighter Suns invite you elsewhere
                                                    F. d'A.

You will have terrible Diñers, alas! but your Godson comes
in for the Dessert.—

184. [1] The comte de Narbonne's letter is not extant, but in his reply to the above,
dated Glaris, Switzerland, 24 Jan. 1796 (Berg; *DL* v. 268–70), he describes his
prospects as much improved ('je passe ici assez doucement ma vie entre Madame
de la Chartre . . . et Madame de Laval'). FBA seems not to have known that he
had been deported (L. 145 n. 1).
    [2] The plan is lost.

185   [Great Bookham,] 26 December 1795

M. d'Arblay
To Madame d'Arblay

A.L. (Berg), 26 December 1795
Single sheet small 4to   2 pp.
Addressed: M^{rs} d'Arblay
Edited by FBA, p. 1, *top margin annotated*: 4
The warm effusion of a noble Heart. / on Occasion of a written offer to his /
favourite friend, M. de Narbonne, to / accept a permanent asylum at /
West Hamble.

Ce 26.^{Xbre} 1795

True Angel!

On disait dernierement à Norbury qu'un homme ne devait
pas pleurer. Que suis-je donc moi qui t'ai lu et qui t'ecris le
visage baigné des plus douces larmes. Il est donc vrai que je
pouvais t'aimer encore davantage! Je ne l'aurais jamais cru et
cependant je le sens. mais comment l'exprimer? jamais plus,
jamais mieux, que je n'ai fait jusqu'à present. car je ne puis
offrir, que ce que tu as dejà. Je rougirais de pouvoir davantage,
que je n'ai fait: car je serais inexcusable, si j'avais quelque chose
encore à donner à celle à qui depuis longtems je dois tout!
Combien cependant ce ᛁ dernier trait me touche! Crois au reste
ma bonne amie que ce dernier trait de generosité ne sera point
perdu. Ta lettre que je copierai et que je leguerai à mon fils lui
sera plus chere, que quelques louis de plus. Comme il adorera
sa mere! Comme je lui en donnerai l'exemple! God bless the
best of the best!

186   [Great Bookham, 22 January 1796]

To Elizabeth (Allen) Burney

A.L. (Osborn), *n.d.*

Single sheet 4to   2 pp. in the original conjecturally a double sheet, the first leaf of which was a letter to Dr. Burney   *pmks* LEATHER / HEAD 22 JA 96   wafer

Addressed: Dr. Burney, / Chelsea College, / Middlesex

Annotated by FBA, p. 1: India Richard

To Mrs. Burney.

Dear Madam,

I must scribble a line or two without delay to say, in case your India Letters are not yet delivered, that nothing can be more comfortable than Richard's last accounts.[1] He is well, & well settled, speaks affectionately of his Wife & Children, & is able to live to his comfort & desire, yet save £400 a year towards times to come.

Thank God, all essential fears I now consider as over for him, both in Character & Fortune. He seems really prospering in both, & I hope you will yet see him, his good Jenny, & his little ones Eating Plumb Pudding, according to his early sermon, of a Sunday with you. I will send you the Letter by Susanna, which I beg you to return me by the next opportunity. I *will* write, if only 3 lines, by this Spring's Ships, I'm resolved.

Your attacks of the poor Doctor[2] always make me Grin. Bringing 6 when he asked for Three! Dr. Fisher[3] is a very good & amiable Man, & I am pleased by his kind Zeal. Miss *Mary Bell*[4] was *not* in your last List. so You have gone on most flourishingly. Dr. Parkenson[5] subscribed to Mrs. Bos[cawen] through the agency of Mrs. Porteus,[6] Bᴾ of London's Lady. |

186. [1] FBA's letter from her half-brother Richard Thomas Burney (i, Intro., lxxiii) of Kiddepore was probably destroyed along with his mother's correspondence (L. 214 n. 1). For his marriage to Jane Ross see i, L. 24 n. 50.
   [2] Unidentified.   [3] See i, L. 3 n. 36.
   [4] Probably Mary Bell (*c.* 1742–1814) of 'the Dean's Yard' or Close, Westminster, a sister of the Revd. William Bell (*c.* 1731–1816), D.D. (1767), Prebendary of Westminster (1765). Like him, she was buried in the Abbey, see J. L. Chester, *Registers of the Collegiate Church or Abbey of St. Peter, Westminster* (1876), pp. 487, 491, 492, and notes.
   [5] Possibly Thomas Parkinson (1745–1830), D.D. (1795).
   [6] See i, L. 13 n. 9.

Susanna bids me say she has seen again the little Footboy,[7] whose Parents now will not let him go to a new place under 8 g[s] & his Cloaths. The Boy, she says, is well spoken of, but she gave him little encouragement. Why does Betty Cook go away? Is it with *Sam?*[8]—are they really *espoused*? Adieu, Dear Madam,— I rejoice in your health bulletins—What a *spring* we have had since last Autumn!—We have Primroses, violets, daisies, wall flowers, all blooming!—& the Rose Trees look like May. Take *courage*—& the *Carriage*—& Peep at us next Summer.

I was very glad to see Mr. Ste[phen] A[llen] so respectably heading the Lynn Address[9]—Pray thank my dear Father for the Brazen Hymn,[10] I have not room left.

Pray, when you see Mrs. Hailes,[11] with my Compliments, be so good as to tell her that a great friend & favourite of hers, *Mrs. Howe*,[12] has been most actively eager for a certain *new work*, & carried a very illustrious List of Names to Edwards,[13] whom she desired to acquaint me with her Zeal. I should be infinitely obliged to Mrs. Hailes if, when she sees Mrs. Howe, she would be so kind as to make my best acknowledgements.

Love to Sally.

[7] Possibly one of the Whitton children (i, L. 6 n. 2).

[8] Samuel Anderson, mentioned as 'house man' or 'man servant' in CB's Account Books (Berg) for this year.

[9] Among the Addresses of Loyalty printed in the *London Gazette* (11–15 Dec. 1792) was a testimonial from 'the Mayor and Inhabitants of the Borough of King's Lynn'. The signatures were not there printed, but presumably Mrs. Burney possessed a copy with the signatories attached.

[10] This was 'a French Hymn' transcribed by Mary Hartley (i, L. 3 n. 99) of Bath and sent *via* CB to the d'Arblays along with a 'pacquet' conjecturally containing her subscription to *Camilla*. CB remembered Mrs. Hartley's having 'copied out for him the commemoration of Handel which was presented to the King in M.S.—'. See SBP's letter (Berg) [*pre* 22 Jan. 1796].

[11] Mrs. Hale, the wife of the Lieutenant-Governor of Chelsea College (i, L. 8 n. 10).

[12] The Hon. Caroline Howe (*c.* 1721–1814), who had married in 1742 John Howe (*c.* 1707–69) of Hanslope, Bucks. She lived at 12 Grafton St., Piccadilly; Mrs. Hale, in St. James's Place.

[13] James Edwards (1757–1816), bookseller in Pall Mall (1784–1804).

187   Great Bookham, 3 February 1796

To M. d'Arblay

A.L. (Berg), 3 Feb. [17]96
Double sheet small 4to   4 pp.   *pmk*   4 FE 96   red wafer
Addressed: Alexander d'Arblay Esqr, / At Capt. Burney's, / James Street, /
Westminster.
Edited by FBA, p. 1, *annotated*: (5)   Written when Alexander was 13
months old.

> Dear—yet now forlorn
> Bookham Hermitage.
> Feby 3^d—96.

We are as well as we know how to be, without our Chief—our
Ami, our Master, our Servant, our Ruler, our Play-fellow—our
best & most deservedly beloved:—but we look about for him
every where.—Yesterday, in the high Wind & Rain, we seemed
desolate without him,—to Day, in this beautiful sun shine, we
still seem solitary. The Mother & The Bambino are already
leagued in the most intelligent sympathy; 'Where, I cry, is
Papa?—He jumps, & points with his little Finger to the
Window,—I carry him thither, & his quick Eye traverses *our
Grounds*,—he sees no one,—& disappointment takes place of
vivacity, & he draws in, with a sorrowful little shake of the head,
& an inquisitive glance at me, that says mais où, où est il donc,
mon Papa?—Then ¦ we go up & down stairs,—&, at every
entrance into a room, he springs almost out of my arms, exclaiming At! At! At!—but no At is there!—Dearest At!—come back
to us on Friday,—J'ai beau vantée mon hermitage,—it won't
do without my Hermit!—

A Thousand kindest Loves to the dear Dwellers where you
will receive this—& at Chelsea—Titchfield—Greenwich—&
Downing St.[1]

I am just going—wrapt up well—to make the *grand tour*.
Bambino is now in the *Great Alley*.

How I enjoy this delicious Day for your long Walks!—Yesterday I wrote 14 Pages. & 1/2. I won't tell you how late I sat up.

187. [1] The addresses respectively of the members of the Burney family, CB, EBB,
CB Jr., and CBF.

You were very good to exact no promises. Come back, & keep me in better order.— |

I long for to-morrow's post.

I am very careful of myself, I assure you, except in the one article of writing late—but—it is so delicious to stride on, when *en verf*! Yet we played a full Hour at Where's My Baby? Where's my Baby?—

I can't tell how to believe you went but yesterday.

I only go to the Parlour to Dine,—I cannot bear to *make my own Establishment*!—nor to look at my opposite side, & see vacancy.—I hurry away as fast as possible.

Pray make our beloved Susanna promise again her Weekly Letters. They are quite *indispensable* to me.

I hope you are writing to Me just at this moment.—Bambino & I have played our Ball up to the Top of the Bed, & nobody can reach it. He points to me to Dance him up there like Papa, —but I tell him he must wait for At. So come home, Dear At!— |

I am now going to give Bambino the Pencil, to write to you himself.

[*here, p. 4, pencilled scratches*]

He has made these scratches unguided—I wish you could see his self-complacency at his own performance:

188   [Great Bookham,] 4 March [1796]

To Doctor Burney

A.L. (Berg), 4 Mar.

Double sheet small 4to   4 pp.   *pmks*   LEATHER / HEAD   4 MR 96
red wafer

Addressed: Dr. Burney, / Chelsea, / Middlesex.

Edited by FBA, p. 1, *annotated and dated*: ✗ ✗ 1796   (2)

The Queen's permission to have Camilla presented to her in Person at Windsor.

In pencil, p. 4: M^rs B⟨oscawen⟩ / L^y Spencer / ⟨Devonshire⟩

4—March—

I know my beloved Father will exactly feel with me the pleasure I have received from what I now write to relate.

In my last *Birth Day Epistle*, I mentioned, that I should earnestly wish to lay at her Majesty's feet the little Work I was preparing for the Press, if she would deign to accept that small mark of my respectful & grateful devotion.—¹

I received no answer, & concluded my *french name* was against the request, or that it must be made more in form.—T'other day, however, came the Reply²—conceived in the ǀ civilest terms possible by Mrs. S[chwellenberg]—to say illness & business alone had prevented her writing sooner, but that *she never took up her pen with more pleasure* than to tell me she had The Queen's Commands to acquaint me with her Majesty's consent to my request.—

And she ends her Letter with every kind wish to *my littel Boy.* Many reasons combine to make this permission a sort of *public protection* on the part of the Queen, for which I am truly grateful.

I shall write this through my friend Miss Cambridge ǀ for the excellent Mrs. Boscawen, whose goodness to me & my Work, & whose perfect orthodoxy for King, Queen, Religion, Laws, & Government—will approve of the 'LICENCE' to her protegée, Camilla. Should you be able to see her *first*, I entreat you, dearest Sir, to make the communication, in my Name, & with my most faithful Respect.

We wish to hear better news of my Mother.—My dear gardiner still cannot bear his head uncovered. He tried to d'off his Cap Yesterday, & suffered severely in returned pain some Hours. I am not quite at my ease yet about it!——He goes on adoring Metastasio,³ & it is to be our first Book of real enjoyment to read to-gether, upon the First of July.⁴

My kind Love & best wishes to my Mother & to Sall—Adieu
most dear Sir ǀ

188. ¹ FBA's request would have been drafted, copied, and sent *pre* 18 Jan. 1796, but no draft seems to survive.

² Miss Schwellenberg, in her letter (Berg) of 26 Feb. 1796, after apologizing for a delay caused by indifferent health and excessive business, came to the point: 'I do assure you I never took my pen in hand with more pleasure then to informe you I have her Majestys Commands to say she gives lave for you to Dedicate youre Books to her.'

CB, convinced that his daughter, by her marriage, could be held only in disfavour at Court, was incredulous to the last with respect to the Queen's permission.

³ CB's *Metastasio* had been advertised as 'published' as early as 24 Feb. 1796 (L. 149 n. 4).

⁴ The date on which *Camilla* was at first advertised to appear, for example, in the *Morning Chronicle*, 7 July 1795 (L. 172 n. 1).

Charles. & Mrs. C. were so kind as to spend Saturday Evening & Sunday[5] with Us.—all talk between Him & M. d'A. upon Copy right &c—full & pleasant. I hope something now will be settled soon. Proof sheets coming hither will require more time,—& I Would not disappoint my Day for the universe. M. d'A. says *NO ROMAN* was ever more *interesting* to him than Metastasio's Letters, his *Character* & *Memoirs* Make such friends of his readers.

My dear *littel Boy* is well, & really '*pretty Enuff*

189   [Great Bookham, 11 March 1796]

Conjointly with M. d'Arblay
To Doctor Burney

A.L. & A.L. (Berg), *n.d.*
Double sheet folio   4 pp.   *pmks*   LEATHER / HEAD   11 MR 96 wafer
Addressed: Dr Burney, / Chelsea. / Middlesex
Endorsed by CB: M. d'Arblay / 1796
Edited by FBA, p. 1, *annotated and dated*: ·⁖· 11 March—96   11 March / 1796 (3) Again on Memoirs of Metastasio. & on Camilla—& presentation to The Queen, & accepted Dedication.—our Happy Happy Bookham Hermitage!

[By M. d'Arblay]

Dearest Sir,

Though I am very much affraid to make you repent of your indulgence by intruding my self so soon on your way, and preying so indiscretly upon your precious time, I cannot prevail upon myself not to say how much I feel my self gratified with your kind & encouraging though dangerous & unmerited praises: dangerous, because self love lends to them a too much pleased & gratified Ear; unmerited, as I must not only own, that I know very little of your *mother's tongue* but that what was really praise worthy in my letter was due to my *Father's work*. In deed I was so amused and so full of your charming work that

5 26 and 27 Feb.

There is no wonder if some expressions and even some sentences have been included in my very well timed trial; so it is that you found in perusing it some words *well* chosen & *well* arranged, & thank God *well* received too. I was not at all sanguine upon their success; and thus I was the more gratified and grateful by hearing from Dear Susan the good reception my scrawl had been favoured with. A thousand thousand thanks for the promised and expected | deficient sheets.[1] I know the few days of men of business, & principally Printers, are to be understood very often as so many months; thus I will bridle my impatience to have my dear dirty-Copy neatly *shelfed*. After many unhappy and very short trials to take off my *night* cap in *day* time, To day I make again this experiment, of which, till now, I have no occasion to repent. True it is that I am very comfortably & very PLEASEDLY writing by a pretty good fire with my hat upon my head, but I have already visited my dear Garden without the least pain. However I will by further precaution keep, some days more, my above cap in the air. The mother of Camilla had left her daughter asleep in order to nurse for a short time her brisk & lively boy, & refresh a little herself by walking before breakfast with her chattering Gardner, when we had your welcome & dearest letter.[2] I leave to her to answer to the article concerning the Camilla's patronage. I wrote instantly, in order to entreat you, after our sincerest congratulations to Mrs Burney, to pray her to send us word in her promised letter, how you are escaped from the pericolous but too gratifying excursion so *temptingly* sollicited by the respectable and respected as much as admired Mrs Boscowen. Her letters are indeed the best pattern in such a delicate situation as hers towards us. T'is delicacy itself associated with kindness & true wit.[3] Poor Mr Twining, I don't know him—but I know enough of him to pity his situation with

189. [1] In a letter (Berg) to FBA and M. d'A, dated 29 Feb.–1 Mar. 1796, SBP had conveyed her father's acknowledgements of a letter that M. d'A had sent to him. CB had been '*delighted*' to find in it '*the best English he ever saw written by a foreigner!*' He 'has charged me with his love & his thanks' and says he will try to procure from his printer the proof sheets of *Metastasio* that M. d'A had found missing.

[2] Not extant.

[3] Mrs. Boscawen had developed an elegant epistolary style. In the letter of 7 Mar. 1796, carefully preserved in the Scrapbook (Berg) 'Fanny d'Arblay and friends. England. 1759–1799', p. 105, she acknowledged with pleasure FBA's 'information'. 'Any thing that is advantageous & agreeable to You' would always be a pleasure, as was 'a Visit from Dr Burney, in perfect good Health'. Her 'respectable Register' or 'green book' she describes as green in the snow and bearing many new poesies, that is, names of subscribers to *Camilla*.

all my heart.[4] Pray, dear Sir, though I am so much happy in receiving your letters, don't suffer the least uneasiness in answering to me, to defeat my purpose, which is to save you all trouble. —You know my sentiments   they are not of the fickly tribe. |

[*By Madame d'Arblay*]

You see, most dear Sir, how happy your kind Letter has made us,[2]—& I must now hasten to *expound* what I have unconsciously made obscure. I wrote to Mrs. Schwellenberg, to tell her my *wish* to lay at her Majesty's feet this new Work, & to ask her counsel, whether she thought *publicly* to do it would be graciously accepted by my ever revered Royal Mistress: the *form* of such a request I well knew was to be made through the Chamberlain; but I wanted encouragement from Mrs. S[chwellenberg] to proceed, or not. — — To This came the answer I have mentioned, —setting aside all *form* & further *ceremonial*, & aquainting me, by the Queen's own commands, that she accepts the public Dedication of my new Work.

I have now sent my most grateful & humble acknowledgements to Her Majesty, for so kindly gracious a permission to Manife⟨st⟩ my devotion & gratitude to her.

This is the exact state,—& the leave has been communicated with so much *Kindness*, to boot, that I have not the least objection to its being named.

I had not meant tormenting sweet Mrs. Boscawen with a separate Letter—but M. d'A. thought to *hang back* was too *English* & *sheepish*, & so I wrote, after your Letter one Day,— but I most extremely rejoice, for it has procured me a *beautiful* answer,[3]—Dearest Sir, speak for me when you next see her, in best manner, & clear my obscurity, & present her my very grateful Respects & Thanks for her Letter. |

⌐⎯⎯⎯⌐

The Queen knows, at full length, & has long known, by an especial Letter, of my Three principals. ⌐By the way, what are the 4 names of Mrs. Crewe that she gave in coming to Town?

---

4 The Revd. Thomas Twining's wife, *née* 1739 Elizabeth Smythies, had died on 3 Mar. 1796. She was the daughter of the Revd. Palmer Smythies (1700–76), Rector of St. Michael's, Mile End, Colchester, and until 1773 Rector of St. Mary Magdalen and Master of the Colchester Free Grammar School.

I have never heard them, nor of any, since the first 3. Ld Macartney, L^y Douglas,[5] & Lady Pembroke.[6] These 6 I shall insert in the general List instantly. I beseech when you see her next you will say as pretty things as you can for me, dear, dear Sir, do!—Poor Mr Twining! I had never thought his wife merited him[7] but as *he* was content, I am truly grieved at his loss—

When Carlos left us, after a very kind visit of consultation with M. d'A—he intended opening a negotiation immediately I fear, by hearing nothing, something has retarded his purpose. And I must begin printing in April as I shall have my proofs all here.

We much want better news of my Mother. Her list grows *superb*, but your readiness to answer for people makes me a little quake too. I hope Mrs. Crewe has the goodness to give receipts, that there may be no mistakes or difficulties about the delivery of the Books, when that dear jumping, freeing Day arrives.

My little Man, who waits till then to skip & spring, is just the thing for the part that you love, romping, playing, begging, good humoured, gay, yet carressing.

Adieu most dear & dearest Sir,—We shall ⟨much⟩ want news of the [Wor]ld & hope to hear it from Susanna, as well as of my Mother. She is naughty, & has not ⟨written⟩ lately.[11]

---

[5] Frances Scott (1750–1817), who married in 1783 Archibald James Edward Douglas (1748–1827), cr. Baron Douglas of Douglas (1790).

[6] Elizabeth Spencer (1737–1831), who had married in 1756 Henry Herbert (1734–94), 10th Earl of Pembroke, Earl of Montgomery (1749/50).

[7] FBA may not have met Mr. Twining's wife. His marriage (3 Jan. 1764), though childless, was a happy one, according to Professor R. S. Walker, who has studied the unpublished Twining papers. Elizabeth Twining (see n. 4 above) was by no means uncultivated, but read a great deal, studied French, and her letters, full of cheerful references to the domestic affairs of the parsonage, show her as lively, humorous, and gay. TT's letters of 1796 reflect his distress during her long and painful illness and his desolation after her death.

190   [Great Bookham, 14 March 1796]

Conjointly with M. d'Arblay
To Charles Burney

A.L. & A.L. (Osborn), *n.d.*
Double sheet small 4to   3 pp.   *pmks*   LEATHER / HEAD   14 MR 96
wafer
Addressed: Dr Charles Burney / Greenwich / Kent

Most noble Carolus!
Neither Cicero, Longinus, nor Dr. Johnson ever wrote so
exquisite a Letter.[1]
     The Copy shall be ready with all speed: but pray let me know
if it will be in time if I send it on Easter Monday,[2] when I have
a safe conveyance by *Mr. Lock*, as I tremble at a mere stage.
I can then, also, send *two volumes*, but sooner *only one*, on account
of poor M. d'A's head, which has retarded Copying;[3] & my
original is not very legible but to ourselves, who, like the Eels,
are used to it.
     We will keep the secret,[4] if they desire it, most punctiliously.
But is it to be ALL secret, or only the *terms*, & not that the M.S.
is sold? To *us* this is indifferent.
     We have communicated the affair to the Idol, who is very
sensible of the trust, & cried, putting his little finger to his Nose,
as I whispered it him 'Har!—Har!' for *Hark*! which is the
only word he has yet attempted.
     I EXTREMELY rejoice Mr. payne has the Work. Pray tell
him so, with my best Compliments, very particularly when you
see him. I should have been really sorry if circumstances had
divided This young lady from her Elder sister.
     How James will *delight* it is Mr. Payne's—but how stare if you
divulge the Ways & Means: My Father will be HIGHLY PLEASED
it is Mr. Payne's, also. In short

190. [1] CB Jr.'s letter is missing.   [2] On 28 March.
    [3] The extant manuscripts of *Camilla*, about 300 pp. (Berg), are in M. d'A's hand
with revisions in FBA's hand. It would seem that he had also made the fair copy
for the press.
    [4] The secret was apparently the sale of the copyright (Ll. 168 n. 5; 178 n. 10).

You are a fine fellow, Charles, a very fine fellow! And let's see now who says you *don't wake well,* if you have been asleep! You were always famous for that you know. ¹

My best thanks to my dear Rosette for her kind, obliging, & confidential Letters.

[*By M. d'Arblay*]

I am quite astonished at your quick and very succesful negociation. Adieu most beloved Ambassador Your God Son sends you his love with many tender kisses to Mʳˢ B[urney].

We send word to Dʳ Burney of the sale without saying anything about the Particulars. We even do not name Mʳ Payne, because we are fearing to trust the business to paper. Thus, my dearest friend, we leave the whole to you, and we depend upon your inexhautible kindness to fulfill that last task

191   [Great Bookham, 21 March 1796]

To Doctor Burney

A.L. (Berg), *n.d.*
Single sheet 4to 1 p.
Edited by FBA, p. 1, *annotated and dated*: ⁂ ⁂ 21 March 1796 (5)
On Edᵈ· Burke's subscr[i]ption to Camilla for 5 Setts himself 5 his Wife 5 his lost Son, & 5 his also dead Brother!

My dearly beloved Father—
The shabbyest little bit will be better than total silence to so very delicious a Letter¹—you judged us *both* right—& for *Me,* my Eyes, as well as Heart swelled at reading those touching

191. ¹ CB's letter is missing, as is also, according to Professor Thomas W. Cope-land, the letter from Burke to Mrs. Crewe. The latter, complying in part at least with FBA's request, 'transmitted [the letter] to the Hermits' (*Memoirs*, iii. 210–11); and that she allowed them, if not to keep the letter, to excerpt the part of it relating to FBA, is indicated by a copy in M. d'A's hand (30 Misc. copies, Berg) and by another (differing slightly) in FBA's hand as preserved in the Scrapbook (Berg) 'Fanny d'Arblay and friends. England 1759–1799', p. 110. Burke's gratifying comments FBA later printed in *Memoirs* (above): '. . . the subscription ought to be, for certain persons, five Guineas; & to take but a single copy each. . . . I am sure that it is a disgrace to the Age & Nation if this [the subscription] be not a great thing for her. If every person in England who has received pleasure & instruction from Cecilia were to ⟨rate⟩ its value at the hundredth part of their satisfaction, Madame d'Arblay would be one of the richest women in the kingdom. . . .'

lines—I feared poor Mr. B[urke] had forgotten Me—but to be *so* remembered warmed yet afflicted me at once. Would it be impossible to obtain for me of dear & always KIND Mrs. Crewe the donation of the Letter? She has thousands from him—I have ONE[2] that is *worth thousands*, in his phrase,—but I earnestly covet *this other.* She will not refuse it, I am sure, if it is not envirroned with some affairs that are not *transferable.* She has an openness & a desire to give pleasure that make me not fear the request, even if it is not feasible.

That charming Mrs. Boscawen amazes me!—Speak for me, Dearest Sir,—I am touched by this Zeal in the Nephew[3] of my honoured & beloved Mrs. Delany. He has sent me one of her *last works*, an elegant mosaic Chimney piece, in cut & stained Paper—which how I prize I need not say.—*could not*, indeed. Her *little* Niece, Miss Port that was,[4] is with Mrs. Lock, & with a list round abergavenny, where she lives. Where can be the D^s of Devonshire, whose name appears no where, though she told M^{de} d'Henin she had entered it? Adieu, Dearest Sir! my Love & best wishes to my poor Mother.

192   [Great Bookham, *c.* 12 June 1796]

Conjointly with M. d'Arblay
To Mrs. Phillips

A.L. & A.L. (Berg), *n.d.*
Double sheet 4to   4 pp.
Edited by FBA, p. 1, *annotated and dated*: ✣ April. May, or June, 1796. N° 10 Genl d'A. to Mrs. Phillips during the last part of the composition of Camilla.
p. 4: My dear most partial ami's account of my writing Camilla, to my darling Susanna!—in May or June, 1796.

[*By M. d'Arblay*]

Un mot seulement à notre bonne et indulgente soeur pour lui dire qu'hier au soir ma femme entre onze heures et minuit a enfin été heureusement delivrée d'une fille qui d'après tout ce que j'en ai vu me paraît devoir, avant peu, jouer un assez beau

---

[2] See *DL* ii. 92–3.
[3] Bernard Dewes (L. 124 n. 8).
[4] i.e. Mrs. Waddington. For her list, see L. 173 n. 6.

rôle. L'accouchement est parfait, et il n'est plus question à present que d'achever promptement l'education de cet enfant appellée à de si hautes destinées. Laissant là le style figuré, j'ajouterai qu'aujourd'hui vôtre soeur est renfermée pour relire et me preparer le 8ᵉ livre tandis que j'acheve le 7ᵉ qui partira lundy matin: car il faut que vous sachiez que Mardy au soir nous avons reçu une demande de l'Imprimeur pour la premiere moitié du 3ᵉ volᵉ et même s'il etait possible la moitié du 4ᵉ pour les faire marcher de front. hier matin donc, nous avon*s* envoyé le 5ᵉ livre et lundy nous envoyons le 7ᵉ Je compte que ¹ le 17⁽ᵉᵐᵉ⁾ ou le 18 de ce mois le 8ᵉᵐᵉ livre sera copié qu'ainsi on pourra commencer à imprimer le 9ᵉ volume le 20 epoque suffisante pour que le tout paraisse à tems si les imprimeurs sont exacts et veulent imprimer une feuille par jour et nous en envoyer deux de chaque volume par chaque stage.¹

D'après cet exposé vous voyez ma bonne chere amie que nous sommes cruellement desapointés relativement au projet de vous faire lire à toutes l'ouvrage avant l'impression. Cependant si Madames Burney et Francis ainsi que Mesdemoiselles Marianne et Salley avaient la bonté de se contenter de l'entendre environ trois semaines avant la publication ce serait pour ma femme une douce recompense de son travail, et pour moi la satisfaction la plus vive. Nous vous prions toutes de penser que c'est la seule occasion où nous puissions avoir un pretexte plausible pour oser esperer une pareille reunion dans notre hermitage—

[By Madame d'Arblay]

Do *you* come as soon as ever it is convenient to you for your *stay*, my beloved, I cannot *invite* you to a mere Chapter or 2 a Day, but when you are *here* you shall read it so, if *agreeable*: but the Printers now demand to go on ¹ with all the volumes, at once, which cruelly thwarts my best ends & views. I *cannot* leave my Babe—so many thanks, but 'tis impossible. Write directly when you can come conveniently. My dearest Etty &

192. ¹ If, of the possible dates (9–12 June) for the writing of this letter, one were to choose the latest, Sunday 12 June, the timetable here supplied for the completion and printing of *Camilla* would be as follows: The printer's request for the first half of vol. iii (book v) and if possible the first half of vol. iv (book vii) was received on Tuesday evening, 7 June. On Saturday morning 11 June book v (vol. iii, first half) was sent; and on that evening between 11 and 12 o'clock, FBA completed the first draft of all five volumes (ten books). On Sunday 12 June she proposed to re-read book viii (vol. iv, second half) while M. d'A copied book vii (vol. iv, first half). Part of vol. v must already have gone to the printer (see L. 193).

Charlotte & Sally & Marianne will still, I trust, come to read it *unpublished*, though not unprinted, except for the last vol. It will be to me a *great* regale, though unhappily no benefit— my Loves to All most tender—& relate this cross &, to me, *great* mortification which I hope they will not make worse by declining the matter as it may still be.—

[*M. d'Arblay continues*]

Vous entendez que *vous* ma chere athanase c.à.d. le cher vous et ce qui s'ensuit vous viendrez quand vous le jugerez convenable à vos arrangemens et jamais assez tôt pour les notres. le thé que vous nous avez envoyé est bon, et vous voudrez bien en consequence en apporter avec vous une livre, plus une livre de celui que prend actuellement M^{de} Locke. nous suivrons votre avis et mêlerons ces deux especes. J'espère que le rhume de Mr Locke est tout à fait gueri donnez nous, je vous prie des nouvelles de James. aurez vous la bonté de lui faire nos remerciemens?[1] Mille et mille [cho]ses tendres à Chelsea, et surtout veuillez être mon interprete auprès du cher et très cher Docteur, et lui dire combien je suis reconnaissant et de son billet à M^{rs} H[artley][2] et de l'extrême bonté qui l'a fait en prendre copie pour nous l'envoyer. Adieu—adieu donc. avez vous des nouvelles de la princesse? J'ai peine encore à revenir de l'extrême surprise ou votre soeur m'a jetté mardy dernier. La demande de l'Imprimeur avait de quoi lui faire tout à fait partir la tête. Ses journées s'etaient jusqu'alors partagées sans la moindre relâche entre 4 travaux très diff^{nts} et son esprit ne paraissait pas être porté à la composition qui languissait. à peine eut elle lu la lettre que se mettant à ecrire infiniment plus vîte qu'il n'est possible de copier, elle ne quitta la plume qu'après avoir achevé la *trentieme* page de composition. Je vous jure que c'est, depuis que j'existe ce dont j'ai été le plus frappè ! ! ! Nous avons changè notre manière de vivre et nous nous en trouvons tous deux très bien. Tous les jours à 5^h $\frac{1}{2}$ au plus tard je me leve Pour elle, Rarement il est plus de 7^h quand elle quitte le lit. Nous dejeunons à 9^h precises le reste comme vous l'avez vu, excepté qu'elle se couche toujours avant 10^h—et même quelquefois avant

---

[2] This was a copy of a letter that CB had written to Mary Hartley (i, L. 3 n. 100) of Bath, acknowledging two letters from her, a subscription to *Camilla*, and the 'Brazen Hymn' (L. 186 n. 10) in honour of the d'Arblays. See a letter (Berg) from SBP to M. d'A [*pre* 12 June 1796], to which the above is a reply.

10½h· Du reste elle ne s'asseoit presque pas dans tout le cours de la journée et elle ecrit debout—

Si comme je l'espere vos arrangemens vous permettent de venir bientot faire votre etablissem^t ici—Que l'heure de dejeuner, ne vous effraye point—parceque, où nous la changerons, où vous dejeunerez quand vous voudrez—*liberté pleniere* est notre devise. qu'elle soit la votre—adieu donc—

Pardon mille et mille fois j'ai tellement griffoné cette lettre que lorsque j'ai voulu la plier il m'a été impossible—

193   [Great Bookham,] 17 June 1796

Conjointly with M. d'Arblay
To Charles Burney

A.L. & A.L. (John Comyn, grangerized *Diary*, vol. vi. 12), 17 June 1796
Double sheet folio   4 pp   *pmks*   LEATHER / HEAD   18 JU 96   wafer
Addressed: Dr. Charles Burney / Greenwich / Kent.
Markings: arithmetic on address page

June 17th 1796

My dearest Agent,—

The whole Copy we have sent to the two Printers this dear & blessed morning. The first vol. is printed all but 8 Pages—The 2^d nearly done,—the 4th d°—the third is more in the back Ground, & the 5th is up to 264.—& if the Printers go on *as sometimes* it will be speedily out of hand.¹

The *Prefatory Matter* is not yet sent; the List will take some arranging, & ceases not collecting till Monday 20th.²

On that memorable Day—Can you have the goodness to complete your agency, by receiving for us the 750?—And, if the

193.   ¹ The date of publication previously advertised as 1 July was, however, lost. In a notice dated 2 July (*The Times*, 6 July), the publishers 'respectfully informed' the subscribers that the publication of *Camilla* would be 'unavoidably postponed till the latter end of next week, when their Books will be ready for delivery from the several Booksellers to whom they have subscribed . . .'. An advertisement 'this Day was Published' appeared in the *London Chronicle* (12–14 July), as also the announcement of a seventh edition of *Cecilia, or Memoirs of an Heiress*. *The Times* did not advertise *Camilla* as this day published until 29 July 1796.
   ² *The Times* (14 June 1796) gave notice that 'THE SUBSCRIPTIONS . . . will be closed on the 20th of June, for the List of Subscribers to be printed'.

5 pr Cents[3] are open, can you deliver it to our worthy *other* Agent, Edward?[4] begging him to place it with the rest with what speed he can? If the *5 pr* C[ts] are shut, will you be so kind as to consign it to your Banker for us, till they open?—

—And besides—

Will you ask of the 3 assembling Pay Masters, when the *First Set* can be ready, for The Queen,[5] & *give orders* for its being conveyed where *you* recommended, for being very handsomely bound, in red morocco?—It must *precede* all else. We shall want 3 other sets bound *exactly alike*, & with the *utmost elegance*,—& 4 others in various ways, bound very *handsomely*, though not for presentation, & shall be greatly obliged to you to give the proper orders for us, that they may be ready before general publication, as they are for particular Book Keepers.

—And moreover—

Will you have the goodness to demand my *complete Lists* from *All* the Booksellers. & Mr. Payne will then be so good as to forward them, for my arranging, by one of the Printer's Packets | & if they proffer the Rhino thence due—you won't refuse it.—

—Also—

Will you be so kind as to settle *completely* with Mr. Payne for us, deducting at once all expences we are to pay, be they what they may, *clear*? |

We have some expectation of our fine original set meeting here next *Monday*, or *Tuesday* at latest, To Read This schtoff before publication in a Group:—I am like the *Princess sleeping in the Wood*[6]—& not *sure* how your Time stands—but *James* said

---

[3] Government 'stocks' at this time usually bore interest at 3 per cent of par value but from time to time the Government floated loans paying as high as 5 per cent, e.g. those offered in 1784 when certain Navy bills were funded.

   In January 1796 the '5 per cents' sold for a high of 104¼ but by 7 June *The Times* gave the price as 94½–94¼. The 5 per cent stock is not listed again until 7 July by which date the price had fallen to 91¾–90⅞ (see Ll. 249 and 250).

[4] See L. 157 n. 1.

[5] Of the eight presentation copies of *Camilla*, two in red and six in white and gold (see p. 195), no trace is now to be found in the Royal Libraries. The sale catalogue (8 June 1819) for Queen Charlotte's Library, however, lists (nos. 2382–3) two sets of a 1796 edition of *Camilla* (5 vols., 12mo.) which sold for 14s. 6d. each (see *A | Catalogue | of the | Genuine Library, | Prints, and Books of Prints, | of | An Illustrious Personage, | lately deceased . . .* (BM, 123. f. 16).

[6] *La Belle au bois dormant* (1724), by Charles Perrault (1628–1703). An edition of 1811 was entitled *La Princesse au bois dormant*.

he *thought* your Holydays were *now*,—James's *son* could probably be *sure*,—If—it would be *possible* you could join the party— what a joy to me such an assemblage!—We can only accommodate Esther here—Charlotte & Marianne will be at one Inn— & James at the other—Do think if it is within any practicability that I could have such a happiness—you will Chum with James in a 2 bedded room—

I dare not name poor Rosette, except to beg my kind love— for we have no room whatsoever—tho I know her kind *bread & cheese rusticity* for such a visit & such an occasion would not be disdainful. I hope she is now better.

[By M. d'Arblay]

Now, dearest brother, we all *id est*, my better half, I, & your God son we send you our best thanks with the news that the rest of the Copy of Camilla is dispatched to both the Printers, who have been very kind & will, I hope, make all that exertions to finish in time. The fifth volume will be of 23 sheets, though your Sister has been as much at work in *pruning*, as many perhaps think she was in *forcing* & *increasing*—There remains nearly 12 sheets of the 5 vol. which was not pruned.

I can hardly hold my pen—but I must tell you that if it was possible to be more grateful for your so much betering our happy condition, I should feel yet more how much the service we have received from your brotherly friendship is beyond all words, since I see what scrape we should have been put in, by the disapointment of not being paid four hundred pounds, which were destined to the printing of Camilla. That sum I had been promised with, and I expected in vain from Ireland, eight months ago.[7] An *hint* to keep our present money in old England.

---

7 FB had lent 400 guineas, evidently *pre* 1792, to Walter Shirley (1768–1859) and his mother Henrietta Maria (Phillips) Shirley (1741/2–92), widow of the Revd. Walter Shirley (1725–86) and a sister of Molesworth Phillips. See further, p. 302.

194   [Great Bookham, 20 June 1796]

To Sarah (Rose) Burney

A.L. (Osborn), *n.d.*
Single sheet small 4to 1 p. *pmks* LEATHER / HEAD 20 JU 96 wafer
Addressed: Dr. Charles Burney / Greenwich / Kent—

My dear Rosette I grieve at the impossibility of meeting this season—for we are *painting*, & driven from the Parlour to the nursery, where we reside, in defiance of a smell very disagreeable to us all, but which to you, in your delicate state, might be even highly prejudicial, if not dangerous. Yet we could not defer it, though we were most sorry to give it to our sister philips—It cost us all severe head aches at first, but we are now more inured to it—but I would not wish an *invalide* for even 3 Hours. I hope it will be quite over by your return—

I have *now* 6 proofs to correct just arrived—& all my list to alphebetize — — & I am extremely hurried, indeed—pray take care of yourself—& when our house is restored to its pure air, it will affectionately welcome you

adieu—adieu

WINDSORIANA, *Part I*

195   [*for* 5 July 1796]

To Doctor Burney

A.J.L.S. (Diary MSS. vi. 4900–[03], Berg), written at Great Bookham on 10 July [1796]

Double sheet 4to   4 pp.   *pmks*   LEATHER / HEAD   11 JY 96   20 JY 96 wafer torn

Addressed: Dᵣ Burney / Chelsea College / Middlesex.

Endorsed by CB: Fanny's / Windsor / Nᵒ 1.

Edited by FBA, p. 1 (4900), *annotated, dated, and a date retraced*: ✥ ✥ ✥ ✥ July 10 *July* 1796 (6) on the Presentation of Camilla to the Queen. Part I

Edited also by CFBt *and the* Press.

Bookham, July 10ᵗʰ

If I had as much of Time as of Matter, my most dear Father, what an immense Letter should I write you!—but I have still so many *Book oddments*, of accounts, examinations, directions ᴵᵀto Mr. ⟨Payne⟩,ᴵᴵ & little household affairs to arrange—that, with Baby kissing included, I expect I can give you, to Day, only Part the First of an excursion which I mean to comprize in 4 parts.¹

So here begins—

The Books were ready at 11 or 12—but not so *The Taylor*!²— the 3 Miss Thrales³ came to a short but cordial *handshaking* at the last minute, by appointment,—&, at about ½ past 3 we set

195. ¹ FBA's 'Windsoriana' or detailed accounts of a visit that she made with her husband to Windsor on 5–8 July, when she presented copies of *Camilla* to the Royal Family, was written in five parts, dated respectively 10, [12], 27 July, 3 and 13 Aug.

This effort FBA made to please CB, whose characteristic clamour for the successive Journals was relayed by SBP in her letter of *pmk* 25 JY 96 (Berg), printed in *FB & the Burneys*, pp. 219–21: 'My dear Father is quite disappointed at the delay of yᵣ Windsor account—for heaven's sake make haste and let him have it. I have not uttered *one word* relative to what passed there—but my Father, who has refrained from asking questions that he might hear all from yourself, will be really mortified if you keep him longer in suspense—if you have the *power* therefore let him forthwith have a new sheet.'

² Her court dress or her husband's.   ³ See i, L. 11 n. 4.

forward. I had written the Day before to my worthy old friend, Mrs. Agnew,[4] the Housekeeper, erst, of my revered Mrs. Delaney, to secure us rooms for one Day & night,—& to Miss Planta, to make known I could not set out till late.

When we came into Windsor, at 7 o'clock, the way to Mrs. Agnew's was so intricate, that we could not find it,—till one of the King's footmen—recollecting me, I imagine,—came forward, a volunteer, & walked by the side of the Chaise to shew the Postillion the House. N.B. No bad omen to worldly Augurers! |

Arrived, Mrs. Agnew came forth with faithful attachment— to conduct us to our destined lodgings ⌐at a Hair Dressers.¬ I wrote hastily to Miss Planta, to announce to the Queen that I was waiting the high honour of Her Majesty's commands,— & then began preparing for my appearance the next Morning, when I expected a summons: but Miss Planta came instantly herself, *from The Queen*, with orders of immediate attendance,— as Her Majesty would see me directly! The King was just gone upon the Terrace, but Her Majesty did not walk that Evening.

I cannot express to you my delight at this most flattering condescendsion of readiness—Mrs. Agnew was my maid—Miss Planta, my Arranger—my Landlord came to my head—& M. d'Arblay was general superintendent—the haste & the joy went hand in hand, & I was soon equipped, though shocked at my own precipitance in sending before I was already *visible*. Who, however, could have expected such prompt admission? And in an *Evening*?

M. d'Arblay helped to carry the Books as far as to the Gates. The lodgings were as near to them as possible. At the first entry towards the Queen's Lodge, we encountered Dr. Fisher, & his lady[5]—the sight of *me* there—in a dress announcing indisputably whither | I was hying, was such an astonishment, that they looked at me rather as a recollected spectre, than a renewed acquaintance.—When we came to the Iron Rails, poor Miss Planta, in much fidget, begged to take the Books from M. d'Arblay, terrified lest *French feet* should contaminate the Gravel within!— while he, innocent of her fears, was insisting upon carrying them as far as to the house—till he saw I took part with Miss Planta, & he then was compelled to let us *lug* in 10 Volumes as we could.

---

[4] Mrs. Agnew (i, L. 9 n. 8) later lived at 21 Park Street, Windsor.
[5] See i, L. 3 n. 36.

The King was already returned from the Terrace, the page in waiting told us;—'O, then,' said, Miss Planta, 'you are too late!' [*tear*], I went into my old Dining Parlour,—while she said she would see if any one could obtain the Queen's commands for another time.—I did not stay 5 minutes—ruminating upon the *Dinners*—'gone where the Chickens,' &c when Miss Planta returned, & told me The Queen would see me instantly. This second surprise really agitated me with so much gratitude & pleasure, that it lost me wholly my voice, when I arrived in the Royal presence. Miss Planta had *orders* to help me in with the Books—which shewed that they were ALL to be presented.

The Queen was in her Dressing Room, & with only the Princess Elizabeth—Her reception was the most gracious imaginable—yet, when she saw my emotion in thus meeting her again, she was herself by no means quite unmoved,—I presented my little—yet not *small* offering, upon one Knee, placing them, as she directed, upon a Table by her ^l side, & expressing, as well as I could, my devoted gratitude for her invariable goodness to me. She then began a conversation—in her old style—upon various things & people, with all her former graciousness of manner, which soon, as she perceived my strong sense of her indulgence, grew into even all its former kindness. Particulars I have now no room for—but when, in about half an Hour, she said 'How long do you intend to stay here, Madame d'Arblay? —'& I answered—'we have no intentions, Ma'am!—' she repeated, laughing, 'You have no intentions?—Well, then, if you can come again to-morrow morning, you shall see the Princesses.—'

Can you paint to yourself a higher satisfaction than this?—

She then said she would not detain me at present—&, encouraged by her extreme condescendsion in all that had passed, I asked if I might presume to put at the Door of the King's Apartment a copy of my little work?—She hesitated—but with smiles the most propitious—then told me to fetch the Books— & whispered something to the Princess Elizabeth, who left the room by another Door at the same moment I retired for the other set—

Here ends part the First. Part the second must wait a future Letter from dearest dearest Sir your

F. ⟨d'A.⟩

We could not return [*tear*] [Y]ou said you would accept a paper narra [*tear*] ⟨gh⟩ unwillingly we came on—but you shall [*tear*]—& my best love & duty to my poor Mother—[*tear*] for some better account of her—& now camm [*tear*]—Sally *should* write it—has she no author's [*tear*] her? Kind love to dear Mrs. d'y.⁶ ᴵ

[*top margin*, p. 1]

One word, dearest Sir, since our Journey allows of no more. If only to say I rec'd my Mother's kind parcel not till *Friday* last, on which day I was really quite ill wth a violent cold & headache or I believe I sh^d have told her how much I was touched by what she sent me immediately. I will write very soon. my kind love & thanks to dear Sally, whose letter I ⟨rec^d⟩ yesterday.

WINDSORIANA, *Part II*¹

196   [*for* 5–6 July 1796]

To Doctor Burney

A.J.L. (Diary MSS. vi. 4904–[7], Berg), written at Great Bookham, [12–17 July 1796]
Double sheet 4to   4 pp.   *pmks* LEATHER / HEAD   18 JY 96   wafer
Addressed: Dr. Burney, / Chelsea College / Middlesex
Endorsed by CB: Windsor audience / P^t 2^d
Edited by FBA, p. 1 *annotated*: ⌗   (7)   Presentation of Camilla   Part 2^d
Edited also by CFBt *and the* Press.

Tuesday Evening
Almost immediately upon my return to The Queen & The Princess Elizabeth,—The King entered the Apartment!—& entered it to receive himself my little offering!—How did I long

---

⁶ Dorothy Young (*fl.* 1750–1806) of King's Lynn, one of Mrs. Burney's earliest friends (*Memoirs*, i. 97–9), who had come to Chelsea to nurse her in her last illness. She was authoress of *Translations from the French* (1770).

196. ¹ 'Your 2nd Windsor acct', SBP reported on 19 July (*FB & the Burneys*, p. 224), 'has been greedily swallowed.'

to present it to him, as to The Queen, upon my knees!—but, as it was not dedicated to him, I had not courage. But my very Heart bowed down to him, in gratitude for this kind condescendsion.

'Madame d'Arblay,' said her Majesty, 'tells me that Mrs. Boscawen is to have the — — *third* set,—but the *First* — — your Majesty will excuse me!—is mine!'

This sweetness was not, you will believe, thrown away upon me; The King, smiling, said 'Mrs. Boscawen, I hear, has been very zealous?'

I confirmed this, & the Princess Elizabeth eagerly called out 'Yes, Sir! & while Mrs. Boscawen kept a Book for Madame d'Arblay, the Duchess of Beaufort kept one for Mrs. Boscawen.'[2]

This led to a little discourse upon the business, in which the King's countenance seemed to speak a benign interest, & the Queen then said 'This Book was begun *here*, Sir.' which already I had mentioned.

'And what did you write of it here? he cried;—how far did you go?—did you finish any part? or only form the — — skeleton?' [1]

'Just that, Sir;' I answered; The skeleton was formed here, but nothing was completed. I worked it up in my little Cottage.'

'And about what time did you give to it?'

'*All* my time, sir!—from the period I planned publishing it, I devoted myself to it wholly;—I had no Episode[3]—but a little baby!—My subject grew upon me, & encreased my materials to a bulk—that, I am afraid, will be still more laborious to wade through for the Readers, than the Writer!—'

'Are you much frightened?—' cried he, smiling?—As much frightened as you were before?'

'I have hardly had time to know, yet, Sir!—I received the fair sheets of the last volume only last night. I have, therefore, had no leisure for fear.—And sure I am, happen what may to the Book from the Critics,—it can never cause me pain in any proportion with the pleasure & happiness I owe to it!—'

I am sure I spoke most sincerely, & he looked kindly to believe me.

---

[2] See Ll. 171 n. 8; 180 n. 4.
[3] Austin Dobson comments on this, the earliest use of *episode* in such a sense (*DL* v. 274 n. 1).

He asked if *Mr. Locke* had seen it: & when I said no, seemed comically pleased, as if desirous to have it in its *first state*: he asked next if *Dr. Burney* had overlooked it,—&, upon the same answer,—looked with the same satisfaction. He did not imagine how it would have *passed current* with my dearest Father!—he appeared only to be glad it would be a *genuine work*: but laughingly said 'So you kept it quite snug?—'

'Not intentionally, sir, but from my situation & my haste; I should else have been very happy to have consulted my Father & Mr. Locke; ¹ but I had so much, to the last moment, to *write*, that I literally had not a moment to hear what could be *said*! The work is longer by the whole fifth Volume than I had first planned:—& I am almost ashamed to look at its size!—& afraid my Readers would have been more obliged to me if I had left so much out—than for putting so much in!—'

He laughed—& enquired who corrected my proofs? Only myself, I answered. 'Why some Authors have told me, cried he, that they are the last to do that work for themselves. They know so well by heart what *ought* to be, that they run on, without seeing what *is*. They have told me, besides, that a mere *plodding head* is best & surest for that work,—& that the livlier the imagination, the less it should be trusted to it.'

⌒

I must not go on thus minutely, or my 4 parts will be 40—but a full half Hour of graciousness, I could almost call kindness, was accorded me, though the King came from the Concert to grant it—it broke up by the Queen's saying 'I have told Madame d'Arblay that if she can come again to-morrow, she shall see the Princesses.'

The King bowed gently to my grateful obeisance for this sweet offer, & told me I should not know the Princess Amelia, she was so much grown, adding 'She is taller than you!—'

I expressed my delight in the permission of seeing their Royal Highnesses; & their Majesties, then, with looks & manners of the most indulgent softness & goodness, returned to the Concert Room. The Princess Elizabeth stayed—& flew up to me, crying 'How glad I am to see you here again, my dear Miss Burney!—I beg your pardon, ¹ Madame d'Arblay, I mean—but I always

N

call all my friends by their maiden names, when I first see them after they are married.'

I warmly now opened upon my excessive happiness in this return to all their sights,—& the extreme condescendsion & sweetness with which it was granted me,—& confessed I could hardly behave *prettily* & *properly* at my first entrance, after so long an absence. '&, I assure you I felt for you! cried she; I thought you must be agitated—it was so *natural* to you to come here!—to *Mama!*—'

You will believe, my dearest Father, how light-hearted & full of glee I went back to my Expecting Companion: Miss Planta accompanied me, & stayed the greatest part of the little remaining Evening, promising to let me know at what hour I should wait upon their Royal Highnesses.

The next Morning, at 8 or 9 o'clock[4]—my old footman, Moss,[5] came with Mlle Jacobi's compliments to *MONSIEUR & Madame* d'Arblay, & an invitation to Dine at the Queen's Lodge. I could scarce believe my Ears—my Senses!—I made Mrs. Agnew run down to him, & enquire if it were not a mistake—but he was gone—& I could only resolve to visit Mlle Jacobi *first*, & make certain whether or not Monsieur were really invited to The Queen's Lodge!

End of Part 2[d]

Sunday morn.

I have just received my beloved Father's Letter,[6] which I have just room to express my most warm thanks for—& my extreme delight my *little large Work* has met with that approbation I *most* prize of all approbations in this lower sphere—dear

[4] On Wednesday 6 July.

[5] The R.H.I., Windsor, has no record of Moss, a *footman*, but from 7 Oct. 1797–1 Jan. 1817 a William Moss, *Chairman*, appears in 'The Treasurer's Account of Her Majesty Queen Charlotte's Household' (BM Add. MSS. 17,876–93).

[6] By Sunday morning 17 July, FBA would have received CB's letters of 12 July (Berg) and *pmk* 14 JY 96 (Berg), in which he describes his 'Glutton-wise' devouring of *Camilla*—'lying in bed a full hour beyond my usual time of getting up, & making the hair-dresser wait without knowing it!' No other novel in his recollection could boast 'such good writing, thinking, & moral lessons'. Mr. Tyrold's sermon (iii, bk. v, chap. v) 'discovers more penetration, delicacy, & knowledge of the female heart, than I have ever seen in any other book in any language'. *Camilla* is 'the best system of *Education*, I ever saw . . . apart from all its wit, humour, and entertainment'.

SBP's accounts of the enthusiastic reading of the novel *en famille* are printed in *FB & the Burneys*, pp. 219–24.

to me & interesting as are many others—indeed I am quite seriously thankful for it, & receive it rather as a *blessing* than a *pleasure*.

my Love to my mother—Mrs-d-Y[oung]—& love & thanks to Sally for her very flattering & kind Letter. ⟨Pray [tell] her We do not⟩ know where to send Ld Macartney's bound sets as I could not get the direction. perhaps you will be so kind as to take them, with *my acknowledgements?*—

WINDSORIANA, Part III

197   [*for* 6 July 1796]

To Doctor Burney

A.J.L. (Diary MSS. vi. 4908–[11], Berg), written at Great Bookham on [27 July 1796]

Double sheet 4to   4 pp.   *pmks* LEATHER / HEAD   27 JY 96   wafer
Addressed: Dr. Burney, / Chelsea College / Middlesex
Endorsed by CB: Fanny's Windsor / N° 3.
Edited by FBA, p. 1, *annotated*: ⁘ ⁘ July 1796.   (8)
PART 3^d PRESENTATION OF CAMILLA TO THE QUEEN
Edited also by CFBt *and the* Press.

Miss Planta arrived at 10.[1] with Her Majesty's commands that I should be at the Queen's Lodge at 12. I stayed, meanwhile, with good Mrs. Agnew, & M. d'A. made acquaintance with her worthy husband,[2] who is a skilful & famous botanist, & lately made Gardener to the Queen for Frogmore—so M. d'A. consulted him about our *Cabbages!*—& so if they have not, now, a high flavour, we are hopeless.—

At 11—M. d'Arblay again ventured to esquire me to the Rails round the Lodge, whence I shewed him my ci-divant Apartment, which he languished to view nearer. I made a visit to Mlle Jacobi, who is a very good Creature, & with whom I remained very comfortably till Her Majesty & the Princesses returned from Frogmore, where they had past 2 or 3 Hours. Almost immediately I was summoned to The Queen, by one of

197.   [1] On Wednesday 6 July.   [2] See i, L. 9 n. 8.

the Pages. She was just seated to her Hair-Dresser. She received me with the utmost condescendsion, instantly putting away the News-papers she was beginning to examine. She conversed upon various public & general topics, till the Friseur was dismissed, & then—I was honoured with an Audience quite alone for a full Hour & half. In this, nothing could be more gracious, more sweet, than her whole manner & discourse. The particulars, as there was no pause, would fill a duodecimo Vol. at least. Among them—was Mr. Windham, whom she named with great favour; & gave me the opportunity of expressing my delight upon his belonging to the Government.[3] We had so often conversed about him, during the accounts I had related of Mr. Hastings' trial, that there was much to say upon the acquisition of administration, & my former *round assertions* of his goodness of Heart & honour.—She enquired how *YOU* did, my dearest Father, with an air of great kindness,—& when I said I well, looked pleased, as she answered 'I was afraid he was ill,—for I saw him but *twice* last year at our Music.' She then gave me an account of the removal of the concert to the Haymarket, since the time I was admitted to it.[4] She talked of some Books, & Authors,—but found me wholly in the Clouds as to all that is new. She then said 'What a very pretty Book Dr. Burney has brought out upon Metastasio![5] I am very much pleased with it.—Pray,—(smiling) what will he bring out next?'—'*As yet*, Madam, I don't know of any plan!'—'But he *will* bring out something else?—' — 'Most probably—but he will rest a little first, I fancy.'—'Has he nothing in hand?'— 'Not that I now know of, Madam.'—'O, but he soon will!' cried she, again smiling. 'He has so active a Mind, Ma'am, that I believe it quite impossible to him to be utterly idle—but indeed I know of no present design.'

[3] As Secretary at War since 1794.

[4] Since their founding date (1776) the 'Antient Concerts' had been held in the New Rooms, sometimes called the King's Concert Rooms, later, the site of the Prince of Wales's Theatre, Tottenham Street, but these quarters proving by 1775 'far too small and inconveniently situated for the . . . subscribing nobility and gentry' (of which in a list covering four years there were 400 subscribers), the concerts were moved to the King's Theatre, in the Haymarket, and in 1804, to the Festino Rooms, Hanover Square.

In 1787 the King himself had offered to enter FB's name among the subscribers (the price being originally £8. 8s. (for twelve concerts)). 'Doubtless I accepted this condescension very willingly' (*DL* iii. 216). In 1804 CB was presented with a 'General Ticket' of perpetual admission (*Memoirs*, iii. 338–9; Lonsdale, 422).

[5] See L. 149 n. 4.

We had then some discourse upon the new connexion at Norbury Park—the Fitzgeralds, &c—& I had the opportunity to speak as highly as I believe her to deserve, of Mrs. Charles.[6]— The Queen had thought Miss Angerstein[7] was dead.—from this she lead to various topics of our former conferences, both in persons & things, & gave me a full description of her new house at Frogmore,[8] its fitting up, & the share of each Princess in its decoration. She spoke with delight of its quiet & ease, & her enjoyment of its complete retirement. 'I spend,' she cried, 'there, almost constantly all my Mornings. I rarely come home but just before dinner, merely to dress. but to Day — — I came sooner.—' This was said in a manner so flattering, I could scarse forbear the air of *thanking her*,—however, I checked the expression, though I could not the inference which urged it.[1]

At 2 O'clock the Princess Elizabeth appeared. 'Is the Princess Royal ready?' said the Queen. She answered yes; & Her Majesty then told me I might go to her,—adding '*You know the way*, M[e] d'Arblay'—And, thus graciously licenced, I went to the Apartment of her Royal Highness up stairs. She was just quitting it; she received me most graciously, & told me she was going to sit for her Picture, if I would come & stay with her while she sat. Miss Bab Planta[9] was in attendance, to read during this period. The Princess Royal ordered me a Chair facing her: & another for Miss Bab & her Book,—which, however, was never opened. The Painter was Mr. Dupont.[10] she was very gay, & very charming; full of lively discourse, & amiable condescendsion.

In about an Hour, the Princess Augusta came in; she addressed me with her usual sweetness, & when she had looked at her sister's Portrait, said 'Mad[e] d'Arblay, when Princess Royal can spare you, I hope you will come to *me*?' as she left the Room. I did not *Flout* her;—& when I had been an Hour with the Princess Royal, she told me she 'would keep me no *longer* from Augusta, & Miss Planta came to conduct me to the latter.

[6] See Ll. 171 nn. 10, 11; 177 n. 4.
[7] Juliana Angerstein (1772–1846) was formerly engaged to Charles Locke but was to marry on 20 Nov. 1804 General Nicholas Sablonkoff (1776–1848).
[8] See i, L. 23 n. 4.   [9] See i, L. 23 n. 81.
[10] Gainsborough Dupont (1767–97), a nephew and pupil of Thomas Gainsborough, best known as an engraver of his uncle's works, was also a portrait and landscape painter. The *Morning Herald* (26 July) announced that the artist was at this time at Windsor painting the Princesses, but according to Mr. Oliver N. Millar, C.V.O., F.S.A., Deputy Surveyor of the Queen's Pictures, the Duponts were never in the Royal Collection.

This lovely Princess received me quite alone,—Miss Planta only shut me in,—& she then made me sit by her,—& kept me, in most sweet & bewitching discourse, more than an Hour. She has a gaiety, a *charm* about her, that is quite resistless, & much of true, genuine, & very original humour. She related to me the history of all the feats & exploits & dangers & escapes of her Brothers, during last year,—rejoicing in their safety, yet softly adding 'Though these trials & difficulties did them a great deal of good! —— —' We talked a little of France, & she enquired of me what I knew of the late unhappy Queen, through M. d'Arblay? & spoke of her with the most *virtuous discrimination*, between her foibles & her really great qualities, with her most barbarous end. ꟾ She then dwelt upon *Madame Royale*,[11] saying, in her unaffected manner—'It's very odd one never hears what *sort of Girl* she is!' I told her all I had gathered from M. d'Arblay. She next spoke of my Bambino, indulging me in recounting his *faits et gestes*: & never moved till the Princess Royal came to summon her. [They were] all to return to Frogmore to Dinner. 'We have detained M^e d'Arblay between us the whole Morning—' said the Princess Royal, with a gracious smile. 'Yes,' cried Princess Augusta, & I'm afraid I've bored her to Death—but when once I begin upon my poor Brothers,—I can never stop without telling all my little bits of glory.' She then outstayed the Princess Royal, to tell me, that, when she was at Plymouth,[12] at Church, she saw so many officers wives & sisters & Mothers, helping their maimed Husbands, or Brothers, or sons, that she could not forbear whispering to the Queen 'Mama—how lucky it is Ernest[13] is just come so seasonably with that wound in his face!—I should have been quite shocked, else, not to have had one little bit of Glory!'

[11] Marie-Thérèse-Charlotte (1778–1851), daughter of Louis XVI. In 1799 she was to marry her cousin Louis-Antoine d'Artois, duc d'Angoulême (1775–1844).

[12] This was the week 23–30 June 1794 (*The Times*, 18, 21, 23, 24, 26–8, 30 June) when their Majesties, the six Princesses, and Prince Ernest went to Portsmouth (not Plymouth) to congratulate Lord Howe on his victory, being accommodated at the Commissioner's house in the Portsmouth Dock Yard (*AR* xxxvi (1794), 'Chronicle', 16–18).

[13] Ernest Augustus (1771–1851), lieutenant in the 9th Hanoverian Hussars (1790), lieutenant-colonel (1793), major-general in the Hanoverian army (1794), who, in hand-to-hand combat at Tournay 10 May 1794 was severely wounded in the right arm and in the face. The critical condition of an injured eye he describes in requests to the King for permission to come home for treatment (*Later Corr. Geo. III*, ii, Letters 1209, 1310). See also Anthony Bird, *The Damnable Duke of Cumberland* (1966), pp. 58–63.

When forced away from this sweet Creature, I went to Mlle Jacobi—who said 'But where is Mons. d'Arblay?' I gave no hint of my *doubts*, but, finding it too late for me to go to my Lodging to Dress before dinner, I wrote him a word, which immediately brought him to the Queen's Lodge!—& there I shall leave my dear Father the pleasure of seeing us, mentally, at Dinner, at my ancient Table—*both* invited by the Queen's commands. Miss Gomm was asked to meet me,—& the Repast was extremely pleasant. ⌜As Susanna ⟨knows,⟩ he has not *peached*, I would go on, but I had stopt, for our bow. I should not like to relate a twice told tale.⌝ adieu most dear Sir,—your indulgence to Camilla is my constant regale all Day long almost all night too.—

[*top margin*, p. 1]

P.S. Best Duty & Love & kindest wishes to my Mother—& Love to Susanna, ⟨Etty, D. Young, & Sall⟩—We shall expect Susan & Fanny on Tuesday—Mrs. Boscawen really expects you now to show her *Green Book*, Miss Cam[bridge] tells me. It is to be delivered to no one else.

WINDSORIANA, Part IV

198   [*for* 6 July 1796]

To Doctor Burney

A.J.L. (Diary MSS. vi. 4912–[15], Berg), written at Great Bookham on [3 Aug. 1796]

Two single sheets 4to   4 pp.   *pmks* LEATHER   3 AU 96   wafer
Addressed: Dr. Burney, / Chelsea College, / Middlesex.
Endorsed by CB: Fanny's Windsor / N° 4
Docketed in pencil, p. 4: 1796
Edited by FBA, p. 1, *annotated and dated*: ✲ July—96   (9)
Camilla presentation continued.   Part 4th
Edited also by CFBt *and the* Press.

Just before we assembled to Dinner,[1] Mlle Jacobi desired to speak with me alone; &, taking me to another Room, presented me with a folded little pacquet, saying 'The Queen ordered me

198.   [1] On 6 July 1796.

to put this into your hands, & said Tell Mad^e d'Arblay it is from *us BOTH.*' It was an hundred Guineas.—I was confounded, & nearly sorry,—so little was *such* a mark of their goodness in my thoughts: She added, that The King, as soon as he came from the Chapel in the Morning, went to the Queen's dressing Room, just before he set out for the Levee: & put into *Her* Hands 50 Guineas, saying, 'This is for MY set!' The Queen answered 'I shall do exactly the same for Mine.' & made up the pacquet herself. ' 'Tis only, she said, for the *Paper*, tell Me. d'Arblay. NOTHING for the *trouble!*—' meaning she *accepted* that. The *manner* of this was so *more* than gracious, so *kind*, in the words *us BOTH*, that indeed the money, at the time, was quite *nothing* in the scale of my gratification: it was even *less*, for it almost pained me.² However, a delightful thought that, in a few minutes occurred, made all light & blythsome,—'We will come, then,' I cried, '*once a year* to Windsor!—to walk the Terrace, & see the King, Queen, & sweet Princesses. *This* will enable us, & I shall never again look forward to so long a deprivation of their sight.' This, with my humble gratitude for this great goodness, was what I could not refrain commissioning her to report.

our Dinner was extremely chearful: all my old friends were highly curious to see M. d'A. who was in spirits, &, as he could address them in French, & at his ease, did not seem *much disapproved* of by them. I went to my Lodging afterwards to Dress, where I told my *Mons.* this last & unexpected stroke, which gave him exactly my sensations—& we returned to Tea. We had hopes of the Terrace, as my Monsieur was quite eager to see all this beloved & benign Royal House—The Weather, however, was very unpromising. The King came from the Levee during our absence; but soon after we were in the Lodge, 3 Royal Coaches came from Frogmore; In the first was the Queen, the Princesses Royal & Augusta, & some Lady in waiting; M d'A. stood by me at a window to see them—&, to my excessive gratification, Her Majesty looked up, & bowed to me. And, upon her alighting, looked again. This, I am sure, was to see

---

² 'More—More—More!' wrote CB on 6 Aug. 1796 in his acknowledgement (Berg) of FBA's 'delightful Windsoriana', part III. 'How glad I am to recollect that I have been all my life loyal to such excellent sovereigns, & fighting & scolding with Wilkites—Foxites—Democrats—revolutionists—Jacobins—& anarchists, without knowing that such gracious goodness to you & your last born child Camilla were in the Womb of time!'

M. d'A. who could not be ¹ *doubted*, as he wore his *Croix*³ the whole time he was at Windsor. The Princesses bowed also,—& the 4 younger, who followed, all severally kissed their hands at *me*, & fixed their Eyes on my Companion, with an equal expression of kindness, & curiosity. He therefore saw them perfectly.

In a few Minutes, a Page came to say 'The Princesses desire to see Madᵉ d'Arblay.' And he conducted me to the Apartment of the Princess Elizabeth, which is the most elegantly & fancifully ornamented of any in the Lodge, as she has most delight & most taste in producing good effects.

Here the fair owner of the Chamber received me, encircled with the Princesses Mary, Sophia, & Amelia,—& *no attendant*. They were so exactly as I had left them—so kind, condescending, open, & delightful, that this was, indeed, a regale not to be appreciated. & the goodness of the Queen, in sparing them all to me thus, without any allay of ceremony, or gêne of Listening Mutes, I felt most deeply. They were all very gay, & *I* not very sad,—so we enjoyed a perfectly easy & even *merry* half hour, in diverse discourses,—in which they recounted to me who had been most *anxious* about *the Book*, & doubted not its *great success*, as *every body* was so eager about it. 'And I *must* tell you one thing,' cried the Princess Elizabeth, 'the King is very much pleased with the Dedication.' This was, you will be sure, a very touching hearing to me,—& Princess Mary exclaimed 'And He is *very difficult*!—' 'O, yes, he's hardly ever pleased with a dedication.' cried Princess Sophia,—'He almost always thinks them so fulsome,—' cried Princess Mary. 'I was resolved I would tell it you,' cried Princess Elizabeth.—

Can you *imagine* any thing more amiable than this pleasure in giving pleasure? 'Colonel Greville,'⁴ said Princess Mary, 'has been quite interested in it; & Major Price⁵ said every body *ought* to come forward upon such an occasion.' 'I assure you,' said Princess Elizabeth, every body we have seen has been quite impatient for it.' 'There have been so many *bad* books published of that sort,' said Princess Mary, 'that every body should be glad of such a good one.' 'Yes,' said Princess Sophia, '& the Writers are all turned Democrats, they say.'

³ The cross of St. Louis.   ⁴ See i, L. 16 n. 14.
⁵ Major Price (i, L. 16 n. 12), formerly of Worcester, had long known the Burneys.

I now explained that *Politics* were, *all ways*, left out: that once I had had an ¹ idea of bringing in such as suited *me*,—but that, upon second thoughts, I returned to my more native opinion they were not a *feminine* subject for discussion, & that I even believed, should the little work sufficiently succeed to be at all generally read, it would be a better office to general Readers to carry them wide of all politics, to their domestic fire sides, than to open new matter of endless debate.

Soon after, the sweet Princess Augusta came in,—smiling & lovely, to join our chattery. Princess Royal next appeared;—Princess Augusta sat down, & charged me to take a chair next her. I resisted, as Princess Royal, & all her sisters, were standing; but the former begged I would not mind her, & Pˢ Augusta would absolutely take no denial, & began clearing me a chair herself. I was forced, then, to submit, though much ashamed. Princess Royal did not stay long, & soon returned, to summon her sister Augusta down stairs, as the Concert was begun. But she replied she could not come yet; & the P. Royal went alone. We had really a more *delicious* chat, then. They made a thousand enquiries about my Book, & when & where it was written, &c, & how I stood as to *fright & fidget*. I answered all with openness, & frankly related my motives for the publicatio[n.] Every thing, of house keeping, I told them, was nearly doubled in price at the end of the first year & half of our marriage, & we found it impossible to continue so near our friends, & the Capital, with our limitted income, though M. d'A. had accommodated himself completely, & even happily, to every species of œconomy, & though my dearest Father had capitally assisted us;—I then, therefore, determined upon adopting a plan I had formerly rejected, of publishing by subscription;—I told them the former history of that plan, *as Mr. Burke's*,[6]—& many particulars, that seemed extremely to interest them. My *Garden*, our way of life, our House,—our *Bambino*,—all were enquired after, & related. I repeatedly told them the strong desire M. d'A. had to be regaled with a sight of all their House—a House to which I stood so every way indebted,— & they looked kindly concerned the Weather admitted no prospect of the Terrace. I mentioned, to the Princess Augusta, my recent new obligation to their Majesties, & my amaze & even shame

[6] See L. 173 n. 5.

at their goodness. 'O, I am sure,' cried she, 'they were very happy ⏐ to have it in their powers.—' 'Yes,—& we were so glad!—' 'so glad!—' ecchoed each of the others. 'How enchanted should I have been,' cried I, 'to have presented my little Book to each of your Royal Highnesses—if I had dared!—or if, after Her Majesty has looked it over, I might hope for such a permission, how proud & how happy it would make me!—' 'O,—I dare say you may—!' cried the Princess Augusta. I then intimated how deeply I should feel such an honour, if it might be asked, after Her Majesty had read it: & the Princess Elizabeth gracefully undertook the office. She related to me, in a most pleasant manner, the whole of *her own* transaction, its rise & cause & progress, in the Birth of Love,[7] but alas I must here abridge, or never have done—I told them ALL my scheme for coming again next July, which they sweetly seconded. Princess Amelia assured me she had not forgotten me,—& when another summons came, Princess Augusta, comically sitting still, &, keeping me by her side, called out 'Do you little ones go!—' But they loitered also,—& we went on, on, on, with our Chat, they as unwilling as myself to break it up, till staying longer was impossible—& then, in parting, they all expressed the kindest pleasure in our newly adopted plan of a yearly visit. 'And pray,' cried Princess Elizabeth, '*write again* immediately!' 'O no,' cried Princess Augusta, 'wait half a year—to rest: & then—encrease your family—*all ways*!—' 'The Queen,' said Pˢ Eliza, 'consulted me which way she should read Camilla; whether quick, at once, or comfortably at Weymouth: so I answered, Why, Mama, I think, as you will be so much interested in the Book, Mᵉ. d'Arblay would be most pleased you should read it now at once, quick,—that nobody may be mentioning the Events before you come to them;—& then *again*, at Weymouth, slow & comfortably!'—In going, the sweet Princess Augusta loitered last but

[7] A series of twenty-four drawings by Princess Elizabeth was engraved by P. W. Tomkins, 'Historical Engraver to her Majesty', and published on 17 Jan. 1795 under the title *The Birth and Triumph of Cupid*, and a second series *The Birthday Gift or the New Doll* appeared in the next year (see Stuart, *Dtrs. Geo. III*, pp. 151–4). The first series supplied the ideas on which James Bland Burges, *afterwards* Lamb (1752–1824), knight marshal (1795), cr. Baronet (1795), constructed an allegorical poem of 109 Spenserian stanzas, published in 1796, along with 'the Original Designs, by an Illustrious Personage'. The title was changed, at least in the second edition, to *The Birth and Triumph of Love. A Poem.*

'The intimate union of the graphic and poetic arts was never more delightfully exemplified', averred the *British Critic*, vii (1796), 475–80.

her youngest sister, Amelia, who came to take my Hand, when the rest were departed, & assure me she should never forget me.—

⌐what adieu, my dearest Father? yet I could not compare all, so I ⟨mus⟩t still give a 5ᵗʰ Parti, if this is not de trop—Susanna joins in kindest Love & wishes to my Mother—I have much to say of all sorts but nothing so good as *Windsor*, therefore I [omit a]ll else apart—adieu, Dearest sir, my m[ate love]s you with *Heart & Soul*.⌐

WINDSORIANA, Part V

199   [*for* 6–9 July 1796]

To Doctor Burney

A.J.L. (Diary MSS. vi. 4916–[23], Berg), written at Great Bookham on [13 Aug. 1796] with interpolations (pp. 2 and 8) by M. d'A

Two double sheets 4to 8 pp. *foliated by* FBA 1–4 *pmks* LEATHER / HEAD 13 AU 96 wafer

Addressed: Dr. Burney, / Chelsea College, / Middlesex.

Endorsed by CB: Fanny's / Windsoriana / Nº 5.

Edited by FBA, p. 1 (4916), *docketed and dated*: ⊞ July—96 (10) Part 5. Camilla Presentation

p. 5 (4920): July—96 (10) Part 5 continued Camilla presentation

Edited also by CFBt *and the* Press.

What encouragement[1] does my kindest Father give my Windsoriana—which thus proceeds.

We spent the remnant of Wednesday Evening with my old friends, determining to quit Windsor the next Day, if the Weather did not promise a view of the Royal Family upon the Terrace for M. d'Arblay, who was most eager to see them There.

Thursday Morn.[2] was lowering, & we determined upon departing, after only visiting some of my former acquaintances. We met Miss Planta, in our way to the Lodge, & took leave,

199.   [1] In the letter of 6 Aug. (L. 198 n. 2).   [2] Thursday 7 July 1796.

with every message of gratitude I could suggest to Their Majesties: but when we arrived at Mlle Jacobi's, we found, from Mlle J. that the Queen expected we should stay, for the chance of the Terrace, & had told Mlle Jacobi to again invite us to Dinner. This was irresistible: &, our visit paid, & our Dinner fixed, we went to the Lower Lodge, to see Miss Gomme There I spent a comfortable Hour, in old revivals, with her, while M. d'A. looked at a Garden of the younger Princesses. Next we visited Miss Goldsworthy[3] together, & she was so kind as to propose shewing M. d'Arblay the Apartment of the Princess Elizabeth, which is the most elegantly decorated of any at Windsor. It was agreed this permission was to be asked of Her Royal Highness against Dinner time, when we were to be at the Upper Lodge. It would be vain to attempt describing the pleasure with which I saw the favourable impression that must have been received of my Chevalier by this proposition. We left the friendly Miss Goldsworthy for other visits;—first to good old Mrs. Planta;[4]—next to the very respectable D^r. Fisher, & his Wife.[5] The former insisted upon doing the honours himself of St. George's Cathedral to M. d'Arblay, which occasioned his seeing that beautiful antique building to the utmost advantage. D^r. Fisher then accompanied us to a spot to shew M. d'A. Eton in the best view, & next walked with us to Mrs. de Luc,[6] whom I was anxious to see; *4 times* she had sought me at our Lodgings, the preceding Day,—little aware we should be so regularly, at all Hours, at the Lodge!—Here I was received with open Arms: but I saw nothing of M. de Luc, who was out, or absconded. Mrs. de Luc walked up the Hill with us back, & then upon the Terrace, & left us to make our own way up to the Round Tower. All this filled our Morning too completely for viewing the Castle, ¹ which M. d'Arblay, finding me *foot*-tired, though mind-alert, relinquished, & we only went to our Lodgings, to Dress for Dinner.

That meal, at[7] my old Table, passed as before, but the Evening lowered, & all hopes of the Terrace were weak, when the

---

[3] See i, L. 16 n. 2.   [4] See i, L. 23 n. 81.   [5] See i, L. 3 n. 36.
[6] See L. 126 n. 8.
[7] Here M. d'A inserted the addition (numbered 1): 'M^de d'Ar. oublie qu'avant le diner M^delle Planta me dit qu'elle avait reçu de la P^esse Eliz. l'ordre positif de me faire voir son appartement qu'en effet j'ai vu. il est tres bon gout.'

Duke & Duchess of York arrived. This seemed to determine against us, as they told us the Duchess never went upon the Terrace but in the finest weather, & the Royal family did not chuse to leave her. We were hesitating, therefore, whether to set off for Rose Dale,[8] when the Princess Sophia, who had permitted M[lle] Jacobi to bring me some of her work, to see how much she was improved since I left Windsor, gave an intimation to me, through the same Channel, that the King, herself, & the Princess Amelia, would walk on the Terrace.

Thither, instantly, we hastened, & were joined by D[r] & Mrs. Fisher. The Evening was so raw, & cold, that there was very little Company, & scarce any expectation of the Royal family: & when we had been there about half an hour, we began to fear the Princess Sophia had conceived false hopes for us; for the Musicians retreated, & every body was preparing to follow, —when a Messenger suddenly came forward, helter skelter running after the Horns & Clarinets & Hallooing to them to return. This brought back the straggling parties, & the King, Duke of York, & Six Princesses soon appeared.

I have never yet seen M. d'A. agitated as at this Moment. He could scarce keep his steadiness, or even his Ground. The recollections, he has since told me, that rushed upon his mind, of His own King & Royal House, were so violent, & so painful, as almost to disorder him. His Majesty was accompanied by the Duke, & Lord Beaulieu,[9] Lord Walsingham,[10] Mr. Digby,[11] & General Manners:[12] the Princesses were attended by Lady Charlotte Bruce,[13] some other Lady, & Miss Goldsworthy. The King stopt to speak to the ┃ Bishop of Norwich,[14] & some others, at the entrance, & then walked on towards us, who were at the further end. As he approached, the Princess Royal said, loud

[8] The residence of Mrs. Boscawen near Kew (L. 180 n. 2).

[9] Edward Hussey-Montagu (1721–1802), cr. Baron Beaulieu (1762), Earl of (1784).

[10] Thomas De Grey (1748–1818), 2nd Baron Walsingham (1781), Groom of the Bedchamber (1771–77), a favourite of the King.

[11] See i, L. 21 n. 8.

[12] Robert Manners (1758–1823), equerry to the King (1784–1800), first Equerry and Clerk Martial (1802–12, 1814–20); Lt.-Gen. (1803); General (1813). (R.H.I., Windsor).

[13] Lady Charlotte Bruce (1771–1816), daughter of the 5th Earl of Elgin. She was Lady of the Bedchamber to the elder Princesses from 7 May 1796 to 27 Mar. 1799 (R.H.I., Windsor).

[14] Charles Manners-Sutton (1755–1828), Bishop of Norwich (1792), Archbishop of Canterbury (1805).

enough to be heard by Mrs. Fisher, 'Madame d'Arblay, Sir.—'
& instantly he came on a step, & then stopt, & addressed me,—
&, after a word or two of the Weather, which, for grateful
surprise, I hardly heard, he said 'Is that Monsieur d'Arblay?—'
& upon my faint *Yes, sir⟨e.⟩* faint from encreasing gratitude &
delight, he most graciously bowed to him, & entered into a little
conversation; demanding how long he had been in England,
how long in the Country, &c &c, & with a sweetness, an air of
wishing us well, that will never, never be erased from our
Hearts.[15] M. d'Arblay recovered himself immediately, upon
this address, & answered with as much firmness as Respect. To
be treated as *he had been treated* seemed instantly to renovate his
best powers, & he acquitted himself as my dearest Father would
have rejoiced to see. Upon the King's bowing & leaving us, the
Commander in Chief [16] most courteously bowed also to M. d'Arblay,
& the Princesses *all* came up to speak to me, & to courtsie to
him: & the Princess Elizabeth cried 'I've got leave!—& Mama
says she won't wait to read it first!—'

Do you think I felt flattered?—penetrated?—Indeed rarely
so deeply.

After this, the King & Duke never passed without taking off
their Hats, & the Princesses gave me a smile & a Courtsie at
every turn: Lord Walsingham came to speak to me,—& Mr.
Digby, & General Manners,—who regretted that more of our
old *Tea-party* were not there, to meet me once more.

As soon as they all re-entered the Lodge, we followed, to take
leave of M[lle] Jacobi: but, upon moving towards the passage, the
Princess Royal appeared, saying 'Madame d'Arblay, I come to
way-lay you!' And made me follow her to the Dressing Room,
whence the voice of the Queen, as the Door opened, called out,
in mild accents 'Come in, Madame d'Arblay!—' |

Her Majesty was seated at the upper end of the Room, with
the Duchess of York on her Right, & the Princesses Sophia &
Amelia on her left. She made me advance, in the most condescending manner possible, & said 'I have just been telling the
Duchess of York that I find her Royal Highnesses name the

[15] This instant FBA recalled in *Memoirs*, iii. 214, as the 'proudest' of her life.
Cf. CB's delight at 'the notice bestowed on our dear Chevalier—How c[d] you keep
such circumstances so long from my knowledge!—' See letter (Berg), 23 Aug. 1796.
[16] The Duke of York, Field Marshal of the Forces (1795), officially appointed
(3 Apr. 1798) Commander-in-Chief of the Army.

first upon This list.—'[17] Producing Camilla. 'Indeed, said the Duchess, bowing to me, I was so very impatient to read it; I could not but try to get it as early as possible. I am very eager for it, indeed!' 'I have read, said the Queen, but 90 pages yet,— but I am in great uneasiness for that poor little Girl, that I am afraid will get the small pox!—And I am sadly afraid that sweet little other Girl will not keep her fortune! but I won't peep! I read quite fair. But I must tell Mad^e. d'Arblay I know a Country Gentleman—in Micklenburg,—exactly the very character of that good old Man the Uncle!'[18] She seemed to speak as if delighted to meet him upon Paper. The King now came in, & I could not forbear making up to him, to pour forth some part of my full heart for his goodness,—indeed I could joyfully have kissed his Garments!—He tried to turn away, but it was smilingly, & I had courage to pursue him, for I *could not* help it.—

He then slightly bowed it off, & asked the Queen to repeat what she had said upon the Book. 'O, your Majesty, she cried, I must not anticipate!' yet told him of her pleasure in finding an old acquaintance. 'Well! cried the King, archly, & what other characters have you seized?—' *None*, I protested, from life. 'O! cried he, shaking his head, you *must have some*!' 'Indeed your Majesty will find none!' I cried, 'But they may be a little better, —or a little worse,—he answered, but still — — if they are not like *somebody*, how can they play their parts?' 'O, yes, Sir, I cried, as far as *general nature* goes, or as Characters belong to Classes, I have certainly tried to take them. But no indiduals!' |

—My account must be endless, if I do not now curtail — — The Duke of York, the other princesses, General Manners, & all the rest of the Groupe, made way to the Room soon after, upon hearing the chearfulness of the voice of the King, whose graciousness raised me into spirits that set me quite at my ease. He talked much upon the Book, & then of the revered Mrs. Delany,—& then of various others, that my sight brought to his recollection, & all with a freedom & goodness, that enabled me to answer without difficulty or embarrassment, & that produced two or three hearty laughs from the Duke of York. Indeed, of what marble must I have been composed, not to have

[17] As is the fact, for two sets.
[18] The characters Eugenia, Camilla, and Sir Hugh, respectively.

been elated by what had passed upon the Terrace? by seeing such generous justice done so unexpectedly, as an introduction so public, by his own device, of M. d'A. to his Majesty, while the Commander in Chief was at his side?—

After various other topics, the Queen said 'Duchess, Mad^e. d'Arblay is Aunt of the pretty little Boy you was so good to.'[19]

The Duchess understood her so immediately, that I fancy this was not new to her: she bowed to me again, very smilingly, upon the acknowledgements this encouraged me to offer, & the King asked an explanation. 'Sir, said the Duchess, I was upon the Road near Dorking, & I saw a little—Gig—overturned,—& a little Boy was taken out, & sat down upon the Road. I told them to stop, & ask if the little Boy was hurt. And they said yes; & I asked where he was to go; & they said to a village just a few miles off; so I took him into my Coach, Sir, & carried him home.'

'And the benedictions, Madam, cried I, of all his family have followed you ever since!—'

'And he said your Royal Highness called him a very pretty Boy!' cried the Queen, laughing,—to whom I had related it. |

'Indeed what he said is very true!' answered she, nodding.

'Yes,—he said—quoth I, again to the Queen—that he saw the Duchess liked him!'

This again the Queen repeated, & the Duchess again nodded, & pointedly repeated 'It is very true!'

'He was a very fine Boy! a very fine Boy indeed,—cried the King, what is become of him?'

I was a little distressed in answering 'He is — — in Ireland, sir.'[20]

[19] On 26 Aug. 1792 Norbury Phillips, then 7 years old, having been taken by the Hooles for a visit to Abinger ('He tho^t it *exquisite* to go & visit the White Swan'), was being driven home on the 27th in a small chaise, which broke down about a mile from Dorking. Norbury, attempting to jump clear, fell, and a wheel ran over his leg. The Duchess of York, travelling with full retinue from Brighton to Oatlands, witnessed the accident and sent one of her suite to offer help; and after Norbury's leg had been bound up with vinegar and brandy procured from an alehouse nearby, the Duchess took him in her carriage to Mickleham and 'wth infinite sweetness & condescendsion' delivered him to his mother, Norbury chatting all the way and excitedly pointing out the Phillips house as the carriage went with full velocity down the hill to the Leatherhead road. 'How uncommonly sweet & benevolent!' The story is told in detail in SBP's letters (Berg), one to FBA, *pmk* 27 AU 92; the other to CBF, 18 Sept. 1792.

[20] This was dangerous ground, as by October 1795 Major Phillips had resigned his commission in the Marines and set out for Ireland.

In a letter (Berg) of 13 Nov. [1795] SBP relates how JB had begged Phillips to reconsider his plan but had received a light-hearted letter from the Major divulging

'In Ireland? What does he do in Ireland?—what does he go there for?'

'His Father took him, Sir,—' I was forced to answer.

'And what does his Father take him to Ireland for?'

'Because — — he is an Irishman, Sir!'—I answered, half laughing; but the King & the Duke laughed more than half, &, most fortunately, this stopt more grave enquiry: though I soon found the King has no knowledge of the resignation,—which I evaded mentioning, though not without difficulty, for General Manners asked if he were in the Army? & the King said 'In the Marines,—is he not?—'

When, at length, every one deigning me a sweet bow of leave taking, their Majesties & Sons & Daughters retired to the adjoining Room, the Princess Amelia loitered to shake hands, & the Princess Augusta returned, for the same condescendsion, earnestly reminding me of my *purpose for next year*.

And, while this was passing, the Princess Royal had repaired to the Apartment of Mlle Jacobi, where she had held a little conversation with M. d'Arblay. |

And thus ends this Charming Excursion—which has filled us with emotions of joyful gratitude & reverence & delight ever since.

We finished the Evening very chearfully with Mlle. Jacobi & Mlle. Montmollin[21] whom she invited to meet us: & the next Morning left Windsor, & visited Rose Dale.

Mrs. Boscawen received us very sweetly, & the little *offering* as if not at all her due!—Mrs. Lewison Gore[22] was with her, & shewed us Thompson's Temple.[23] Mrs. Boscawen spoke of my

---

that the resignation was already in effect. JB had since heard from William Marsden (1754–1836), second secretary of the Admiralty (1795), first secretary of the Admiralty (1804–7), 'that the step had been taken, & the resignation accepted, before [we] were informed of its being in agitation'. SBP herself had been 'a good deal shook by it—but after 3 or 4 days & nights of mental & bodily suffering, I have gradually found my quiet returning, & I have slept during the last two nights nearly as well as before this interruption'. She had then undertaken the painful task of acquainting CB with the event before he should 'suddenly hear it at Sir J. Banks's or elsewhere'. 'He & James have *more* than acquiesced in my wish of remaining silent concerning this business, at least, till there may be a Peace—.'

[21] Julie de Montmollin (1765–1841), originally of Neufchâtel, was appointed in July 1791 French teacher to the younger Princesses, receiving from 1791 to 1811 a salary of £200 a year (R.H.I., Windsor).

[22] Mrs. Boscawen's daughter Frances (1746–1813), who had married in 1773 John Leveson-Gower (1740–92), Rear-Admiral (1787).

[23] James Thomson, the poet, lived till the year of his death (1748) 'at the upper end of Kew Lane' in a cottage, one room of which was incorporated in Rosedale,

dearest Father with her usual true sense of *how* to speak of him. She invited us to dinner—but we were anxious to return to Bambino, & M. d'Arblay had, all this time, only *fought off* being ill with his remnant cold. Nevertheless, when we came to Twickenham, my good old friend Mr. Cambridge was so cordial, & so earnest, that we could not resist him, & were pressed in to staying Dinner. I have not seen him more pleasant many years.—& M. d'A. was much taken with his original humour, when he told him 'he knew he should not like Camilla, —for Cecilia was a work to have wholly exhausted its writer's powers, & that *no Characters* could remain for her.

We next repaired to Charlotte's, at Richmond, & saw her lovely Children, & poor altered little namesake, & she accompanied us to dear Aunt Beckey,—who received us with very strong emotion, but the utmost kindness. Here we sent for Etty,—& drank Tea.

And, at a little before Eleven, we arrived at our dear Cottage, & to our Sleeping Bambino, delightfully well under his excellent superintendant's care:[24] but *she* was in bed,—& we would not speak with Baby till Morning, though he awoke, lest we should hurry his little intellects. In the Morning, we watched over his Cradle till he awoke. He then stared at us, with infinite Surprise; we would not aid his recollection by our speech; it seemed soon to come to him— | but with doubt & uncertainty—he looked from one to the other, & then looked down, as if ashamed,— then again examined us—& then suddenly smiled, & held out his little hands, & sprung forward to our arms.

⌐——⌐

I wrote immediately to order 6 setts, bound in White & Gold, for the 6 Princesses:[25] & I have had A Letter from Miss Planta, with all their Thanks, most condescendingly expressed, & further Words of the graciousness with which the Queen

---

the house later built on the site. A 'little rustick seat' in which he was popularly said to have written some of the *Seasons*, Mrs. Boscawen found in ruins in 1787, but 'reserving all the materials', she explained in a letter of 1797, 'I have replaced it in a retir'd part of the garden, much enlarg'd and hung round with votive tablets or inscriptions in honour of [the] admir'd poet. His bust is on the pediment of the seat, and in front is written "Here Thomson sung the seasons and their change." In the alcove is a little old table, which I am assur'd belonged to him.' See Aspinall-Oglander, *Admiral's Widow*, chap. xix, and p. 142.

[24] In the care of SBP. [25] See L. 193 n. 5.

received the acknowledgements I left behind for all her goodness.[26]

Thus deliciously all has concluded—& now I want 2 sheets more to thank my dearest Father for his most kind Letter & communication. I was quite touched by this fresh testimony of the Queen's graciousness, to Mr. Langton,—& very highly gratified by Mr. Langton's approbation.[27] I have things to say you will kindly take part in, upon that Camilla subject,—but nothing to come home to me like what drops from your own generous pen, my kindest Father—your pleasure in giving delight redoubles its power over the receiver. My Mother's partiality, which I hear of all round, is truly flattering,—& most sincerely welcome—you will easily believe!—Love to Her & Sally & Mrs. D[orothy] Y[oung] I hope you go to *Mr. [illegible]*—He has been my best Bookham Friend!—adieu, ever dearest Sir. Susanna is at Norbury Park for a few Days, with Fanny. Willy we still durst not see, for the Cough is not wholly gone. Bambino is much plagued with his Teeth, [but kno]ws no other care.

[26] Here M. d'A made a second addition (numbered 2): 'j'ai été obligé de repaier en français une petite omission de M$^{d\langle e \rangle}$ d'Ar. qui est restée à diner à Norbury où nous etions allés faire une visite'.

[27] In a letter (Berg) of 6 Aug., CB had related how on a visit to Edmond Malone he had met Bennet Langton, who obligingly reported a conversation he had had with the Queen on the subject of *Camilla*. Asked what he was reading, he had replied: ' ". . . Madame d'Arblay has occupied me so much, day & night, of late, that I have been able to read nothing else"—When the Q^n brightening up, & expanding both her hands, say—"& do you like it so much?—I am so glad!" '

To Mrs. Waddington

A.L.S. (Berg), 18 July [17]96
Double sheet small 4to   1 p.   *pmks*   LEATHER / HEAD   20 JY 96
wafer
Addressed: Mrs. Waddington, / Lanover Court, / Abergavenny.

Bookham,
July 18.—96.

once again I hav[e] the pleasure of writing to my ever dear
Marianne *expressly*—though I shall now say but 5 WORDS—for
I would not so utterly monopolize her, much as I am in arrears,
as to add more to the 5 immense Volumes I conclude her now
wading through. Yet I cannot with a safe conscience content
myself with giving her only public employment, till I have
thanked her in private for her Letters, her Zeal, & Kindness.
I could not be ready exactly to my Day—but when you see the
size of the volume I have entirely added to my first intentions
of length,[1] you will acquit me of being dilitory, or unpunctual,
—for the promised 4 vols might have been ready some months
before they could have been demanded.

I hear of your Abbé Lajard[2] with the same praise you bestow
upon him—but I have never seen him—but I can enter upon
nothing now, save enquiries after your health—& rejoicings at
your late accounts of it—& of your flourishing little ones—
& Mr. W[addington]—My Bambino I now indulge myself
with having endlessly around me in his little sportive plays—
God bless you, my dear friend—ever tenderly yours is

F. d'A.

200.   [1] Volume v, the thickest, runs to 556 pages.
   [2] L. de Lagéard (1754–1845), abbé de Cherval, former grand Vicar of the
diocese of Rheims, Abbé commendataire de l'abbaye de la Cour Dieu, Orléans
(1780), whom Mrs. Waddington had probably met in Bath in this year (see Bunsen,
i. 31–2), where he is described as 'M. Lajand de Cherval, an emigrant, and a man
of brilliant conversation, who had been in the intimacy of Talleyrand when he was
in his ecclesiastical splendour'.

201   [Great Bookham, *post* 31 August 1796]

To Mrs. Phillips

A.L. (Berg), *n.d.*
Double sheet large 8vo   3 pp.
Addressed: Mrs Phillips
Dated in pencil: 1795(?)
Edited by FBA, p. 1, *annotated*: ⁕ M. de Lally—

⌐I can make no ⟨cove⟩nants, my Susan, ⟨more⟩.¬

M. d'A. will write about the money—but join our names
most cordially in the invitation to Edward, whom we long to
thank *here* for his kind exertions. We cannot now return the
Letter of attorney,[1] as we wait for Mr. Locke to sign it. We
imagine it will only defer receiving the interest, & that the delay
is there fore immaterial, as we are just now in possession of
Money we mean—hope, at least, to replace by that very interest.

We shall write to Charles of the £82 — — & beg he will take
of you what is wanted.

Surely the Letters shall be always yours,[2] my beloved Susan!
—we have put the things from the bag safe — — — we have
just made a larger bag, & therefore shall re-place the original
one, & re-fill.

I grieve to return M. de Lally's incomparable Book—I have
been delighted and enlightened by the Letters to the Electors,
& the pieces justificatives[3]—I think *never* more by any ⏐ writing
I ever read. there is a nobleness of *MIND* & of *STYLE*, of thought
& of expression, so strikingly combined, that eloquence has
rarely seemed to me so natural, & never more penetrating.
That any Country can voluntarily throw away such a statesman
—such an Orator—such a Citizen?—You know how forcibly I
was struck by M. de Lally from the first—you will not therefore
wonder I am now quite enthusiastic for him. Warmth &
sensibility such as his, joined to a candour that seems above all
prejudice, on any side, or for any party, or purpose, or even

201.   [1] See L. 157 n. 1.
   [2] Probably the Journal-Letters that SBP had written in the 1780's and 1790's to
FBA, by this time running to hundreds of pages (see *Catalogue*).
   [3] *Mémoire . . . ou seconde lettre à ses commettans.* (*Pièces justificatives, contenant différentes
motions de M. le Comte de Lally-Tolendal.*), published in Paris in 1790.

wish, make me reverence now as before I admired him. always, when you can, remember me to him, & to your adored Princesse,[4]—how I wish you could spend more time with such consolatory beings!—That poor Me de Chav[agnac] should go, at last, without her husband amazes & concerns me—[5]

We are seeking every where in the dorking | vicinity a new dwelling—but the difficulty of finding any thing is immoderate. Nevertheless, as this is the sole period in which we can hope to bear the expense of removing, we are ardent in the search: for the dearness of provisions & the difficulty of obtaining the common comforts of the family board, milk, butter, &c, makes us unwilling to establish here for life: & the *sight* of M[r] Locke oftener is well worth a few Guineas a year. God bless my ever dearest—dearest Susan!—I could say too much more to venture at any thing. Thank my beloved Father for his charming Letter[6] —& his Susy for her dear bit. Bambino is pretty well.

202   [Hill Street, Richmond,
                                post 3 September 1796]

To M. d'Arblay

A.L. mutilated (Berg), *n.d.*
Single sheet 8vo 1 p. one line sliced off at the bottom
Edited by FBA, p. 1, *annotated and dated*: Aug[st] or Septr 1796   (6)
Sent back Express to my kindest Friend from Richmond whither I had gone to see my sisters Esther & Charlotte conveyed by Mrs. Cooke—

My most beloved Ami will find he had more foresight than myself in supposing this excursion might lead to an interview

[4] The princesse d'Hénin (ii, L. 68 n. 17).
[5] Agathe-Françoise de Montecler (1773–*pre* 1808), who had married in 1790 Louis-Vigile, comte de Chavagnac (1765–1819). The couple had emigrated, living for a time in Brussels, where their son Henri was born in the summer of 1794. With the French conquest of the Netherlands, however, they fled to England, landing at Harwich *c.* 22 Jan. 1795 (PRO, H.O. 1/3), and their daughter Adrienne was born in London *c.* 3 Dec. 1795 (L. 215 n. 12).
   Encouraged by the establishment of the Directory (27 Oct. 1795), many of the *émigrés* were now returning to France in the hope of reclaiming property or establishing inheritances, and apparently among them, Mme de Chavagnac. See also Mme de La Tour du Pin, *Journal*, ii. 99–101, and chap. vi.
[6] This is CB's letter (Berg) of 23 Aug. 1796, acknowledging Part V of FBA's 'Windsoriana'. M. d'A's reception 'upon the Terrace' was an event beyond the Doctor's 'hopes' and 'fondest desires' (*Memoirs*, iii. 214).

with my poor Susanna—I hear she is so deeply afflicted,[1] that I have accepted my dearest Ami's permission that I should prolong my stay, if it could lead to a meeting. Charlotte will go, purposely, with me to Town immediately—but we shall be only in Downing Street, & not make known the journey, that Susanna may come to me there alone:[2] & to-morrow I shall return to my most cherished & cherishing Home—My Heart's beloved,—& my darling Bambino.—

[*part of line sliced away*] I shall come back

203 [Great Bookham, 10–11 October 1796]

To Mrs. Phillips

A.L.S. (rejected Diary MSS. 4930–[3], Berg), *n.d.*
Double sheet 4to 4 pp. wafer
Addressed: Mrs. Phillips, / at Capt. Burney's, / James Street, / Westminster.
Endorsed by SBP: rec^d Octr 12^*th* 96.
Edited by FBA, p. 1 (4930), *top margin, dated*: Octr 10th & 11th 96.
Edited also by CFBt *and the* Press.

How touching is every line of my beloved Susan's Letter![1]— but what a pang was the Day named—the *Friday*—to my Heart!

202. [1] The Major had returned from Ireland, arriving in London on Saturday evening 28 Aug. *without* Norbury but with immediate plans of returning to Bel-cotton, County Louth, with his wife, daughter, and youngest child.
The circumstances are related by SBP in a letter (Berg) of Wednesday 31 Aug.: 'The Major wrote to me from Buxton no doubt to prepare me for not seeing my poor Norbury—and yet a lingering hope remained—that a wish might exist for once to surprise me delightfully—I acknowledged it scarce to myself—but c^d not crush it—Saturday eve^g however on returning home with Fanny from Mad^e de Chavagnac's—I heard the Major was arrived—& that he was alone—finding me absent he was gone out in the expectation of meeting with me—I was not sorry to have thus a little while alone to subdue an excess of chagrin before out meeting—He says he *wished* to bring me Norbury—but he was out of town . . . & Mr Maturin [his tutor] thought he would lose ground by such long holydays—'.
[2] As may be seen from SBP's despondent letter of [11]–15 Sept. 1796 (Berg), the meeting between the three sisters had taken place on [11] September in CBF's apartments in Downing Street. Apparently encouraged to 'wifely submission', SBP later assured FBA (see same letter) that 'the terrible struggle is over—I think I shall be capable of submitting as you would have me—not from *mere* despondence—but from something better—that despondence may not at times seize me I do not presume to hope . . . but I intend to subdue it when I can, & to make such efforts as I am able to support myself for the sake of those who w^d make every effort for me—'.
203. [1] This letter (now missing) had apparently been written on SBP's return to London on Friday 7 October after a farewell visit to Great Bookham and Norbury

little as I wish it retarded from elemental reasons, since to retard is not to obviate.—Prosperous may it prove to my darling sister —in the sight of her Norbury,[2] in finding him all he left her, & all she wishes him. I think of the dear fellow with added fondness from the good I feel I shall owe him in his Mother's revival. What claims, too, are those of Fanny! — — I think, too, accutely of the sinking of our beloved Father when you are gone—what ties has my Susan for care! to renovate her strength, brace her nerves, & support all her fatigues.—I have a thousand things to say, & nothing I like to write but benedictions of the little Boy whose smiles & raptures await you, & earnest, earnest recommendations to excessive attention to warmth, dryness, & all that best contribute to restore & preserve health. Bear us all in mind, my most loved Susan, forever & ever upon this most interesting of all worldly concerns.

When you were gone—& I could not see the Chaise from the gallery Window—whither I ran from the many Eyes in the Hall, I could only go to your deserted room—& only pray for your safety & restoration—till our angel friend followed me up —& would take upon her sweet self all of consolation, in rosiest hopes, which she mixed with praises so soothing & so just & so touching of my dearest Susan, that soon I found all the benefit her benign heart could wish me from her participated feelings. Norbury, still, was the theme of comfort to both—

About an hour after, we went to the drawing room, to dearest Mr. Locke, where, very soon, we were interrupted by Mr. Hartsinke, the comtesse de Bylande, his Sister, & the Comte & Admiral, his Brother in Law.[3] They had given orders to let in

Park. Friday 14 October was the day first set by Major Phillips for his departure from London, as see SBP's letter (Berg) of 8 Oct. 1796 to CBF.

A view of the preparations is given by CB in his inquiry (Berg) of [Sept.] 1796: 'Your 2d recd of our poor dear Susan's health has comforted me a little for the present; though it cannot extend to the future, with such a journey, such a voyage, & such a season before her! I am fearful that this half mad & unfeeling M[ajor] means to travel to the seaside in a strange kind of open carriage, wch is constructed with a basket that is to contain the whole family! . . . such a one he has been driving about. If I find that his plan, I shall remonstrate, though ⟨Susan⟩ & prudence wd not let me attempt to interfere abt the Irish Journey: as I had no hope of working upon his wrong-headed & tyrannical spirit by anything I cd say or do; & there was great reason to fear the making bad worse, by putting him out of humour, since we *must*, circumstanced as we are, submit.'

[2] Norbury, it was felt, was purposely left in Dublin to ensure SBP's acquiescence in the journey.

[3] Jan Casper Hartsinck (1755–1835), lately Minister at Hamburg for the recently deposed Prince of Orange, had migrated to England in August 1796, and,

no one,—but these were persons they could not refuse. They regretted extremely all interruption ⌐ to the only subject we could any of us keep in mind. The Bylandes seem very good sort of people. She is perfectly well bred, & he bears an excellent character. They are nearly ruined by the French Revolution in Holland, whence they came over to England with the Stadtholder.[4] They are going to pass 3 Months at Mr. Boucherette's.[5]—I escaped as quickly as I dared, for my Monsieur loves not my shyness, which I try to vanquish therefore: I stole to dear Amelia, who had been seeking me—& took refuge in her room & sweet sympathy for the rest of the morning. We spoke scarce an instant but of my Susan.—one thing, however, struck me; in speaking of Miss White[6] & the amiable young man whose regard for her you have heard of, she said—'I question if ever she may meet with another man who may shew her so sincere a partiality, with so fair a character—' & afterwards, she added, as if with regret, 'she knew very little of him—very little, indeed!—' this with an expression that appeared to mark some regret of having been obliged to take a decisive part, before certain if it were right or wrong. I really believe the young man in question lost Miss White more by his own unguarded impetuosity than by cool judgment on her part. Had he quietly kept back from *all* overtures, & followed without such obvious views, I very much suspect he would have succeeded. The *Cadeau*, too, a la sorella seemed very kind. Miss White also,

related by marriage (i, L. 16 n. 10) to John Julius Angerstein, often visited Norbury Park. His sister Susanna Cornelia Maria Hartsinck (1758–1824) had married in 1786 Frederik Sigismund, graff van Bylandt (1749–1828).

[4] William V (1748–1806), Stadtholder of the Netherlands, Prince of Orange-Nassau-Dietz, left the Netherlands on 18 Jan. 1795 after the French conquest of his country. Crossing to England, he 'arrived and left Harwich, all facilities being offered to him' by 22 Jan. 1795 (PRO, H.O. 1/3). At this time the comte de Bylandt had directed the escape of the Princess of Orange, Frederica Sophia Wilhelmina (1751–1820), who had married in 1767 William V (above). See letters between Jan Casper Hartsinck and the Princess, in one of which he thanks her for allowing 'his sister to accompany her in the fishing boat' (*Family Papers*, ed. Samuel H. Day, 1911).

[5] See L. 150 n. 14.

[6] A pseudonym for Amelia Locke (1776–1848). Cf. the epithet 'white-souled Girl' used by SBP in her reply of 13–14 Oct. (Berg).

The parable here concerns the Irish family: Elizabeth Cuffe (1746–1830), who had married 2 Oct. 1769 James William Wall (1744–1819) of Coolnamuck, County Waterford, but who, for the years 1795–6, had rented a house in Mickleham (so shown in the Land Tax Assessments); her son Charles William Wall (1772–1843); and their daughter Elizabeth 1776–1823). Evidently Charles Wall's courtship of Amelia Locke, though approved by his mother, failed through the precipitancy described. For the conclusion of the history, see L. 222.

she said, wished extremely that the Mrs. Madre should know how sensible she was to her great kindness, & feared she doubted or disbelieved it; but she felt it very strongly nevertheless, though she was awkwardly situated for expressing it. 'Indeed, she very sweetly said, Miss White must always be *very* grateful for such marks as she received of esteem, where most parents would have consulted only fortune, & have been ¹ against such a connection.'—

I made my escape at dinner time, & we returned to our dear little Home, yet harping only upon my darling Susan—& there my Bambino revived me beyond all else—his playful unconscious gaiety absorbed me nearly till his early hour of rest—but my Night was *troublous* & Saturday & Sunday⁷ I was head-ached, & compelled to keep my room—blessing Heaven for such a dear refuge—so uncommon & so consolatory. Monday I thought it requisite to go to the Fair⁸—& the exertion & air & pretty scene cheered me extremely: & since then I have been quite *well* in health—& studied all the roses of our ange Amie to reconcile me to being better in mind & hopes. Forced spirits aid real ones, where the *will* assists—& mine has every motive to assist.

Miss Ogilvie⁹ came to the Fair & looked very lovely.— Amelia was still a little saddened by your departure even in air & manner—Augusta is returned in perfect health [& Mrs.] Charles looking well, but much *worsted* by sea air—her husband all fond devotion to her, & both thoroughly happy. I believe the sufferings of 3 successive *losses of promise* occasioned the little changes we heard of in disposition¹⁰—for I have seen her this morning as interesting & as sweet & soft & amiable as I ever thought her. She is *indeed*, I believe, a truly sweet Creature— William is very serious, but very gentle, he retires from all to painting, & mixes scarce at all with the party now at Norbury.

This is going to ⟨save⟩, if possible, the pacquet—if not for the post—My Bambino will not quit me, in fear I ¹ should again

---

⁷ The days 7 and 8 Oct. following SBP's farewell visit.
⁸ The Fair at Leatherhead.
⁹ Emily Charlotte Ogilvie (*c.* 1779–1832), who was to marry in 1799 Charles George Beauclerk (1774–1846).
¹⁰ Cecilia and Charles Locke (L. 177 n. 4) had spent the summer of 1796 at Lavant, a country house near Chichester lent to them by the Duke of Richmond, where boating had been their chief amusement. Augusta Locke had visited them there and in the autumn the party returned to Norbury Park. Cecilia was expecting a child, Emily Frederica, to be born on 12 Dec. (*Locks of Norbury*, pp. 115–16).

leave him—for I made off this morning to West humble. Mrs. Cooke has been here with kindest enquiries, & full of gratitude for your note, & admiration for its writer—

My other self is full of sanguine expectations of a speedy return—& we mean to struggle hard for the occupation of a new habitation this Winter. I conjure you to write a *single line* at all opportunities upon the journey, from beginning to end. It will be most gratefully & solicitously received & watched for. O how shall we long for news

And now adieu, my own most beloved Susan!—God Almighty return you to us speedily & well? & again & again—& ever & ever let me supplicate the utmost care of a health & existence precious to so many! My tenderest love to my very dear Fanny & kiss honest affectionate little William for your true—faithful —anxious & fond sister

F. d'A.

204   Great Bookham, [14] October 1796

To Doctor Burney

A.L.S. (Diary MSS. vi. 4924–[7], Berg), Oct. 1796
Double sheet 4to   4 pp.   *pmks*   LEATHER / HEAD   17 OC 96   wafer
Addressed: Dr. Burney, / Chelsea College, / Middlesex.
Endorsed by CB: Octr 1796
Edited by FBA, p. 1 (4924), *annotated*: ⁂ (10) (12) Mrs. Phillips. astonishing Sale of Camilla
Edited also by CFBt *and the* Press.

Friday, Oct.—96.
Bookham—

How well I know—& feel the pang of this cruel Day[1] to my beloved Father! my Heart seems visiting him almost every minute in grief & participation. Yet I was happy to see it open with a smiling aspect, & encourage a superstition of hoping it portentous of a good conclusion. All here are persuaded that the Major is *already* tired of Ireland, ⌜& mostly returns because he cannot in any decency remain in England, after his *retiring*

204. ¹ The day fixed by Major Phillips for departure.

upon half pay when the pretence was his insuperable avocations in Ireland.¹¹ This dear Soul, therefore, we suppose taken to *lighten* to him his banishment, by making him a *chez lui*; & raising his credit by his but too excellent choice. That he loves her I still believe, though with a selfishness so imperious, tyrannical, & absorbing, that not one mark of regard can break out of the adamantine fortifications of his egotism that could oppose, or restrain, his own smallest will or wish. —— —

I am almost afraid to ask how my poor Mother bore the last farewell—indeed I hope She was *virtuously* cheated of a leave-taking. I advised Susan to avoid it if possible, as the parting impression would be lighter by such management; &, much as she is recovered from her *very* terrible state, she cannot be too cautious of emotions, of almost any sort—much less of such a separation. Our ⌐ sorrow, however, here, has very considerably been diminished by the Major's voluntary promises to Mrs. Locke of certain & speedy return. I shall expect him *at the Peace*! —not before. I cannot think it possible he sᵈ appear here during the War—except, as now, merely to fetch his family.

But I meant to have begun with our thanks for my dear kind Father's indulgence of our extreme curiosity & interest in the sight of the Reviews.² I am quite happy in what I have escaped of greater severity, though my Mate cannot bear that the palm should be contested by Evelina & Cecilia, his partiality rates the *last* as so much the highest. So does the News paper I have mentioned, of which I long to send you a Copy.³ But those immense Men whose single praise was Fame & Security, who established, by a Word, the two elder sisters, are now silent—Dr. Johnson &

---

² FBA little knew what an active part CB had been prepared to take in 'fixing' the reviews. See Appendix B, p. 368.

³ This newspaper has not been located; but by this time two criticisms had appeared. The *English Review*, xxviii (Aug. 1796), 178–80, and the *Critical Review*, xviii (Sept. 1796), 26–40, quoted generously from *Camilla*, but, while respectful of its moral purpose and its author, were restrained in praise. 'This novel is not such as we expected.'

To follow were the *Monthly Review*, xxi (Oct. 1796), 156–63, with its long list of verbal and grammatical inaccuracies (L. 211 nn. 1 and 2); the *Scots Magazine*, lviii (Oct. 1796), 691–7, with a reprinting of 'The Public Breakfast' (6 pp.); the *British Critic*, viii (Nov. 1796), 527–36, with seven pages of quotations; and a brief laudatory paragraph in the *Monthly Magazine, and British Register*, iii (Jan. 1797), 47.

The reviewers in general praised the heroine, the 'invention', the 'highly animated scenes of life and manners', and the value of the work as a '*warning*' guide to youth, but deplored the 'immoderate length' of the novel, the improbability of many of the characters, Gallicisms, errors in grammar and diction, and the use of dialect.

Sir Joshua are no more—& Mr. Burke is ill, or otherwise en-
grossed.[4] Yet,—even without their powerful influence, to which
I owe such unspeakable obligation, the *essential* success of
Camilla *exceeds* that of the Elders: the sale is truly astonishing,—
Charles has just sent to me that 500 only remain of 4000!—& it
has appeared barely 3 Months!—

The first Edition of Evelina was of 800.—The second of 500
—& the 3d. of 1000.—what the following have been I have
never heard. The sale from that period became more flourishing
than the generous Publisher cared to announce.[5] Of Cecilia the
first Edition was I reckoned *enormous* at 2000.[6]—& as a part of
payment was reserved for it, I remember our dear Daddy Crisp
thought it very *unfair*. It was printed, like this, in July, & sold
in October,—to every one's wonder. Here, however, the Sale
is encreased in rapidity more than a third. Charles says

Now heed no more what Critics thought 'em

Since this you know—All People bought 'em. — —

⌐How very much M. d'Arblay is obliged to you for the
Peltier[7] & the kind promise of more in future exchange. It is a
work of highest possible interest to him. He meant to have
written *this Letter* himself but my Heart is so full of what I know
my dearest Father's to be filled with also, that I have taken *all*
the paper & shall make over to him the next time. He is, all this
morning digging up his last crop, I fear, of Potatoes from our
orchard.

We have not been able to find any small House that could
replace this, & This requires a hundred pounds for repairs, 'tis
in such bad winter plight.⌐ We have therefore resumed our

4 CB, reporting in a letter of 23 Aug. 1796 (Berg) the favourable reactions to
Camilla that he was able to elicit from his acquaintances, had regretted extremely
that 'Poor Mr Burke has been too ill to read your book! A complaint in his bowels,
brought on by grief & fretting wch has driven him to death's door—He has been
at Bath for some time—'. According to *Memoirs*, iii. 215–16, Mrs. Crewe had quoted
him as saying: ' "How ill I am you will easily believe, when a new work of Madame
d'Arblay's lies on my table, unread!" '

5 Thomas Lowndes (1719–84), in the Strand. Cf. his letter to CB of 27 Jan. 1779
(Barrett, Eg. 3695, f. 12): 'I'll soon get ready 500 of the 1500 for wch the Cuts are
ingraving. This 500 must come out as 3d Edition & the remaining 1000 may be
ready for the Cuts.' Also a letter of 5 Sept. 1782 (*DL* ii. 481–2): 'I printed 500, and
afterwards a Second Edition of 500. . . .' Between this evidence and FBA's recollection of the business, the total will be seen to fall between 2,500 and 2,300 copies
for the first three editions.

6 Cf. *Burford Papers*, pp. 74, 81; *ED* ii. 307.

7 Probably parts (or fascicles) of the series, *Paris pendant l'année 1795-[1802]*
(35 vols., 1795–1802). Cf. ii, L. 68 nn. 25, 37.

original plan, & are going immediately to build a little Cottage for ourselves. We shall make it as small & as cheap as will accord with its being warm & comfortable. We have relinquished, however, the very kind offer of Mr. Locke, which he has renewed, for his Park: we mean to make this a property *salable* or *lettable* for our Alec—& in Mr. Locke's park we could not encroach any Tenant, if the youth's circumstances, profession, or inclination should make him not chuse the Spot for his own residence. M. d'Arblay, therefore, has fixed upon a field of Mr. Locke's, which he will rent, & of which Mr. Locke will grant him a lease of 90 years.[8] By this means, we shall leave the little Alex: a little property besides what will be in the Funds, & a property likely to rise in value, as the situation of the field is remarkably beautiful. It is in the valley, between Mr. Locke's park & Dorking, & where Land is so scarce, that there is not another possessor within many Miles who would part, upon any terms, with half an Acre. My kindest Father will come & give it, I trust, his benediction. I am now almost *jealous* of Bookham for having received it.—Imagine but the extacy of M. d'A. in framing All his own way an entire new Garden! He dreams now of Cabbage Walks—potatoe Beds—Bean perfumes & peas' blossoms. My Mother should send him a little sketch to help his Flower Garden, which will be his second favourite object. Alex has made no progress in *phrases*, but pronounces single words, a few more—adieu, most dear Sir,

My Love to my Mother & to Clarentine[9]—I hope to see her in the next paccellone—

ever most dutifully & most affectionately your

F. d'A

8 Refusing a parcel of land offered in the Park, M. d'A had accepted in the outer part of Mr. Locke's lands a field of 5 acres, which with the possible adjunct of an adjoining field of 7 acres would make an estate, of which the disposition might be separate from that of the Park. See M. d'A's statement (Barrett, Eg. 3700B, ff. 88–9b).

9 Sarah Harriet Burney's first novel *Clarentine* (3 vols.) was published anonymously by G. G. and J. Robinson, Paternoster-row, appearing, according to *The Times*, c. 7 July 1796, at the price 10s. 6d. It was favourably reviewed in the *Monthly Mirror*, ii (Nov. 1796), 416; and the *Monthly Review*, xxi (Dec. 1796), 452–6, commended its ease in language, 'vivacity of dialogue, and morality of sentiment'. 'To say that some of the conversations are insipid, and some of the characters unimportant, would be to censure the manners of the age, rather than the novel.'

205   Chelsea College, 22 October 1796

To M. d'Arblay

A.L. (Berg), 22 Oct. [17]96
Double sheet 4to   3 pp.   *pmks* ANDERSON   22 OC 96   wafer
Addressed: Alexander d'Arblay Esqr, / Bookham, / near Leatherhead, /
Surry.
Edited by FBA, p. 1, *annotated*: (7)   on my arrival at Chelsea College after
the Death of my Mother in Law.

Chelsea College,[1]
oct^r 22d.—96.

How sweet a surprise was this Morning's post!—dearest &
most kind I felt it, & doubly that to-morrow will be a blank—no
post comes in, & I shall think it very long indeed to wait till
Monday even now that the separation is thus solaced.—I found
my beloved Father tolerably composed, & most truly kind.—He
has kept me by him uninterruptedly, & by him I am now writing. He goes, however, this afternoon to Greenwich, to spend a
few Days with Charles, at his most eager solicitation. He wishes
me to stay here mean while, & till after the Funeral,—This it is
impossible to refuse, or to wonder at, for he holds it a duty that
the last remains should not be abandonned. Sally stays also, &
Marianne is come from Titchfield Street to pass here this
interval. I will write further particulars on Monday. I am not
without hopes of prevailing | with my dearest Father to come to
us after his return from Greenwich. I am inexpressibly glad he
will quit this melancholy scene for the present: & he goes more
contentedly for leaving me in the house. James has the charge

205. [1] At the news of Mrs. Burney's death on Thursday morning 20 Oct. 1796, FBA
had gone immediately to Chelsea College, where she was to remain for the funeral
(27 Oct.), returning to Bookham only on 31 Oct.
   CB's grief and desolation emerge in the letters he wrote to those friends who,
having been entertained through the years at his home, best knew Mrs. Burney,
i.e. Ralph Griffiths, 2 Nov. (Bodleian), Christian Latrobe, 14 Nov. (Osborn), and
Thomas Twining, 6 Dec. (Berg). Arthur Young also, whose friendship went back
to the days at King's Lynn and who had promoted the union, could now conceive
of his sorrow (7 Feb. 1797, Berg): 'When I am at home, I shut myself up in the
room where every thing I see reminds me of what I can see no more! I sit in the
same chair wch used to be occupied by the dearest part of myself! . . . ' See also
'Memoirs' (Berg).

of all the Mourning orders & regulations.² My Father talks with pleasure of our Alexander — — he says he thinks him the most *fascinating Child* he ever saw.—Do you believe this sours me much? And he is as anxious as ourselves about the innoculation; & permits me to run over to him all the dear Bambino's words, & *faits et gestes*, & always smiles & listens to that exhaustless strain. He names my best friend with sweet affection—& has given me 3 more vaillant's³ for him—& bids me say he *PRESENTS* him the two Reviews,⁴ to bind up ⌐ as the new volume of *Camilla Jugemens*. ⌐He will get two more to compleat his own set. But pray take great Care of Vaillant & Peltier volumes he will have returned by the first opportunity.

No French papers have appeared these 13 Days past, yet a pacquet is already returned from Calais with news of the safe arrival of Lord Malmsbury.⁵ The paper to Day has nothing official, but general foreign news of Moreau's⁶ continued difficulties, & Buonaparte's reverse of fortune with the deaths of General Berthier, & General Serrurier in Battle.⌐⁷

Write my tenderest Love to my dearest Mrs. Locke & her's,—

² Mrs. Burney was interred in the old burial ground of Chelsea Hospital, her epitaph reading: In Memory of / Elizabeth Burney / died 20ᵗʰ October 1796 / Aged 68. The registers of St. Margaret's Church, King's Lynn, however, give the date of her birth as 23 Jan. 1725.

³ This refers to François Le Vaillant (1753–1824) and his *Second Voyage dans l'intérieur de l'Afrique* (1795). Translations of 'the 3d, 4th, and 5th Volumes, in Octavo' were advertised in *The Times* (24 June 1796) under the title *Travels into the Interior Parts of Africa by the way of the Cape of Good Hope*.

⁴ Probably the *English Review* and the *Critical Review* (L. 204 n. 3).

⁵ James Harris (1746–1820), K.B. (1778), cr. Baron Malmesbury (1788), Earl of (1800), M.P. (1770–4, 1780–8), who, having gone over with 'the old Whigs' to Pitt, was employed as a diplomat (see *DNB*). High hopes were placed in his mission when on 18 Oct. 1796 he set out for Paris (*The Times*, 20–28 Oct.) 'as a Minister Plenipotentiary' to 'negotiate a Peace'. 'Of Lord Malmesbury's mission, we augur the happiest consequences', wrote the *Oracle* (9 Nov.). 'Convinced of the sincerity of the British Government, we have reason to think that the Directory have, in some degree, receded from their inordinate projects of ambition.'

Great, in converse, therefore, was the disappointment when, at the insistence of the British Government that the Directory return the Netherlands to the rightful rulers, the negotiation failed. War was the alternative, and the diplomat was ingloriously recalled in December. 'This Mongrel has been whipped back to the Kennel yelping & with his Tail between his Legs', wrote Burke, 25 Dec. 1796, to Mrs. Crewe (Add. MSS. 37,843, ff. 125–6).

⁶ Jean-Victor Moreau (1763–1813), General, and Commander-in-Chief of the French Army on the Rhine and the Moselle (1796), had lately suffered reverses at the hands of the Austrians (*The Times*, 22 Oct.).

⁷ Louis-Alexandre Berthier (1753–1815), prince and sovereign of Neufchâtel (1806–14), prince de Wagram (1809), maréchal de l'empire; and Jean-Mathieu Philibert Sérurier (1742–1819), maréchal de France (1804), both of whom were with the French armies in Italy and both reported by *The Times* (22 Oct.) to have been 'killed in action'.

but don't send away my Letter—keep for yourself what for yourself is written, my First, best, & MOST dear of all that I prize upon Earth—& HOPE for in Heaven!—

Kiss my Alexander *very softly*, & sans barbe, for his Maman.

206   Great Bookham, 23 October 1796

M. d'Arblay
To Madame d'Arblay

A.L. (Berg), 23 Oct. 1796
Originally a double sheet 4to, of which FBA later discarded the second leaf   2 pp.
Edited by FBA, p. 1, *annotated*: 8
Received ⌐written⌐ on my arrival at Chelsea College after the Death of my Mother in Law.

Bookham 23. October—96
à 2ʰ après midy

Quelle bonne, aimable, charmante, et delicieuse lettre![1] Je ne puis dire qu'elle me tiendra lieu de celle qui l'a ecrite, mais je sens qu'elle me rend son absence plus supportable. J'y aurais repondu à l'instant même mais j'en ai été empeché par l'arrivée du Jeune Alphonse[2] qui en ce moment est à lire au coin du feu, car je ne veux pas perdre cette poste, et Jenny[3] portera elle même ma lettre à Leatherhead. Je lui ai donné permission d'aller voir son oncle.

Quand ton epître est arrivée, j'etais à dejeuner avec Babey qui me tient fidele compagnie. Je venais de lui verser sa tasse de lait, que j'ai posée sur la table pʳ rompre le cachet. Il commençait a se plaindre—je lui ai dit en ouvrant la lettre—c'est une lettre de Maman—aussitôt il m'a repeté pour la 100 fois au moins—*Mama all gone!* avec un petit air, qu'il n'a jamais eu avant; et il ᴵ est resté tranquille. Au milieu de ma lecture il m'a tiré par le pan de mon habit en disant—'Papa? Mama all

206. [1] FBA's letter of the previous day, L. 205.
   [2] Here FBA later interpolated: 'le fils du vicomte, apres Duc de La Chartre, & ambassadeur en angleterre' (ii, Intro., p. xvi).
   [3] An unidentified servant.

gone!' Alors je lui ai dit de baiser la lettre, et il me l'a laissée achever; puis je lui ai donné sa tasse. A peine avait il fini de boire qu'il a pris la lettre. 'Hum Hum.' et il me la tendait. Je lui ai dit 'Yes Mama's letter!

Aussitôt il l'a portée à sa bouche et l'a baisée deux fois mais avec une expression qui m'a fait eprouver une sensation qu'il me serait impossible de decrire. à cela j'ajouterai que cette nuit, à deux fois differentes il a parlé en rêvant et, c'à été pour dire mam—mam—mama! ce qui m'avait aussi beaucoup touché, mais non pas autant. [xxxxx *3 lines*]

[*the second leaf is missing*]

207   Chelsea College, 24 October 1796

To M. d'Arblay

A.L. (Berg), 24 Oct. 1796
Originally a double sheet 4to, of which FBA later discarded the second leaf   2 pp.
Edited by FBA, p. 1, *annotated*:   (9)
From Chelsea before the Funeral of my Mother in Law

Bookham—
Chelsea—oct. 24. 96

What sweetly touching traits of my little darling![1] & how sweetly told!—keep me still in his dear mind, & let me find him as I left—& as you paint him. O how do I long & languish to have you give him again to my arms—

⌐I am a little surprised at the dispensation granted by our Mrs. Locke but doubt not its being right.[2] I honor it; on *Wednesday*; *Thursday* I must hope you will not leave home as it is the day of the Funeral, ⟨alas⟩, that once past, there will be no longer any want of attention.¬

My dearest Father is at Greenwich, with Charles; he lives entirely in an Apartment made sacred to him, & has his own servant alone, [only he] & my Brother, ever approach him at

---

207. [1] As narrated in M. d'A's letter, L. 206.
    [2] Some relaxation in the etiquette of mourning or of mourning dress?

present. This Week over, I am convinced he will accept every comfort that his family can propose him. I have strong hopes he will return with me, but no | promise. Sally is returned again to that softer & fairer character I have told you I so much loved formerly. I foresee in her a change the most favourable in all respects from living only with so sweet a Nature as my dearest Father's. It is now my own Ami will know that Father. He evidently wishes to call all his Children about him, to receive & bestow the affections long pent or restrained, rather than manifested & indulged. His Heart has never been shut, but his ARMS now are opened again—as affectionately, as tenderly as Mine will be to my Alexanders *alMOST*.

I fancy I shall be back on Friday.[3] My Father comes on Thursday,—& that Day I shall surely devote to him: but I believe no longer.

⌐What will you do about your Mourning? have it made at Dorking—or shall I order it for you of Mr. White?[4] He has your measure, I conclude Mine has been brought¬

[*the second leaf is missing*]

---

208   Great Bookham, 25 October 1796

M. d'Arblay
To Madame d'Arblay

A.L. (Berg), 25 Oct. 1796
Single sheet 4to   2 pp.   cover missing
Edited by FBA, p. 1, *annotated*: 10
Received at Chelsea College, ⌐whither I went alone to see¬ while I remained with my dear Father upon ⌐the news of¬ the Death of my Mother in Law.

Bookham ce 25. Oct^{bre} 1796

Pourquoi mon amie, en achevant ta lettre ne suis-je pas aussi content qu'aprés avoir lu la derniere?[1] Dis moi franchement etais tu bien dans les mêmes dispositions en les ecrivant? Yes

---

[3] On Friday 28 Oct.
[4] Possibly White & Son, Breeches-makers, 23 Old Bond Street (1810), but there are other Whites listed as tailors in the commercial directories of the time.
208. [1] FBA's letter, no. 207.

you *must hope*—You must even be sure I will not leave home to morrow.

Si tu as le moindre doute sur la maniere dont tu es desirée, et dont tu seras reçue in the dear hermitage, Jamais dans aucun culte l'objet de l'adoration de ses sectateurs n'a du compter sur la sincerité de l'hommage et des voeux qui lui etaient offerts. Mais non, je me trompe il est de l'essence de la divinité de ne pouvoir etre trompée! Que n'as tu comme elle le pouvoir de lire au fond des coeurs—Tu n'en verrais aucun aussi bonnement aussi tendrement aussi entierement à ce qu'il aime! |

Oui tu seras *aumoins* accueillie à ton retour par ton petit Alexandre qui plus joli que jamais ne passe pas une heure sans parler de *Mamma*, dont il vient encore de baiser la lettre pour la 7ᵉ fois. Je te jure que c'à été sans que je le lui aye dit. Dès qu'il a su qu'elle etait de toi, et surtout après que je lui ai eu lu, *Mama loves babey very much & will return, I hope, very soon*; il me l'à prise des mains et s'est mis à la baiser, puis à lire lui même, ensuite à la baiser encore et à me la donner pour que j'en fisse autant; ce qu'il a repeté à differents intervalles.

Tu m'enchantes en me repetant que tu n'es pas sans esperances d'amener le cher docteur. Songe qu'il faut que je le sache afin d'avoir un lit et une *grate* / un gril / que je ferais arranger dans *la book room.*

209 [Great Bookham, 1 November 1796]

To Doctor Burney

A.L.S. (rejected Diary MSS. 4934–[7], Berg), *n.d.*
Double sheet large 4to   4 pp.   *pmks* LEATHER⟨   ⟩ 2 NO 96
wafer
Addressed: Dr. Burney / Chelsea College / Middlesex
Endorsed by CB: N°1 1796—after last / quitting Chelsea.
Edited by FBA, p. 1, *annotated and dated*: ⊞ 2 Novʳ –96 ⌜(11)⌝ (13)
Alex, under two year's of age—reception of his Mother after a few weeks parting from her. Spending them with her honoured Father after the Death of his Second Wife.

I can make no delay in writing to my most dear Father though I know he will have heard of my safe arrival at my Hermitage from his Coach man. But I leave with him so much of my heart that I yearn for immediate intercourse—for intercourse almost unbroken. Yet my journey,[1] though safe, was *very near having an accident*; after we had passed Leatherhead, & the postilion had received his final directions for Bookham, & I knew we had only to go strait forward, I read without looking up, till some jolts in the road surprised me; I then sent round my Eyes, & saw unaccustommed objects; saw, in short, I was upon an open & extensive common, & upon a rarely beaten track. Luckily, my £33:0.0. for our Workmen did not occur to me, or I might have been still more *consternated*; however, my sugars & soaps, [& various stores, for winter consumption, were too nearly my Companions to be forgotten, and][2] I called to ask the driver what way he was going? The right, he answered; however, I begged he would enquire, as it was an unknown track to me; & he | alighted, & went back to a Barn, where he saw some people; the Horses being sufficiently gentleized by 18 miles at a stretch not to be alarmingly frisky. He returned, & said he had turned short out of the road, & was on the Kingston Common.—Thus I was near a nocturnal visit to Chesington, that would not there have given more surprise than at home excessive inquietude. The Man was too civil & obliging, however, to let any other sort of terror mix with that of a late arrival, & a little consideration of the uses of my pacquets to others as well as myself, had I encountered any one who had a knack at that sort of calculation.

My Hermit came to the Chariot with his little Companion; but I motioned that the latter might be carried back, lest I should lose the soft pleasure of his recollection from my changed & melancholy attire. And when all was entered, & the carriage & the Postilion were exited, I had him put into the parlour where we sat, without a word of introduction. He came frisking forward, | expecting to see only his Papa; but at sight of me, stopt short, & stared. I had slipt a loose long Gown on, over my other; yet he seemed at first uncertain who I might be. I kept still & silent. So did his Father; he looked from one to the other for some explanation; but, meeting none, advanced, slowly, but with brightening Eyes & rosier Cheeks, pulling his little fingers

209. [1] Evidently on 31 Oct.
  [2] The lines in brackets FBA substituted for two lines that in her editorial capacity she had obliterated. Of the original there can be read: 'which had so recently escaped the [xxxx *3 words*] I was [xxxx *4 words*] exertion, as'.

with mingled embarrassment & agitation. Still I kept quiet, &
he came close up to me; when, running away again, he fetched
his little arm Chair, &, sitting down upon it immediately next
me, affected to fall out of it, crying 'O—h dea!—' which was
his last favourite play with Me previous to my quitting him. We
were not, then, very long from each other's arms; & he soon
grew so happy, so affectionate, & carressing, that he would not
leave me a moment: except when the Maid came into the
Room upon any errand, to dart forward, & push her out again,
with vehement testimonies that he was not to be fetched away.
But when at last, the fatal knell of Seven rang in our Ears, & his
nurse-Maid came to claim him, he could | scarcely endure the
horrour with which he was seized upon regarding another
separation as settled. He tried again his little Forces of resistance,
but, finding them ineffectual, flew to seek refuge in a Closet;
there she followed, & he left her, to plant himself at my sides,
where he appealed to me with looks of such reproach at my not
supporting him, that—it is *not nothing* that I did not let him stay
by me till Midnight! Then he tried remonstrance with his
Betty,[3] in a language he seemed to invent as he spoke, of energetic prayer. She told him his supper was ready—he kissed her,
as if to thank her, but fearfully, & keeping his little figure back,
while his face was thrust forward: & then he retreated again,
yet more earnestly seeking a reprieve. — —

This has occupied a[ll] my paper & time—my anxious hopes
of speedy News of your health, & my kindest love to Sally is all
that remains. I have not a minute or a space left for the much
my Monsieur commissioned me to say for him—nor for the
Sincere & kind Compliments &c of Mr. & Mrs. Locke, who
sent to me immediately to enquire how you did. Lady Rothes[4]
& Lady Harriet Leslie[5] have just been here but I could not see
them. Heaven bless my most dear dear Father! prays his dutiful
& affecte

F. d'A.

[3] Elizabeth Parker, possibly the nursemaid employed for a time by SBP.
See SBP's Journals for 1787 (Osborn).

[4] See i, L. 12 n. 13.

[5] Lady Harriet Leslie (1777–1839), daughter of the Countess of Rothes and Sir
Lucas Pepys, who, like her brothers and sisters, took the name Leslie. She was to
marry in 1804 William Courtenay (1777–1859), 10th Earl of Devon (1835).

210   Great Bookham, 7 November 1796

Conjointly with Mrs. Locke
To Mrs. Phillips

A.L.S. & A.N. the first leaf and a part (2·7 to 2·8 × 7·4″) cut from
the second leaf (Diary MSS. vi. 4946–[7b], Berg); and the remainder
(5·9 × 7·3″) of the second leaf (Barrett, Eg. 3690, f. 171–b), 7 Nov. 1796
    Originally a double sheet 4to (8·7? × 7·3″) 4 pp. mutilated as described
in Textual Notes   *pmks*   LEATHER / HEAD   9 NO⟨   ⟩
12 NO ⟨96⟩   black seal
    Addressed: Mrs. Phillips, / at George Kiernan's Esqr, / Henry Street, /
Dublin
    Endorsed by SBP: Novr 13th / –96.
    Edited by CFBt.

[*By Madame d'Arblay*]

Bookham, Nov. 7th
—96.

Yes, my most beloved Susan, *safe landed at Dublin*[1] was indeed
all sufficient for some time—nor, indeed, could I even read any
more for many minutes. That, & the single sentence at the end
'My Norbury is with me—' compleatly overset me, though only
with joy: After your actual safety, nothing could so much touch
me as the picture I instantly viewed of Norbury in your arms.
Yet I shall hope for more detail of so dear a circumstance
hereafter.

The last Letter I had from you addressed to myself shews me
your own sentiment of the fatal event[2] which so speedily followed
your departure, & which my dear Father has himself announced
to you; though, probably, the News-papers will anticipate his
Letter. I am very sorry, now, I did not write sooner; but while
you were still in England, & travelling so slowly, I had always
lurking ideas that disqualified me from writing to Ireland.—
of all that now no more—

The minute I received from Sally, by our dearest Father's
desire, the last tydings, I set out for Chelsea. I was much

210. [1] SBP's letter (Berg) to FBA, dated 31 Oct. 1796, with *pmk* 3 NO, had
reported her arrival ('*safe landed at Dublin*').
    [2] Mrs. Burney's death on 20 Oct.

shocked by the News, long as it has been but natural to look forward to it. Affliction, indeed, I felt not,—it was impossible where so unearned—but concern I felt, in various ways, both for herself & my Father. The better part, also, always rises highest after the worse part can no more displease. *My* better part spoke even before myself upon the propriety of my instant journey, & promised me a faithful nursing attendance during my absence. I went in a Chaise, to lose no time: but the uncertainty how I might find my poor Father made me arrive with a nervous seizure upon my voice that rendered it as husky as Mr. Rishton's. While I settled with the Postillion, Sally, James, Charlotte & Marianne came to me in the little yard. Esther & Charles had been there the preceding Day; they were sent to as soon as the event had happened. My dearest Father received me with extreme kindness; but though far—far more calm & quiet than I could expect, he was much shaken, & often very faint. However, in the course of the Evening, he suffered me to read to him, various passages, from various Books, such as conversation introduced, &, as his nature is, as pure from affectation as from falsehood, encouraged in himself as well as permitted in us whatever could lead to chearfulness. Had this fatal Scene past a few years ǀ sooner, I am convinced he could not Thus have borne it—that poor self tormentor had not an *Enemy* ⟨cleared⟩ from the House by my quitting its residence!— I am satisfied that, from that period, our so long-enduring Father became more clear sighted to her frailties, &, indulgently as he continued to bear them, ceased to persuade himself he had nothing to bear. The happiness of sweet recollection upon his own patience & sweetness is now indeed, & evidently, his, & this poor soul uttered thanks for them ultimately in the most touching manner, before sally & the maid, upon their last —as it proved, parting, at 11 or 12 at night. I am much rejoiced at this, which is also an awakener to very suffering feelings towards the poor departed, as well as a source of constant peace to the reflections of the beloved survivor.

Let me not forget to record one thing that was truly generous & tender in my poor Mother's last voluntary exertions. She charged Sally & Molly[3] both not to call my Father when she appeared to be dying—& not disturb him if her death should

---

[3] The servant Mary More (ii, L. 68 n. 30).

happen in the Night, nor to let him hear it till he arose at his usual time. I feel sensibly the kindness of this sparing consideration & true feeling.

Yet — — Not so would *I* be served! O never should I forgive the misjudged prudence that should rob me of one little instant of remaining life in one who was truly dear to me! Nor do I believe my poor Father would have been any more thankful than myself had this been tried by *our* Mother—for his unmixed adoration covetted living upon her parting breath to its last sigh—but here, alas—so much was previously gone of happiness in the Union,[4] that the tenderness of his pitying nature, not the penetrated affections of his heart, was all that seemed remaining.

Nevertheless, so yielding is his temper, so unapt to seize, & yet less to retain any thing ungentle, that I shall not be surprised to have his first shock succeedd by a sorrow it did not excite. He will forget all that was alienating, by dwelling only on what was formerly attractive, & I fear he will require much watching & vigilance to be kept as well as I have quitted him.

I had had some little hope to draw him to Bookham—but he had already ┃ engaged himself to Charles for Greenwich, & I was well contented, as his removal from Chelsea was all I most earnestly desired. He wished me to remain upon the spot, with Sally & Marianne, till after the Funeral—& till his return. I was gratified to discover any wish, & stayed that time, & 5 Days longer; & then felt very reluctant indeed to leave him, though very solicitous to return to my own Treasures—I was most unceasingly sorry you were gone—You would have proved to him such a comfort!—However, I now hope looking forward to your return may be an exhilarating point of view always before [him.]

I delighted to see our worthy & dear James once again there upon his own proper & deserved footing. All the funeral arrangement was put into his hands, & left to his care.

The Letter of the good Mrs. D[olly] Y[oung] upon this occasion, though extremely tender & full of affection & grief,

---

4 FBA's opinion is much at variance with the testimonies of past happiness to be read in CB's letter of 2 Nov. 1796 (Bodleian), for instance, wherein he speaks of his bereavement 'of a bosom friend & rational companion of 30 years, who had virtues, cultivation, & intellectual powers, sufficient to make home not only desirable, but preferable to places where amusement is sought & promised; add to this a similarity of taste and coincidence of opinion in all matters of wch the discussion is apt to ruffle the temper and alienate affection, & who can calculate my loss'.

is by no means the Letter she would have written before her last visit!⁵ —— I obtained 5 Days of our dearest Etty at Chelsea. Think of the sweetness of my Father—the very night of my arrival, he wanted her to come, that I might see her, &, when he expressed his wish she should be in the house The Day of the burial, he added '& ask her to come as soon before as possible— you may be together here so happily—' This was an inexpressibly touching proof of observations long dormant that had stopt any such proposition ever from being made before—

This subject has engrossed all my paper—I am sure, however, you will wish for all intelligence upon it that give you any information of our dearest Father. Sally behaves very amiably & affectionately. I perceive she will rise into a much fairer & smoother & more pleasing character from this change. Her independance, from my Father's excessive indulgence, may, indeed, be feared; but her intentions are good, & her temper & her manners are both most sensibly improved. I have the happiness—& it is a very considerable one—to feel myself loving her again as before the alteration in her had estranged the partiality I originally conceived for her. *Partiality* I only thought it from the period her mingled flippancy & bluffness had lessened my regard.—

I have said nothing in answer to your dearly welcome Letter though I could have filled one with only my joy,—but I feel this will be interesting, & I hope to have another Call for writing very soon. Our Ange will begin the next, & the tag end will be mine

[*By Mrs. Locke*]

Sunday even^g

When I wrote my scrap 2 hours ago I fervently hoped that my beloved Friend was safely landed & now Heaven be praised! I have the blessed certainty of it—my joy was so great that it was not till a second reading that I thoroughly comprehended all she suffered—the good was so uppermost—our dearest kindest Fanny came herself with the precious letter she arrived

⁵ It is difficult to see what FBA could have found lacking in Dorothy Young's tributes to her lamented friend or in her estimates of the value of a life 'devoted to the endeavour of making others happy; a benevolence alltogether divested of every thought of self; a whole system of virtuous habits, approaching the nearest to perfection of any character I ever knew' (see her letter to CB [20 Oct.], Osborn).

with her dear Partner just as we had done dinner, & what a desert!! and now in the short space I have left I must say how vexed I feel that my own best Friend shou'd have expected to hear from me & been disappointed.—our Fannys sudden departure & all her melancholy business while at Chelsea prevented her communicating how I was to direct, & I took it for granted that till your arrival in Dublin we shou'd not have a direction— I suspect that a miserable half sheet written on in every possible & *impossible* corner never reached you it was directed to James Street—it was written immediately

our dearest Fanny looks delightfully well altho she had had a cold. *our*, your Amelia insists upon a particular mention of her in that you have seen your Norbury—after I had folded the dear Manuscp^t Music to my heart—God bless you most precious Friend all mine joy with the tenderest joy—

[*Concluded by Madame d'Arblay*]

Give m[y l]ove to the Major—& to my dear Fanny Norbury [& W]illy. My Monsr is forever in his Field—the house [not] Yet begun, but the orchard planted. The well is 6[o f]eet deep, yet no sign of water!—adieu, my most dear precious Sister! He[aven] bless you ever & ever!

F. d'A.

My Bambino is flourishing in [health] looks & spirits.

211   Great Bookham, 8 November 1796

To Doctor Burney

A.L.S. (Diary MSS. vi. 4942–[5], Berg), 8 Nov. [17]96
Double sheet 4to   4 pp.   *pmks* LEATHER / HEAD   9 NO 96   black seal
Addressed: Dr. Burney / Chelsea College / Middlesex
Endorsed by CB: N° 2 / 1796
Edited by FBA, p. 1 (4942), *annotated and date retraced*: ⁑ 8.—96   (14)
On the Reviewers on Camilla—after a visit of Condolence to Dr. B on the Death of Mrs. Burney his 2^d Wife.
Edited also by CFBt *and the* Press.

Bookham,
Nov. 8.—96

I had intended writing to my dearest Father by a *return of
Goods*; but I find it impossible to defer the overflowings of my
Heart at his most kind & generous indignation with the
Reviewer.[1] What Censure can ever so much hurt as such compensation can heal? And, in fact, the praise is so strong, that,
were it neatly put together, the writer might challenge my best
Enthusiasts to find it insufficient; the truth, however, is, that
the criticisms come forward, & the panegyric is entangled, & so
blended with blame, as to lose almost all effect. What of *verbal*
criticisms are fair, I shall certainly & gladly attend to in the
second edition: but most of them are of another class, & mark a
desire to find them that astonishes me; for I have no consciousness of any enemy, & yet only to enmity can attribute the
possibility of supposing 'A man & Horse *was* sent off—' could
be other than an error of the press. A Chambermaid, *now adays*,
would have written *were*. 'An *admirable* good joke', also, is the
cant of Clermont, not of the author; who might as well be
accountable for the slip slops of Dubster. '*Nor* have I *no* great
disposition'—must be an *invention*, I should think. Certainly I
never wrote it, whether it be I in the Book or not. I had not time
for an errata—which might, methinks, have been observed, in
some candid supposition that, otherwise, a few of the verbal
errours might have been corrected.[2]

211. [1] On reading the critique of *Camilla* by William Enfield (1741–97) and Ralph
Griffiths (see Appendix B, p. 368), which had appeared in the *Monthly Review*,
xxi (Oct. 1796), 156–63, CB had written the indignant letter of [2] Nov. (Diary
MSS. 4938–40; partly printed in *DL* v. 296–7). Part of his reaction is in print
('J'enrage! Morbleu!') but one part FBA had later scratched over with obliterating
marks: 'There is praise', CB had written, '& now & then handsome praise; but it
seems given designedly with a sparing hand; though the *strictures* are numerous, &
often severe & unfair. Well, but this praise will never be supposed to come from
Dr Charles—as was predicted. Sall shall make a *parsellina*, & inclose this Review for
your inspection & M. d'Arblay's collection of *Jugemens*—If no better than this are
in store I sh^d wish it to be the *last*.'
  Approved were 'the highly animated scenes of life and manners' by which the
plot was brought forward; 'the rich and varied groups of characters'; and the
'general structure' or 'succession of painful and delightful images', all of which
'must deeply interest the feeling heart'. Among serious faults, however, were
inconsistencies in character portrayal with resultant improbabilities in action.
Moreover, the novel was too long. As FBA remarked, praise and blame were
inextricably mixed. See further L. 214 n. 3.
  [2] What troubled FBA most and 'enraged' CB (see above) was the list of grammatical errors, Gallicisms, colloquialisms, and dialectal words (op. cit., p. 162).
FBA's attribution of the errors to the printer will not, however, stand investigation.
In such corresponding parts of the manuscripts of *Camilla* as are extant (Berg) at least

The Reviews, however, as they have not *made*, will not, I trust, *mar* me. Evelina made its way all by itself: it was well spoken of, indeed, in all the Reviews, compared with general Novels;[3] but it was undistinguished by any quotation, & only put in the Monthly Catalogue, & only allowed a short single paragraph.[4] It was circulated only by the general public, till it reached through that unbiassed medium, Dr. Johnson—and thence it wanted no patron. This circumstance made me easy about Cecilia, which, however, was extremely well treated, though not by them, but by Mr Burke brought forward to the high station its supporters have claimed for it. Camilla, also, will live or die by more general means. Works of this kind are judged always by the *many*: works of science, History & philosophy & voyages & travels, & poetry, frequently owe their fate to the sentiments of the first Critics who brand or extol them. |

Miss Cambridge asked me, early, if I should not take some care about the Reviews? No, I said, none. There are two species of Composition which may nearly brave them; Politics & Novels: for these will be sought & will be judged by the various Multitude, not the fastidious few. With the latter, indeed, they may be Aided, or injured, by Criticism; but it will not stop their being read, though it may prejudice their Readers. They want no Recommendation for being handed about but that of being NEW, & they frequently become established, or sink into oblivion, before that high Literary Tribunal has brought them to a trial. She laughed at my composure; but, though I am a good deal chagrined, it is not broken. If I had begun by such a perusal, I might indeed have been disturbed: but it has succeeded to so much solace & encouragement, that it cannot penetrate deeply. The respected opinion of Mr. Langhton,[5] the perpetual praise

six of the errors of which the reviewer complained may be clearly seen (with no correction) in the copy. The copy is in M. d'A's hand with corrections and revisions in FBA's hand. In her reading of this copy at least, she had failed to pick up the errors.

Vol. v, bk. x, chap. 8: she laid down in her cloaths
Vol. iii, bk. vi, chap. 3: one of the horses laid dead
Vol. i, bk. i, chap. 1: born to almost nothing
Vol. iv, bk. viii, chap. 7: not equally adroit as Henry

[3] e.g. the *London Review of English and Foreign Literature*, vii (Feb. 1778), 151, allowed *Evelina* 'much more merit' with respect to 'stile, character and incident, than is usually to be met with among our modern novels'.

[4] 'The Monthly Catalogue, for April, 1778', the *Monthly Review; or, Literary Journal*, lviii (Apr. 1778), 316. There was a long review, however, in the *Critical Review*, xlvi (Sept. 1778), 202–4.

[5] As reported by CB in his letter (Berg) of 6 Aug. 1796 (L. 199 n. 27).

of Mr. Cambridge, the continual histories of three readings, the triumphal criterion of nearly 4000 Copies soled in 4 Months—& the unbounded kindness of my dearest Father,—more dear to me than all else—have surely ill played their parts, if they have not braced me for a little castigation, though I affect not to say they have ⎪ rendered me invulnerable.

But I wanted to write a Whole Letter upon my earnestness that my beloved Father would find some new *Canons*:[6] I sigh at the picture of his lowness. I long to be with him again—in aid of Sally,—I know how my dearest Father accepts from *ALL* the offerings of affection.—But how could he name the *journies* that saved me from an anxiety I should have found insupportable? & that gave me the comfort of witnessing his mild fortitude in sorrow, & the *self-consolation* his reflections on all that is past with the poor departed Sufferer in his constant indulgent kindness *must* & *do* occasion him—with a reception so sweet it still soothes me—how could I have purchased a hundredth part of such satisfaction any other way? When I peep at you again, I must bring my little Boy,—*for he is worth us all* as a Consoler, & he begins now to grow manageable without a Maid. I hope the melancholy Inventory has been made? I know what a *lift* the News of our Susanne's safety will prove. She has sent me a little Letter, her *second*[7]—for she was sure her *First* would be spread in Town through my dearest Father. My Chevalier almost lives in his Field. Lady Rothes, Sir Lucas Pepys & Lady Hariet Leslie have been to see it. No Water yet in the Well!—yet 60 feet deep! —I want to say something of a *Dictionary of Music*—it would be an unrivalled work in your hands. My kind Love to Sally— I shall write to her soon—we go on slow, from resolving to read together,—I like her Book[8] very much—so does M. d'A.—but it is well worth a Letter to herself. I hope Sophy is still at Chelsea? Adieu My most dear—dear Father—may Heaven support & preserve you—prays your affec^te & dutiful

F d'A.

P.S. ⌐Mrs. Locke made me promise not to forget to name her compliments & sincere solicitude to hear of you further.⌐

[6] Cf. *XII Canzonetti a due voci in Canone. Poesia dell' Abate Metastasio*, composed by CB in 1790 (Scholes, ii. 350). Also in manuscript in the Osborn Collection, a 'Canon / 4 in 2 / Recte et Retro / Retro et Recte.' Most of CB's unpublished scores are in the British Museum.

[7] See *Catalogue*.   [8] *Clarentine* (L. 204 n. 9).

212   Great Bookham, 9 Nov. 1796

To Mrs. Francis (*later* Broome)

A.L.S. (Barrett, Eg. 3693, ff. 65–6b), 9 Nov. [17]96
Double sheet 4to 4 pp. *pmks* LEATHER / HEAD 10 N⟨O⟩ 96 black seal
Addressed: Mrs. Francis, / Hill Street / Richmond / Surry.—
Endorsed by CBF: Sister d'arblay / Novr 11th 1796 / ans.— —

Bookham
Nov. 9.—96.

On *Sunday* I received news that our beloved Susan was just arrived; my dearest Charlotte's Letter of yesterday,[1] desiring to hear by return of Post, should instantly have been answered, but that I was engaged to Norbury Park, & could not get time for three words. So I deferred one Day, to exchange them for as many pages. I entreat you immediately to convey this intelligence to my dear Miss Cambridge, with my kindest love; & an assurance I should have sent it strait forward to herself, had I not this dependance. How I rejoice my dearest Charlotte sees so much of that invaluable Friend:—do not fear your Clement's fondness; nothing is so captivating as a Child's partiality, & your Children are amongst the least troublesome existing. They all do their dear Mother honour, who will have nothing else, I trust, from them: though perhaps she must guard her own heart from suffering the extraordinary talents & character of her eldest love to take so much hold of it as to permit her being brought too early forward. My dear Charlotte will forgive a hint which, from similar reasons, | I am already watchfully giving to myself.

You are very good to seize all the opportunities of letting me hear from you.—Pray never neglect any: when you have only time to say *I am well*; *how are you?* it will always be bestowing a pleasure worth the moment. I regret not having the same means to return what I have perfect confidence would meet the same welcome. But you will not be *punctilious*, I know. To wait for an

212. [1] SBP's letter of 31 Oct. (op. cit.) had reached Great Bookham on Sunday 6 Nov. CBF's letter is missing.

answer is a plea only to be urged where we write from mere civility.

The Safe[2] is a most delicious ease of mind to me: it came in my absence, & is a constant memorial of your kindness.

I am extremely pleased with your plan of a Weekly visit to Chelsea. I would the distance, &c, from hence, did not disable me from making the same arrangement! our dearest Father will be cheared by the sight of us, & his manner of calling us so immediately around him was a touching proof what his heart would always have dictated. With what delight shall we all shew our sensibility to his affection!

I felt exactly what you describe from missing you on Monday,[3] it was *provoking*, yet *right*. I think Sally will considerably improve both in manners & character. She is excessively fond of our dearest Father, which, however natural, is loveable, & I hope he will have much comfort from her.

I truly partake in your satisfaction with your Governess:[4] it is one of the most essential points to all that is most dear to you. And I congratulate *you*, as well as herself, that Miss Day is again settled. She had behaved so well & worthily, that I think her welfare & success must be important to you.

Pray let me know when any thing is decided concerning the money dilemmas. I heard, through James, of the unsatisfactory papers relative to the mortgage from Mr. Parmentar,[5] & I fear you & that good soul will both be tormented, between your desire to oblige good people, & your just apprehension of hurting your little charges, or yourselves. James however, seems as cautious as he is friendly. You could not possibly have been all placed in more excellent hands.

[2] 'Safes' were confidential notes written on slips of paper and enclosed in, but detachable from, letters that might be put in public reading.

[3] On 31 October, the day of FBA's return to Bookham.

[4] Elizabeth Morton (*fl.* 1796–*post* 1848) had succeeded Ann Day (L. 164 n. 9) as a governess to CBF's children. For long years a friend of the Francis and Barrett families, she is mentioned in drafts of CFBt's will (Barrett, Eg. 3708, ff. 62–6). Clement Francis had left to each of his children £100 a year for their maintenance and education (P.C.C. Fountain 607).

[5] Robert Parmeter (1764–1831), a successful miller or 'Flour dresser', originally of Ingworth, but later a considerable citizen of Aylsham. He had married on 28 June 1787 Clement Francis's sister Sarah (1764–1815), whose M.I. with that of her husband is in the chancel of the parish church of Burgh-next-Aylsham. A schedule of the estate left by Clement Francis of Aylsham (Barrett, Eg. 3708, ff. 87–92b) lists among his debtors: 'Notes of hand from Robert Parmenter £300 at 4½ per Cent Interest paid to Decr 1791.'

Do you see any plays? go to any assemblies? make any new acquaintances? gather any more bon mots from Mrs. Purgatory?[6] Let me know how you go on; all will be interesting to me.

Remember my best love to my dear Aunt Becky when you see her. I am very glad to hear of her intended visit to Titchfield Street: I hope she will also be called for a while to Chelsea. What a blessing for that dear & good soul is your residence at Richmond! whether she sees you or not, she is now always sure of a friend as near as she is dear. I should else wish her to remove back to London.

Our Susanna had but just seen Norbury—but she seems, by half a ǀ phrase, to have found him what she hoped. Tell this also to Miss Cambridge, who knows—like ourselves—the reward of her conduct & excellence seemed all hanging upon that lovely boy.

Tell my dear little Charlotte I love her very much, & for nothing quite so well as her just fondness for a dear sister of mine who is her Namesake. My Love to Marianne & Clement.

M. d'A. sends his, abundantly, to you & his fair little Mistress. We must contrive a meeting both at Bookham & Richmond early in the summer. My Bambino has a 4th double tooth, & begins, now, to grow *above minding the pain*, to his Father's great triumph.

God bless my Charlotte—Ever her's is
F d'A.

213   Great Bookham,
2 October–11 November 1796

To Mrs. Waddington

A.L.S. (Berg), 2 Oct.–11 Nov. [17]96

Double sheet small 4to 4 pp. *pmks* LEATH[ER / HEAD] 12 NO 96 black seal

Addressed: Mrs. Waddington, / Lanover Court / Abergavenny.

[6] Mrs. Paradise (L. 134 n. 6), whose singular conversations and behaviour often emerge in CB's letters and CBF's letters and Journals (e.g. *ED* ii. 314–17).

Bookham,
oct. 2ᵈ—96

You allow so little, my dear Marianne, to even the Manual labour of bringing forth the 5 huge volumes with which I have burthened so many shelves, that I must plead a wearied hand no more—though I will not promise you will no more feel its consequences. I thank you for the honesty of your confession. When I cease to prize sincerity, how must I be metamorphosed! I have not, however, any great philosophy to boast in sustaining heroically partial censors, while the Public reception is beyond all possible expectation. The sale has been one of the most rapid ever known for a Guinea Book: it is 4 times that of Evelina, & nearly double that of Cecilia. Of the First Edition, containing the immense quantity of 4000, 500 only remain: & it has been printed but 3 Months.—

We have parted with the Copy right,[1]—very reluctantly, as guarding it was our motive to the subscription: but all our friends interfered, representing our ignorance of money ǀ concerns, & the risks we should run from piracies & double dealings. The Publishers give 1000 pounds for the Copy—but this you must not mention from me at present, as they desire to keep it secret, from affirming a similar price has never yet been given, & fearing to offend cotemporaries. I doubt not, however, it will soon be known, as the very extraordinary quick sale will make the Purchasers think it incumbent upon their characters to proclaim an extraordinary price. We know not, yet, what the subscription will prove, from certain non-payments, & various expences not yet settled: but we have reason to believe it will nearly, if not wholly, clear another thousand.

I confide what I am sure will be highly interesting to you without scruple; & now I will go back to your Letters.

I am truly delighted with the account you give me of your health, & I hope the little *excess* of which you were guilty in overstraining your strength is already forgotten. 'Tis the only excess to which I am myself ever tempted, & certainly were I in the circle of your beautiful Welsh Mountains, I should not be more likely to escape it. The description of ǀ your little Girls is all alive, & brings them forcibly to my view & knowledge.

213. [1] See Ll. 168 n. 5, 178 n. 10, 190.

Fanny seems, by it, *la plus aimable*—Emily, *la plus aimée*—not from your partiality, but from the very construction of their characters.

Nov. 11.—Thus much has been written this Month—& I meant to have added some little account that might have been interesting to you of my visit to Windsor with my little big work —but circumstances have stopt my writing—The papers will have announced to you the late fatal end at Chelsea[2]—it took me instantly to my dearest Father, with whom I spent a fortnight—& for the few days since my return I have not had a moment from my Hermit or my Bambino—a bewitching little suducer of time!—or Norbury park, even to add these few miserable words which hasten—thus tardily—to assure you of my constant affectionate tenderness through all absence & all silence—

F. d'A. [|]

All Mr. Lock's charming family are well, & always love you.

214	Great Bookham, 14 November 1796

To Doctor Burney

A.L.S. (Diary MSS. vi. 4948–[51], Berg), 14 Nov. [17]96
Double sheet 4to   4 pp.   *pmks*   LEATHER / HEAD   16 NO 96   black seal
Addressed: Dr Burney, / Chelsea College, / Middlesex.
Endorsed by CB: 1796
Edited by FBA, p. 1 (4948), *annotated*: ⁖· ᴨ(14)ᴨ   (15)
Alex's first visit to Lady Rothes & Lady Harriet Leslie. now Courtney
Edited also by CFBt *and the* Press.

Bookham
Nov. 14. 96

ᴨI think my dearest Father will wish to hear of the safe arrival of our argent, & it would not be fair to make poor Sarah pay for

---

² e.g. the *Morning Chronicle* (22 Oct. 1796): 'DIED . . . On Thursday last, Mrs. Burney, wife of Dr. Burney, of Chelsea College, whose virtues and intellectual powers will be long remembered and deplored by her family and friends.'

her trouble. I shall therefore take the opportunity to confab a little again with my most dear Father.⁷

I covet much to hear that the melancholy task of ransacking, examining, depositing, or demolishing regretful records is over.¹ Sometimes I wish this search could be mixed with collecting for Copying your numerous—& so many of them beautiful—manuscript poems.² Some particular pursuit is absolutely necessary. How I wish we could engage in any conjointly!—If Mr. Twining—& 2 or 3 other such—(only where are they to be found?)—would bear a part, I know nothing that might better interest my dearest Father, nor in which he would more, & in a thousand ways, excel, than superintending some periodical work.

Upon a second reading the Monthly Review, I am far in better humour with it, & willing to *confess the Case* to the criticisms, if I may claim by that concession any right to the eulogies. They are stronger & more important, upon re-perusal, than I had imagined, in the panic of a first survey, & an unprepared for disappointment in any | thing like severity from so friendly an Editor. The recommendation at the conclusion of the Book as a warning Guide to Youth would recompense me, upon the least reflection, to whatever strictures might precede it.³ I hope my kind Father has not suffered his generous—& to me most *cordial*—indignation against the Reviewer to interfere with his intended answer to the affectionate Letter of Dr. Griffiths?⁴

I must now inform you of a grand event. Alex has made his

214. ¹ CB's 'Memoirs' (Berg) and his letters of this time tell of the 'heart-rending task' that after the death of his wife he had imposed upon himself 'of looking over & burning old letters & papers'. 'I have destroyed near 500 letters of my own writing to the dear soul [and presumably] an equal number from her.' See A.L.S. (Berg) to Thomas Twining, 6 Dec. 1796. See also i, Intro., p. xxii.

² With this suggestion, CB complied. See his letter (Berg) to FBA, 2 Dec. 1796; and Lonsdale, p. 384. Extant, e.g., in the Osborn Collection is a notebook (*c.* 7·8 × 6·2″) containing a collection of manuscript poems in the hand of CB, paged 1–273, plus an index, but with pp. 1–47, among others, cut way. The work has been edited by FBA.

³ The highest praise was reserved for the last paragraph, that in which Griffiths recommended the novel 'as a *warning* "picture of youth;"'—as a guide for the conduct of young females in the most important circumstances and situations of life'. Elaborating obligingly on CB's opinion, he concluded with 'the truly *Reverend* Mr. Tyrold's *Sermon*', a 'brilliant' so 'large and lustrous' that it could not be cut (quoted from) without '*diminishing* its value'. See further Appendix B, p. 368.

⁴ Dr. Ralph Griffiths (1720–1803), LL.D. (Dartmouth, 10 Sept. 1790), founder (1749) of the *Monthly Review*. 'So different from the generality of mechanical enquiries' was his letter of condolence (now missing) that CB had replied at once. See his letter of 2 Nov. (Bodleian) and a copy (Osborn).

entrance into the *polite Circle*. Last week he accompanied me in returning about the *6ᵗʰ* visit for one of Lady Rothes. I left him in Mr. Lock's Carriage, which I had borrowed for the occasion, till I was preparing to take leave, & then I owned I had a little beau in waiting. You will suppose he was immediately demanded. His Nurse set him down at the Drawing Room Door, where he stood very gravely, but quietly; easy from seeing me, but not willing to advance, as Lady Rothes & her Daughter, Lady Hariet Leslie, were to be passed if he approached. This was his first visit,—except to Norbury Park—for we would not bring him out *too soon*,—& he now wants but 5 Weeks of being Two Years old! — —

The two Ladies, with all sort of civil blandishments, sought to allure him forward; but he put his little hands up to his face, shy, serious, & *all but* frightened. 'What may I give him?' cried Lady Rothes. He is allowed nothing, I answered, but Bread & Milk & Water. 'May I not offer him this?' cried she, taking an Apple from the Table,

No sooner was this perceived by the little retreater, than, concluding it, I suppose, the spoil of his own orchard, (where he is taught to play with the Apples as with Balls,) he started suddenly, & rushing up to Lady R[othes] snatched the Apple

(Throw it away.

from her hand, &, exclaiming '(*Tro it evay*' cast it with violence to the other end of the Apartment.

This extreme cavalier treatment of her offering surprised as much as it diverted her, till I explained what must have occasioned his apparent disdain of her present. Put at his ease, meanwhile, by this exploit, & the laughing it raised, he looked round him, & espying an hearth broom, again imagined it his own property, & flying to seize it from its hook, began sweeping & beating the Carpet with all his Might.

From this time, he was compleatly freed from his timid apprehensions, & amused himself with chucking the apple backwards & forwards, to his two hostesses, with an airy merriment that soon brought them both to the Carpet to play with him, almost as delighted as his little happy self. But his first rejection of the fruit, with so scornful a repulse as *Throw it away*, when I had just announced he could not yet speak, will not easily be forgotten, & was very comic in its immediate effect. |

⌜M. d'Arblay is enchanted with this fresh supply of Peltier,[5]—but we are both scandalized at all the parcels with our own goods, being post free—I pray, dearest sir, END such an imposition. I entreat you to thank my dear Sally for not deferring the pacquet, she judged very wisely in her cogitation upon the agreeableness of expedition.⌝

The Well—for *Water*, seems impervious. I grow rather uneasy about it. It is now at near 90 feet depth. M. d'A. works all Day long at his new Garden & Orchard, & only comes home to a cold spoiled Dinner at Tea time. Baby & I are just going to take a peep at him at his work, which various affairs of *menage*, joined to frequent evenings at Norbury, to meet the excellent & most worthy Count de Lally Tolendal, have hitherto prevented.

Adieu, my most dear, Dear Father!—⌜you will write all you can I know—but I have no comforting accounts as yet of the effect of ⟨those⟩ exertions. We hear nothing more of ⟨Sarah J‹r› ina⟩[6]—but we have written—James ⟨has⟩ called though at Titchfield Street when at Chelsea.

most dutifully, & affectionately—⌝

your F.d'A

215   Norbury Park, 15 November 1796

Conjointly with Mrs. Locke
To Mrs. Phillips

A.N. & A.L.S. (Berg), 15 Nov. 1796
Single sheet 4to 2 pp. 12 lines of Mrs. Locke's section crosswritten (p. 1)
Docketed in ink, perhaps at time of writing, p. 1, top margin: Mrs. Phillips
in pencil, p. 1, line 24: Letter from Mrs. Lock

[*By Madame d'Arblay*]

Norbury Tuesday even‹g› No‹r› 15‹th› 1796

How sweetly does my Susan spread a Sun beam when warmed with it herself! the dear—dear Letter of this morning[1]

⁵ See L. 204 n. 7.
⁶ The infant expected by JB's wife Sarah was to appear on 17 Nov. (L. 217 n. 14). Named Sarah, she was baptized on 15 Dec. 1796 at the font of St. Margaret's Church, Westminster.
215. ¹ This was SBP's letter (Berg), dated Henry Street, Dublin, 7 Nov. 1796, with the London *pmk* 14 NO 96. Printed in *FB & the Burneys*, pp. 231–5, it describes

has been one continued gratification to me all Day. That Norbury should be even improved surpasses indeed my every hope, & gives me a pleasure inexpressible: & that Mrs. Kiernan[2] seems so amiable delights me. I shall write again the latter end of next week—but now only thank my beloved Susan, & beg to be kindly remembered to the Major—Fanny, Norbury & Willy. My dear Father is very low, but well. adieu, my dearest love.

[By Mrs. Locke]

It was yesterday morn[g] my own beloved Friend that my heart was gladdened beyond my power of telling—I had been with my Aug[ust][a] Am[elia] & W[illia][m] to the Darking Ball & all my sleep from 4 o'clock had been saddened by some fancied misfortune to my beloved Friend. I was actively employed with her some times, & at others the most sinister feelings took her place—in short tho I have no superstitions I was involuntarily saddened when I awoke, & remained so till my Locke appeared at the foot of my Bed with the precious heart chearing sheet[3]— bless you for it my most loved & kindest! and now I must begin I believe with a Bulutin of myself—I had forgotten that I had a bad cold when worse than any cold happened to me—well—the cold went away & then I was very imprudent I believe, & stood out in my Garden making it so beautiful by thinning y[e] trees that I could not bring myself to go in—tho I had repeated warnings—the next day I met the Gardener again—& as the 1st Darking Ball was approaching I was obliged to sally forth & make visits by dozens—but I believe I told all this before. in short what with the imprudence that was pleasant & the visits that were unpleasant, I became so stiff with Rheumatism that for the last 3 weeks I have been obliged to spend half my day in Bed — — I should like to tell you all & every thing I have done if the paper would hold it—poor Alphonse[4] came to us & stayed near a fortnight. we were extremely pleased with him—

SBP's meeting with her son and the family of Cartlands with whom his father had placed him.

[2] Molesworth Phillips's sister Magdalene Dorothea (1752–1824), the wife of George Kiernan (1754–1811), *pharmacopola*, of Henry Street, Dublin, and formerly of Drumcondra. The family included Augusta (*c.* 1782–1854), who had visited Mickleham; Selina (*c.* 1784–1859); Harriet (*c.* 1781–1835); Sophie Dorothea (*c.* 1789–1820); and George (*c.* 1792–*post* 1833).

[3] SBP had included a sheet for Mrs. Locke.

[4] Alphonse de la Châtre (L. 206 n. 2; also ii, Intro., p. xvi).

& my Locke thinks very highly of him—has any body told you what saved his life when he was beset by all those Villains?—his *Mothers picture*! that he always wears in his bosom. it was the breast plate that prevented the assassins knife from piercing his heart—is it not beautifully touching?—he left us on Friday ye 4^{th}Nov^r—Fuseli[5] came to us for 3 days while he was with us & was as usual extremely entertaining—Alphonse copied many of William's drawings surprizingly well.—my Locke has encouraged him very much.

Thursday morn^g 17 Nov^r—Now my beloved Friend I will take up my account, interrupted yesterday by dinner & after it as we are now quite en famille & that our Willm much wished a little music I could not continue without I making the evening unsocial—my own Friend understands me for after the music & Tea, reading commences & I think it essential not to interrupt or break that social plan if I can possibly help it.—How I have more than ever wished for my beloved Friend the last week which the dear et bonne Princesse & ye delightful Mr de Lally spent here—she was particularly pleased to write from hence to you whom she tenderly loves[6]—you will believe that. we talked of our loss, of our hopes, she is worthy to rehearse my darling Friend — — with what satisfaction she would have heard the truly comfortgiving account of your sweet Boys situation with that excellent family[7] where it seems to me that he has the constant advantage of home with his classical instruction.—All mine heard it with delight but most especially his friend Amelia who has a *maternal* feeling for Every thing that concerns him—

[5] See L. 178 n. 3; also i, L. 24 n. 8.

[6] The princesse d'Hénin and SBP, in their mutual concern for the destitute French *émigrés*, often met in London in the months June 1795–Oct. 1796. See SBP's letters of that period (*Catalogue*) as well as eleven letters (Berg) from the princesse to her. The letter written from Norbury Park is, however, missing.

[7] That is, the family of George Cartland (1735–88), B.A. (1758), M.A. (1767), and called to the Irish Bar in 1767. He had married c. 1778 Elizabeth Dawson, the widow of the Revd. Charles Robert Maturin (1729–76), rector of Rathdrummin near Duncleer (1765). Of the Maturin marriage there were five daughters, and two sons, Gabriel (1767–1840) and Henry (c. 1771–1842), Fellow of Trinity College (1792), M.A. (1793), and Senior Fellow until 1802, the date of his marriage to Elizabeth Johnston. It was under this brilliant young Fellow of Trinity that Molesworth had placed his son, at this time 11 years old.
Of the Cartland marriage there was a son George (born c. 1779), described by SBP's letters of the time (e.g. 7 Nov. 1796, Berg), as a youth about 17: 'I will not defer saying', she had written, 'that I very much like ⟨all⟩ the Family, & am *more* than satisfied with the manner in wch my Norbury is treated—they are all evidently extremely fond of him; yet not willing to spoil him, or to pass over anything he says or does amiss'.

perhaps he will not like that term so well as his dearest Mamma
—What an exquisitely touching account is hers of her first
meeting with that beloved Child[1]—it filled my eyes with the
softest tears — — but I have so much to say that I can follow no
method & shall be quite incoherent I fear—I began with the
charming people whose society I so longed my Friend should
share—the 1st eveng Tuesday 8th Mr de Lally read a most
extraordy Play called Le *Comité du Salut Public*[8] now acting at
Paris which is a terrible & burelsque picture of the horrible
tiranny of Robespierres reign where a set of the lowest mechanics
who can neither write or read—& have assumed the names of
Cato, Brutus Saevola / Saevola is a hairdresser & comes in
saying 'qu'il a peigné toutes ses pratiques' & can now attend to
the Nation— / &c make out the most iniquitous denonciations
against the most worthy & virtuous family—Father, Mother
Son & Servants—this is said to be an exact transcript of these
shocking opressions, & is represented with the consent of ye
present Governmt. It wou'd not have been possible to listen to
this horrid Drama if it had not conveyed the certainty of an
entire change—the next eveng Wednesday Mr de Lally (who I
could almost worship) read a *divine* (that word is neither too
strong for the performance or intention) Work of his—a
Plaidoyer for the Emigrés—an address to the Government &
People of France to reverse the decrees against them[9]—there
was but one voice amongst us that it was le chef d'œuvre de
l'Esprit humain the perfection of reason & pathos that speaks
equally to the head & ye heart—our Fanny & her good Mr
d'Arblay assisted & the first was almost too much affected by
it—on Thursday our Wm went to London. & Mr de Lally not
haveg quite prepared ye second part of this inspiration it was
kindly adjourned to Friday eveng—our Fanny & Co attended,
& the enthusiasm of admiration was if possible greater than
before—he has still a concluding & most difficult part remaining but such talents overcome every difficulty.—such talents &
such benevolence—my Locke conversing with me the next

---

[8] Charles-Pierre Duncancel (1766–1835), *Intérieur des comités révolutionnaires, ou
les Aristides modernes* (1795). After 200 performances the play was withdrawn late
in 1796. Mrs. Locke has confused Scévola's entrance in Act I, scene ii, with his
soliloquy in scene v: 'Et moi—qu'est ce que je vais faire? J'ai peigné toutes mes
pratiques. . . .'
[9] *Défense des émigrés français, adressée au peuple français* (1797) and translated by
John Gifford (1797).

morn^g on the noble & exalted use of his Talents said 'I envy M
de Lally's Pillow!—'What a repose must his be indeed, & how
soothing every thought!!—he delighted us in another way, by
his paternal fondness for his little girl[10]—he brought us 2 letters
which he had rec^d from her excellent Governess containing 2
also from his Eliza with her hair & her height—they are pretty
natural & affectionate, she is not yet 11 y^{rs} old—my best Friend
would have entered into the joy of this poor Father whose eyes
were filled while the letters were reading—by having this good
Governess Mad^{me} Campan[11] who speaks English like an english-
woman we saw at Versailles, she was particularly civil to us, &
shewed us the poor Queens apartments she was one of her femmes
de Chambres & a personne très distinguée as you wou'd think by
her letters which are charming.—Poor Mr de Chavagnac came
on Thursday even^g & it was very gratifying to us to see him
enjoy the improvements of his little adrienne[12] & spend a few
days comfortably—he stayed till Sunday noon when ye bonne
Princesse conveyed him back to London—he desired his Wife
when she wrote to be affec^y remembered to my beloved Friend
—my Locke—my William & George were very pressing to be
very affec^{ly} mentioned Take now my darling Friend a most
tenderly affectionate Embrace from your own

F L ^l

I must tell you that my Locke is in the most blessed health &
goes out every day in ye Phaeton. all mine are perfectly well, we
expect our Charles & his sweet wife on Saturday—ye Duc^{ss} of
Richm^d is dead[13]—Kiss your dearest Children for me every one
—How I wish I could peep at Belcotton. I am sure it is Elegant

---

[10] Elisabeth-Félicité-Claude de Lally-Tolendal (1786–1883), who was to marry
in 1807 Henri-Raymond d'Aux de Lescout (1782–1870), later marquis d'Aux-
Lally (1815).

[11] Jean-Louise-Henriette Genest [or Genet] (1752–1822) had married in 1774
Pierre-Dominique-François Berthollet, *called* Campan (*fl.* 1774–92). Ruined by the
Revolution, she had opened a school for young ladies at St. Germain-en-laye on 31
July 1794. In 1802 FBA was to attend the closing exercises of the school (v, L. 530).

[12] Adrienne-Adélaïde-Anne de Chavagnac was born in London *c.* 3 Dec. and
baptized 4 Dec. 1795 (for her parents, see L. 201 n. 5), the princesse d'Hénin being
one of her godparents. SBP's letters of that time (Berg) recount the arrival of a
wet-nurse, sent by Mrs. Locke, and the placing of the infant with a foster nurse in
Surrey. Adopted informally and reared at Norbury Park, Adrienne was sent to
Paris, at the request of her father, only in 1802 (*Locks of Norbury,* pp. 86–7).

[13] Lady Mary Bruce, daughter of Charles, 4th Earl of Elgin, 3rd Earl of Ailesbury,
had married on 1 Apr. 1757 Charles Lennox (1734/5–1806), 3rd Duke of Richmond
and Lennox. She had died on 8 Nov. 1796.

what ever the Major works at always is so—I need not beg a particular account of it & the sort of Country that I may a little know where to look for you—I sent a large paquet to the good de La Landelles[14] last week with the happy news of your safe arrival—tell me if you find any difficulty in reading this cross writing because if you do not it would give more space always.— I think our Fanny in the best health & looks & her dear Husband & Baby *perfect*—Don't imagine I am in the least ill only but Rheumatic & I am going to try a Mustard medicine of which they relate wonders. |

216   Great Bookham *and* Norbury Park,
                              25–7 November 1796

Conjointly with Mrs. Locke
To Mrs. Phillips

> A.L.S. & A.L. (Diary MSS. vi. 4952–[5], Berg), 25–27 Nov. 1796
> Double sheet 4to 4 pp. *pmks* DARKING 29 NO 96 3 DE 96 wafer
> *Addressed*: Mrs Phillips, / at Major Phillips, Belcotton, / Drogheda / Ireland
> *Endorsed by* SBP: Decr 8th / 96,
> *Edited by* CFBt *and the* Press.

[*By Madame d'Arblay*]

Bookham, Nov. 25.
1796.

Never was a sweeter Letter written, my dearest Susanna, than that I have this moment read[1]—& though my quinze jours are

[14] Among the destitute *émigrés* assisted by the princesse d'Hénin and Mrs. Locke and visited by SBP on errands of mercy in London in 1795–6 (see her letters, *Catalogue*) was a family that seems to have included the 'Mesdames de la Landelle', an elderly father, and a son lately '*shot* at Quiberon', probably René-Vincent-Marie de la Landelle de Roscanver, an *émigré* who was condemned to death on 27 July 1795, see Le Garrec, *Les Vrais Martyrs de Quiberon 1795* (1935). A Register of the Laity (1798–9), included in the records of government assistance to *émigrés* (PRO, T. 93/28), shows (item 330) the two signatures 'de LaLandelle' and 'hue de La Landelle', of no. 35, Ladington Street, Portman Square, formerly of ⟨Tréquier⟩ in Brittany, but no other record has as yet been found.

216. [1] This is SBP's letter of four folio pages (Berg), dated Belcotton, 14 Nov. 1796, with the London *pmk* 24 NO 96, a copy of which (Armagh) is printed in *FB & the Burneys*, pp. 235–40. The letter gives a full account of the members of the Kiernan family.

PLATE II

The farm-yard of Belcotton, Co. Louth, Ireland, as it appeared in 1960

but half over, I cannot forbear answering it immediately, to tell you of my delight in all your accounts, especially of the Kiernan Family, which is so peculiarly interesting to you. I was well prepared to love it from the fair branch I saw at Mickleham;[2] pray make her remember me, & assure her She has a friend in England who—though but of a few Hours growth, thinks of her always with pleasure, & every sort of presentiment of good.

⸺⸺

The anxiety I have been in to know how the Weather agreed with you, in so trying a journey, makes what you say a relief, though alas—anxiety must still live in such a season!—I want to know more of Belcotton. A description of every room, when nothing else occurs more pressing, would much gratify me, by giving me a nearer view in idea of how & where my dearest Susan is seated—standing—or walking.—The interview, as you describe it, with Mrs. Hill,[3] brings fresh to me my tendency of loving that respectably singular & amiable character: but you do not seem to think her Mate otherwise worthy of her than by his attachment, which I regret. Mr. K's plan for the Empress[4] made me laugh heartily—&, when my Builder comes home from his field, will be a comedy to him, I am sure. From what other Country could such a proposal be made to a known Constitutionel! *You'll excuse me*—You know how sincerely I can admire & honour as well as be wicked, where Hibernians are in question: witness my favourite Lord O Lerney.[5] ⸺ ⸺ I must tell you,—as I should thank you to be so told—that after I had given your first dear Letter to our beloved Friend, & she had read it, & I had told its principal contents to Mr. Locke, & she

---

[2] Augusta Kiernan. See L. 215 n. 2.

[3] Elizabeth Kirwan (*c.* 1760–1840), who, in London with her father Richard Kirwan (1733–1812), LL.D. (1794), became a great favourite with the young Burneys (*ED* ii. 267, 305, 313–17). 'Bessy' had married on 16 Feb. 1792 Hugh Hill (1770–1850), 'Deputy Commissary-Gen., and formerly Col. of the Battle-axe Guards' (*AR* xcii (1850), 'Chronicle', 253). She was the mother of three children, lived ten miles from Dublin, and on visiting SBP 'her countenance spoke so much affection, such warmth of heart and shewed marks of such tender emotion, that the pleasure I rec^d from her visit was extremely great' (SBP, op. cit.).

[4] After attesting to the friends that FBA's *Brief Reflections* had gained in Ireland for the emigrant French clergy, Mr. Kirwan (above) proposed that she should write a pamphlet in defence of the 'grossly calumniated and libelled' Empress of Russia. Failing FBA, he asked if M. d'A might not be engaged to undertake a work of this kind, which would undoubtedly procure him '*a handsome pension from the Empress*'.

[5] The kind and cavalier Irishman in *Camilla*.

had added, with sweetest interest, her comments, & the Letter was again in YOUR pocket Book—Mr. Locke, [a] little hesitating, said 'May *I* — — read her account of her meeting with Norbury?—' To be sure I did not say no!—Indeed I had myself twice cried over it with strong pleasure & emotion.—Amelia then advanced—& said 'O—if I might just see that part!—' & was gratified, & her sweet Eyes spoke even more than her expressive voice ┃ how much it touched her.

You will have heard, from herself, that the Princesse d'henin & M. de Lally have spent a few days at Norbury Park. We went every Evening regularly to meet them, & they yet contrive to grow higher & higher in our best opinions & *affections*. They force that last word—none other is adequate to such regard as they excite. M. de L. read us a pleading for *Emigrés*[6] of all description, to the People & Government of France, for their re-instatement in their Native land, that exceeds, in Eloquence, Argument, taste, feeling, & every power of oratory & Truth united, ANY thing I ever remember to have read. It is so affecting, in many places, that I was almost ill from restraining my nearly convulsive emotions. My dear & honoured Partner gives me, perhaps, an interest in such a Subject beyond what is its mere natural due & effect, therefore I cannot be sure such will be its universal success; yet — — I shall be nothing less than surprised to live to see his Statue erected in his own Country, at the expence of his own restored Exiles. 'Tis, indeed, a wonderful performance. And he was so easy, so gay, so unassuming, yet free from *condescendsion*, that I almost worshipped him. M. d'A. cut me off a bit of the Coat in which he read his pleading— & I shall preserve it, labelled! The Princesse was all that was amiable & attractive & she loves my Susanna so tenderly, that her voice was always carressing when she named her. She would go to Ireland, she repeatedly said, on purpose to see you, were her fortune less miserably cramped. The Journey—voyage— time, difficulties, & sea-sickness would be *nothing* for obstacles. —O, indeed, you have made, there, that rare & exquisite acquisition, an ardent Friend for life.

---

[6] *Défense des émigrés français* . . . (1797), as in L. 215 n. 9.

I have not heard very lately of my dearest Father—all accounts speak of his being very much lower in spirits than I left him. I sometimes am ready to return to him—for my whole heart yearns to devote itself to him—but the babe—& the babe's Father—& there is no going *en famille* uninvited,—& my dear Father does not feel equal to ¹ making the invitation. The only Letter he has written me since my return was chiefly animated by his dear generous indignation against the Monthly Review, for having made some *criticisms* upon Camilla, though mixed with the highest panegyric.⁷ Camilla continues still his most ardent passion. He cannot name it without enthusiasm, neither when I am absent nor present. And he told me it was the last *real pleasure* the poor departed seemed to find, & helped on the Summer, & afforded her a vivacity of occupation & delight that nothing long before, nor ever after, had given. This is, to me, you will be sure, a very great satisfaction.

One of the Titchfield dear Girls⁸ seems to be constantly with Sally, to aid the passing Hours: but our poor Father wants something more than chearfulness & affection, though nothing without them could do: he wants some one to *find out* pursuits; to *entice* him into reading, by bringing Books, or starting subjects; some one to lead him to talk of what he thinks, or to forget what he thinks of by adroitly talking of what may catch other attention. Even where deep sorrow is impossible, a gloomy void must rest in the total breaking up of such a long—& such a last connexion. I must always grieve at *your* absence at such a period!—our Esther has so much to do in her own family, & fears so much the cold of Chelsea, that she can be only of Day & occasional use: & it is nights & mornings that call for the confidential Companion that might best revive him. He is more sweetly amiable—more *winningly* himself, than—if possible— than ever.—God long preserve him to bless us all!

Our new House is stopt short in actual building, from the shortness of the Days, &c—but the Master Surveyor has still much to settle there, & 3 workmen to aid preparing the

---

⁷ See L. 211 n. 1.　　　　⁸ Sophia Elizabeth Burney.

Ground for agricultural purposes. The Foundation is laid, & on the 1ˢᵗ of March, the little dwelling will begin to be run up. The Well is just finished; the water is 100 & odd feet deep—& it costs near £22—which this very Morning, thank Heaven, has been paid. ˡ

I shall keep this till Monday,[9] as we mean, when not prevented by accident, to dispatch a sheet every other Monday. We depend on a further account of sweet Norbury I rejoice la chere petite philosophier—my tenderest love to my dearest Fanny[10]—& a kiss or two for dear Willy. I must not fatigue the Major with messages yet cannot omit my love to him. M. d'A. intended writing, but my Pen has played him false. Remember me to good Susan.[11] My Bambino is flourishingly well, gay, & teeming with new ideas, & new methods of communicating them: but still no speech beyond a few words. adieu, my own dearest dear!—Heaven bless & preserve you!

F.d'A.

My special Compᵗˢ to Mrs. Hill when you see her—& my best Compᵗˢ to Mr. Kirwan.

[*By Mrs. Locke*]

Sunday 27ʰ Novʳ Norbury Park.

With what delight I read your precious Letter of yᵉ 14ʰ my beloved Friend—our Fanny spent Friday evenᵍ with us & brought it me—I wish you could have seen the faces how they brightened—every one—news from our beloved Friend has a most animating effect—! how many comforting circumstances! —The Keirnan family are charming—a most interesting sweet family—I love all those that manifest affection—I feel obliged to them for what they cannot help & what I was certain would be every where as soon as that dearest made her appearance but I forget how limited my powers of prating are—I must hasten to say that we are all perfectly well our precious chief never was in more perfect health & continues his airings in yᵉ Phaeton

---

[9] On 28 Nov.

[10] Fanny Phillips, now about 14 years of age, and referred to in SBP's letter (op. cit.): 'Ma pauvre petite commence à se faire un peu à sa destinée, et devient moins triste—Ma bonne Susanne aussi . . . Willy n'est pas trop content de notre chateau—Mais s'amuse beaucoup à suivre les chevaux . . .'.

[11] Susan Adams (bapt. 5 June 1768 at St. Martin's Church, Epsom), SBP's faithful servant.

daily in all most unpromising weather & returns always the better for them—our sweet Cecilia & her Charles are with us & I never saw such perfection of health as that dear creature is in —such activity—*notwithstanding*—The dear Duchess[12] spent 2 nights with us on her way to her brother ye D. of Richmonds[13] Goodwood where she is gone to meet L^{dy} Louisa Conolly[14] who is come over on ye Duchess of Richmonds death—I have a precious hostage left with me ye sweet Mimi[15]—yesterday even my dearest L^y Templetown[16] came to us with her 3 charming girls on their way from Tunbridge—she is delightfully well—all mine say tenderest most affec^{te} remem^b to my beloved Friend. Heaven bless & preserve her.

I never saw such robust health as our dearest Fanny & her little darling,—she brought him yesterday morn^g to see Cecilia & then walked to their building & back here & woud hardly set down—& then with the brightest alacrity walked to Bookham —take the tenderest [of care]—my own beloved Friend every creature th[at knows] you enquires after you with warmest soli[citude]—our bonne Princesse was delighted with y^e [firs]t news I gave her—

How I was amused with ye E. of Russias champion & his expectations. Kiss your dearest children for me & bless them— our Fanny is perfect &—hers

[12] The Duchess of Leinster (L. 171 n. 11).
[13] See ii, L. 60 n. 6.
[14] The Duchess of Leinster's sister, Lady Louisa Augusta Lennox (1743–1821), who had married in 1758 the Rt. Hon. Thomas Conolly (1738–1803) of Castletown.
[15] Emily Charlotte Ogilvie (L. 203 n. 8).
[16] One of Mrs. Locke's earliest friends Elizabeth Boughton (1746–1823), who had married in 1769 Clotworthy Upton (1721–85), cr. Baron Templetown (1776). Her daughters Elizabeth Albana (1775–1844), Caroline (1778–1862), and Sophia (1780–1853) had from childhood been frequent visitors at Norbury Park. See also i, L. 16 n. 13.

217   Great Bookham, 29 November 1796

To Doctor Burney

A.L.S. (Diary MSS. vi, not numbered, Berg), 29 Nov. [17]96
Double sheet 4to (8·8 × 7·5″)   4 pp. From the bottom of the second leaf a
segment (1·4 × 7·5″) has been cut away   *pmks*   30 NO 96   30 NO 96
black seal
Addressed: Dᵣ Burney, / Chelsea College, / Middlesex
Endorsed by CB: 1796
Docketed: C. 20
Edited by FBA, p. 1, *annotated*: al—O [all out?]
Edited also by CFBt.

Nov. 29.—96.
Bookham.

Most dear Sir,

This uncommon & so total silence begins to give me great
uneasiness. Morning after Morning the hope of a line from Sally
has regularly awoke with me,—& regularly been disappointed—
Let me entreat a few words with as little delay as possible, to say
merely how you now are—The thousand other things I should
wish to know—of your occupations—whom you admit—What
you can bear to read—&c &c may wait more leisure. But I am
panic struck & saddenned by this ignorance of your *health*, &
can only rest at Night by saying *To-morrow will bring me news*.[1]

Yesterday my Bab, for the first time, *spoke in reply*; & I
deemed it an Epock worthy Record to his dear Grandpapa. He
was eating some bread, & let a piece fall; I presented it to him,
saying 'Will Bab have it?—' He looked irresolute, &, to help
him, I added 'Say Yes, Mama.—' He then turned round, with
a look more decisive, & instead of ecchoing me as heretofore,
pronounced '*lo*, Mama!' *Lo* stands for *NO*.

I was extremely delighted by his negative: any other person's
affirmative will with difficulty be received with more compla-
cency: & ǀ soon after, I gave him a bit of Cake, which, as I told
him, was sent him by Mrs. Locke, bidding him, at the same
time, repeat after me 'Thank you, Mama.—' He took it with

217. ¹ This concern elicited CB's rather melancholy letter (Berg) of 2 Dec.
He is apathetic, lethargic, and able to think only of his loss.

great glee; but, conceiving I had misplaced his gratitude, in-
(Dear Locke!)
stead of repeating my words, called out 'Dea Ock!—'

This opening of his powers of elocution by a phrase that shews them preceded by those of reflexion, has not, I will confess, induced us to dub him a blockhead.—But I shall have no spirit to go on with his improvements, & the wonderful wonders with which he makes *even his own parents* astonished by his wit & vivacity, till I hear how my dearest Father is in health, & whether such narratives have any chance to beguile a few minutes of sadness.

I have had a Letter from Miss Thrale containing much concern, & the utmost desire I would convey both her own & her sisters' kindest Respects & condolances to my dear Father. I find some very unpleasant circumstances have again arisen between them & their Mother; relative to Cecilia's affairs in her new connexion.[2] I am very sorry: but Miss T[hrale] assures me nothing shall again provoke her to a total breach.

Our Cottage stops now, from the shortness of the Days, till the beginning of March. The foundation is laid, & it will then be run up with great speed. The Well, at length, is finished. It is 100 & odd feet deep. The water is said to be excellent.[3] But M. d'A. has had it now stopt up, to prevent accidents for hazardous Boys, who, when the field is empty of owners, will be amusing themselves there. M. d'A. has just compleated his grand plantations—part of which are in Evergreens, part in fire wood, for future time, & part in an orchard.

But—My dearest Sir, I think I would risk *my new Cottage* against sixpence, that I have guessed the Author of The pursuits of Literature. Is it not Mr. Mason? The verses I think equal to Any body—those on Shakespeare '*His pen he dipt in Mind*' are demi divine—& who else could so well interweave

---

[2] Cecilia Margaretta Thrale (1777–1857) had married on 9 June 1795 John Meredith Mostyn (1775–1807). Miss Thrale's letter on the subject of the settlements is missing.

[3] On receipt of this news CB was to send a set of congratulatory puns to the 'persevering ground-architect': 'I really feared that he was digging a bottomless pit. I heard the otherday of somebody boring a 1000 feet (what a *bore*!) without finding water—Your naiad . . . had only hidden herself at the depth of a 100 feet. and I yet hope that she will *rise* in your favour, & shake hands with you or your domestics at half that distance; & then, if there sh^d happen to be a company of strollers in any neighbouring barn, you ought in gratitude to entreat them to play —"All's Well, that ends *Well*!"' (A.L.S., 2 Dec., op. cit.).

what concerns Music? could so well attack Dr. Par for his
severity against *Dr. Hurd*, who had to himself addressed his
Essay on the Marks of imitation?[4] who be so interested or so
difficult to satisfy about the exquisite *Gray*?[5] who know so well
how to appreciate Works upon *Gardening*?[6] who so singularly be
for *The Sovereign, The Government*, yet palpably not for George the
third, nor William Pit?[7] And then the lines which form his sort
(Mason
of Epitaph, seem for *(HIM* alone designed. How wickedly he has
flogged all around him! & how cleverly! but I am very angry
about the excellent Marchioness of Buckingham.[8] The fear of
Popery in these Days seems to me most marvellous ! The fears of
INFIDELITY seem a thousand times more rational. 'Tis, however,
a very first rate production. The Hymns,[9] in his open Name, are

---

[4] Dialogue I of *The Pursuits of Literature* (L. 171 n. 7), with notes, by Thomas James
Mathias (*c.* 1754–1835), had appeared anonymously in May 1794; Dialogues II
and III, assiduously advertised by the publisher, J. Owen, of Piccadilly, had
appeared in June 1796, but still anonymously, and there was much speculation
for some years still on the identity of the author. Immensely popular, the poem ran
to sixteen editions by 1812.
     The lines on Shakespeare that FBA mentions occur in Dialogue II. Mathias's
satiric lines on 'Parr, THE GUIDE OF PUBLIC TASTE', emerging in all three Dialogues,
were understood as a castigation of the 'Whig Doctor' for his attack on Bishop Hurd
(1720–1808), which attack consisted in the malicious publication of *Tracts, by
Warburton, and a Warburtonian; not admitted into the Collections of their respective works*
(1789), being a reprinting (with an ironic dedicatory epistle) of pieces that Parr
knew that Bishop Hurd would now very much like to suppress. The causes and
course of this controversy (with amusing quotations from Dr. Parr) are supplied by
Warren Derry, *Dr. Parr, a Portrait of the Whig Dr. Johnson* (1966), pp. 81–6. FBA had
also recollected Bishop Hurd's familiar epistle, *A Letter to Mr. Mason, on the marks of
imitation* (1757).
     [5] As to 'The self-supported melancholy Gray' (Dialogue I), the satirist was
dissatisfied not with the poet and his work but with the lack of royal patronage for
it: 'Dark was his morn of life, and bleak the spring, Without one fostering ray from
Britain's king'. Mason also stood neglected 'While great Augustus pass'd unconscious
by'. The note to this line carries the sly comment: 'The discernment of His Majesty,
GEORGE THE THIRD, in poetical merit, is acknowledged in the patronage of Dr.
Beattie, . . . and of Mr. Cowper. . . . Mr. Mason must have been overlooked for
a particular reason.'
     [6] The few lines on gardening ('Raise lust in pinks', etc.) in Dialogue I, their
satiric bent notwithstanding, had evidently suggested to FBA *The English Garden*
(1772–82) and aided her delusion with respect to the authorship of *The Pursuits*.
     [7] Epithets like 'honest statesmen', 'majesty, in Pitt', 'firmness', 'courage',
'serene', and 'just' indicate the satirist's approval of the ministry, if not of the King.
     [8] Lady Mary Elizabeth Nugent (d. 16 Mar. 1812), daughter of Robert, 1st Earl
of Nugent (*c.* 1720–88), who had married on 16 Apr. 1775 George Nugent-Temple-
Grenville, 1st Marquis of Buckingham (1753–1813). FBA, who knew of CB's
friendly association with the Marchioness in their mutual efforts for the French
emigrant clergy (*Memoirs*, iii. 184–8; Lonsdale, pp. 367–8) and had herself married
a Roman Catholic, was little pleased with Mathias's prejudiced mention of the
Marquis and his lady (Dialogue II, n. 68) and his crude satire on the Mass.
     [9] Probably *Collection of the Psalms of David* used as anthems in York Cathedral and

most gratefully accepted by my excellent Neighbour Mr. Cooke. We have not yet read Le Vaillant.[10] Peltier[11] is so greedily swallowed by my Mate, that he much regrets my forgetting, at last, the 2 bound first volumes you so kindly put me out for him. We are not much struck with the Creole;[12] it is too full of trite observations introduced sententiously. Clarentine is written with better taste. We have just been lent Caleb Williams, or *Things as They ARE*.[13] Mr. Locke, who says its *design* is execrable, avers that one little word is omitted in its title, which should be thus—or Things as they are *NOT*.—

Adieu, most dear—dear sir—I shall be very unquiet till I have some news of your health. Most dutifully & affect[ly] ever your

F. d'A.

Where has Martin's little Brother or Sister hid itself?[14] I expected to hear of its birth a fortnight ago. M. d'A. has just planted a Golden Pippin, which he calls *L'Arbre à M. le cher docteur*.

I have had another very comfortable Letter from our dear Susanna.

published under the direction of William Mason, by whom is prefixed a 'Critical and Historical Essay on Cathedral Music' (1795).

[10] See L. 205 n. 3.

[11] See L. 204 n. 7.

[12] Samuel James Arnold, Jr. (1774–1852), *The Creole; or, the Haunted Island* (1796).

[13] William Godwin, *Things as They Are; or, the Adventures of Caleb Williams* (1794).

[14] The infant had appeared on 17 Nov. (L. 214 n. 6) and JB, evidently conscience-stricken to hear of FBA's ignorance of the birth, wrote comically, if belatedly on Wednesday [1 Dec. 1796]: 'I will not lose another moment in acquainting you of the arrival of your niece. . . . She shall be [Alex's] Statira, that is when he can speak and she is able to say, Good Gods, how he can speak! . . . M[rs] B. is doing very well & desires her kindest love to Brother D'Arblay & yourself. The little damsel is likewise in a good way and inclined to thrive—and I too, *am as well as can be expected*.'

218   Great Bookham, [9] December 1796

To Doctor Burney

A.L.S. (Diary MSS. vi. 4958–[61], Berg), Dec. [17]96
Double sheet 4to   4 pp.   *pmks*   LEATH[ER] / HEAD   9 DE 96   black
seal
Addressed: Dr. Burney, / Chelsea College / Middlesex.
Endorsed by CB: 1796
Edited by FBA, p. 1 (4958), *annotated and dated*: ⋗ 1796   (16)
Babe Alex, M. de Lally Mdlle de Lally—Mr. Mason. Pursuits of
Literature   Mrs Delany Sacharissa.   sweet Susanna!
Annotated p. 2 [4959], *top margin*: ⌜∞ Mason ∞⌝
Docketed in pencil: 491 . 1796
Edited also by CFBt *and the* Press.

Bookham, Dec.
96

What cruel & most unnecessary disturbance might I have
been spared if accident had not twice stood my Enemy! ⌜yester-
day arrived the kind reassuring letter below & to Day's was
dear Sarah's long & satisfactory Epistle & those precious lines
of my beloved Father which would have kept me in peace if sure
they were entrusted to Miss Cambridge, who, by unlucky
chance, saw us March past & had no way to get at me till
yesterday.⌝ All's Well that ends WELL,[1] however, ⌜as my
dear Father—so much more as Sally, though not more truly,
has just said, & I will⌝ forget the inquietude, & all else that is
painful, to dwell upon the sweet meeting in store, & the sight
that my Eye's Mind, equally with my Mind's Eye, presents to
me continually of my innocent Alex restoring, by his playful
spirits, the smiles of his dearest grandfather whose Heart—were
it made as hard as it is soft, could not resist what all Mankind
consent to find irresistible, the persuasive gaiety of happy
Childhood.

M. le C^t de Lally Tolendal, who has been upon a visit to
Norbury Park, says he can never forgive me the laugh I have
brought against him by the Scene of Sir Hugh on the Birth day,[2]

218. [1] This is CB's conclusion with respect to the water at length rising in the
well (L. 217 n. 3).
   [2] *Camilla*, i, bk. i, chap. 2.

'tis so exactly the description of himself when an amiable Child comes in his way. He left an only Daughter in Paris, where she is now at school,[3] under the superintendence of La Princesse de Poix,[4] whose infirmities & constant illness have detained in that wretched City during the whole Revolution—though under the compulsion of I a pretended divorce from le Prince, who is in London. M. de Lally had just received, by a private hand, a Letter from his Daughter, now Eleven years old, extremely pretty & touching, half in french, half in broken English, which language he has particularly ordered she may study; & enclosed a ribbon with her Heigtht & breadth. She tells him she has just learnt by heart his translation of Pope's universal prayer;[5] & she hopes, when he comes to fetch her, he will meet her upon the Terrace, where she walks with her companions, & *know her at once from every body*.

I, too, thought the *prose* too spirited & good for Mr. Mason, when compared with what I have seen of his general Letters: but he has two styles in prose, as well as poetry; & I have seen compositions rather than Epistles, which he wrote formerly to Mrs. Delany, so full of Satire, point, & Epigrammatic severity & derision, upon those of their mutual acquaintance whom he confidentially named, that I feel not the least scruple for my opinion. In those Letters—with which that revered old friend entrusted me, when her Eye-sight failed for reading them herself, there were, also, many ludicrous sketches of certain persons, & caricatures as strong of the Pencil as of the Pen. They were written in his Season of democracy, & my dear Mrs. Delany made me destroy all that were mischievous. The highest Personages, with whom she was not, then, peculiarly, as afterwards, connected, were held up to so much ridicule, that her early regard & esteem diminished as her loyalty encreased, & immediately upon I taking possession of the house given her at Windsor by the King she struck the name of Mr. Mason from her Will, in which she had bequeathed him her Sacharissa— which he had particularly admired—& left it to me. I did not

[3] Elisabeth de Lally-Tolendal was attending Madame Campan's school (L. 215 nn. 10, 11).

[4] Princesse Anne-Louise-Marie de Beauvau (1750–1834), who had married in 1767 Philippe-Louis-Marc-Antoine de Noailles, prince de Poix (ii, L. 112 n. 1). See also v, L. 526.

[5] Lally's translation *La Prière univèrselle*, is printed in volume xvii of Jacques Delille's *Œuvres* (18 vols., 1821), pp. 199–207.

know this till she was no more, when Mrs. Agnew informed me of the period of the alteration.[6]

My little Man waits for your lessons to get on in elocution; he has made no further advance, but that of calling out, as he saw our two Watches hung on two opposite hooks over the Chamber Chimney piece 'Watch, Papa—Watch, Mama,—' So, though his first Speech is English, the idiom is french. We agree this is to avoid any heart-burning in his Parents. He is at this moment so exquisitely enchanted with a little Penny Trumpet, finding he can produce such harmony *his own self*, that he is blowing & laughing till he can hardly stand. If you could see his little swelling cheeks, you would not ačuse yourself of being a misnommer in calling him cherub. I try to impress him with an idea of pleasure in going to see Grandpapa but the short visit to Bookham is forgotten, & the permanent Engraving remains, & all his concurrence consists in pointing up to the Print over the Chimney piece, & giving it one of his concise little bows.

Are not people a little revived in the political World by this unexampled honour paid to Mr. Pitt?[7] Mr. Locke has subscribed £3000. How you rejoiced me by what you say of poor Mr. Burke,—for I had seen the Paragraph of his Death[8] | with most exceeding great concern.

The Irish reports are, I trust, exaggerated[9]—few things come quite plainly from Hibernia—yet—what a time in all respects, to *transport* thither, as you too well term it, our beloved & most thrown away Susan! She writes *serenely*, & Norbury seems to repay a world of sufferings. It is delightful to see her so satisfied there, at least. But they have *all*, she says, got the brogue!

ᴵᵀMy Builder intends working hard at the Encyclopedia when at Chelsea we hope, also, Cᵗ Rumfords new treatise for Cottages

6 Mrs. Delany's will (P.C.C. Calvert 239) shows no such change.

7 This was the 'voluntary Loan' of 'EIGHT MILLIONS STERLING' subscribed on 1 Dec. for the support of 'His Majesty's Government' (*The Times*, 2 Dec. 1796).

8 This paragraph has not been located but according to Professor Thomas W. Copeland, such a false report was printed in *The Times*, 20 Jan. 1797.

9 Always anxious about Ireland, FBA may have noted in *The Times* (9 Dec.) or elsewhere that, on information laid by eighteen J.P.s, the Lord Lieutenant had on 3 Dec. issued a Proclamation declaring certain parishes 'in a state of disturbance'.

& Cabbages[10] will be printed before the building goes on.ᴛ Our Building is to be resumed the 1ˢᵗ of March. It will then soon be done, as it is only of lath & plaister, & the Roof & wood work are already prepared. My indefatigable superintendant goes every Morning for 2, 3 or 4 Hours to his field, to work at a sunk fence that is to protect his Garden from our Cow. I have sent Mrs. Boscawen, through Miss Cambridge, a history of our plan, & I have just heard she is quite gratified the dwelling is destined by M. d'A. to be called the Camilla Cottage. ᴛI am very glad good & dear James has promises [of] an addition to his comfort. James [is] quite shocked poor Martin should [come] to dread what is his best happiness, his holydays. I beg my kindest Love to Sally, ⟨James⟩ & Titchfield Street Comps ditto ⟨join⟩

adieu most dear Sir, ever your
most affectᵉ & dutifulᴛ
F.d'A.

219   Chelsea College, 30 December 1796

To Mrs. Phillips

A.L. (rejected Diary MSS. 4962–[3], Berg), 30 Dec. [17]96
Single sheet 4to   2 pp.
Edited by CFBt *and the* Press.

Chelsea College—Decʳ 30
—96.

I know how my beloved Susan will rejoice to *see* me thus with our dearest Father, whom I had indeed most cruelly longed to embrace, for several accounts subsequent to my leaving him had been so extremely melancholy as to excite a severe uneasiness.

---

[10] Widely advertised in newspapers of the time were the diversified essays of Sir Benjamin Thompson (1753–1814), Graf von Rumford (1790), F.R.S. (1779). See *The Complete Works of Count Rumford*, 4 vols., Boston, 1870–5. Volume i of his collected *Essays, Political, Economical, and Philosophical*, which had appeared in 1796, included a treatise 'Of Chimney Fireplaces' that concluded with a promise of a future 'essay on *cottage fireplaces*, which I am now preparing for publication'. This essay 'On the Construction of Kitchen Fire-places and Kitchen utensils; together with Remarks and Observations relating to the various processes of cookery, and proposals for improving that most useful art' did not appear, however, until 1799–1802.

I find him, I thank God, restored again to tranquility & chearfulness, hoarding rather a tender than bitter sorrow, & never
withdrawing from whatever may mitigate it. His private employment is still revising, copying, or burning old Letters &
Papers,[1] which, though filling him with regret, *occupy* his mind,
& keep off the foulest & most dangerous of all our enemies,
inactive despondence.—We came hither on Thursday;[2] Babkin
is an excellent Traveller, & was perfectly good. When we stopt
to change Horses, I enquired for some Cakes; a woman brought
a large basket full, & when I prepared to see its contents, Bab,
espying them, darted forward, & seizing one in each hand,
exclaimed 'Ock! Ock!—dea Ock!' & began munching both at
a time, to the great & staring amazement of the Maid. He is
firmly persuaded there is ONE owner & distributer of Cakes for
all England, & That is our sweet Friend. Here, when my Father
shares his Morning biscuit with him, I can never prevail with
the little Rogue to utter any thanks, or take any other notice of
it, than to cry out, delighted, 'Ock! Ock!—dea Ock!' & I
believe he thinks me rather reprehensible for endeavouring to
induce him to say *Thank you, Grandpapa.*—He still has no other
phrase to boast than *Tow it eay*—& has acquired very few even
single words. *Gan*-pappa is our last attainment: but he has a
little *Gibberish lingo* of his own, which is so very intelligible, by
his variety of looks & modulation, that he makes himself comprehended with very little difficulty. His Father fears his
pantomimical facility will retard his faculty of speech, by
rendering it less necessary to his wants.—Sally answers my
expectations in her general amelioration of manners, to my
great satisfaction. Her Heart & Hand have always been good, &
the *exterior* being softened, will make the *interior* better credited,
& more productive to the service of others, & to pleasant sensations for herself.—I have seen our Etty but once, when I dined
& spent the day in Titchfield Street. She looks tolerably well,
& was sprightly, & seemed at ease though very, very thin, &
making me long to bestow upon her dear meagre face & form
a portion of my rustic acquisition of fat & robustness. I could
soon recover any such deprivation, at Bookham, & under my
peculiar Physician. Mr. Burney looks remarkably well. So does
the excellent Edward. Marianne is again, selon moi, in beauty;

219. [1] See L. 214 n. 1.   [2] On Thursday 22 Dec.

Fanny considerably improved in health, & healthy appearance, but much altered for the worse, selon moi, in prettiness. Sophy rather bettered. | We had some exquisite Music, of Staebalt,[3] a Composer to me quite new, & very delicious. Fanny's voice & expression are both very much improved, & her singing is extremely pleasing. Sophy, also, is coming forth very prettily. They have both such native advantages, & native talents, that application alone can be wanting to make them shine above most others.—James appears very amiably as the fond Father of his little one; but it is a very plain, or rather most ordinary Baby. A Baby, however, is always interesting: & the Mother looks unusually well, & seems employed to her Heart's content in constant nursing.—Charles I have only seen for a minute; he is gone to Bath for Christmas, & could only call here *in his way*, for one quarter of an Hour. He is pretty well, & was gay & good humoured à son ordinaire. His wife & Mrs. Bicknel & little Charles were of the party, & all in high spirits, & hope of happiness.—our good Charlotte came to greet us the Day after our arrival, with her *sensible* little name-sake—who will surely soon be signalised as The *Thensible one of the Family*, for she has parts, & a thirst of knowledge, & a power of combining information, very extraordinary—very *strange*, indeed; & she is softer & of a more modest demeanour with respect to her acquisitions than formerly. I pray God for her preservation, as her health is *all* that her fond Mother need be much solicitous about. That poor Mother, on her return to Richmond found her Clement unwell; the next day he was worse, the 3^d she sent for Mr. Dundas,[4] & the 4th—the Measles appeared.—so now the poor thing will have all 3 to Nurse, No doubt, & our promise of spending a few days with her, in our way home, is broken up, to our mutual disappointment. Thus much for our own dear House; what little I have opportunity or inclination to arrange for seeing others, I shall defer to another Letter; I will enclose in this a half sheet of our beloved Friend, which she sent me to deliver to the Princesse d'Henin; but that charming woman is not well, & there is no requesting her to write for our convenience, when she forbears holding a Pen, she says, even a moment

---

[3] Daniel Steibalt (*c.* 1756–1823), a German pianist and composer, little known in England before 1790.

[4] David Dundas (1749–1826), cr. Baronet (1815), sergeant surgeon to the King (1791).

for her own. I hope it is only such a Cold as caution & a little time will remove. Were she less distant, I should like to see her every day, for she is engaging & winning by intercourse more at every interview, & she loves my Susan as if she had known her as *I* know her. What a charm in a warmth of Heart so generous in *believing* worth, before it can be proved? & how *rare* is that warmth, even in *tried* attachments! I see less of it than of almost any attraction, & I feel it the *single* one the most endearing.—We all grow *rather* anxious for a Letter from my dearest —it seems as if we had all been unusually long without one; I know how many are her claims, & only *wonder* at the power she has *made* to satisfy us as she has done. *Nobody* writes so interestingly, we *all agree*,—but I have brought none of my dear pacquets here, & therefore have written strait on, without any *responses*. I hope, however, our *lying-in* Letter[5] is now arrived. My Mate is not within, or would sign a name. He is well, thank Heaven, in all ways, & in all ways what my tender Susan wishes My Mate. Adieu—Kiss your Loves for me, Remember me kindly to the Major—& watch over *your-My* Health, my beloved—

220   Great Bookham, 8 January 1797

To Doctor Burney

A.L.S. (Diary MSS. vi. 4964–[7], Berg), 8 Jan. [17]96 [*sic*]
Double sheet 4to   4 pp.   *pmks* LEATHER / HEAD   9 JA 97   black wafer
Addressed: Dr. Burney, / Chelsea College, / Middlesex.
Endorsed by CB: Fanny 1797
Edited by FBA, p. 1 (4964), *annotated, date corrected from* 96 *to* 97 *and* Bookham *retraced*: ⁖ —97   (1)   Journey Home from Chelsea visit. Susanna & Ireland   Baby Alexander
Edited also by CFBt *and the* Press.

Bookham—
Jany 8th—96.

I was extremely vexed at missing our uncertain post yesterday, & losing, unavoidably, another to Day, before I return my

⁵ Announcing the birth of the first Locke grandchild Emily Frederica (L. 203 n. 10).

dearest Father our united Thanks for the kind sweet fortnight passed under his Roof.[1] Our adventures in coming back were better adapted to our departure than our arrival, for they were rather rueful. one of the Horses did not like his business, & wanted to be off—& we were stopt by his gambols continually, &, if I had not been a *soldier's wife*, I should have been terribly alarmed; but my soldier does not like to see himself disgraced in his other half, & so I was fain to keep up my courage,—till, at length, after we had passed Fetcham, the frisky animal plunged till he fastened the shaft against a Hedge, & then, little Betty[2] beginning to scream, I enquired of the Postilion if we had not better alight. If it were not, he said, for the *dirt*, yes,— The dirt then was defied, & I prevailed, though with difficulty, upon my Chieftain to consent to a general dismounting. And he then found it was not too soon, for the Horse became inexorable to all menace, carress, chastisement, or harangue, & was obliged to be loosened. Meanwhile, Betty, Bab, & I. trudged on, vainly looking back for our vehicle, till we | reached our little Home,—a Mile & half. Here we found good fires, though not a morsel of food; this, however, was soon procured, &—our walking apparel changed for dryer raiment,—& I sent forth our nearest Cottager, & a young Butcher, & a Boy, towards Fetcham, to aid the Vehicle, or its contents; for my Traveller had stayed, on account of our Chattels. And about 2 Hours after, the Chaise arrived, with ONE HORSE, & pushed by its Hirer, while it was half dragged by its driver. But all came safe, & we drank a dish of Tea, & Eat a Mutton chop, & kissed our little darling, & forgot all else of our journey but the pleasure we had had at Chelsea with my dearest Father & dear Salkin.—

And just now I receive a Letter from our Susanna, which tells me the invasion has been made in a part of Ireland where all is so loyal there can be no apprehension from any such attempt;[3]

220. [1] Apparently from 23 Dec. 1796 to 6 Jan. 1797.   [2] See L. 209 n. 3.
   [3] In a long folio letter of 25 Dec. 1796–2 Jan. 1797 (Berg), *pmks* 4 JA 97 7 JA 97 and printed in *FB & the Burneys*, pp. 252–8, SBP had relayed such inaccurate rumours as had by this time reached Drogheda of the appearance of French ships in Bantry Bay.
   Tabled conveniently by E. H. Stuart Jones, R.N., *An Invasion that Failed* (1950), pp. 106–61, is a list of the 45 ships (17 sail of the line, 8 transports, etc.) that, carrying an army of 15,000 troops, had set out from Brest on 16 Dec. to invade Ireland. Easterly gales of 'cyclonic strength' scattered the ships and prevented the landing of troops. To avoid being driven on the rocks the flotilla tacked off to sea, making a storm-tossed return to Brest *c.* 27 Dec.–2 Jan. 1797.

but she adds that if it had happened in the North, every thing might have been feared. Heaven send the Invaders far from all the points of the Irish Compass! & that's an Irish wish for expression, though not for meaning. All the intelligence she gathers, all around, is encouraging with regard to the ˡ spirit & loyalty of all that surround her. But Mr. Brabazon[4] is in much uneasiness for his wife, whose situation is critical, & he hesitates whether or not to convey her to Dublin, as a place of more security than her own habitation. What a period this for the cruel journey of our invaluable Susan! That dear Soul has had the delight, however, of her charming Norbury these last 3 weeks, & speaks of him with a satisfaction soothing to read.

⌐Mr. Lock & his eldest Daughter came to see us the morning after our return, but to forbid our going to Norbury park, as dear Mrs. Locke has a sore throat, which though trifling, she thinks should not be risked for the few who are always embracing a certain little Man, a Man she loves as if he was her own. Amelia is her head Nurse, & sends me good accounts, & M. d'Arblay is just gone for further inquiries to the house, though not to the Invalid.⌐

One of the Letters sent me on from Chelsea is from the good Mrs. Chapone,[5] who writes with / flattering / kindness her regret at not seeing me when I called, & her desire to *hear* from me, till I can call again. I am proud as well as glad of her constant regard, & shall answer her with all speed.

Alec looks rather displeased now when we call the Engraving *Grandpapa*, & will not repeat it after us: but he doats upon having me talk to him of Chelsea, & remind him of his visits to ˡ the Bed Room, & his Ock Cake, & clapping of hands, & playing & romping,—& Sally's singing, & dancing, & milk & water presents on her Knee. He has it all fresh in mind, & sometimes takes my Hand, when we are upon the subject, to lead me out of the Room, as if meaning to go to the right spot: & when he sees our journey ineffectual, & that no spacious apartment, nor Grandpapa, nor Aunt Sally, nor nodding figures appear, he pouts his little mouth, with one of his *oooea's*! & looks grievously disappointed, & half angry. He has quite left off *falling down*,

---

[4] Wallop Brabazon (ii, L. 44 n. 6) of Rath House, a mile or so distant from Belcotton. In 1796 he had married Jane Dupré (d. 1800), who was now pregnant. A daughter Rebecca was born in April or May of 1797.

[5] See L. 232 n. 5; also p. 320.

since he cannot call for your pity, except from his Horse, which still is formed of every thing he can contrive to mount. But *you* had so exactly hit his tone of commiseration, that he disclaims any other, & has forborne to demand one single 'poor Gentleman' since his return.

⎯⎯⎯⎯⎯⟶

I have just got a Friday's Mail from Mr. Cooke; but I wait my Monsieur's coming home to read it together. Mrs. Cooke is just set off to Oxfordshire, to a sick Sister.[6] Miss Cambridge writes me word she has a *pocket volume* of an account of our visit to Mrs. Boscawen from that kind lady.

adieu, most dear sir—I must now look forward to a Summer's Bookham to console my late parting—I recommend it to my dear Sally's influence with my kindest Love.

> Ever most dutifully & aff^ly your
> F. d'A.

I have a Letter from poor Mrs. R[ishton][7] who will make one more trial, upon a plan prepared, before she flees her own destiny.

221   Great Bookham, 26 January 1797

To Doctor Burney

A.L.S. (Diary MSS. vi. 4968–[71], Berg), 26 Jan. [17]97
Double sheet 4to   4 pp.   *pmks* [LEATHER] / HEAD   28 JA 97   black seal
Addressed: Dr. Burney, / Chelsea College, / Middlesex.
Endorsed by CB: 1797
Edited by FBA, p. 1, *annotated and date retraced*: ✳· 26   97   (2)
on verses upon Camilla &c—addressed to their honored Author. M^e de
⟨Tobale⟩. Dr. B.'s Astronomy   Cerulia
Edited also by CFBt *and the* Press.

> Bookham,
> Jany. 26. 97.

How is it, my dearest kindest Father!—you have made me so in love with my own Tears that no laughter ever gave my Heart

---

[6] See L. 179 n. 7.   [7] See L. 222 n. 10; iv, L. 269.

such pleasure as those I have shed—even plentifully—over these sweet sweet lines?¹—How do they endear to me my little Books —which with the utmost truth I can aver, never, in all their amazing circle of success have procured me any satisfaction I can put on a par with your approbation of them. My little Boy will be proud, hereafter—however POOR a Gentleman now— to read such lines, addressed by SUCH a Grandfather to his Mother. M. d'Arblay himself could not keep the Tears within his Eyes—*hard as is his Heart*—when he perused what so much touched me. He confesses your English *grows upon him*; & he does not *much wonder* if I, like Mr. Courtney,² class it with the very first class:—though I cannot boast quite as disinterested a generosity as that democratical Friend.

By the way, I hope soon to receive some copies of some of the early effusions of my Partner;³ after he had left you, yesterday, he saw a lady formerly very high in his good graces, who told him she had brought over with her, in her flight from her unhappy Country, several of his juvenile pieces; & he begged them for his Hermit. She thought him, probably, horribly John Bullyfied—yet promised to look them out. Indeed, she asked him if he did not find her *bien changée?*—& he replied 'Ma foi— Je ne peux pas vous le cacher—'

221. ¹ Seventy-six lines in heroic couplets, entitled 'To my daughter Fanny (Mʳˢ d'Arblay) Author of Evelina, Cecilia, & Camilla', postdated 1797, are extant in a collection of miscellaneous holographs (Berg); and, inscribed by CB in a note-book of occasional poetry (Osborn), is an earlier version of the poem. The lines, evidently written with carping reviews of *Camilla* freshly in mind, extol the un-exceptionable morals of the book. The Queen ('That prudent Mother, freed from usual dread') had allowed the novel 'unread' to be presented to her daughters.

> . . . spotless vestals might peruse secure
> Such harmless humours, & such passion pure.

The verses describing FB's youthful talents are perhaps the most interesting:

> In state of childhood, innocently gay.
> Thy voice & looks cᵈ folly well display;
> Could Affectation see where'er it lurk
> In face or limb, of Christian, Jew, or Turk
> Though neither wise nor learn'd thyself, couldst see
> Each subject true of risibility:
> The pedantry & petulence of wits,
> The vulgar ignorance of clowns & cits,
> The lies & cant of tradesmen thou couldst trace
> As well as Coxcomb's, or Coquet's grimace.

² See L. 150 n. 10.
³ A number of M. d'A's occasional poems, portraits, imitations, etc., if not his 'Juvenilia', are extant in both the Berg and Osborn Collections. In earlier times he had published *Opuscules du Chᵉʳ d'Anceny, ou anecdotes en vers recueillies et publiées Par M.d'A****. (Metz and Paris, 1787).

This lady also, who still, he says, is *une des plus elegantes*, & who is a thorough aristocrate, gave him the pleasure of informing him that M. de Bouilli[4] wished much to meet with him, & had declared he would wait upon him whenever he heard he was within reach. M. d'Arblay's acquaintance ^l with M. de Bouilli in France had been but slight, yet, as it was chiefly Professional, it could not, I believe, be but to his advantage. To ME it is always a very sensible gratification to see even party spirit stand still to do justice to the worth & intentions of my honourable Companion, M^e la Marquise de ⟨Tobale⟩[5] has promised they shall dine together with her when my Monsieur is again in her vicinity.

I delight in the reference my dearest Father has made to the Queen's trust for her Daughters in his most sweet lines. I am quite enchanted to hear of the 200 additionals to my very favourite poem on astronomy,[6] or rather its history. Yet I am provoked you have found no scattered verses to help on, for so many could never have been completed & refined, without many more sketched & imagined—at least, not if you compose like any body else. Pope had always *myriads* half finished, & dispersed, for future parts, while he corrected & polished the preceding.[7]

I am *very* glad indeed you proceed with this design, which is likely—according to the best of my judgement, such as it is,—to add very considerably to the stock of literature, & in a walk perhaps the most unhackneyed. To conduct to any science by a path strewed over with Flowers is giving beauty to labour, & making study a luxury.

When left alone the other day with the *poor Gentleman*, in the

4 Général François-Claude-Amour, marquis de Bouillé (1739–1800), who had associated himself with Louis XVI's attempted escape; or, with less probability, his son Louis-Joseph (1769–1850), aide-de-camp to his father. The failure of the plot forced both father and son to emigrate, the former dying in London.

5 Written confusedly and illegibly, as was sometimes FBA's spelling of foreign names.

6 For the long poem on the history of astronomy that was to occupy CB for some years, see Lonsdale, pp. 384–406; Scholes, ii. 155–6; *Memoirs*, iii. 415–17. In a letter of 7 Feb. (Berg) to [? Arthur Young], CB explained how 'from the urgent entreaties of Fanny, that I w^d occupy my mind with something that was likely to fasten on it, & help to wean reminiscence from unavailing regret & sorrow, I have collected together my astronomical books; extended my plan; and made a further progress in the work, chiefly in bed of a night . . .'.

7 FBA's acquaintance with Pope's practices was probably derived from Dr. Johnson and his 'Preface to Pope', the proof sheets of which he had presented to her (L. 176 no. 2).

interval of our sports, I took it into my mind to look at a certain melancholy ditty of 9 acts,[8] which I had once an idea of bringing forth upon the stage, & which you may remember Kemble had accepted, but which I with drew before he had time to shew it to Sheridan, from preferring to make trial of | Edwy & Elgiva, because it was more dramatic—but which I must always aver, *NEVER WAS ACTED*. This other piece you have seen—& it lost you, you told me, a night's rest—which, in the spirit of the black men in the funeral, made *me* all the gayer!—however, upon this re-perusal, after near 3 years interment, I feel fixed never to essay it for representation. I shall therefore restore it to its first form, that of a Tale in Dialogue, & only revive, & endeavour to make it readable for a fire-side. And this will be my immediate occupation in my Episodical moments taken from my companions & *maisonnette*: for since Camilla, I have devoted myself, as yet, wholly to them, as the solace of the fatigue my engagement with Time occasioned me. An engagement which I earnestly hope never more to make; for the fright & anxiety attending it can scarce be repaid.

⌐Nevertheless the abominable second ⟨horad post⟩ to your abominable Mr. Lewis[9] makes me waver from my original intent of *lying fallow* for some years to come. And therefore I shall prepare my Dramatic Tale as well as I can, & then ponder & consult upon its production probabilities.⌐

I rejoice Mrs. Crewe is in Town. I hope you will see her often. No one can be more *genial* to you. I rejoice, too, Mr. Coxe has got hold of you. I know his friendly zeal will be at work to do all that is in his power to chear you—& my dearest Father has all the kind consideration for others that leads to accepting good offices. Nothing is so cruel as rejecting them. My Monsieur was very sorry to see so little of you, but he would not disappoint my expectations of his return. He did not imagine what a *gem*

---

[8] This was 'Hubert De Vere / A Dramatic Tale', two manuscripts of which are extant in the Berg Collection of the NYPL. One version (126 pp.), originally transcribed in 5 *cahiers* (9·1 × 7·8″), has been heavily revised, the revisions having been written on slips of paper and pinned or pasted over the original pages. This text also shows obliterations, cancellations, and emendations, as does the 2nd version (110 pp.), written in 5 *cahiers* (7·8 × 6·4″).

[9] Possibly Matthew Gregory Lewis (1775–1818), author of *The Monk* (1795), M.P. (1796–1802), to whom CB apparently lent money. See L. 226 n. 10. It must have been he (or his father) who offered CB (or the d'Arblays) a frank used by the latter in writing to SBP on 17, 29 Aug. 1797. The letter that CB apparently wrote to him is missing.

he brought me into the bargain. My own little Gem—as Etty (*ill-naturedly*) calls the poor Gentleman, is blyth & well.— ⌐

⌐[He] has gained nothing new in eloquence since that excellent moral order which he uttered on the Morn of his Father's departure 'Get up'—except that to Day, after saying Grandpapa to your portrait, which he has again taken into favour, for want of the original, he looked at Mr. Locks which he is accustomed to call '*Ock, ock*,—& suddenly said *At's* Lock's' This surprised me into a laugh at the moment, whereupon its repetition; I confess the second to be rather cavalier & familiar for so young a personage. However, *Alas*, he at present so little allows us of leisure that I will not even *write* when it is [a] question of him. But Dick, I remember, would never be persuaded, when double my Alec's age, to call Sir William Brown anything but *William Brown*.[10] I am sorry poor Lord Orford is so ill & much obliged by his recollection of *Mr. Hayes*.[11] I received another very miserable Letter from our poor Mrs. Rishton, even more unhappy, because hopeless I learn & even such as she tells of that Misery in her last Letters, is *much*, & of his manner of detention. I was truly grieved for her!—Adieu, my most dear Father, again & again accept the grateful thanks of your most dutiful & affectionate

F. d'Arblay⌐

[10] Sir William Browne (1692–1774), M.D. (1721), F.R.S. (1738/9), knighted (1748), President of the College of Physicians (1765–6), who, like Dr. Burney, had spent some time in King's Lynn and, like the Burneys in the early 1770s, lived in Queen Square. In May 1772 he is seen (*ED* i. 184–5) in Dr. Burney's parlour gallantly quoting his own verses on love, 'a most extraordinary old man, . . . a very renowned physician . . . near eighty, [who] enjoys prodigious health and spirits'. In 1772 FB's half-brother Richard Thomas would have been 4 years old, as FBA says, twice her son's present age.

[11] John Hayes, reputedly the natural son of the 1st Earl of Oxford (Scholes, i. 71; also i, L. 10 n. 10).

222   Great Bookham, 29 January 1797

Conjointly with M. d'Arblay
    and Mrs. Locke
To Mrs. Phillips;
and Amelia Locke *to* Charles Norbury Phillips

A.L. & A.L. & A.L. (Berg), 29 Jan. [17]97
Double sheet folio   4 pp.   *pmks*   LEATHER / HEAD   1 FE 97   4 FE
97   red seal
    Addressed: Ireland / Mrs. Phillips / Belcotton / Drogheda / Ireland—
    Endorsed by SBP: Feby 5th / —97.

[*By Madame d'Arblay*]

Bookham, Jany 29.—97

And can you, my beloved Susan, reproach yourself about
Letters? when one of yours seems to me to contain, for real
matter, for all its readers love & long for, more than 10 of
almost any writers, even amongst the select? I fear you will have
wondered, I hope not have been uneasy, at *my* silence: I have
heard of so many Letters travelling towards you, I thought you
would be sure all was well, & I henceforth purpose writing
longer Letters & less frequently. But you must tell me *honestly*
whether this large sheet is charged any more than a small one.[1]
Otherwise I shall reverse my plan.

I must now own to my dearest beloved that we have been
under some anxiety for the sweet Friend of both our Hearts:[2]
she has had a very severe suffering indeed, from a nervous
rheumatism of the most excruciating kind: such, almost, as you
may remember Mr. FitzGerald of Poland Street[3] to have

222. [1] Quarto double sheets (4 pp.) cost SBP 11*d.* on arrival at Belcotton; double
folio sheets (4 pp.), being still one sheet of paper, seem to have been carried for the
same price.
    [2] Mrs. Locke of Norbury Park (i, L. 1 n. 3), and presently alluded to, Amelia
(her third child), Mr. Locke, and the youngest son Frederick (i, L. 15 n. 8), who,
like his brothers, was sent to Cheam.
    [3] Keane FitzGerald (d. 29 June 1782), F.R.S. (25 Mar. 1756), an experimental
scientist, best known for his invention of a barometer, and duly mentioned by
William Ellis, 'Brief Historical Account of the Barometer', *Q.J.R. Met. Soc.* xii

described. She bore it with extremest patience & sweetness; but as the seizure began with a sore throat, she would not admit me to see her: & I was banished a full fortnight after my return to my dear Hermitage. Last Saturday however, I had the delight of embracing her,—& her looks were such as to remove every remaining apprehension,—bright, glowing, & clear as if the inside were turned out. I thank God I can assure you I am perfectly at ease about her—I leave you to judge, therefore, how well she must be. I have had notes from her ever since our meeting; till then her lovely third self wrote constantly, often 2^{ce} a day, & was as anxious to give comfort as if only a looker on for my sake; though she was almost ill with affectionate cares & attentions. The Oracle—or Ange—or whatever else best pictures all that is most wise & most Good, has held up surprisingly, though living only by her life—for that is, after all, the case, dear to him as is all the rest of his family, & some favoured few besides. He has had, & still has a Cold, but nothing of fever, & looks well. Poor little Frederic has had the same sore throat, & a fever with it, & a great indigestion; but he is getting over it, & happy that it chanced just as his holydays were waning away; I really believe the detention at home has recompensed the evil. There has been much illness round about, but none other that peculiarly affects us, & not one of our own race has suffered. My dear Father I think particularly well; & he is now eagerly employed, once more, in literary business.

———

O how do I rejoice my dearest Susanna has escaped all but colds! The Duchess of Leinster told me the climate about you was soft & mild, & that she believed, from what she had been

(1886), 134–53. Drawings and explanations of his barometer are to be found in the *Phil. Trans.* lii (1761), 146–76; and lx (1770), 74–9. He published *A Letter to the Directors of the East India Company* (1777) and seven papers, besides the above, in the *Phil. Trans.*, though none on rheumatism.

The Collectors' Books (for Property Taxes and Watch Rates) for the Great Marlborough Ward (Archives Department, Public Library, Buckingham Palace Road, Westminster) show Keane FitzGerald living in Poland Street as early as 1753. Dr. Burney, having moved from King's Lynn to London in 1760, appears in the Rate Books of 1761–70 as next-door neighbour to Keane FitzGerald and in his 'Memoirs' (Berg) refers to him as his 'landlord'.

His son Keane (*c.* 1748–1831), a Bencher of the Inner Temple (1808), appears in *ED* ii. 144–5, but of the Burney family it was SBP who called regularly on the FitzGerald family in her visits to town (Journals, see *Catalogue*).

informed of concerning your constitution, it would agree with you. Heaven grant it! & grant its trial may be short!

———

Mrs. Wall's[4] Letter touched me. I saw in it the true estimation she had made of our sweet Amelia, & I fear her very deserving son has made one as true, by the words *restless*, & *hasty*, & by the *agitation* of his sister, which seems to have arisen from *regret*, & from the apprehension her Brother had been premature in his decision. I heartily wish him happy, & hope the precipitance of his choice & fixture may turn out fortunately. I should much like you should see *her*, & you would soon gather what his future prospects promise, & whether mere rash desperation, or Judgement aided by good luck, have impelled him.

———

our poor Charlotte has had a very severe trial; her two little Girls had the measles just as their Mother recovered, & just as they were themselves getting well, after having had the disorder most favourably, Clement was taken ill of a very violent Fever. He is now, thank God! almost well again, but he has suffered long & dangerously, I fear, by accounts which, though smothered, seem to prove it. He is an extremely fine Boy, & his Mother doats upon him, & she has been very much alarmed; but Miss Cambridge, who has visited her daily in this period, writes me word she held herself up with great courage, & was indefatigable in her nursery. Her Governess continues all she can wish.[5]

———

Every account of little Charlotte Francis confirms my early opinion of her.[6] Miss Cambridge gives me 2 traits of her that are charming. A protegée of her own, a poor little kind of foundling, was invited to spend the Day with the Francis's; Miss Cambridge

---

[4] Mrs. James William Wall's letter is missing, but to continue the story (L. 203 and n. 6), her son Charles William Wall, rejected a few months earlier by Amelia Locke, had married on (1 Nov. 1796) Eliza, only daughter of Richard Butler-Hamilton-Lowe (1742–1821) of Lowe's Green, near Cashel. Her portion, £8,000. 'What will you say', SBP had written on 28 Nov. 1796 (Berg), 'when you hear Mr Wall is—married?' 'It was I find suddenly concluded, & his mother seems not without anxiety tho she says she c^d make no objections & that her son had been unhappy—was restless—& perhaps a little hasty—' (*FB & the Burneys*, p. 251).

[5] Elizabeth Morton (L. 212 n. 4).

[6] Charlotte Francis was now 10 years old.

told Charlotte she must not spoil her, but make her keep her distance properly, & always remember her poor & dependant situation. Charlotte, looking up in her Face with great concern & sensibility, frankly answered 'O!—indeed—I don't know how I shall do that!—' Afterwards, when the little protegee arrived, Miss Cambridge repeated her lessons, & gave some to the poor Child itself, charging her not to forget what she was, but keep in mind the honour Miss Francis did her by letting her be her play fellow, & the favour she must think it all her life. Charlotte then, running up to Miss Cambridge, whispered her, but in an animated manner '*Take care*, Miss Cambridge, or while you're at all this pains to make her not think herself a Gentlewoman, you'll make *ME* think myself a fine lady, with your honours & your favours!—'

Pray read this to my dear Children of Belcotton. They would all have had the same desire to raise a little Creature brought to them for her happiness. Miss Cambridge would not thus have insisted for any common poor Child, but a long story hangs to this, who is under her care, & whom she means to provide for, & desires to bring up with the utmost humility & modesty.

An infinitely dear friend of mine, whom I think I need not name, has sent me a description of her abode that has interested me beyond all measure,[7]—saddened me too, in many instances, but in all contented a longing desire I had had of painting her such as she is at the very spot where I can only with my mind's Eye behold her.

You have been prophetic about James's babe,[8] which I hear is considerably improved already, & from M. d'A. who was shocked by its excessive plainness.—A certain little Being after whom you enquire does not yet, I confess, give *that* sort of shock to beholders. But I have no expectation his present appearance will last: He still does not speak, except a few casual words, & 2 or 3 phrases, of which, however, he make the most that is possible, for he contrives to be understood as well as if all Dr. Johnson's dictionary was at his command. He has got a new &

[7] On 15 Jan. 1797 SBP had sent a letter (Berg) of four folio pages describing *inter alia* the unfinished farmhouse of Belcotton, the views from its windows over level lands to the Boyne and the sea, and the outlying semicircle of barns, sheds, and workshops (see *FB & the Burneys*, pp. 258–62; and Plate II). A second description is given in SBP's letter of 23 Nov. 1796 (Berg) to Mrs. Locke.

[8] Sarah Burney, born 17 Nov. 1796.

curious play now, of his own invention, which is sending us to Coventry; for when he is affronted, he calls out with great energy *'do! do! do!'* for *Go,* Go, Go,—& then, turning his little head away, sedately adds *'Papa aw—dawn!—Mama aw dawn!—'*

Charles & his family are returned to Greenwich, but I have not heard of them, since. I had 2 flourishes from the lady all diamonded over with pink,[9]—but they remain unacknowledged. I have very melancholy Letters from a connexion of ours once the most intimate[10]—what of misery is there in the world from mis-alliances!— Nor is the single state much more exempt—the Daughter of my once most dear friend[11]—surrounded with all that is *apparently* to be desired, writes me word she sees *all black*, from the unhappiness she experiences!—To how very few spots has my view of felicity been directed! I should almost blush at my own, but that no one is the worse for it, & that *my* life, also, had only *apparently* been happy, since almost Childhood, till its present date.

Mrs. B[urney] of Greenwich writes me word a charming Letter has been received from You—& expresses herself warmly

[9] 'Quite . . . DIAMONDED WITH *pink* ribband', a phrase used by Norbury Phillips (aged 4) in his efforts to describe the dress 'all flaring & flaming wth gause & pink ribbands' worn by CB Jr.'s wife 'Rosette' on her visit to Mickleham in July 1789 (SBP's Journals, Barrett, Eg. 3692, ff. 61b–6b).

[10] Maria (Allen) Rishton (i, Intro., p. lxxiv), whose unhappiness FBA had been aware of since her visit of 1792 to Thornham (i, L. 38 n. 2). In a long letter (16 pp.) written on [24 Dec.], *franked* Anson 29 Dec., *pmk* 30 DE (Barrett, Eg. 3697, ff. 237–44b), Maria, now resolved to separate from her husband, had applied to FBA for 'Candid Advice'. 'Be My Ghostly Father on this Occasion . . . I never will trouble you again if you will be my Guide and Monitress this once—'. It was Rishton's 'capricious Tyranny' in separating her from her family that had caused her 'dejection', estranged her 'Affections', and made life a 'burthen' to her, and so she had recently told him, her plan being to seek 'An Asylum' at Chelsea with her half-sister SHB and her stepfather Dr. Burney, 'the Man I reverence and love above All other men' (see also her letter of 9 Jan. cited below).

Though FBA's reply is missing, she had apparently sent the 'rigidly Virtuous Advice' to which Maria respectfully refers in her letters of *pmk* 7 JA 97 and Monday 9 Jan. 1797 (Barrett, Eg. 3697, ff. 245–6b, 247–50b). Counselling 'Chearfulness' and urging the duties of marriage, FBA seems to have represented Death as the ' "only *Indispensible* Cause of Marriage Seperation" ' though conceding that it might not be ' "the only *Justifiable* one" '. In a later 'history' of the separation (iv, L. 269), FBA states that her clear opinion and advice to Maria had been that, whatever her wishes, 'she had forfeited, by her marriage vow, the right of positively quitting [her husband], if she could not obtain his consent'.

And this Maria was long in attaining. Her letters (above) report Rishton's anguished efforts to keep her and his attempts at reform. Though he could allow Maria long visits to Holkham, he could never bring himself to receive her brother's family at Thornham.

[11] Hester Maria Thrale, the affluence of whose circumstances can be deduced from the clauses of her father's will (Clifford, p. 200).

in your praise. She conducted herself extremely well upon a late fatal event, & won upon my Father extremely by her quiet & amiable behaviour in the melancholy days he spent at her house.

How delighted have we been at the brevity of the alarm about Ireland! Pray tell the Major I mentioned his proceedings & loyalty & all that in a Letter—one of my half-yearly Epistles— to the lady who thought him so *abrompt*.[12] |

Every word you tell me of Mr. Mathurin[13] charms me—what exquisite good fortune he should prove so every way deserving! how much of sweet Norbury's future happiness must hang upon so very important a circumstance! My almost daily wish rises to my little darling in the shape of Norbury,—it is my hope's model for him. I often believe they will not be very different. My tender love to him, & my dearest Fanny. You were very considerate about the *scrip*, which was quite beyond us. We have been forced to resist one to M. Montlosier,[14] except for half a Year, on account of its being the same sum. But there *is* a subject on which a little thing of that kind though not *literary*, is fulfilled with the utmost pleasure,—& James was certainly right about it. O my Susanna! how could you frame the sentence in which

[12] Miss Schwellenberg and the word she used to describe Captain Phillips when in former years (1786–9), 'dear', 'indulgent', and helpful, he used to call on FB at St. James's Palace.

[13] One sheet of the letter of 15 Jan. 1797 (op. cit.) FBA later destroyed, but from the first SBP had expressed satisfaction with her son's tutor Henry Maturin (L. 215 n. 7), 'one of the best young men in the world' (*FB & the Burneys*, pp. 237, 249). In spite of her assurances that Maturin's 'Methodistical' bent would not affect Norbury, CB thought differently, as may be seen in his letter of 10 June 1808 (Bodleian) to Edmond Malone in reply to a congratulatory letter of 8 June (Folger Shakespeare Library) that Malone had sent to him, relaying a good report that he had had from Ireland on Norbury Phillips and detailing the rigours of the system of studies at Trinity College, from which Norbury had graduated B.A. in 1806.

I am very happy in the acc^t & grateful for it, that your learned correspondent Dr Mich. Kearney gives of Norbury Phillips. He was a shy timid boy from being put into the hands of a methodistical tutor at the beginning of his education and though the most beautiful, spirited, & ingenious child, during the life of his poor mother, he became so sheepish, scrupulous, & unfit for the world, That I had no hope of his ever figuring in classical learning or science, or indeed anything but Music, for wch he had an early passion, to w^h his puritanical Tutor allowed him, at leisure hours, to apply; but he seldom had an instrum^t of his own to practice on, & never was allowed a Master. But after he was entered of Trinity College, his good conduct & sweet temper, gained him friends, particularly Dr Allet, Dean of Raphoe—a great dilettante Musician with a Fine base voice. . . .

[14] SBP's offer is lost with the missing part of the letter 15 Jan. (op. cit.) but evidently it related to a subscription to a periodical like the *Courrier de Londres*, edited by François-Dominique de Reynaud, comte de Montlosier (1755–1838), who emigrated to England in 1794.

you allude to it?—all giving & all good as you are to the UTMOST stretch of your powers,—how could you frame it?

⸻

I had a few lines from Etty through M. d'A, who will tell you himself of his visit, la charmante Princesse, &c—& he calls for my pen & Paper—& you will not hate his hand—Remember me kindly to the Major—

& adieu, my very—very dear!—

[*By M. d'Arblay*]

C'est, en verité with the greatest diffidence, my dear Sister that I take upon myself to write—allons Courage. Pendant notre séjour à Chelsea j'ai bien peu joui du plaisir d'être rapproché de la Princesse et de Lally. Vous avez surement vu le charmant enfant qu'avait laissé à cette excellente amie, sa Niece Mme la C^esse de V[audreuil]?^15 Eh bien quand ma femme est allée visiter la p^esse le pauvre petit etait fort mal. Le lendemain quand j'y-suis passé, il n'était plus; et la douleur que M^e d'H[enin] et La[lly]—en ressentaient ne peut être depeinte. à present encore il est impossible de leur en parler sans les faire fondre en larmes. Neanmoins la Princesse qui avait un gros rhuem et la poitrine très souffrante est reelem^t beaucoup mieux, et assez tranquille. Quant à Lally sa santé est *couci-couci*. Je crois qu'il aurait besoin d'être distrait de ses eternels travaux. Vous savez sans doute qu'il est occupé en ce moment à donner la dernière main à un plaid-oyer en faveur des Emigrés:^16 Cet ouvrage actuellement sous presse lui fera infiniment d'honneur, mais ne diminuera pas le nombre des criailleries. *&c*— *&c*— Après avoir diné avec lui chez la Pri^sse je l'ai mené (avec le jetton d'argent de Charles) à L'Opéra où nous avons vûs Evelynn^17 suivi du ballet de

---

^15 Madame la comtesse de ⟨V⟩ (if M. d'A actually wrote *V*) may have been the prince d'Hénin's niece Pauline-Victoire de Riquet de Caraman (1764–1834), who had married in 1781 Jean Louis Rigaud (1762–1816), vicomte de Vaudreuil. On meeting 'this very lady-like agreeable person' in Paris on 7 Jan. 1818, Glen-bervie recalled (ii. 285–6) having met her first 'with that aunt of hers at Richmond, and afterwards in 1793 at Brussels'.

^16 *Défense des émigrés français* (L. 215 n. 9).

^17 *Arvire et Evelina*, a lyric tragedy in three acts, by Antonio-Maria-Gasparo Sacchini (1734–86), of which there were 87 performances by 1811. He did not live to complete the score, and the final act was constructed from other compositions of his by Jean-Baptiste Rey (1734–1810).

Psiché,[18] qui tout au plus la parodie du Spectacle enchanteur qui porte ce nom à l'Academie Royale de Musique de Paris, offre neanmoins un ensemble assez divertissent qu'anime surtout la jolie Parisot. Cette course que j'ai faitte à Londre où je suis resté trois jours et dont je ne suis revenu que le 25, a été occasionée par la necessité où le manque de parole de Mr Shirley[19] m'a mis de vendre des fonds dans le moment le plus defavorable p^r faire honneur à des engagemens que j'ai pris pour ma batisse qu'en honneur je n'aurais pas entreprise si j'avais pu supposer ca qui même à présent ne me parait pas croyable. il m'a fait passer chez un avocat qui devait me payer dure une somme de 500£ que lui prêtait sa soeur: mais il s'est trompé sur l'age qu'elle a &c— &c—&c—

D'après le conseil de James, j'avais ecrit p^r representer qu'il etait tout simple que la vente que sa manque de parole occasion- erait fut supportée par celui qui s'en etait rendu coupable mais *SA CONSCIANCE* ne lui permet pas de trouver juste ma re- clamation je ne sais pas même où prendre les *intérêts* ! ! !

[*By Amelia Locke*]

For Norbury Phillips

There has hardly passed a day my Norbury, since I rec^d yours & ^ry dearest Mama's joint sweet letter, that I have not *longed* to tell you how grateful I felt for your affectionate remembrance of me; & it has grieved me more than I can express to have been so long without the power of telling you how *very* dear it was to me—But while Mama was so ill, I could not endure to make you uneasy about her, & since her Recovery, but very lately com- pleted, this has been my first opportunity. I have however endeavoured to comfort myself by relying on my dear Norburys kindness & his *I trust*, entire persuasion of my affection for him, & the pleasure that such a proof of his must consequently give me—How I have enjoyed in idea my Norbury's meeting with his (& my) beloved Mama, with the dear Fanny, not forgetting poor little Willy, who tho' so long absent from you never ceased loving you, & used when he was here perceiving I suppose I that I did not *dislike* the subject, continually to entertain me with

---

[18] *L'Amour et Psyché* (1769), a *ballet-héroïque* by Jean-Joseph Cassanea de Mondonville (1715–73), originally the third act of *Les Festes de Paphos* (1758). This piece was presented at the King's Theatre on 27 and 28 Jan. (see the *Morning Chronicle*). [19] See L. 193 n. 7.

what dear Brother Norbury used to do he remembered at Mickleham—I long to be acquainted with all the kind friends where you are that love you, & particularly with y^r favorite *Janey paney*[20] whom I love for that title par avance, without feeling any inclination to *envy it* her, which is perhaps less generous than it may appear, as I only allow her to maintain it in Ireland—D^r M^{rs} d Arblay has I dare say given y^r Mama a very minu[te] description of all little alexanders pretty ways, I will therefore only say that I enclose to you a little Cutting,[21] one out of many unsuccessful attempts to give you an idea of him, which is thought very like & however indifferent the performance I am sure my d^r Norbury will value it on that acc^t. He yesterday returned here from our little Nieces Christening,[22] who was called after her two Grandmamas, Emily-Frederica. she is a very pretty little fat Girl, but you will I think admire her more a few months hence than just now. I am sure you will be happy to hear that poor Frederick is recovering from his fever. He is just now asleep or I am sure were I to tell him to whom I am writing w^d send you many messages All here were delighted with y^r kind remembrances. Y^r *foster* mother who is Thank God perfectly recovered sends you many loves. & Mr Lock Augusta W^m Ma Bonne[23] & all whom you mention, desire to be very affectionately remembered—Pray give my tenderest love to y^r dearest Mama—& tell her if possible how I valued every line from her the letter contained, & that her kind partiality & affection are one of my *very* most precious treasures. As I am writing to you I must not commission you to tell her how her Norbury's letter delighted me Sir Hughs excellent speech[24] & indeed every line [*tear*] But how poor a return is this!

[20] Jane Brabazon (*fl.* 1798–1808), daughter of Philip Brabazon of Mornington (1733–1828), a second cousin of Molesworth Phillips, whose 'flagrant' and assiduous pursuit of her, apparently unrewarded, is described by SBP in her letters of 1798 (see *FB & the Burneys*, pp. 267–75). One of SBP's most devoted friends, Jane was to marry on 22 Nov. 1798 the Revd. Robert Disney (*c.* 1769–1832), 4th son of Brabazon Disney (1711–90), D.D. (1746), Chancellor of Armagh. Disney was the curate of Kilcullen (1797–1800), of St. Mark's, Dublin (1807), of Glasnevin (1809), and Prebendary of Brigowne (Cloyne), 1809–32. The arrangements for the marriage are described by SBP (op. cit., pp. 290–2).

[21] Cuttings of Alexander in petticoats are still extant in the Berg Collection, the NYPL.

[22] Charles Locke's daughter, Emily Frederica, born 12 Dec. 1796, was baptized at Marylebone Church on 29 Jan. 1797.

[23] The French governess at Norbury Park, identified in the record of her burial at Mickleham (2 Oct. 1808) as 'A. C. Monbrun, widow,—Bergonier'.

[24] A character in *Camilla*, but the allusion is lost with Norbury's letter.

I am so stinted for [*tear*] I can hardly add how truly I am my Norbury['s affection]ate Wife.

Amelia Lock

& pray remember us all to y^r Papa—

[*By Mrs. Locke*]

31st Jan Norbury Park—my own dearest Friend will I know be made happy by the assurance of my entire & perfect recovery I have no sort of complaint remaining but weakness which every day lessens—I am seated where she is accustomed to look for me in the Picture Room—over against our Ange who tho' not absolutely free from cold is nearly so, & wou'd now be quite well but for the great anxiety which we have had on our poor little Frederick's account, who has been dangerously ill. about 10 days ago he caught cold walking home late in the evening a very cold foggy night, & a malignant fever & sore throat declared itself—Dr Moore[25] was still with us & he after he had left us, from my Lockes Letter with ye account of the state that dear Boy was in, was so much alarmed that he sent his Son Mr James Moore down immediately. he arrived Friday & immediately gave our poor Frederick large quantities of Bark & Wine —& staid till Sunday when he thought him in so fair a way that he returned to Town & now thank God altho confined to his Bed still, he is progressively amending but you may imagine my beloved Friend the anxiety that we have been in—Our dear Girls have had colds but are well—they returned to us yesterday from Town where they went, with our Willm & my good Rich[26] for ye X^{ng} *of our* little Grand daughter &, to represent us as we could not be present—ye Duchess & your two Friends were Godmothers & Godfather & she is named *Emily Frederica* she is the most flourishing *little large* Persona with eyes which they report are like Grandmama Locke!—& her Mother sees a strong likeness to that same Grandmama—*you* will not hate for it—God bless you my ever dearest—I have been solaced & delighted with your exquisite Letters—poor Susan's sister[27] lives at Swansea & is well

[25] Dr. John Moore (ii, L. 68 n. 4) and his son James, *afterwards* Carrick-Moore (1762–1860), a member of the Corporation of Surgeons of London (1792) and the biographer of his brother Sir John (1761–1809).

[26] Ann Rich (ii, L. 68 n. 27), the housekeeper at Norbury Park.

[27] Either Elizabeth Adams (bapt. 30 Mar. 1760 at St. Martin's Church, Epsom) or Rebecca (bapt. 21 Sept. 1765), who married on 13 Oct. 1784 Edward Edgeler.

223   Great Bookham, 30 January 1797

To Mrs. Francis (*later* Broome)

A.L.S. (Berg), 30 Jan. [17]97
Double sheet small 4to   4 pp.   *pmk* LEATHER / HEAD   black seal
Addressed: Mrs. Francis, / Hill Street, / Richmond, / Surry.
Endorsed by CBF: Sister d'arblay / Feb. 1ˢᵗ—1797 / ans: Feb. 17ᵗʰ

Bookham,
Janʸ 30.—97

What a grievous & most unexpected disappointment, my
dearest Charlotte![1] I thought so much of your worst cares over
—I felicitated you so sincerely—I thanked you so heartily for
the wishes of seeing me quit of the same inflexible disorders—&
now, to find your relief so short, your joy so transitory! And I
greatly fear the dear Clement has been yet more seriously ill
than my kind Miss Cambridge positively mentions.[2] for it is only
by degrees she hints at what has passed; & chiefly gives me to
understand the sweet little fellow's sufferings by what I may
infer from her praises of my dear Charlotte's *bearing up so well*, &
supporting her courage & spirits & health. alas, I am truly
grieved there should have been a cause for such exertion—but
I know my dear sister endures great & real evils with far more
fortitude than small vexations, | which teize & worry her so
forcibly, that those who know her less would not expect the
efforts of which she is capable upon great Calls & trials.—May
she be spared the sad experience that may shew this to others
as to me!

what an exquisite comfort must my Miss Cambridge have been
to you! Every Day, she says, she has seen you. How infinitely
kind! I know well the invaluable goodness of her heart to ALL;
but her zeal for those she once loves is boundless—& by no one
excelled,—by very few indeed equalled. My dear Charlotte is
now of that number—& will be of it for-ever. she is as constant
as she is warm—& that is most rare indeed!—Pray thank her
for her Letter, when you see her,—she will forgive my answering

223. ¹ See L. 222.   ² This letter is missing.

it to you, upon such an occasion. She tells me you mean to write speedily, & I now write to urge you not to forget a design I shall be still uneasy | till I see executed, though the assurance that Clement was a Coachman again has rested most pleasantly upon my imagination.

I delight in hearing Miss Morton[3] has been so amiable & consoling upon this occasion. This is a period in which such conduct will knit you; I trust, to each other. I wish to see & know her. And how do I rejoice in all Miss C[ambridge] tells me of my dear little Charlotte![4] she is seen by her as she has always been by me—as a *wonderful Child*, as uncommon in heart as in head, & loving her dear Mother as that Mother deserves to be loved. What a treasure—what a comfort to you for ever!—And her health, now, I trust will be perfectly re-established.

It was indeed most fortunate you came to me with such prompt kindness at Chelsea,—it is all that softens the *unseasonableness* of the Measles to me,—for that they should come, & speedily, I could not regret; I wish my own little soul to have them at the age of Marianne. I am so glad I *saw* Charlotte, & satisfied myself of her real recovery. I shall now as much long to see them all again—& the summer will not, I hope, be | ungenial to our long projected double meetings. All goes on as well as it there can in Ireland—I had a Letter yesterday,[5] very satisfactory in all she could devise to make it so. she charges me to thank you for a very '*kind & amusing* Letter'—knowing your aversion to writing, she will not yet answer it *directly*. I have had a sweet copy of verses upon Camilla by my dearest Father,[6] which I will shew you when we meet comfortably. How unfortunate our good Aunt[7] should not be well enough to visit you at this Season! My kindest love to her I beg. Miss Cambridge gives me hopes Sally whitton may re-fit again.[8] Is your *good Scrub*, as Miss C[ambridge] calls her, to remain, or Sally to try again? If the latter, do you think *Scrub* would do for me? Can she cook a little, wash, & keep a house clean?

---

[3] See L. 212 n. 4.
[5] This is SBP's letter of 15 Jan. (op. cit.).
[4] Cf. L. 222.
[6] See L. 221 n. 1.
[7] CB's sister Rebecca (1724–1809). She was living in Richmond but the allusion to her is lost with the letter to which this is the reply.
[8] Conjecturally a daughter of 'Nurse Whitton', Fanny Phillips's foster mother. The children of Mary and Thomas Whitton (i, L. 6 n. 2), formerly of Chessington but living in later years at Leatherhead, were from time to time domesticated with members of the Burney family.

Don't stay within too much, I entreat; take walks with your little ones as a *duty*, due to them, & us all, for it will be the best preservative of your health. *My* Treasures, Great & Little, are all you can wish them,—in all ways. M. d'A. is in his field, or would send Loves endless to you, & his favourite little mistress. Mine pray give most tenderly—& most tenderly & truly receive.

F d A.

James has had M^r M[athias]'s receipt.[9]

224   [Great Bookham,] 10 February [1797]

Conjointly with Amelia Locke
To Mrs. Phillips

A.L. & A.L. (Berg), 10 Feb.
Originally a double sheet 4to (already dated 21 Jan.), of which FBA later discarded the second leaf   2 pp.
Edited by CFBt.

[*By Madame d'Arblay*]

Feby. 10th.

My most beloved Susan will, I trust, be relieved from her anxiety completely before this arrives, by a folio sent off some time ago[1]—& I can now assure her that all accounts, & daily sweet billets, from Norbury, confirm every best & most wished security of the entire restoration of our dearest Friend, whom nevertheless I have seen but once, owing to the illness of poor Frederick, which began the day I was there, & which, though *finished*, being reckoned of a contagious nature, has made them desire me to abstain till the house & all are quarantined. You will believe one thing only could make me tractable—my terror of any possible danger to my little darling; who, by the way, has this very Day cut a tooth, & is now enjoying himself in undiscribable gaiety, after a few Hours of great suffering, though no indisposition. The little soul will never speak—he has now

---

[9] Apparently some claim had to be presented before the quarterly payments of FBA's pension (of £100) could be collected.

224. [1] This is L. 222.

made himself a dialect so intelligible & so expressive, all his own, that, finding we comprehend it, he is at no further trouble in making any essay at elocution. It will be odd enough if he should grow up a Mute![2] I am sure it will not be to adapt himself for performing that solemn part in a Tragedy, for his spirits are the most Camillaish I ever saw. He has a new likeness to my dear Norbury gaining ground, which is such a passion for *sociality*, that he prefers staying within, if I will listen to his mock discourses, & reply, to any pleasure the Garden can procure him, though, when once he has entered it, he is wild to stay & run & dance & skip from end to end. I think you will leave off reproaching me that I do not give you an account of the little Pet.—

All danger of even threats to Ireland is, I now think, over; England has her turn, & is menaced ferociously;[3] but I hope our shipping will keep off any deeds of contest, as I own I am not very valiant for Men unused to arms opposed to those who have triumphed in them, & who exist but by plunder. God keep them off, I cry, for Militia men would find it difficult. our dearest Father writes me word he has been ballotted to find a Man & Horse for the Chelsea Cavalry.[4] I think I hardly know how to pity *him*,—those who abhor the War must come in first for my commiseration; though the War, *now* is no fault on our side, for the Directory *shew* what we have all long suspected, I that they *will not* make peace.[5] The Journals from France evince now a rising veneration for the martyred King that will never, I think, suffer the anniversary of his murder to be again held as

[2] A slowness that can be attributed perhaps to the difficulty of learning two languages simultaneously, Alexander's mother speaking English at home, his father, French.

[3] Reports of the massing of French troops at the coastline constantly fanned English fears of invasion.

[4] Among the measures proposed by Pitt on 18 Oct. 1797 for the defence of the realm was 'a supplementary levy of militia' to the number of 60,000 and a considerable increase in the irregular or yeomanry cavalry. *Parl. Hist.* xxxii. 1209–13.

According to a bill passed on 2 November 'every person who kept ten horses, should be obliged to provide one horse and one horseman, to serve in a corps of militia: that those who kept more than ten should provide in the same proportion: and that those who kept fewer than ten, should form themselves into classes, in which it should be decided by ballot, who, at the common expence, should provide the horse and the horseman. These troops were to be provided with an uniform and accoutrements, formed into corps, and put under proper officers.' See *AR* xxxix (1797), 119–26; and *CJ*, lii. 93.

[5] Lord Malmesbury's failure to conclude peace with the Directory was a disappointment widely felt.

a feast. My last accounts from Charlotte[6] spoke of nothing but recovery, & I hope Clement is now as well as Frederick. I have delivered your messages to Charlotte. I have already, I hope, told you how well your Letter to Greenwich was taken. I delight you find the Climate less against you than I had feared. God soften it for you, my most beloved!—my Partner has recommenced his planting, & is out all the morning at hardest work. Poor Mrs. Hamilton is dead.[7] I have written to the worthy Kitty, but not yet heard her plan of future proceedings, nor where she will reside. Mrs. Leigh is also dead,[8] as a Letter tells me from Mrs. Cooke, who was called to her, & who always enquires with the warmest esteem after my dearest Susan. My dear Father is quite revived, I flatter myself. He has renewed his old social habits: he has dined with Mrs. Crewe, Mr. Coxe, Mr. windham, Sir Joseph Banks, & soon, I hope, will go about to all as formerly.[9] He has also much literary business on his hands —which is absolutely necessary for his private hours. I am very glad you hear sometimes from your excellent friends among the *Emigrés*—I only hear of them through you. Me de Monthron has discovered that the Marquis, her son, has constantly sent her remittances, which have been embezzled, while all his Letters were intercepted! how attrocious & she was working for her livelihood at 60! The truth is found out, after 3 years fraud, & 150 £ has been received by her, & she is in heaven already with maternal joy—[10]

[6] CBF's letter is missing as are also the relevant letters to CB Jr.'s wife 'Rosette'.

[7] A monumental tablet in the parish church at Chessington respectfully records the death of Sarah Hamilton (i, L. 22 n. 4), who died on 14 Jan. 1797, aged 92 years. She had been nursed by her niece the faithful Papilian Catherine Cooke (*c*. 1731–97), who was to survive her aunt by less than a year (L. 247 n. 17).

[8] Mary Leigh (L. 179 n. 7) had died on 9 Feb. and was buried on the 11th at Adlestrop, Glos., of which parish her husband was the rector.

[9] The letter that CB had evidently written telling of such visits is now missing.

[10] Angélique-Marie comtesse de Montrond (L. 145 n. 3). Emigrating at the close of 1790, she took refuge first at Neufchâtel, later crossing to England, in which emigrations *'elle perdit son mari â et la plus grande partie de sa fortune'*. After 1799 she settled at Besançon, *'où elle ne cessa plus de résider'* (Malo, op. cit., pp. 8–9). For twenty-eight of her letters (1794–7) to M. d'A, see *Catalogue*.

Of her three sons Denis-François-Edouard (1768–1843), Philippe-François-Casimir (1769–1843), and Claude-Hippolyte (1770–1855), it was perhaps the second who was most able to supply his mother with funds. 'Aide de camp du général Mathieu Dumas, de Lameth, de Latour-Maubourg' et 'Bel homme, il prodiguait une fortune aux origines mystérieuses et était . . . l'inséparable de Talleyrand qui l'appelait "L'Enfant Jésus de l'Enfer".' See Madame de Staël, *Lettres à Ribbing*, ed. Simone Balayé (1960), p. 355 n. 1).

My tenderest love to my Fanny, & Willy & Norbury—& best Compt^s & kindest to the Major   I have written with immense bad tools—adieu, my sweetest & dearest Susan! God bless & preserve you!

[*By Amelia Locke*]

It is impossible to see the least blank space going to my dearest Mrs Phillips & not fill it up with Assurances of that affection & gratitude with which I could fill many many pages. There is not one of those precious remembrances *never forgotten* in any of her letters that I do not long to thank her separately for a thousand times—But most of all for that most kind most flattering permission that I might partake with Mama & our M^{rs} d'arblay of some part of the comfort those sweetest of letters afford in her absence. I cannot reconcile myself to the having made my Norbury so pitoyable a return for his truly lovely letter[11] & his beloved Mama none at all for hers I have in it— Altho I ought to be thankful that any means of thanking them however shabbily was afforded me by those Who have so much with which to fill each sheet that goes to her—But what made my wretched answer still more unsatisfactory was that dear naughty M^r & M^{rs} d'Arblay to whom I sent my precious letter the day I rec^d it have mislaid it among their papers, so that to this day I have not recovered my d^r property, altho great has been my outcry. Thank that dearest boy again & again when you write to him for it. I wish you had seen *how* the cleverness of of it delighted Papa & W^m to whom I read it, & I need not add (for I know you are assured of it) how its touching kindness delighted me. In short it is the same nature it always was cest tout dire receiving daily the improvements that such a nature is capable of—I must now say adieu to my Mrs Phillips & Heaven bless her. It has been an unexpected treat   My best love to my d^r Fanny, to that estimable Girl—

[*Mrs. Locke added interlinearly*]

in the lines allowed me only my kindest love to Norbury & to Willy many kisses
    Ma Bonne intreats to be most tenderly remembered

[11] See L. 222, pp. 267–8.

275

225   Great Bookham, 13 February 1797

To Mrs. Waddington

A.L. (Berg), 13 Feb. [17]97
Double sheet 4to   2 pp.   *pmks*   LEATHER / HEAD   15 FE 97   black seal
Addressed: Mrs. Waddington, / Lanover Court, near / Abergavenny.
Docketed in ink, p. 1: Feby 1797

What is become of my dear Marianne? I know well how little claim I have to punctuality, & indeed I ought never to expect— though I always desire it: but this is a silence so long it makes me rather uneasy—You received, I hope, a Letter I wrote to you just after the fatal event at Chelsea?[1]—write me one of your scraps, at least, my dearest Mary, if some impediment prevents a real Letter.—Acquaint me how you are in health—spirits— &c—& how your little Loves are, & Mr.W[addington]—My little Man, though 2 years & 2 months old, does not yet speak, —*except with his Eyes*—& those are never, but when sleeping, silent. They are the most talking, varying, laughing, playful, scrutinizing little chatterers you ever saw, or by Imagination, heard. My dear friends of Norbury park are all well, & have a little pet rising up of their own, from Mrs. Charles Locke. My Sister P[hillips] & all hers are stationed—alas!—across the Channel. M. d'A—our Bambino & myself spent our Christmas at Chelsea—whence we made scarcely any visits, not to lose a moment from my Father—but we called upon Mrs. Boscawen, who enquired about you. Do write, I beg, & quick, & give me the good tydings, however short—Though | I won't *quarrel* if they should be long—remember that:—

I heard of you, but nothing very recent, from Mrs. Browne,[2] whom I saw at Chelsea, where she called upon me, to renew an acquaintance dropt for 16 years!—

Adieu, my ever dear Mary—*be well*, & tell me you are so.

Bookham—Feby 13.—97.

225. [1] L. 213.
   [2] Henrietta *née* Hay, the first wife of Isaac Hawkins Browne, Jr. whom, however, FB had met at Mrs. Ord's on 1 June 1792 (i, L. 24 n. 6). The couple, between them, had subscribed for three sets of *Camilla*.

226   Great Bookham, [26] February 1797

To Doctor Burney

A.L.S. (Diary MSS. vi. 4976–[9], Berg), *n.d.*
Double sheet 4to   4 pp.   *pmks* LEATHER / HEAD   27 FE 97   black seal
Addressed: Dr. Burney / Chelsea College, / Middlesex.
Endorsed by CB: Fanny / Feb. 27 / 1797 / ab^t Emigrants & / proposal of Mrs Crewe
Edited by FBA, p. 1 (4976), *annotated and date retraced*: ⋇ ⋇ Feb^y ⟨26th⟩— 97. (4) Reply to a proposal for a periodical Work from Mrs. Crewe
Edited also by CFBt *and the* Press.

⌐This is the week's abominable wait, I hope, in ⟨the evening⟩ —news. Not a word heard I of the parcel till the account of my dearest Father's Letter made me send for it!¹ & then a stupid business mistake that would fill all my Letter to explain was my sole consolation. I am so discouraged by the repeated failures, that, notwithstanding all the promises really made, I shall beg my dear Sally to forewarn every future pacquet by a line, engaging that it may not torment her, & to be quite *satisfied* if she only writes *Parcel set off*—& the date according to our Carte blanche or—agreement, though I shall be better than satisfied if she generously adds a line.⌐

I hardly know whether I am most struck with the fertility of the ideas Mrs. Crewe has started,² or most gratified by their direction: certainly I am flattered where most susceptible of pleasure when a mind such as her's would call me forth from my retirement to second views so important in their ends, & demanding such powers in their progress. But though her opinion would give me *courage*, it cannot give me *means*: I am too far removed from the scene of public life to compose any

226. ¹ Apparently a recent letter (now missing) had made mention of a parcel having been sent from Chelsea. The parcel had evidently contained, *inter alia*, CB's letter, dated 6 Feb. 1797 (Berg), of which FBA in her later editorial capacity obliterated some 46 lines, the literary parts that she allowed to stand being printed in *DL* v. 317–19.
² Ideas for a new periodical, or anti-Jacobin weekly, to be called 'The Breakfast Table' (*or* 'The Modern Nestor' *or* 'The Old Gentleman' *or* 'The Spying Glass') Mrs. Crewe gave at great length in four undated letters (Berg) of [1797] addressed to CB. She was hoping that a fictional character like FBA's Sir Hugh might be made to comment on the times, somewhat in the manner of Sir Roger de Coverley.

thing of public utility in the style she indicates. The 'manners as they rise', the morals, or their deficiencies, as they preponderate, should be viewed, for such a scheme, in all their variations, with a diurnal Eye. For though it may not be necessary this *Gentleman-Author* ∣ should be a frequenter himself of public places, he must be sufficiently in the midst of public people to judge the justice of what is communicated to him by his correspondents. The Plan is so excellent it ought to be well adopted, & *really* fulfilled. Many circumstances would render its accomplishment nearly impossible for *me*;—wholly to omit politics would mar all the original design;—yet what would be listened to unabused, by a writer who is honoured by a testimony such as mine of having resigned royal service without resigning royal favour? PERSONAL abuse would make a dreadful breach into the peace of my happiness—though censure of my works I can endure with tolerable firmness: the latter I submit to as the public right, by prescription; the former I think authorised by NO right, & recoil from with mingled fear & indignation. I could mention other embarrassments as to politics—but they will probably occur to you, though they may escape Mrs. Crewe, who is not so well versed in the history & strong character of M. d'Arblay, to whom the misfortunes of his General & Friend are but additional motives to invincible adherence. And how would Mr. Windham, after his late speech,[3] endure a paper in which M. de la Fayette could never be named but with respect & pity? You will feel, I am sure, for his constancy & his Honour; his *profession de foi* in politics is exactly, he says, what you have so delightfully drawn in what you call your liliputian Verses[4]—& his attachment, his reverence, his gratitude for our King are like my own. His arm—his life is at his service—as I have told the Princess Augusta—& he has told Lord Leslie.[5] ∣

To a paper of such a sort, upon a plan less extensive, I feel no repugnance, though much apprehension: I have many things by me that, should I turn my thoughts upon such a scheme,

---

[3] On 16 Dec. 1796 Windham had argued in the House against a motion that would implore His Majesty to intercede with the Emperor of Germany for the deliverance of Lafayette and other Constitutionalists from the prison of Olmütz. The original motion was negatived, Ayes 50, Noes 130 (*Parl. Hist.* xxxii (1795–7), 1348–86).
[4] Possibly the poem CB included in his letter of 17 Nov. 1794 (L. 156 n. 1).
[5] See i, L. 13 n. 8.

might facilitate its execution—& there *her* admirable Mother's
—& let me proudly say *MY* admirable *God*-mother's work,[6]
might & should,—as I know she wishes, appear with great
propriety;—but even this is a speculation from which my
agitated & occupied Heart at present turns aside, from incap-
ability of attention—for I am just now preparing our little
darling for his first sufferings & first known danger.

Our difficulty *how* to accept the most kind offer of Sir Walter[7]
prevents our dwelling upon it, & the many objects the little soul
must perpetually see this summer, from our building & removal,
makes all delay hazardous.—He is so—so precious to us!—& he
is more lovely without & within every minute—&, in short,
Mr. Ansell,[7] the first man for such business in this neighbourhood, is engaged to come from Dorking for this purpose in
about a week or 10 days time.

That this, till it is passed, will shackle all my faculties my
kindest Father will forgive, who knows—& has seen—& has felt
what a little prize our lottery of bantlings has drawn. Your Eyes
have so often indulged mine with the liveliest approbation of
this little Creature, that I do not fear thus letting myself loose
to you.—I wish you could see him once again before the change
that may come—but we have no time for waiting. ǀ

I had a letter from our dearest Susan lately,[8] in which she
laments your silence, & expresses a distress that makes me fear
your *interest* rather in arrears: but she is not explicit. our's is

---

[6] Frances *née* Macartney Greville (i, L. 24 n. 62). Well known for her *Ode to
Indifference*, she had written, according to CB, many other poems in the White
Album at Crewe Hall, of which a few are printed in *Barthomley* (p. 313). She had
also written a novel that Mrs. Crewe hoped might (with FBA's help) appear in
print (see i, 205–6). See also copies made by CPB from the White Album (Osborn)
and CB's letter of 26 Oct. 1797 to SBP (Barrett, Eg. 3700A, ff. 13–14b).

[7] Sir Walter Farquhar (i, L. 23 n. 82), who had evidently offered to inoculate
Alexander against the dreaded smallpox. William Ansell was the apothecary at
Dorking (i, L. 6 n. 4).

[8] This letter would seem to be missing but a Bond of Indemnity to CB, Jr.
(Osborn), dated 25 Mar. 1815, relates how 'Molesworth Phillips, being seized in
fee simple in certain lands hereditaments and premises situate and being in . . . the
parish of Termonfeighan in the County of Louth', had on 12 and 13 Mar. 1795
mortgaged the lands to CB in consideration of £2,000. By 19 Nov. 1814, this
indebtedness to CB and his heirs had mounted to £2,917.

CB's Account Book for 1796 (Berg) had recorded in July the receipt of £40 being
'1/2 yrs interest from Major Phillips due 3 inst'. In a letter of 26 Oct. (op. cit.) to
SBP, CB tells of JB's having paid '£25 on the M——'s acct' and last week 'his own
draught for the remaining £15—& I have written off, on the bond—the 1/2 year's
Interest up to the 3d of last July'. That the payments became still more slack is
indicated in CB's complaint in his will (Scholes, ii. 272) of a 'stoppage . . . of £80 a
year by Col. Phillips'.

wholly left unpaid since the disputation about the principal. I long to have Mr. Shirley[9] & Mr. Lewis[10] engaged in money matters with *one another*. They are not fit for any third person. I am dying to see James's pamphlet.[11]

Do, I entreat, dearest Sir, tell Mrs. Crewe I am made even the *happier* by her kind partiality. Had matters been otherwise situated, how I should have delighted in any scheme in which SHE would have taken a part. I long to see the 600—pray work up Ptolemy—but don't ask me *how*! I can hardly imagine any thing more difficult for poetry. Tell dear Mr. Tw[ining] I shall receive most gratefully his strictures,[12] & beg them with all the speed his leisure will allow. I am proud HE thinks the work *worth flaggelating*. Your Camarade is now Seriously shocked at the expence, & *very* sorry, since his first exultation & merry *fun* subsides upon your fraternity. So can I, dearest Sir—

⌐Adieu, most dear Sir—I am intolerably provoked by these delays of the post. My best Love to Sally & dear love if with you, & Remain ever—⌐

dutifully & affect^{ly}

your F. d'A.

[top margin, upside down, p. 1]

⌐What I can command of time from my little seducer goes still to the Tale in Dialogue.[13] if to shew that to Mrs. Crewe before publication would ⟨mark⟩ the confidence & regard she inspires me with I will convey it you previously.⌐

---

9 See L. 193 n. 7.
10 Also mentioned in CB's will (Scholes, ii. 272) as a defector is a Mr. Lewis, (possibly Matthew Gregory Lewis) L. 221 n. 9), who failed in his payments of £50 per annum, presumably on a mortgage. See also CB's letter (Berg) to FBA, 6 Feb. 1797: 'He [Phillips] & Mr Lewis are a couple of pretty cattle! They neither keep Quarter, nor any track but one of their own making—.'
11 *PLAN | of | DEFENCE against INVASION* (Ll. 139 n. 4, 229 n. 5, 236 n. 2).
12 In a double folio sheet (Berg) addressed to CB, *pmk* 1 JU 97, and entitled 'Commas & Points I set exactly right', Mr. Twining offered four folio pages (double columns) of grammatical and verbal corrections for *Camilla*:
    dose her eyes *for* close her eyes [an obvious mistake in setting M. d'A's hand]
    laid dead *for* lay dead
    who she painted *for* whom she painted
He objected to Gallicisms, especially to the excessive use of the preposition *of* (all of beauty, all of deformity . . . What of virtues are gone). 'I hardly dare say', interjected TT, 'how much I dislike these "ofs". But what of that?'
These corrections FBA later incorporated, she says, in revisions for a second edition of *Camilla* that she records sending to Cadell and Davies *c.* 12 Apr. 1799 (iv, L. 314) and again *c.* 18 Nov. 1800 (iv, L. 397). See further an A.L.S. (Comyn), M. d'A to CB Jr., 20 July 1812. The second edition appeared in 1802.
13 See L. 221 n. 8.

227   Great Bookham,
                       27 February–15 March 1797

Conjointly with M. d'Arblay
    and Mrs. Locke
To Mrs. Phillips

A.J.L., A.N.S., & A.L. (Barrett, Eg. 3690, ff. 172–3b), 27 Feb.–
14–15 Mar. [17]97
    Double sheet folio (12·4×7·8″) 4 pp. *pmks* DARKING 18 MR 97
20 MR 97   red seal
    Addressed: Ireland. / Mrs. Phillips. / Belcotton / Drogheda
    Endorsed by SBP: March 3ᵈ / 97. [*in error for 3 Apr.?*]
    Edited by FBA, *with marks preparatory to mutilation.*

[*By Madame d'Arblay*]

                                 Bookham—Febʸ 27.—97.
    I rejoice that at least this our only converse may be indulged
in folio length. How great a difference it makes in its comfort. I
have often feared beginning a subject in *quarto*, lest I should have
no room to make it intelligible: but I will *now* keep a sheet on the
stocks, & send it off as soon as I hear the last pacquet is received.

                              ⟵————⟶

    In how many ways does almost every line of my beloved's last
Letter come to my Heart![1]—the depression *caused by the news from*
Norbury is truly affecting. I conceive it but too well. Distant &
uncertain alarm harrows us even in the most perfect situations
— — I must not enter upon all that rises within me to say here,
lest I should run any risk[2] — — of tiring you, shall I suppose?
I know you will not tire—but still I will turn to other subjects.
However, not till I mention how completely I concur in your
horrour of concealed illness during separations; & I EARNESTLY
CHARGE & IMPLORE the most scrupulous truth from my dearest
Susanna upon this point. It will not be *unnecessary* anxiety to
inform me if you are ill, for my Partner in all—how truly!—has

227. ¹ This letter is missing.
    ² FBA's phrase 'run any risk' refers to the fear of the Major's reading the com-
ment she would like to make on the sorrows or troubles related in SBP's missing
letter.

assured me, were that the case, he would not spare, but accompany me to my Heart's dearest sister immediately. This soothing promise will lose all its effect, if my Susan does not join to it her solemn honour not to fail giving me such intelligence, by the Major, or by my Fanny, should she,—most unhappily—have it to give. Do not, in such a case, wait for *danger*, I supplicate! *your* Fevers are always frightful—so are your Coughs,—remember, therefore, I beseech, that you may easily be ill enough for me!—& that a tour to Ireland, should we find you amended, or recovered, will not, by that means, be made the more disagreeable. Answer this by an engagement you cannot break, my dearest Susanna, if my peace is dear to you.

Our beloved Father writes me word he sends you Letters but seldom, lest they should be ruinous—or— —de trop—vous *comprende*,[3] like Mrs. Schwell[enberg]? He pursues his new literary work with vigour, & refuses no select parties. The excellent Eliz.[4] of worcester is just now at Chelsea with Marianne, & I believe they do much good there. He speaks most tenderly—& d'une maniere attendrissente of his Susey in every Letter I procure.

Have you heard of a new work I have just seen advertised *by Capt. James Burney, of His Majesty's Navy*, relative to means of Defence against an Invasion? I was all astonished, from never having heard such a design was formed. I have not seen and long to see it. My Father says he is much more satisfied with it than he expected, which has given me infinite pleasure.[5]

March 14. What an age since I began this! & how I long to hear if my most loved Susan is well again—& all hers & how they are.—how she does in all respects, & if she has ever received a pacquet in which we all writ, & which has induced me to defer finishing this sheet till I could recount a history in which she will take nearly the same interest as myself. I would not awaken useless inquietude in your kind bosom by telling you our fixed

---

[3] Ruinous with respect to postage and unwelcomed by the Major.
[4] Elizabeth Warren Burney (i, lxxv) and her niece, EBB's daughter Marianne.
[5] See L. 226 n. 11.

design of innoculating our little love this spring—but Mr. Ansell
was bespoke a Week before this Letter was begun, & the last Day
of last month he came—& performed the dreaded operation.
The dear little soul sat on my lap, & he gave him some Barley
sugar; this made him consent to have his Frock taken off. Mr.
Ansell pressed me to relinquish him to Betty; but I could not
to any one but his Father, who was at his field. When the
Lancet was produced, Betty held him a favourite Toy, of which
I began discoursing with him. It was a maimed young Drummer,
of whose loss of Eyes, Nose, Chin & Hair he always hears with
the tenderest interest. But, while listening attentively, he felt
Mr. Ansell grasp his arm to hold it steady—he turned quite
away from his Drummer, & seeing the Lancet, shrunk back. Mr.
Ansell bid me help to hold him tight,—he then shriekt, & forcibly disengaged his arm from my hand—but, to my utter
astonishment, held it out himself very quietly, & looked on, &
suffered the incision to be made without a cry, or any resistance,
only raising his Eyes from his arm to Mr. Ansel, with an expression of the most superlative wonder at his proceedings. Mr. A.
forced out the blood repeatedly, & played upon it with the
Lancet for some minutes, fearing, he said, if particular caution
was not used, the little soul was so pure his blood could not be
infected. The Child still made no resistance, but looked at the
blood with great curiosity, in the most profound silent rumination. Mr. Ansel still was apprehensive the disorder might not
be imbibed, from the excessive strictness of his whole life's diet:
he therefore asked my leave to innoculate the other arm also.
I left it to his own decision,—& he took off the shirt from the
other arm.—The little Creature fixed him very attentively, &
then turned to me, as if for some explanation of such conduct;
but still made not the smallest resistance, & without being held
at all, permitted the second wound.— —I own I could hardly
endure the absence of his Father, to whom the actual view of
this infantine courage & firmness would have been such exquisite delight. Mr. Ansel confessed he had met no similar
instance.—You will not, I believe, expect an equal history of
his Mother's intrepidity—& therefore I pass that bye. But she
behaved *very well indeed* before COMPANY!— — —

This beloved little object had taken—with me—his leave of
Norbury Park the Day before, for the fine little Baby Emily

283

Frederica was there, &, of course, must be guarded as he himself has been guarded hitherto. He had one double tooth just pierced, & 3 teeth threatening—but we could not defer our purpose, as the season was advancing, & would have been lost by waiting. But one very material comfort immediately preceded the experiment; he had shewn the power of repeating sounds, & could make us understand when he wished to drink or eat.

This stroke was given on the Tuesday; & on the following Sunday, after Breakfasting with us in a gaiety the most animating, & with Eyes & Cheeks brilliant with health & spirits, he suddenly drooped, became pale, languid, hot & short breathed. This continued all Day, & towards evening increased into a restlessness that soon became misery—he refused any food—his Eyes became red, dull, & heavy, his breath feverish, & his limbs in almost convulsive tribulation. His starts were so violent, it was difficult to hold him during his short sleeps, & his cries from pain & nameless sufferings grew incessant.—I expected a fit—& indeed my terrour was horrible—but his Father—my support—made me put his feet in warm water at about 10 o'clock at Night, & he fell into a soft slumber, which lasted 4 Hours. This was a relief that made the renewed pain with which he awoke better endured, & he again slept some Hours afterwards. The Night was far better than the Day which followed, which was a repetition of that I have ⎮ described.—but so was also the succeeding Night of similar relief. The spots began to appear, but yet Tuesday also was very suffering—however, I will not go on with this triste journal, but tell my dearest dear Susan that *now* all is deliciously well! They began to turn yesterday, & this Day, which makes but the fortnight from the operation, many of them are already fading away,—his appetite is returned, his gaiety is revived, all fever is over, & if his face was not changed, the disorder would not be suspected. I know how you will feel for our excessive joy at this conquest of a dread that has hung cruelly over our best happiness. We have been so much frightened, that we would have compromised with fate for the loss of all his personal recommendation, to have *ensured* his life. yet Mr. Ansel says there never was a better sort, & that all my apprehensions have been groundless. He yesterday took from his little Arm *4 Lancets of matter*—& the dear darling Hero suffered the 4 cuts unmoved, except, as before, by astonishment & curiosity. He would not be held, & his Father, this time, had the satisfaction to see I have not spoiled his race.—Mr. Ansel then took his leave, giving me general directions, & assuring me all was safely & happily over as to the distemper.—

Thank God!—repeat for me thank God, my own dearest Susan. And read of his prowess to his dear little Cousins.

You will not wonder this subject should engross both me & my paper,—but I could fill another such with his opening powers of elocution—which have begun, like his Mother's reading, all at once, & ⟨sim⟩ilarly. But this must rest for my next folio. He will be but slig⟨htly, if⟩ at all, marked, though he has more than he will yet let me count of these frightful boutons. Only one, however, has risen in order; the rest come up half way, & seem dying off for want of nourishment: Mr. A. says this is the recompence of his state of blood. He has 13 upon his Face; 3 upon his Nose, in particular, which disfigure it most comically. They give him, his Father says, the air d'un petit Ivrogne—I fear this feature will never recover entirely from this triple association to destroy its delicacy; but I could bear, just now, to see him turned negro without positive repining. He is thinner & paler considerably, & his Hair I have been forced to chop rather than cut in a way that helps the alteration most unfavourably. My poor Partner will tell you his own history—I grow very anxious for yours, my own darling Susan!—Answer me very solemnly to the opening of this—give my kindest Love to my three dears, best comp[ts] to the Major,—& take care of yourself with all your might, I conjure.—adieu, my beloved—Sweet Norbury will write for Itself.

[M. d'Arblay added a paragraph]

C'est avec une extrême impatience, ma bonne soeur que j'attens l'heureux jour où le Major, fidele à sa promesse, se rapprochera de ce pauvre *Surry* bien moins aimable depuis votre depart. Dites, je vous prie, à Fanny qu'il entre dans mes projets sur *Camilla-cottage*; d'avoir, sous les grands arbres qui couronnent cet Hermitage, une excellente balançoire pour elle et ses deux Freres. Qu'elle se depêche donc de revenir de peur qu'en tardant trop, elle n'aille plus trouver mon escarpolette digne d'elle. J'aurai soin d'avoir tout auprès de jolis arbustes et quelques fleurs que l'aimable trio pourra offrir à l'aimée maman. Amen! En faveur de ces projets qu'il me tarde beaucoup de mettre à execution tout en surveillant ma batisse, qui, j'espere, est reprise d'aujourdhui, je compte un peu sur les bonnes prieres de mon excellente soeur, pour que bientôt je puisse *get rid* d'un maudit rheumatisme sans le quel je voudrais bien pouvoir me dire, ce que je suis et serai in saecula saeculorum votre bien sincere Ami

d'A. ¹

[*Mrs. Locke concluded the letter*]

Norbury Park Wednesday 15ʰ March—my beloved Friend must take my heart felt congratulations that all anxiety is for-ever past concerning one dangerous distemper & that this most loved darling has gone so prosperously thro it.—Heaven be praised, his dearest Mother has been spared any unusual alarm altho I fear this fortnight has been a severe trial of her fortitude —with this letter I recᵈ the bligthiest note from her—she has had for this week past the added anxiety of her dear Partners suffer-ing from a Rheumatic attack similar to that he had 2 yʳˢ ago but I fear still more severe—I hope he has at least purchased prudence—he is much better she says—& now that I have ended my thanksgiving & rejoicing I must begin a lamentation—your silence my best & dearest Friend alarms me—I fear you are ill —*very* ill perhaps—God send such a suspicion may be without foundation but your silence is so unusually long—I must briefly tell you that we are *all perfectly* well—our poor Frederic returned to School 3 weeks ago⁶ in ye rosiest health & our little Grand-daughter thriving delightfully with her sweet Mother both in rosiest prosperity—you may imagine that I do not venture any communication with Bookham but by a note that is most reluc-tantly committed to the flames as soon as my anxiety is relieved —when you write my dearest direct to me that I may fully enjoy it without reproach for as I have my little Emily a great deal— I fear to hold long a paper that has been much at Bookham—this very letter I ought not to touch were I to see the little darling, but I shall be aired before I hold her—God bless & preserve you my most dear, dearest Friend—our ange⁷ is delightfully well & every day braving the wind, in his Phaeton   I take an humble

---

⁶ To Cheam.   ⁷ i.e. Mr. Locke, Sr.

walk not daring to be so bold.—our Amelia or Augusta accompany him—give me some comfort *very* soon my own Friend concerning your precious health—poor Mr de Chavagnac is safe in France with his family[8]—dont you rejoice—Adrienne is as prosperous as possible—I had a letter from his amiable Wife desir⟨ing to⟩ be remembered to you in ye kindest manner [*tear*] remember us all to the Major

228   [Great Bookham, 3 March 1797]

To Mrs. Waddington

A.L. (Berg), *n.d.*
Double sheet small 4to   4 pp.   *pmk* 3 MR 97   black seal
Addressed: Mrs. Waddington, / Lanover Court, / Abergavenny.
Docketed in ink, p. 1: 1797

I am too desirous to hear you are well, & free from alarm at the descent in Wales,[1] to wait for time to fill the large paper you *claim*, once more, therefore, take a few—but kind words—of earnest enquiry, & answer them speedily.

[8] See L. 201 n. 5.

228. [1] On 22 February a French squadron (two frigates, a corvette, and a lugger) had entered Fishguard Bay and on that exceptionally calm and beautiful evening 1,400 soldiers of the *Légion Noire* made an unopposed landing in Pembrokeshire. For the most part of gaol-birds, banditti, and renegades, they were no sooner sent out on a foraging expedition for carts and horses than they fell to a disorganized plundering and pillaging of the cottages in the Pencaer peninsula, eating voraciously of the well-stocked larders and, since with the recent shipwreck of a smuggler on the coast there were plentiful supplies of wine, they drank to excess as well, sleeping off the effects on beds of goosefeathers.

The peasantry armed with pitchforks, pokers, and 'Sythes straitined', the Fencibles (290, in number), the Yeomanry Cavalry (50), the Cardiganshire Militia (100), and the Milford Seamen (150) played their appropriate parts gloriously and ingloriously, as described by Commander E. H. Stuart Jones, R.N., *The Last Invasion of Britain* (Cardiff, 1950). Not the least significant part of the episode was the appearance of 400 women, who, dressed in traditional scarlet cloaks or mantles ('Red flanes') and 'low crowned round felt hats' and spied out on the roads and hills as their curiosity brought them near, were mistaken by the French leader for red-clad British regiments of the line, thus contributing substantially, it is thought, to the French capitulation.

On Friday 24 Feb., before any battle was fought, the *Légion* surrendered, laying down arms on the Goodwick Sands. Imprisoned as accommodation could be found in Haverfordwest, Carmarthen, Milford, and Pembroke, they were shipped or marched off as soon as possible to the prison hulks at Portsmouth, and, much to the disgust of the Directory, used in exchanges of prisoners of war.

But for this anxiety, I should not, I confess, so soon have written, since I find you estimate my Letters by their size, not their affection.

And this is not a period for long Epistles with me—I have *JUST* innoculated the little darling of two Hearts, & your mind, which in maternal feelings at least sympathizes with mine, will readily imagine I must in truth want some account of you to write even a word at this epoch.—God bless you—naughty Girl as I think you.

229   Great Bookham, 16 March 1797

To Doctor Burney

A.L.S. (Diary MSS. vi. 4980–[3], Berg), 16 Mar. [17]97
Double sheet folio   4 pp.   *pmks*   LEATHER / HEAD   18 MR 97   black seal
    Addressed: Dr. Burney / Chelsea College, / Middlesex
    Edited by FBA, p. 1 (4980), *annotated and the day 16 and the year 97 retraced*:
⁘ ⁘   97   16–97   (5 / 1)   on the Innoculation of Alexander & his singular courage
    Edited also by CFBt *and the* Press.

Bookham
March 16—97

My dearest Padre

Relieved at length from a terror that almost from the Birth of my little darling has hung upon my Mind, with what confidence in your utmost kindness do I call for your participation in my joy that all alarm is over, & Mr. Ansel has taken his leave? I take this large sheet, to indulge in a Babiana which dea Gandpa will, I am sure, receive with partial pleasure upon this most important event to his poor little Gentleman.

When Mr. Ansel came to perform the dreaded operation, he desired me to leave the Child to him & the Maid: but my agitation was not of that sort; I wished for the experiment upon the most mature deliberation, but while I trembled with the suspence of its effect, I could not endure to lose a moment from the beloved little object for & with whom I was running such a risk. He sat upon my lap, & Mr. Ansel gave him a bit of Barley sugar, to obtain his permission for pulling off one sleeve of his Frock & shirt. He was much surprised at this opening to an Acquaintance—for Mr. Ansel made no previous visit, having sent his directions by M. d'A.—however, the barley sugar occupied his Mouth, & inclined him to a favourable interpretation; though he stared with up raised Eye brows. Mr. Ansel bid Betty hold him a play thing at the other side, to draw off his Eyes from what was to follow; & I began a little history to him of the misfortunes of the Toy we chose, which was a Drummer, maimed in his own service, & whom he loves to lament, under the name of *The poor Man that has lost his Face*; but all my pathos, & all his own ever ready pity, were ineffectual to detain his attention when he felt his Arm grasped by Mr. Ansel; he repulsed Betty, the soldier, & his Mama, & turned about with a quickness that disengaged him from Mr. Ansel, who now desired me to hold his arm myself. This he resisted; but held it out himself, with unconscious intrepidity, in full sight of the Lancet, which he saw hovering over it, without the most remote suspicion of its slaughtering design, & with a rather amused look of curiosity, to see what was intended. But when the incision was made, he gave a little scream; but it was momentary, & ended in a look of astonishment that exceeds all description, all painting, & in turning an appealing Eye I to me, as if demanding at once explanation & protection. My fondest praises now made him understand that non-resistance was an act of virtue, & again he held out his little arm, at our joint entreaty, but resolutely refused to have [it] held by any one else. Mr. Ansel pressed out the blood with his Lancet, again & again, & wiped the instrument upon the wound for two or three minutes; fearing, from the excessive strictness of his whole life's regimen he might still escape the venom: the dear Child coloured at sight of the blood, & seemed almost petrified with amazement, fixing his wondering Eyes upon Mr. Ansel with an expression that sought to dive into his purpose, & then upon me, as if enquiring how I could approve of it.

When this was over, Mr. Ansel owned himself still apprehensive it might not take, & asked if I should object to his innoculating the other Arm. I told him I committed the whole to his judgment, as M. d'Arblay was not at home. And now, indeed, his absence from this scene became doubly regretted, for my little Hero, though probably aware of what would follow, suffered me to bare his other arm, & held it out immediately, while looking at the lancet; nor would he, again, have it supported, or tightened; & he saw & felt the incision without shrinking, & without any marks of displeasure; but though he appeared convinced, by my carresses, that the thing was right, & his submission was good, he evidently thought it as unaccountable as singular, & all his faculties seemed absorbed in profound surprise. I shall never cease being sorry his Father did not see him, to clear my character from having adulterated the chivalric spirit & courage of his race.—Mr. Ansel confessed he had never seen a similar instance in one so very young, & kissing his Forehead when he had done, said 'Indeed, little Sir, I am in love with you.'

Since this, however, my Stars have indulged me in the satisfaction of exhibiting his native bravery where it gives most pride as well as pleasure; for his Father was in the Room when, the other day, Mr. Ansel begged leave to take some matter from his arm for some future experiments. And the same scene was repeated; he presented the little Creature with a Bon Bon, & then shewed his Lancet; he let his arm be bared unresistingly, & suffered him to make 4 successive cuts, to take matter for 4 lancets, never crying, angry, or frightened, but only looking inquisitively at us all in turn, with Eyes *you* would never have forgotten had you beheld, that seemed disturbed by a curiosity they could not satisfy, to find some motive for our extraordinary proceedings.

The disorder was, upon the whole, the most rapidly over that its nature ever admits. The operation, & the leave taking of the operator was a Day within a fortnight. Some part of this time was cruelly suffering to the dear little Patient, but none of it dangerous, as I *now* know, though I was frequently & dreadfully of another opinion in the progress of the business. But he had not one *very* bad night, & therefore we were *all* recruited for bad Days. It was a most grievous circumstance, at that period, that My Partner was forced to relinquish his most willing share in wiling away the little Sufferer's moments, from his own terrible seizure, which not only disabled him from assisting, but divided my own attention & solicitude very painfully. All, however, is so happily terminated, that I feel in Paradise!—My dear little angel is almost quite well, & his pappy is returned to his Champ; with assertions he is wholly recovered.

Alec is now no longer the *lovely* love you *saw* him—3 of 13 spots that visit his Face have fastened upon his Nose,—& the change they have produced is comical: His Hair also had so many, I have been forced to chop it off in little square & round compartments, that have rather more of use than grace for their recommendation: & as his Father would not let me muffle his hands, he has anticipated the departure of them *all* in a manner that will probably fix their marks ever after. His Eyes, however, are uninjured—& his Cheeks, & the form of his face & head have met with no alteration: so he may still escape an attack in Mr Dubster's Summer House,—though, had he been liable to it, I had studied that misfortune so thoroughly under Eugenia,[1] that I was prepared to meet it with philosophy.

Immediately before the Innoculation, the faculty of speech seemed most opportunely accorded him, & with a sudden facility that reminds me of your account of his Mother's reading. At noon, he repeated after me, when I least expected it, '*How do do?*' & the next morning, as soon as he awoke, he called out '*How do, mama? How do, papa?*'—I give you leave to guess if the question was inharmonious. From that time, he has repeated readily whatever we have desired, & yesterday, while he was eating his dry toast, perceiving the Cat, he threw her a bit, calling out '*Eat it, Buff.*' Just now, taking the string that fastens
(That's
his Gown round the Neck, he said '(*At's tie it on*, Mama.' And when, to try him, I bid him say naughty Papa, he repeated 'Naughty Papa,' as if mechanically, but the instant after,
Good
springing from mine to his arms, he kissed him, & said 'dood papa—' in a voice so tender it seemed meant as an apology—

Thus, the powers of elocution having been opened, I may flatter ǀ myself a MINE is sprung that will furnish a Monthy Babiana that my dearest Father, with his universal Baby philanthropy, will not despise.[2] The little soul still recollects you, though imperfectly, for when we carried him to Norbury Park to take leave before innoculation, as soon as he saw Mr. Locke

229. [1] The child in *Camilla* who had been disfigured by smallpox.
[2] For CB's encouragement of infantine biography, see L. 169 n. 9.

sitting back on his easy Chair, with his hands held like my dear
Father's, he called out, with vivacity, 'At's Ganpa!' And nothing
quieted him so frequently during his illness as the history of his
adventures at Chelsea, & how he ran into Ganpa's room, &
how Ganpa gave him a Cake, & how aunt Sally danced & sung,
& ʜow Ganpa clapped his hands—& at that part he always
calls out 'adda!—' & tries to provoke a romp, which ends the
narrative.

ᴦYour poor Camarade is still feeble, but is returned from his
champ uninjured by the walk, though yet unable to resume his
labours. He is quite incensed about your cavalry business,[3] &
could with infinite satisfaction give his notions of things à l'antique
in France to Master Cauchy,[4] whose abominable behaviour
merits no good & I find an authority for reaction. James has
sent us his pamphlet, which we generally like very much. I am
excessively sorry at the paragraph on the Irish visit naming
[H.R.] H'ess.[5]

I have not heard from Susanna this long while. I wish
ardently to know if you or Hetty or Charlotte have had any
news of how she had been suffering with a rheumatic cold when
she wrote here last, which is near a Month since, but affirmed
she was then quite well. I am sorry for your sake as I am glad
for Mr. Burke that Mrs. Crewe still stays at Bath[6]—But I am
anxious to know you are recovered from that vile Cold à l'an
that you mention my dearest Sir, & that the Stars roll brightly
round your head. I had great pleasure in hearing Richard had
been kindly received by the Bishop, tho', it is impossible to doubt
it, his claims & the good Bishop's probity & worth considered.[7]

[3] See L. 224 n. 4.   [4] Unidentified.

[5] PLAN | of | DEFENCE against INVASION (Feb. 1797). In the closing pages,
those on the defence of Ireland, JB had approved the suggestion repeatedly made
by the Opposition (see The Times, 17 Feb. 1797) that the Prince of Wales be sent
as Lord-Lieutenant to Ireland. 'If it is intended to act justly and liberally towards
that country, the plan is truly wise, and cannot by any other means be done with
so good a grace.'

[6] CB's letter has not survived but the Burkes had been in Bath since late January
and were to depart only on 24 May. Mrs. Crewe after a long visit with the Burkes
had left Bath just before this date.

[7] EBB's son, Richard Allen Burney (i, Intro., lxix) was at present by the kindness of his grandfather, CB, at Oxford. It was probably the Bishop of Winchester, Brownlow North (i, L. 3 n. 10), who procured for him an 'eligible
situation' for the Oxford vacations with the Revd. Francis Severne (c. 1751–1828),
rector of Abberley (1780) near Worcester, which position Richard took up on
5 June 1797 ('Worcester Journal').

I am glad Blue remains in Town. She is a most excellent & generous character, & full of qualities that grow more & more into affection by being shown, for her abord is cold, & does little justice to the real worth of her Heart. Adieu, my dearest dear Padre—our joint Loves to Sarah⁊—

ever most dutifully & most affect^{ly}
Your F. d'A

230   Great Bookham, 18 March 1797

To Mrs. Waddington

A.L. (Berg), 18 Mar. [17]97
Double sheet 4to   1 p.   lower left corner of second leaf torn away
pmks LEATHER / HEAD 20 MR 97   black seal
Addressed: Mrs. Waddington / Lanover Court / Abergavenny.

Bookham, March 18.
—97

I have been too much engrossed, mind & hands, for two *WORDS* ever since I wrote last—but my dear Boy is now delightfully recovering, & the diminution of my agitation for his safety is the immediate augmentation of my anxiety for similar news. May you but be able to send it me!—My little angel has suffered very cruelly, but without danger, I am assured, though for some painful Days I could credit no such comforters. He had many dispersed, but only one that has gone through the usual forms: the rest half rose, & then faded away. Yet they all, at present, hold their Marks. He has 13 upon the face, 3 of which upon the Nose are very disfiguring. I am so thankful, however, for his recovery, & that a terror so severe is now removed from my spirits, that I look at them all with good will, I might almost say fondness, as proofs this dreaded risk is at an end. I shall truly rejoice if your lovely Emily[1] has been spared still more indulgently—for indulgent, at last, I regard whatever spares life, after fears such as I have experienced. Do pray let me hear as soon as possible. My fervant & most affectionate wishes are with the sweet child & its Mother. |

230. [1] Emelia, born 3 Feb. 1794 (L. 129 n. 2).

231   [Great Bookham, 1 April 1797]

To Sarah (Rose) Burney

A.L. (Berg), *n.d.*
Double sheet 4to   3 pp.   *pmks* LEATHER / HEAD   1 AP 97   black
seal
Addressed: Mrs. Burney, / at Dr Cha⁵ Burney's, / Greenwich, / Kent.

I ought to have given a more immediate answer to your
affectionate invitation, my dear Rosette, but I had hopes to
accept, as well as thank you for it, & that better part of the
acknowledgment hung upon circumstances that could not be
decided for some days:—mean while, however, an accident has
happenned that removes, at present, all power of yielding to your
temptations & those of my dear Brother—M. d'Arblay, a few
mornings ago, in cutting some Wood, let the ax slip, which fell
upon his foot, & has given it so deep a wound that I have only
to be most thankful it left it, at least, entire. He was compelled
to call in a surgeon,[1] & I am assured time & patience will effect
the cure, without any thing to alarm—the surgeon has dressed
it every morning, & charged him not to let it hang upon the
ground for a week at least—the pain of my Invalid has been
nothing compared with his mortification from not attending
to his workmen—but still he submitted, & we hoped to
compleat his re-establishment, as well as ¦ that of his son, by
the Greenwich Air—

But alas—This Morning a Letter arrives that acquaints him
a person is in Town who brings him intelligence of some of his
Friends—probably of his Brother,[2] or of an Uncle[3] whom he
adores—His wound was forgotten, the pain braved, the surgeon
resisted—& the chaise sent for instantly from Leatherhead, in

231. [1] As will appear in L. 233, the surgeon in attendance was George Lowdall
(*c.* 1741–1825), who seems to have practised formerly both in London and Brighton
(see the list of surgeons in Bailey's *Western, Midland, and London Directory* (1783) and
The Medical Register for the year 1783 (1783)). The Land Tax Assessments (Surrey
County Record Office, Kingston upon Thames) show, however, that he had
acquired *c.* 1792 considerable property in Great Bookham, and the parish registers
record his burial there on 9 June 1825.
    [2] François Piochard d'Arblay (L. 122 n. 11).
    [3] Jean-Baptiste-Gabriel Bazille (1731–1817) of Joigny, Auxerre, from whom
letters are shortly to be received giving news of his family (see Ll. 245, 246).

which he is now set off for an interview big with expectations impossible to repress.—

He promised me to return to-morrow—& I will wait till then, not to leave you in the same suspence in which I write.

⟶

He is come—after a fruitless, expensive, & cruelly disappointing journey, in which he has learnt nothing of all he wanted to know.

We can fix no time for seeing you—M. d'A. is again seated by me on an easy chair, with his foot on a cushion & stool—& our poor Cottage without any superintendant—when he may be able, however, to move, he will be most willing, ǀ & if his workmen do not inevitably detain him, our journey will take place immediately upon his restoration to the power of walking alone. But as I know the uncertainties of your Rooms, & of the avocations of my Brother, you may depend upon no surprise. I shall write to enquire into your conveniences. I should have been particularly glad to have *proved* how truly I spoke in praising my dear Rosette for her very amiable manner of doing the honours of her house, by a speedier repetition of our visit—but the Fates—& their Axes—are unkind, & we must submit.

our best Love to my dear Brother—& to Carlino—& kind Comp^ts to Mrs. Bicknell.

Adieu, Dear Rosette—& pray tell my Brother much as I wish him to take exercise, it is not by *hewing of Wood*—

And pray write a note to Lord Derby,[4] & tell him I shall never forgive him if he makes the divine Farren[5] a Countess before I see her again. He must positively postpone the Marriage till we can take leave of her.

[4] Edward Smith-Stanley (1752–1834), 12th Earl of Derby (1776), whose first wife Elizabeth (1753–97), daughter of James Hamilton (1724–58), 6th Duke (1743), had died on 14 Mar. 1797. Separated from her for many years, Lord Derby had become in some circles (e.g. at Richmond) somewhat a figure of fun for his faithful devotion and finally marriage (1 May 1797) to his mistress, the actress, below.

[5] Elizabeth Farren *or* Farran (*c.* 1763–1829), the daughter (see *DNB*) of 'a surgeon and apothecary in Cork'. For about fifteen years she had been received with the 'warmest favour' in London for her playing of comic fine ladies (Lady Betty Modish, Lady Townly, Lydia Languish, etc.). FBA would doubtless have liked to join the crowds who thronged to Drury Lane on 8 Apr. 1797 for her final appearance as Lady Teazle. When speaking the last lines of the role, she burst into tears.

232   Great Bookham, 3 April 1797

To Esther (Burney) Burney

A.L.S. (Diary MSS. vi. 4984–[7], Berg), 3 Apr. 1797
Double sheet 4to   4 pp.   black seal
Addressed: Mrs. Burney / Upper Titchfield Street / Portland Place
Endorsed by EBB: april—97
Edited by CFBt *and the* Press.

Launcelot Gobbo—or Gobbo Launcelot—was never more cruelly tormented by the struggles between his Conscience & the fiend than I between mine & the Pen.[1] says my Conscience: Tell dea Etty you have conquered one of your worst fears for your little Pet.—Says my Pen: she will have heard it at Chelsea: Says my Conscience she knows what you must have suffered, call, therefore for her congratulations: Says my Pen, I am certain of her sympathy, & the call will be only a trouble to her. Says my Conscience, Are you sure this is not a delicate device to spare yourself? Says my Pen—Mr. Conscience, you are a terrible bore. I have thought so all my life for one odd quirk or another, that you are always giving people when once you get possession of them,—never letting them have their own way, unless it happens to be just to your liking, but pinching & grating & snarling & causing bad dreams for every little private indulgence they presume to take without consulting you. There is not a more troublesome inmate to be found. Always meddling & making, & poking your Nose into every body's concerns. Here's ME, for example, I can't be 4 or 5 Months without answering a Letter, but what you give me as many twitches as if I had committed Murder; & often & often you have consumed me more time in apologies, & cost me more plague in repentance, than would have sufficed for the ǀ most exact punctuality. So that either one must lead the life of a slave in studying all your humours, or be used worse than a dog for following one's own. I tell you, Mr. Conscience, you are an inconceivable Bore.'

232. [1] In construction, the paragraph is an imitation of Launcelot Gobbo's soliloquy in *The Merchant of Venice*, ii. ii.

Thus they go on, wrangling & jangling, at so indecent a rate I can get no rest for them, one urging you would like to hear from myself something of an event so deeply interesting to my happiness, the other assuring me of the pardon of perfect co-incidence in my aversion to epistolary exertion. And, hitherto, I have listened—whether I would or not, to one, & yielded—whether I would or not, to the other. And how long the contest might yet have endured I know not, if Mrs. Locke had not told me, yesterday, she should have an opportunity of forwarding some Letters to Town to-morrow. So now—

I wish you were further! I hear you cry, so now you get out of your difficulties just to make ME get into them!

But consider, my dear Esther, the small pox—

I have considered it at least 6 times, in all its stages, God help me!

But then so sweet a Bantling—

I have half a dozen every one of which would make 3 of him—

I was interrupted in this my pathetic appeal, & now I must finish off hand, or lose my conveyance—So I can only say I am *sure*, seriously, of your hearty felicitation that our little Pet ¹ has escaped the sufferings of your poor Amelia²—& that, though I have been terrified to Death, I believe I had no cause, & am content to be 'Set down an Ass'³ for my pains. But he is cruelly thin, & has not any appetite. He lives wholly upon Milk. He is gay, however, blythe & active, & has such animating spirits I can entertain no real uneasiness for him.

Charles wants us to try change of air for him at Greenwich—& perhaps may think his air not marred by being breathed by his Parents also,—but my poor M. d'A. has hurt his foot, & is lame, & our Cottage besides calls for his superintendence at present. Nevertheless, we are not without plans which I hope will bring me to a view of my dearest Esther ere long. Our cottage is now *running up a legs bravely*, as they say in Norfolk, & when you Will trust yourself there, & deem it sufficiently aired, you will be paid for your journey by the first walk you can take, turn which way you will.

---

² Amelia, now nearly 5 years old, had had smallpox (L. 150 n. 4).
³ A part of Dogberry's speech, *Much Ado about Nothing*, IV. ii.

I fancy Mrs. Rishton is at Chelsea now[4]—do not be cold or backward to her advances, from however just remembrances, my dear Esther, for she loves us all at heart, & has been forced into a conduct that has done the utmost injustice to her real feelings. She is *ashamed*, I know, with respect to you in particular —but longs even ardently to regain your kindness & affection. You may believe I do not speak at random, though I can say this *only to yourself*, from the delicacy of her situation with Him who has the power—& has thus used it—to withdraw her from ALL her first connexions. She has declared to me—however— that they are entwined around her heart-strings & cannot be broken!—Ah—again let *you & I* drink, according to your toast, to ALL good Husbands! Who besides can you give it to without exciting a sigh?

I entreat whenever you see Mrs. Chapone[5] you will present my affectionate respects to her, & ask if she received a long Letter I directed to her in Francis St—Tottenham court Road?

All Norbury is well—I told your Message to the lovely Amelia, who said she would much rather have had a Letter instead.

I had a sweet sheet from *our beloved* yesterday,[6]—she seems well—but sad!—so insulated!—alas!—how would *our toast* choak there!—God restore the sweet soul!—that is my now most ardent wish & prayer on earth. I hope you go to Chelsea a little more liberally than in my time when I thought you horridly shabby[7] our dearest Father speaks of colds & coughs, but I hope they are over

Mr. Burney keeps well, I hope, also,—& hope must not stop there, but extend to dear Edward—Marianne—Sophy—&

4 Perhaps not as early as this. Through the extreme possessiveness of her husband (L. 222 n. 10) Maria had been isolated from her brother's family and from the Burneys, the friends of her girlhood (*ED* i. 113 n., 136, etc.).

5 FBA's letter is missing, but typical of Mrs. Chapone's kindness to FBA and her husband is her social note of Jan. 1797 (Barrett, Eg. 3698, f. 120): 'I would have born a week's illness to have been well when you call'd; the rather because I cannot hope for another opportunity of seeing you. . . . They have put my *name* in your [subscription] list with M[r] before it—leaving out the *S*. so that it appears not to be there—a disgrace I could not bear.' For this correspondence, see *Catalogue*.

6 This would have been SBP's folio letter (Berg) of Friday 24 Mar., of which FBA in her later editorial capacity obliterated thirteen lines of the first sheet and destroyed the second. The residue is printed in *FB & the Burneys*, pp. 262-5.

7 Cf. SBP's regret that 'Esther is not more frequently at Chelsea. . . . I think she has great powers of chearing and soothing our dearest Father and I lament they sh[d] not oftener be together' (*FB & the Burneys*, p. 262).

Amelia. Fanny & Cecilia—Adieu, dearest Esther, God bless you—& don't forget, little as you see your never endingly affectionate

                                    & faithful
                                          F d'A.

Bookham,
   April 3ᵈ 97

This is called for in a horrid hurry—

233   [Great Bookham, 1] April [1797]

To Doctor Burney
and Sarah Harriet Burney

A.L.S. (Berg), Apr.
Double sheet 4to 4 pp. *pmks* LEATHER / HEAD 1 AP 97 black seal
Addressed: Dr. Burney / Chelsea College / Middlesex
Edited by FBA, p. 1, *annotated and dated*: 4 9⟨7⟩ M.d'A.'s Call to Town on false News— ⟨a⟩ 1 O [*all out?*]

                                          April

My dearest Father will have wondered I have not sooner thanked him for his most welcome felicitations;[1] but an unkind accident has damped my satisfaction & my spirits. M. d'Arblay, in cutting some Wood, about a week ago, let the Ax slip, & it struck upon his foot.—Heaven be praised without material, or rather lasting consequences,—but with great pain, both from the force of the instrument in its fall, & the depth of the Cut. It bled most violently, which, the surgeon says, will probably save a Fever, & alleviate the suffering: The good Mr. Lowdall[2] came to our call, & dressed it. He charged the poor Patient to keep quiet, constantly seated, & with his foot upon a high stool. He has come to dress it himself every Morning since, & assures me it requires only time & stillness to be well. But Time, you will believe, can ill be accorded, when, the very day of the wound the little Building was re-commenced; it had been deferred for

233. [1] This letter is missing.   [2] See L. 231 n. 1.

fine Weather till that unlucky Morning; & stillness—to one so eminently his own labourer, is a cruel requisite. | Nevertheless, the great escape by which his foot has been saved, & my thankfulness, upon the danger Mr. Lowdall pointed out, that nothing yet more serious ensued, induced him to submit with a patience no one could have exceeded,—till Yesterday, when a Letter arrived, telling him a person was in Town who could give him news of *some of his friends*. He instantly concluded—judging by his wishes, these Friends were his Brother, & an Uncle whom he quite worships.[3] All his command over his feelings was now at an end, & he resolved to go immediately to Town,—at all hazards, & all expence. We sent for a Chaise from Leatherhead, —& he was helped into it—I would fain have accompanied him, but did not dare leave our little Treasure—& he set off in an agitation of hope & fear that almost made him breathless— & that nearly kept me so for him till Noon to day, when he returned—dejected, saddenned, disappointed beyond all expression. The Person who had summoned him knew nothing at all of his family,—nothing of any friend for Whom he is much interested, & only brought him a translation of Camilla![4]—And his helpless state had made it impossible to him to seek any one else,—getting even in & out of the Chaise was so | dangerous, & so contrary to the charges of Mr. Lowdall, that I had engaged his previous promise not to make one exertion that was avoidable. He arrived at London after 8 o'clock last Night, & had a Lodging to seek, as well as this officious person, whom he could not meet with till this Morning: & his Night, in the expectations then alive, was spent quite in agony. After the explanation, he felt so crushed, he was glad to commit his poor lame foot & dispirited person to the Chaise which he had engaged to bring him back. And now he is here again, by his own fire side, more depressed than I have hardly even seen him, from the sudden fall of hopes of information concerning all that he left most dear to him in his unhappy country. The kindness of his Nature, however, which nothing can injure, will soon, I know, as heretofore, make him seek to revive himself, that he may not deject his Companion. | He was much vexed not to get to Chelsea—

[3] See Ll. 122 n. 11, 231 n. 3.
[4] *Camilla, ou la Peinture de la jeunesse. Traduit de l'anglais de Miss Burney* . . . par J. B. Denis Deprés et J. Mar. Deschamps (5 tomes, 1797).

but his Coach hire, independant of his Chaise) cost 14^s & he could not put a foot to the Ground. But basta!—How I enrage at the 30£ for the Irish enquiries!^{5} & how tantalizing the *seniority*!^{6}—Crosdal & Parsons were not young enough to supersede it—& so now *Croch* must take his place. I hope my dear Mrs. Rishton is now with you^7—Charles presses us to Greenwich, with his Godson, for change of air, & *other reasons*—or any other—but this accident is wholly disabling for the present. Adieu, most dear Sir—pray excuse this morne Epître—& what Times are these, when ever I hear of them!—

ever most dutifully & affect^{ly} your F. d'A.

Miss Burney.

Thanks my dearest Sally for your kind congrats^8—I hope you have now Mrs. Rishton with you—I should write if I were sure —I want to know her stay & plans—I must positively see her, tell her—though we are all here in our worst plight,—but I shall be too glad to be proud. I entreat to know her designs. I fear we must give the Irish invitation of a Bed at the Inn—for we have only a Summer House, & I dread damp horribly—but a most cordial welcome to our Bread & Butter & Cheese—Beg her to write to me—& pray let me know about the mourning, which I think ends next Month—God bless you dear Girl—

^{5} Possibly into the affairs of Molesworth Phillips and the mortgages and remortgages he had placed on his lands in County Louth, one of which CB held.

^{6} Lacking CB's letter, one can only speculate that the rivalries may have been related to the professorship of music at Oxford left vacant by the sudden death on 19 Mar. 1797 of Philip Hayes (see *DNB*), to which post the musical prodigy and composer William Crotch (1775–1847) had succeeded. CB's paper on the wonders of Crotch's abilities as a child is printed in *Philosophical Transactions*, lxix (1779), 183–206.

John Crosdill (*c.* 1751–1825), principal cellist from 1776 at the Concerts of Antient Music and from 1778 violist at the Chapel Royal, was well known to the Burneys. William Parsons (*c.* 1748–1817), D.Mus. (Oxon., 1790), and knighted (1795), had in 1786 been appointed (over CB's own hopes) to the Mastership of the King's Band (Lonsdale, pp. 320–2).

^{7} As one knows from the letters of 24 Dec. 1796, [7], and 9 Jan. 1797 (op. cit.), Rishton had agreed to Maria's visiting Chelsea for ten days. She was not to arrive, however, until *c.* 3 May (L. 237 n. 14).

^{8} SHB's letter is missing.

234   Great Bookham, 11 May 1797

To James Burney

A.L.S. (PML, Autog. Cor. bound), 11 May 1797
Double sheet large 8vo   4 pp.   *pmks*   Up Seymour St / U.P.P.
12 MA 97   seal
Addressed: Captain Burney, / James Street, / Westminster.

                                                    May 11. 1797
                                                    Bookham.
Dear Brother,
    I hate to torment you—but what can poor folks do?
    We really stand abominably in need of that same £25 which
we begged you to receive for us of Mr. Mathias—
    The extreme uncertainty of the workmen's proceedings, & the
absolute necessity of superintending them, defers our journey to
Greenwich, for which we can yet fix no day.
    You never told us if you had received the X^mas £25.—
    I tremble lest any seeming carelessness of payment should
involve an idea we can do without it—This would be really
ruinous. We must therefore entreat you, dear James, to have
the goodness to ask Mr. Mathias for this 2^d receipt, which he
will deliver into *your own hands* with the [s]ame readiness as the
first, but which, *I know*, I must sign before I claim.[1] And if you
can send it [u]s by post, We may receive the monies by Mr.
Locke's [l]ittle Garden Cart, which brings & carries parcels
once [a] Week. This billet goes by that conveyance.
    M. d'A. has written another remonstrance ǀ to Mr. Shirley,
& received a rather more satisfactory answer. He promises to
exert himself with respect to his sister's offered loan, & apolo-
gises with some air of concern & sincerity for what is passed.[2]
    But we have no news of our Susanna & we are very ill at ease.
She has never yet been so long silent to me. If you have had any

234. [1] See Ll. 157 nn. 5, 6; 223 n. 9.
    [2] See L. 193 n. 7, for the loan of £400 that the Revd. Walter Shirley was at last
attempting to repay. Frances Anne (1770–1838), who had formerly visited Mickleham, may have been the sister most inclined to help with the debt to the d'Arblays.
She had married in 1789 the Revd. John Going (d. 23 Oct. 1829), rector of
Mealiffe, Tipperary.

account whatever from or of her, pray mention it. Mr. Shirley
says he has *seen the Major lately*, but does not name our sister.

M. d'A. has acknowldegd to Mr. Shirley the receipt of the
Jany half year's interest.

I have read with real instruction your Measures, & though
I am sorry you support the project of send^g the P. to Ireland,[3]
whi[c]h ˡ I do not think a proper view to all action can govern,
& which calls for Experience as well as ability,—yet I see many
things in which I concur, & several strokes which I sincerely
admire. And M. d'A.—a far better judge, upon matters of
calculation especially, speaks warmly in praise of the Measures
proposed, & the depth of reflection they combine.

Alas! what melancholy times!—

The Sailor's Mutiny[4] seems to me the most dreadful & alarming menace of all—exceeding whatever is passed—& boding
more than I dare think of—

I suppose our dear Father must be almost sunk—or on the
rack—by the present turn of affairs. For God's sake preserve
HIM & *YOURSELF* from entering upon these subjects at this sore
period!—& forgive, my dearest James, this earnest injunction
as well as plague & trouble from

Y^r most affe^t·

F d'A.

My Love to Mrs. B[urney]

I hope the Nursery continues thriving.

Is our dear—original—inscrutable & Heart-staunch Mrs.
R[ishton] still at Chelsea? I hope so. ˡ

You never told us how ⟨often⟩ you were robbed & murdered
in your way home

M. d'A's Kind Love—

defying this new winter, he is constantly at the house—

---

³ See L. 229 n. 5.
⁴ By this date a second mutiny had broken out at Spithead (i.e. on 7 May, the
mutiny on the *London*). There was trouble at St. Helen's and the outbreak of
mutinous symptoms at the Nore. JB's analysis of the cause of the mutinies, a holograph manuscript in the possession of the Pierpont Morgan Library, has been
recently edited by Hugh D. Sproule, 'James Burney's Opinion on the Naval
Mutinies of 1797', *The Mariner's Mirror*, xlvi (1960), 61–2.

235   Great Bookham, 11 May 1797

To Mrs. Francis (*later* Broome)

A.L. (Barrett, Eg. 3693, ff. 67–8b), 11 May [17]97
Double sheet 4to   4 pp.   *pmk*   11 MA 97   wafer
Addressed: Mrs. Francis, / Hill Street, / Richmond, / Surry.
Endorsed by CBF: Sister d'arblay / 1797

Bookham,
May 11.—97.

No news yet from Ireland — —

I am a good deal disappointed, my dearest Charlotte,—not
at the delay in itself, for I shall have equal pleasure in all parts
of the summer as now to embrace you here, but because I had
pleased myself with the hope of contributing to your recovery.
The so entire return we could now enjoy of our first & happy
social comforts & confidence & *badinages*, I think might materi-
ally hasten that wished for event; your stay would not be
so considerable as to give you pain from the separation with
your three treasures, & the perfect quiet with your so long &
early favourite *crony*, might have exhilarated the spirits so much
fatigue has harrassed, & so much business almost exhausted.
However, perhaps the shake of a London journey may be as
well. I wish you, at all events, to remove as speedily as *circumstances* will permit you, for I am certain nothing will so effectually
aid your general health as *any* change of air, a slow lurking
fever sooner yielding to that than to all other care or medicine.

Be perfectly at your own choice, my dear love, as to your visit
to us,—we would put no other constraint upon you but that of
insisting we ARE *to have it this summer*. And for as long as you can,
& with dear little Charlotte if possible. From all but that one
bond [we] ¦ release you. Our own time, with respect to Greenwich, is still uncertain. We wish it to be *quick*, for many reasons
—but the House & Workmen are not yet in a state to be left.
M. d'Arblay spends great part of every day in the field, & has
never yet returned without finding a necessity of yet further
postponing our journey. Make your own plans & proposals,
therefore, exactly to suit your own convenience, & if the excur-

sion hither should unfortunately happen to suit you at the period we are able to go to Charles, we will honestly confess it, upon promise you will reconcile us to so provoking a circumstance by endeavouring to return with, or speedily follow us. We can be absent but a week, happen when it may, from the great want of superintendance our Cottage requires.

Tell my dear & very dear Friends Miss Cambridge & Miss Baker[1] I beg them to take the same carte blanche, upon the same conditions. We have no other restriction, even in our wishes, than that of ascertaining that we shall see such dear persons *undoubtedly*. The sooner or later we will not torment about.

Your Godson, *though not in breeches*, as you must tell Clement, is all alive & prosperous. Nothing will, I trust, prevent our presenting ⟨hi⟩m to his little Cousins at Richmond this summer or Autumn,—& to my dear ǀ Aunt. Do pray give my kindest love to that dear aunt, & tell her so, & how delighted I shall be to shew her my little Boy, & beg her to kiss & bless him. Love him, I am sure, her kind Heart will make her do even unseen. Remember me, too, kindly to good Miss Brookes.[2]

I am very glad my dear sister Esther has a plan to spend days amongst you so soon—when she arrives give her my best love, & thanks for her kind Letter.

M. d'Ar. still wears a gouty shoe, though he has no remaining pain, except if the foot has not great & entire liberty.

You will go, I hope, soon to Town, & see our dearest Father, & *all the World* besides, a *little*: don't shut yourself entirely up, with an idea it is necessary. A gentle exertion, sufficient to allow you some amusement, will be productive of good, not mischief, to your health, I am firmly persuaded. I do not fear your flying into *dissipation*— —& a little *dulcet recreation* will be enlivening to your spirits, which cannot revive without removing this sluggish feverette.

I wish you, also, to catch Mrs. Rishton at Chelsea[3]—she will be sincerely glad to see you. She has come once more into the family with all her first & fondest partiality for every part of it. And she is all she *then* was—delightfully entertaining while essentially good.

235. [1] See i, L. 10 n. 6.   [2] See L. 150 n. 6.   [3] See L. 233 n. 7.

My best of loves to my little Charlotte, & to Marianne & Clement—& M. d'Arblay to *all Four*. Heaven bless you, my dear love. Come exactly when you will—you will be s⟨ure⟩ to come to open arms.

236   [Great Bookham, *pre* 11 May 1797]

To James Burney

A.L. (PML, Autog. Cor. bound), *n.d.*
Single sheet 4to   2 pp.   trimmed
Postdated in pencil, p. 1: 1797

My dear Brother,
I have the joy to tell you a Letter is arrived this Morning from our dearest Susan,[1] who gives no particular reason for her long silence, & says nothing of her health; but writes in her usual serene & interesting manner. All about her is still pretty quiet— & should it be otherwise, she is to remove, she understands, to some safer place—but she does not say where—Would to God she were home again!
We shall be very much obliged to you to transmit this to Mr. Mathias as soon as you possibly can,—& the *argent*, in small Notes, or dollars, or as you can get it best, in a small pacquet directed
                    For M. d'Arblay
                        at W. Lock's Esqr,
                            No 247. oxford Street, Hyde Park Corner.
& it will be forwarded by their cart, which comes back again friday Evening. Else we must wait till friday se'night. which will be rather *unked*.
I know this plagues you terribly—but what can we do with these odious Butchers & Bakers & Candle Merchants? not to mention Bricklayers & Carpenters, & t'other gang? There's no persuading them to serve us gratis, in a handsome manner. They have not the smallest notion of such a thing. And, to say the truth, I am not quite sure I should do better in their place.

236. [1] This letter is missing.

We have got the two good Charlottes with us. I hope the change of air will help the lingering fever that hangs upon the elder. Yesterday they came, with Miss Cambridge & Miss Baker, who spent the Day here & returned, after a visit to the Cottage. I heartily wish you & Mrs. B[urney] & Sally could have given us such another Day.

Alas—as to Ireland—'tis dismal indeed: That they may do better without us is possible—but what are we to do without them? Even if your plan of making Guards for the Country of all its Inhabitants were adopted,[2] I do not think they could protect it should Ireland, first being Free, next prove INIMICAL.

I cannot help, now, being egotist enough to rejoice you have not a Ship, as I pity all the officers who have to serve at such a time of insubordination, & I should be dreadfully anxious if any one I loved were now in any command. Yet M. d'A. says you are the *just the Man* for the present business, for he is sure though you love liberty, you a friend of order & discipline.

God send us PEACE! I am ready to finish & club & join with you in the end of your Pamphlet with all my Heart & all my Mind & all my Might, PEACE! PEACE! PEACE!

My Mate sends you his Kind love—& bids *ME* write these Letters, because they are *troublesome*, & may be unwelcome.

The two Charlottes greet you most kindly. Alec will one of these days. Mean time, I believe he would greet his little Cousin Sarah still more courteously.

All our loves to Mrs. B[urney]

Adieu, dear James.

NB. The 200 being drawn from Mr. Coutts, we dare not draw for the odd 25 till you tell us whether 'tis deposited there,

---

[2] James Burney's PLAN | *of* | DEFENCE *against* INVASION (L. 229 n. 5) had apparently appeared in February (L. 226 n. 11); and the second edition PLAN | *of* PREPARATION *against* INVASION (1797) took note of some of the objections made to the first.

Beginning with the axiom 'SECURITY is the first blessing of life; without it no other good is permanent, and life itself is scarcely a benefit', JB proposed that all the men between the ages of 18 and 55 residing in the parishes near the eastern and southern coasts and capable of bearing arms should be called up, enrolled, armed, and drilled regularly, thus supplying a reserve force of 200,000 men who, in addition to the regular armies, would be prepared to defend the country; while the knowledge that such a force existed would act as a deterrent to invasion.

The pamphlets were favourably mentioned in the *Monthly Magazine*, iv (July 1797), 35, and in the *Monthly Review*, xxii (Mar. 1797), 338–9, as 'moderate' and 'sensible', the latter opining that JB's plan might be 'less objectionable than the measures lately adopted to meet the exigences of the moment', namely, the militia bills of 2 Nov. 1796, see *AR* xxxix (1797), 119–26; and *CJ* lii. 93.

as M. d'A. wished, or kept ready for us in James Street, as was wished by his Rib. Did you ever know greater Plagues than *we two is?* as our friend Kitty would say: for I remember her exclaiming of Hetty & me, formerly—'Lord, what Toads you two is!'—

237   —3 April—17 May 1797 [Great Bookham,] To Mrs. Phillips

A.J.L. (Barrett, Eg. 3690, f. 174–b; Diary MSS. vi. [4987], Berg),—3 Apr. —17 May [17]97.
Originally a double sheet folio (12·4 × 7·8″), of which the first leaf is now missing and the second, extant in three pieces (see Textual Notes)
Edited with mutilations by FBA.

[*first leaf missing*]

April 3ᵈ—97

Yesterday I joined to our beloved Friend's Letter a brief acknowledgment of my Susan's dear last folio;[1] I will now begin at once to answer what calls for reply, as I am terribly apt, when the time for sending arrives, to fill up all my paper with some preponderating subjects, & to recollect afterwards how much I have omitted. In the first place, les trois femmes were received by M. d'Arblay safely and thankfully[2]—I must own I have not yet read them—not having curiosity enough to combat want of leisure from the million of things claiming my long arrears with Time, & with all employments but one. of course the Willyite Cadeau must be received, as the 3 femmes came safe. The pacquet for Esther ⟨Ponself⟩[3] went shortly after we lost its beloved donor,—& Betty will certainly call there when the weather will let her in her home visits, & deliver your kind messages. I have delivered, repeatedly, my good little Norbury's love to Nanny,[4] which she always hears with Tears of pleasure. Pray tell Susan, with my kind remembrance, I heard of her

237. [1] The last extant folio was that of Friday 24 Mar. (op. cit.).
  [2] Probably Charles Albert Dermoustier, *Les Femmes* (1793), a verse comedy in three acts.   [3] Presumably one of SBP's former servants.
  [4] Anne (Oxley) Richbill, who in April 1787 had succeeded Betty Parker as nursemaid to the 2-year-old Norbury but who was eventually driven away by Phillips's unkindness and unreasoning rages (*FB & the Burneys*, pp. 132–204, 248; and SBP's MSS. Journals, Osborn).

sister the other Day from Betty,[5] whose sister Mary is married, & is planning to live with Mrs. Newton,[6] at Mickleham. Both their husbands have work that employs & absents them all the week except Sunday, & they think they can bear their widow-hood more chearfully each by living together. Mary's husband is John Woodyear, formerly a footman, now a Day workman in Mr. Locke's Garden. How touching is your Letter from M. de Ternay![7]—I am sure our truly good & ever generous-hearted Esther will have much pleasure if she can soothe or serve the worthy de la Landelles:[8] & Sally will surely be glad to cultivate with such a woman as M[e] de Maureville,[9] now she has time & a carriage she can almost command.

May 2[d] I was interrupted,—& I have waited Day after Day till now with inexpressible | impatience & anxiety for another Letter to acknowledge—& be soothed by—before I write on: for after a very few days, I feel as if I had had no news for a month. What is this silence, my dearest beloved? the longest we have yet had, & w[ch] under such circumstances as the present is becoming now cruelly inquieting. God send some Letter may have miscarried that may soon find its right road!

‾‾‾‾‾‾⟶

[5] John Woodyear had apparently married a Mary Parker but the parish registers have so far yielded no further information.

[6] This is Ann Adams (bapt. 8 May 1754) of Epsom, who had married Robert Newton of Mickleham (see also, iv, L. 262 n. 1).

[7] Among the French *émigrés* on whom SBP called on Monday 7 Mar. 1796 (*FB & the Burneys*, p. 218) was Marie-Jeanne-Geneviève de Losse de Bayac (*post* 1750–1812), who had married in 1771 René-Henri-Louis-Jérôme d'Arsac *dit* le comte de Ternay (b. 1730). Emigrating in 1791, he had served as a volunteer in the 4th *compagnie de la noblesse du Poitou à l'armée des Princes* and had died in London on 21 July 1796. SBP records Madame de Ternay having come to visit her in December 1795 from an 'immense distance (she lives at *Somerstown*) on foot, & alone!—' (A.L., SBP to FB [27 Nov.–4 Dec. 1795], Barrett, Eg. 3692, ff. 194–5b).

[8] See L. 215 n. 14.

[9] Henriette-Marguerite Guinot de Soulignac (*c*. 1761—*post* 1825), widow of Jean-Louis-Bernard Bidé de Maurville, 'capitaine des vaisseaux de Roi, chevalier de St. Louis', who, having emigrated and taken service with England in the Regiment de Mortemart, died in London and was buried in St. Pancras Parish on 2 Aug. 1796 (Woelmont de Brumagne, iv; and A.L.S. (Berg) from Lally–Tolendal and Mme de Maurville to FBA, 26 May 1825.) With two young sons to educate, Madame de Maurville kept a small school for a time in England but returned to France in 1801 and later (in the year 1814) resided in Brussels. See A.L.S. (PRO W.O./43/61/5112) FBA to Charles Chamier Raper, 5 Aug. 1814.

Related to the princesse d'Hénin (*née* Guinot de Monconseil), Madame de Maurville was as well a 'cousine' of Frédéric-Séraphin, marquis de La Tour du Pin (1759–1837), whose wife, Henriette-Lucie Dillon (1770–1853), comments in her *Journal*, ii. 229–30, on Madame de Maurville's destitution at this time and her ᴇᴠbsequent history.

I have been reading over again all my Susan's Letters since her arrival in Ireland[10]—How they have penetrated me—Want of new ones obliged me to this resource for a little consolation. I have always forgotten to mention that I have 7ˢ—6ᵈ for you, paid me by Mrs. Locke just after you went—It is some remnant of a returned commission, but I know not what. I keep it for directions.—I have read with infinite pleasure over again what already I had read repeatedly, the account of the very amiable Kiernans, the excellent Mr. Maturin, & the good Mrs. Cartland —as well as of Jany Pany. Few people have more reason to be proud of their Relations than the Major,—tell him so, si vous en parliez de moi—& that he ought to forgive others who feel what he has a right to feel himself. His sisters & his nieces are certainly well deserving the warmest affection.

May 17ᵗʰ—This dear Morning has given me a pleasure amounting to a blessing—one for which I have sighed indeed, & am most—MOST thankful in the sight once more of my darling Susan's hand.[11]—I had become so terribly uneasy, that—had I not drawn from you the promise (your last contains,) to suffer me to be summoned if you were ill, & had I not known your integrity, the most exact of all your engagements,—I should have written to Mrs. Kiernan,—or the Major himself,—& with difficulty have refrained from meeting the Letter of answer by a nearer post than Bookham. Thank Heaven my terrors have been unfounded—I scarce ever received a Letter more joyfully —My dearest Soul! I am indeed delighted that illness, at least, has not added its cruelty to our separation—& that the second dearest little Boy in the world has *blessed* it so lately. The disturbances of Ireland, as recounted in the papers that we meet with here,[12] are so tremendous, I know less than ever how to

[10] Most of these can be read in sequence in *FB & the Burneys*, pp. 228–305.

[11] SBP's letter (Berg) of 24 Mar. contained the promise that FBA, never trusting her sister to report faithfully on her health, had exacted: 'it wᵈ be painful to me to resist anything so urgently demanded—depend therefore on my sincerity in all points relative to health—' (*FB & the Burneys*, pp. 262–5).

[12] On the very day that FBA was writing *The Times* reported the arrival yesterday (16 May) of 'two Mails from IRELAND' of an alarming nature. A Secret Committee of the Irish House of Commons had learned from papers lately seized in Belfast that 'the conspiracy of the United Irishmen extends far and wide; that there is a regular system of assassination and plunder; and that their avowed object is the overthrow of his Majesty's Government'.

Reported under the captions Dublin, May 11, 12, and Edenderry, May 7, were the arrivals of English regiments to the number of 8,000, fencible cavalry and even

reconcile myself to your abodes there. God speed *October* to our hopes & wishes, & may we embrace the Major for the happiness he will then, we trust, restore to us! O may no cruel circumstances intervene to break the pact he kindly fixed for that period! *Volti* The Letter shall go on this Evening, which, luckily, is that on which Arter[13] comes for pacquets for the last.

You will be pleased to hear our dear Charlotte & her charming little Girl are now with us for a few Days. Miss Cambridge & Miss Baker came with them yesterday, & visited our field, & took a rough rustic Dinner, & spent �... with us most kindly & cordially the Day. The two Charlotte's take your room & accommodations, to keep them in airing & employ. Though we do not build upon your resuming the *Apartment* any more, but prepare one for you in our new Chateau, where, however, the same brilliant *equipage & ornaments* must travel. our building goes on apace. The spot is so beautiful, nothing can help being pretty that grows upon it: & the Cottage has an architect that is not apt to mar advantages. Thank God, his foot is well, though he still wears a gouty shoe. He will write to you himself of what I am longing to communicate.

We have had a long & very comfortable Day with another party here,—Mrs. Rishton has spent some weeks at Chelsea,[14] & she came thence, with Sally & James, to spend a Day here. They set out at 5 o'clock in the Morning, & were At our breakfast at 8. We took them, also, to our field,—for M.d'A. delights to shew his Lions, & Sally was curious to behold them, & Mrs. Rishton was full of spirit, & in all her original humour of fun & sport. She was excessively entertaining, & played off her whims upon James just in her old way—with '*Lord bless the poor Noodle? What does he mean, now? does he know himself. Pray, Mr. Jem, do be so good to hold your tongue: you know you never know what*

artillery, and, not unrelatedly, the desperate raids of the 'Defenders' on private homes in their efforts to procure arms.

13 Probably William Arter (*fl.* 1771–97), the burial of whose wife on 18 Dec. 1771 is recorded in the parish registers of Mickleham.

14 Mrs. Rishton seems to have arrived at Chelsea *c.* 3 May (L. 222 n. 10).

you say.' And James, who adores her & her merry flights, was
in the most perfect harmony with her, himself, & all the world,
I have ever seen him. She *positively* orders him never to touch
upon politics, except when she is disposed to that subject herself. And then, as they very much agree in sentiments, I believe,
they can discuss them without quarrelling. James' two pamphlets[15] are both written with excellent good sense, & contain some
very good strokes—but it grieves me he should publicly write
against the administration, & offer his political counsel upon
what steps ought to be adopted as to Ireland & the Peace.
Otherwise, the two ostensible subjects of his two pamphlets,
The security against invasion, & Measures for restoring public
credit,—seem fairly open to all, & are so treated, with respect
to perspicuity & sagacity, that they could only have done
him honour. But all beyond will seem presumption, in one who
has had no opportunity of studying the hard business of a
statesman—a business which no experience or ability can teach
as to please two parties, or scarcely two persons in a nation.

M^e de S[taël]'s Book[16] was sent by herself to Mr. Lock, with
a short note, in which she calls herself pathetically to his
remembrance. She begs him to get the work well translated.
She then desires I, also, may read it,—& says she demands
aloud my own performance. She recommends herself to his
family, claims his friendship, begs him to accept her public
homage, & concludes. The Letter is touching enough. The
public homage is in the work.[17] It is in the chapter upon

---

[15] James's second pamphlet *Measures Recommended for the Support of Public Credit*
was praised by the *Monthly Review*, xxii (Apr. 1797), 465–6, as a 'well intended and
sensible pamphlet . . . delivered in concise and strong language' and by the *Monthly
Magazine*, iv (July 1797), 35, as 'a manly pamphlet, concisely and energetically
written'. The Yale Library, New Haven, has a copy, notwithstanding Scholes
(ii. 353).
[16] *De l'influence des passions sur le bonheur des individus et des nations* (Lausanne, 1796).
[17] Madame de Staël's 'short note' is missing but 'her public homage' to Mr.
Locke occurs, not, as FBA says, in the chapter 'De la tendresse filiale, paternelle et
conjugale' (Section II, chap. iii, pp. 263–75) but in the chapter 'De l'amour'
(Section I, chap. iv, pp. 148–78):

> J'ai vu, pendant mon séjour en Angleterre, un homme du plus rare mérite,
> uni depuis vingt-cinq ans à une femme digne de lui: Un jour, en nous prom-
> enant ensemble nous rencontrâmes . . . des *Gipsies*, des Bohémiens, errants souvent
> au milieu des bois, dans la situation la plus déplorable; je les plaignais de réunir
> ainsi tous les maux physiques de la nature. *Eh bien*, me dit alors M.L., *si, pour passer*

CONJUGAL affection, & relates a little dialogue she had with Mr. L[ocke] upon his own peculiar happiness. The Work has many Striking & most beautiful passages, & one or two whole Chapters that are *admirable*: but it has others that one may blush ⟨she⟩ has written, or made one read. All sort of principle yields to passion & impulse. She seems to have no idea of any moral *decency*, though the highest & most sublime of moral *virtues*. She is a very *great* woman, but thrown out of her sphere by an ambition that has no bounds, & no exact point of view, & a passion that is much in the same state, & both disappointed.—[18] Blame her as I may, *I* never can hate her, nor dislike her,— praise her as I may, must & will, I never can vindicate nor esteem nor respect her. Yet I can never recollect her many endearing, as well as superior qualities, & be sure I never again could love her.—But O M. de Lally!—what a divinity he is! I have written him a Letter such as I never wrote before of enthusiasm,—could not resist. And O I have had such an Answer![19]—La Pr^sse [d'Hénin] is not yet gone; difficulties have retarded her.[20] The work is much too considerable for *many* franks. It must wait some friend. I long for you to have it. I am so sure we shall feel alike in it, if you can but read it de suite. I hear good accounts alltogether of my dearest Father, though he has a cough. We should go to Green⟨wich⟩ but for the Palais, which occupies all tim⟨e⟩.

> ma vie avec elle, il avait fallu me résigner à cet état, j'aurais mendié depuis trente ans, et nous aurions encore été bien heureux! Ah! oui, s'écria sa femme, ainsi même encore nous aurions été les plus heureux des êtres!

The author goes on to applaud this sentiment, which, she says,

> fait éprouver une passion peut-être plus profonde encore que dans la jeunesse; une passion qui rassemble dans l'ame tout ce que le tems enleve aux sensations; une passion qui fait de la vie un seul souvenir . . .

[18] Cf. Madame La Tour du Pin, *Journal*, i. 204–5. 'Ses grandes qualités étaient seulement ternies par des passions auxquelles elle s'abandonnait d'autant plus facilement qu'elle éprouvait toujours une sorte d'agréable surprise. . . .'

[19] This correspondence is not extant, but see *Catalogue* for later letters from Lally-Tolendal to FBA.

[20] According to Madame de La Tour du Pin (*Journal*, ii. 138), the princesse returned to France in the summer of 1797 under an assumed name ('celui d'une marchande de modes de Genève').

238 [Great Bookham, *pre* 18 May 1797]

To Mrs. Locke

L., imperfect copy in hand of CFBt (Diary MSS. viii. 4928–9, Berg), 1796
Double sheet 4to   2 pp. *misdated*
Edited by the Press.

1796

To Mrs Locke

You are too good my dearest Friend—almost literally *too* good, which you know, like all extremes, is naught.

My Mate wants to send you a Daisy—but says he will carry it. What can *I* send you? Only what you have got already, which is very Irish, for I have but my *old* Heart, with not one *new* thing in it for you these many years. I have had this morrning a Letter that has quite melted me with grateful sensations, written *by command*.[1] I will shew it you when these eternal rains will take a little rest. A private letter from Windsor tells me the P[rince] of Wirtemberg has much pleased in the royal house by his manners & address upon his interview; but that the poor P[rincess] R[oyal] was almost *dead* with terror & agitation & affright at the first meeting—she could not utter a word—the Q[ueen] was obliged to speak her answers—The Prince said he hoped this *first* would be the *last* disturbance his presence would ever occasion her. She then tried to recover, & so far conquered her tumult as to attempt joining in a *general* discourse from time to time. He paid his court successfully, I am told, to the Sisters, who all determine to like him, & the P[rincess] R[oyal] is quite revived in her spirits ǀ again now this tremendous opening—& Sight—is over.—[2]

238. [1] As is explained in iv, L. 255, the Queen had sent FBA almost immediate notice of the death of Miss Schwellenberg (d. 7 Mar. 1797); and this with the present 'command', FBA was to interpret as a hint on the part of the Queen that she (FBA) might supply the vacancy. She delayed, therefore, in obeying the summons (see L. 242 and n. 9.)

[2] On 3 May a Marriage Treaty had been ratified by Parliament between Charlotte Augusta Matilda (1766–1828), Princess Royal of Great Britain, and Frederick William Charles (1754–1816), Hereditary Prince of Würtemberg (of which in this same year he was to succeed to the dukedom). The meeting here described took place on 13 May. See Stuart, *Dtrs. Geo. III*, pp. 15–68. A 'Scrapbook on Marriages' (BM Add. MSS. 6332) has a selection of clippings tracing the progress of the negotiations from the arrival of an Envoy from Württemberg on

You will be pleased, and my dearest Mr Locke, at the style of my summons: 'tis so openly from the dear Queen herself. Indeed she has behaved like an Angel to me from the trying time to *her* of my marriage with a *Frenchman*[3]—*So odd!* you know, as L^y Inchiquin said.[4] |

239   [Great Bookham, 2 June 1797]

To Mrs. Waddington

A.L.S. (Diary MSS. vi. 4988–[91], Berg), *n.d.*
Double sheet 4to   4 pp.   *pmks* LEATHER / HEAD   2 JU 97   red wafer
Addressed: Mrs. Waddington / Llanover, / Abergavenny / Monmouth.
Edited by FBA, p. 1 (4988), *postdated*: June 1797
Edited also by CFBt *and the* Press.

It was a very sweet thought to make my little namesake[1] write to me, & I beg her dear Mama to thank her for me, & to tell her how pleased I should have been at the sight of her early progress, had it not proved the vehicle of anxious intelligence. Yet I could not sooner contrive to enquire further news, much as I wish to hear, unless I had contented myself in a way that so ill contents *you*—namely by a few *lines,*—with which I should have begged a few *words.* Let me, however, have a Letter as speedily as you can spare time for writing it, I entreat. I shall wish much to have a confirmation of your assurance that the illness is over, & that your maternal tenderness has the recompence of your own & your Cherub's returning bloom & health.

It is but lately I have thought my little Boy entirely recovered, for his appetite had never returned since the eruptive fever till this last fortnight—or returned only by fits, & announced a frightful ⟨fever⟩ devourer which has since, thank Heaven, been routed. He is now compleatly restored to all his strength & good

12 Nov. 1796 to the Printed Ceremonials, the Order of the Procession, etc., for the Nuptials in the Chapel Royal at St. James's on 18 May 1797. On 2 June the Prince and Princess set off for Harwich, all scenes being 'highly affecting'.
   [3] See L. 124 n. 5.   [4] *Née* Mary Palmer (i, L. 23 n. 26).
239. [1] See i, L. 22 n. 8.

looks, & to all my wishes—for 'tis the gayest & most companion-able little soul I ever saw.

And now—what shall I tell you?—you ask me *What informa-tion any of my late Letters have given you, except of my health & affection?*—None, I confess!— —yet they are such as all my other friends have borne with, since my writing-weariness has seized me, & such as I still, & upon equally *shabby morsels of paper*, continue to give them. Nor have I yet thought that to accept was to abuse their indulgence. When they ǀ understood that writing was entirely irksome to me, except as the mere vehicle to prevent uneasiness on their part, & to obtain intelli-gence on mine, they concurred not to make my silence still more oppressive to me than my writing, by a kind reception of a few words, & returning me LETTERS for *NOTES*.

And why are YOU so much more severe? & tenacious?

Why, rather, you will perhaps ask, should YOU, because you see me thus spoilt, join in spoiling me?—

My faithful attachment, I am sure, you cannot doubt—holy & sacred I hold its origin,[2] which my memory brings back to me with reverence almost every day of my existence. And why should that *affection*, in your estimation, be so little, which in mine—where I dare believe I possess it—predominates over all things save my opinion of the worth of the character from which I may receive it?—by *little*, I only mean *little satisfactory*, unless unremittingly & regularly proved by *length* of Letters. I do not imagine you to slight it in itself—but I see you utterly dissatis-fied without its constant manifestation.

It appears to me—perhaps wrongly—you have wrought yourself into a fit of fancied resentment against a succession of *short* Letters, which could only have been merited by Letters that were *unfriendly*. You forget, meanwhile, the numerous Letters, I have, at various epochs, received from yourself not merely of half pages, but of literally three lines—& you forget them, because they were never received with reproach, nor answered with coldness. By me they were equally valued with the longest, though they gave me not equal entertainment; for I prized them as marks of *affection*, & I required them as *bulletins*

---

[2] This was a vow of 'eternal regard' given to Miss Port at the deathbed of her great-aunt Mrs. Delany in April 1788 (*DL* iii. 484). 'Sacred shall I hold it!—sacred to my last hour. I believe, indeed, that angelic being had no other wish equally fervent.'

of Health. Entertainment, or Information, I never considered
as a basis of correspondence, though no one, you may believe,
can more ⏌ delight to meet with them. The basis of Letters, as of
Friendship, must be *KINDNESS*, which does not count lines &
words, but expressions & meaning, which is indulgent to
brevity, puts a favourable construction upon silence, grants
full liberty to inclination, & makes every allowance for convenience. Punctuality with respect to writing is a quality in
which I know myself deficient,—but which, also, I have to no
one ever promised. To Two persons, only, I have practiced it,
my Father & my sister Phillips—There is a third whose claims
are still higher; but uninterrupted intercourse has spared all
trial to my exactness: my other friends, however near, & however tender, have all accepted my *Letters* like *myself* for better &
for worse, &, finding my Heart unalterable, have left my Pen
to its own propensities.

Nor am I quite aware what species of 'information' you repine at not receiving. An *elaborate composition* written for admiration, & calculated to be exhibited to strangers, I should not be
more the last to write, than you—quick & penetrating to
whatever is ridiculous—would be the first to deride & despise:
a *gay & amusing rattle* you must be sensible can flow only from
the humour of the moment, which an idea of raised expectations
represses rather than promotes: a *communication of private affairs*
— — —no,—the very Letter which produced this complaint
contained a statement of personal concerns the most important
I have had to write since my marriage:[3]— —

From all this, which reluctantly, though openly, I have
written, you will deduct That while you think me unkind (as I
apprehend) I think you unjust.

But I have *written*, now, as well as *read*,—& have emptied my
mind of all ⏌ ungenial thoughts—hasten, then, dear Marianne,
to fill up the space once more with those fairer materials which
the estranged style of your late Letters has woefully com-
pressed. You will think of me, you say, always '*as you ought*'—if
you do, I may venture to send you again the shabby Paper, or
wide margin, you have received so indignantly, by reminding
you—in the first place, That the zealous Advocate for Public
Liberty must not be an imposer of private exactions,—&, in the

[3] See L. 230.

second, That though the most miserable of correspondents, I am the most unchangeable of Friends.

And now, if I could draw, I would send you The Olive Branch, with our arms mutually entwining it.—Enclose me the Design—& I will return you its inscriptions. F. d'A.

I find my Father has heard just the same high character of the super-eminent powers & eloquence of the Abbé Lajard that you sent me in a former Letter.[4]

The Lock Family have not yet returned from Town. They did not go thither till late in April. Have you seen Mr. William's beautiful sketch of Lady Templetown's two eldest Daughters?[5]

We have begun, at last, the little Hermitage we have so long purposed rearing for our residence, & M. d'A, who is his own Architect & Surveyor, is constantly with his workmen—whom Bab & I do not spare visiting & admiring. God bless you—

240   Great Bookham, [29 June] 1797

To Esther (Burney) Burney

A.L.S. (Berg), Midsummer Quarter, 1797
Double sheet 4to   4 pp.   *pmks*   LEA[THER] / HEAD   29 JU 97
wafer
Addressed: Mrs. Burney, / Nº 2. Upper Titchfield Street, / Portland Place.
Endorsed by EBB: answer'd / July 1ˢᵗ / —97

Midsummer Quarter.
—97.
Bookham.

I agree to your Quarterly payments, my dearest Etty, but must add a clause to allow law to the end of the Month of each pay Day. Your proposal struck me at first to be shockingly niggardly; but I found, when Midsummer Day arrived, I was only

---

⁴ See L. 200 n. 2.
⁵ Unidentified, but perhaps very much like William Locke's pencil and wash of two young women, the possession of the Print Collection of the British Museum, which on accession (1906-7-19-4) was described as 'two studies of Lady Hamilton dancing the tarantella combined in a group, Pen outline and watercolour'. Engraved and published by Mⁿᵒ Bovi of no. 207 Piccadilly, 2 May 1796, it bears the added title 'Grace is in all their steps. &c. Milton'.

provoked I had not oftener to *receive*, not to *write*. So, upon the whole, I close with the proposition unmurmuring.

Alas, my dear Hetty, I was much more shocked than surprised by the cruel extracts you have given me.[1] Grief & indignation for that beloved of our Hearts never subside,—but astonishment is *all gone* for him who produces them. O that she were out of his hands, & partaking, under our little Roof, such fare as we can afford for ourselves! M. d'Arblay loves her with so truly a brother's tenderness, that he would rejoice like myself in obtaining her,—& our extremest frugality (though then a little more *extremed*) would to her be as chearful as to us.—Sure I am that, with her exemplary fortitude & resignation & sweetness of mind, we could console her into far more happiness, in a retreat the most œconomic, than she can ever experience as mistress of 30 workmen! — — How abominable such projects & risks, where no provision is made for either wife or Children! that dear lovely Fanny has a happiness of temper that will make her endure any change of situation better than almost any one so extremely young,—but how horrible to have her put to such proof thus wantonly!—the poor Boys,—Norbury particularly, brought up | with *nothing spared* to give them high notions of themselves & their conditions!—the uncommon parts of Norbury are all that have saved him from being arrogant & haughty & supercilious to ALL but people of the first rank or consideration. What a *Father* to instill notions at all times insolent, & then trifle away the situation which alone can make those who have imbibed them supported by the world! Had not Nature, in her mercy, given them all their Mother's blood, how doubly unhappy, because doubly disgraced, must they have become from any reverse of fortune! I have not dared mention your communications in my Letters: I write with constant dread of not writing to *her* alone—& though she complains I am *too* guarded,

240. [1] The letters written by SBP from Ireland to her eldest sister were, a quarter of a century later, destroyed for the reasons explained to FBA in EBB's letter of 13 May 1823 (Barrett, Eg. 3690, f. 142): The 'dear & confidential Letters—after repeated readings and lamentations over them,—I have with a repugnance indescribable thought it unsafe to keep—and many have I been compelled from common prudence to sacrifice!'

The series sent to FBA, printed in large part in *FB & the Burneys*, pp. 228–305, supply a consecutive record of the years 1796–9 at Belcotton, the debts, wild schemes, tyrannic cruelties, infidelities, and rages of the spendthrift, erratic, and ruined Irishman Phillips, whose career in many ways could have supplied fair copy for Maria Edgeworth's Irish tales.

I dare not be otherwise. The flames that would blaze forth at sight of any thing I could write naturally would be tremendous. —As to our own portion of Irish punctuality,—it has been a heavy disappointment, & may prove a severe evil. We should not have begun our Cottage but from an engagement of Mr. Shirley that he would pay his Mother's & his own debt. The 400 Gˢ was lent to *both.*[2] He has again promised, however, to expedite payment in a short time, & remonstrated against M. d'A.'s hint of putting his claim into the hands of a Lawyer. This latter Method would make *me* quite unhappy, from 1000 reasons. Yet 'tis cruel to be thus distressed for one so wholly without right or claim to our property. But I think so much more of our darling sister, in all that relates to Money Matters, that I only feel oppressed by *this* upon *occasion,* & where *circumstance* forces the debt to embarrass, or alarm. Certainly we must combine to hold the corrosion of this business from our dearest Father's breast. He is already but too much disturbed by all he knows of it.—But I must not let this sad subject wholly engross my paper. |

I have had infinite pleasure & satisfaction in the accounts of Richard, & the intention of the good (& Merry) Bishop to ordain him so speedily.[3] His frolic with your supper implements diverted me very much. I shall really be obliged to you to remember my sincerest felicitations upon Miss North's marriage,[4] both to herself the Bishop, when you have opportunity. I mean if Mr. Garnier appears to be worthy of so excellent & amiable a Wife. And I hope, as the choice has in it no glare of splendour to dazzle, it is really made upon motives that will ensure happiness.

You don't tell me if you have ever seen Mrs. Chapone, & given my message; & I have no other way to know any thing of her, & yet a constant wish for intelligence, & her remembrance.

I join very much in what you say of Mrs. Rishton, that she now seems a more *pleasing* character than ever: as well as that she has not been wholly blameless in suffering for so long a time her earliest friends to remain in doubt whether she had a *Heart or not*: I own this now, because she has boldly come forward to

---

[2] Ll. 193 n. 7, and 234 n. 2.   [3] Cf. L. 229 n. 7.

[4] Henrietta North (1771–1847), who had married on 9 June 1797 the Revd. William Garnier (*c.* 1772–1835), prebendary of Winchester (1800) and rector of Droxford, Hants (1801–35).

shew it: but as, formerly, & regularly, I have been exempted from *sharing* in this doubt, I have always felt a tie of personal gratitude that has silenced me upon the subject, though it could never reconcile me to it.—Could she *get free*, how happy she might still be, with those admirable & unimpaired spirits which she has preserved through all seasons & all trials!—

M. d'A. was much pleased with your account of the marriage of M. le Marquis Sigy,[5] & will endeavour to congratulate him when next he *emerges from his solitude*. I extremely regret the good & dear Betsy B.[6] was not in Town at the time I spent at Chelsea. I should rejoice with my whole Heart to meet her again. |

Our sweet Mrs. Locke—with whom we are going to spend the Evening—tells me you looked better than usual—& speaks with animated pleasure of what she calls *your kind reception of her*, in the few minutes she spent with you. It doubled her concern, she says, that she could see you no more. If I had a frank, I should enclose her own words about the little meeting written me from Town. My Partner is quite well, & free from accident, just now, & working Daily at his Cottage & Grounds. My little Love is alas but *too interesting to view* now,—for he looks as delicate as ever his little Cousin Cecilia did. He has never been thoroughly flourishing since the small pox. I don't believe enough of their malignancy came out. He has had a worm since, & but rarely has the least appetite. You will believe we are not always at our ease about him, thus circumstanced! Yet, between whiles, he is so perfectly well, in spirits, gayity, playful- ness, & even strength, that we are never suffered to be alarmed seriously—Heaven be praised!—for if we were — — but adieu, without finishing what no language could express. M.d'A. sends you—& yours, Love, & so does she who scribbles it, most cordially. Is dear Marianne returned from Halsted?[7] Sophy I hear is at Chelsea, & rejoice for Sally's sake, but not for yours & Amelia's. I hope dear M^r B[urney] keep well. & must beg parti- cular remembrance to our Cousin Edward. What a beautiful Drawing he has sent us! Adieu, Dearest Etty—you are a terrible

[5] Frédéric-Auguste-René du Roux, marquis de Sigy (*c.* 1758/60–1847), a captain in the *émigré* regiment de Mortemart (1794–6), who had lately married Antoinette-Anne-Laure de Perpignat (1776–1849).

[6] FBA's cousin Elizabeth Warren Burney, *called* 'Blue'.

[7] Marianne spent much time with her aunt Ann *née* Burney (1749–1819), the wife since 27 Jan. 1780 of the Revd. John Hawkins (d. 17 June 1804), rector (1792) of Halstead, Essex (i, Intro., p. lxxiv; and L. 7 n. 23).

29 June 1797

shabberoon, as Kitty Cooke would say, if your last is to serve for all Mids^r quarter! Y^{rs} ever, ever & ever

F.d'A.

Love to the two dear Charlottas if with you.

241 [Great] Bookham, 20–24 July 1797

Conjointly with Mrs. Locke
and Amelia Locke
To Mrs. Phillips

A.L.S. & A.N. & A.N. (Berg), 20–24 July 1797
Double sheet folio   4 pp.   *pmk* 5AU 97   red seal
Franked: W Free Windham / London August first 97.   *pmk* FREE 1 AU 97
Addressed: Mrs Phillips / Belcotton / Drogheda

[*By Madame d'Arblay*]

July 20$^{th.}$—97
Bookham

Your dear Letters, my most beloved Susan, are received with a joy even in the mere sight of your hand, that prevents almost *any* contents from immediately depressing—otherwise we had hoped some intelligence relative to the Month to which we *must* still / subject of our last paquet, Some word of that return to which we so anxiously / look forward would have cheared our prospects in the last,—but however, our Anchor is our Hostage, & we have recourse to it in all our fears & anxieties.[1]

The enquiries & doubts the most interesting I leave wholly to our dearest of Friends to answer, merely saying, once for all, myself, that the *termination* has been all I could wish, & will be always what I shall most rejoice in. And now I will open upon nothing more, that I may give the Alexandriana you so kindly believe will be pleasant to you, for if once I enter upon other matters, my paper will again be gone ere I know where I am. I only wish I could send you a Babiana to my Father,—but he is

241. [1] No letters of these dates have survived, and FBA's comment is obscure. The anchor to which FBA tied her hopes was Phillips's promise to the Lockes that SBP could return at the end of the year, that is, October 1797.

322

so fond of Babys, he would not like to part with it. I must therefore *write it all over again*—& remember how often my beloved
Susanna did just the same for me.

When you left us—alas! —— you may recollect he had not
above 4 words at his command, & not even one sentence, though
nearly 2 years old: &, though he could comprehend, apparently,
whatever was said to him, either in French or English, he was
still so backward of speech, that he made not one volunteer
effort towards conversing, except by his Eyes, & by signs, till
the last Day of February, when he was 2 years & 10 weeks old:
& then, suddenly, upon awakening in the middle of the night,
he called out '*How do, Mamma?—How do, papa?*' A phrase he
had learnt by rote the preceding Day, to use to a stranger: but
of which this application was not more unexpected than—you
will believe,—welcome. We were, in truth, enchanted at this first
use of his best faculty, that of expressing his own meaning.

—March.—

Certain nocturnal infirmities—which must be nameless—
occasioning Betty's first words to be, commonly, 'Come, my
dear, come & have a dry Gown on,'—he has conceived an idea
that DRY is a term for whatever is desirable & perfect, & he uses
it accordingly—saying, when I am in a visiting Garb '*Mamma
got   dry cap
dot a dye tap on!*—' & '*Mamma dot a dye Hat!*' And still, when he
trots about the Garden with us, claiming his allowance of Fruit,
Give   currant
he says 'Dive a dye turran, mama,' '*Dive a dye piece onnange, papa!*'
onnange, you must know, is his technical term for what is best,
adopted ever since he had oranges presented him during the
small pox. He most particularly, however, appropriates it to
strawberries Nor is his fashion of classing animals at all less
concise; a Dog being the first Quadruped he noticed, he no
sooner saw a Horse, after he was able to speak, than called out
'*A Bow wow, Mamma!*' And perceiving, in the same Meadow, a
Another
Cow, he added '*Annonner Bow wow, mamma!*' And having learnt
that the Robins & Thrushes that sing around us are called
Birds, he gave no other Name to our Poultry, caperring after
stop
the Cocks & Hens as he cried '*Birds! Birds! top, Birds!*'

When I put him in a closet for any misdemeanour, he claps his little hands, by way of begging pardon, & says '*Won't do any more, mamma!*' |

During his confinement with the small pox, the ever kind Amelia sent him a Horse & Chaise, which he was passionately fond of, & always called '*Amenie Horse—*' & afterwards a little Dog. Of this latter I informed him as he awoke in some suffering,—which it instantly made him forget, to exlaim 'O, dood good
Boy, Amenie!'

As soon as he was able to repeat after us, upon meeting occasional passengers in our Walks, *That's a Man*, he began to say it for himself, & still does the same, by every *person of that sort* we meet, in a matter that not a little amazes them—for when he says, full in their face, & stopping short to look at them
'*At's a Man—*' they seem to demand why, what should I be? That's
He does it, too, equally without ceremony to the Gentle as the Simple, & the former think it as democratic a liberty as the latter queer & *out of the way.*

One of the first desires he manifested, upon receiving the power of speech, was to be called Boy: if we said my dear Baby, he immediately cried, 'my dear *Boy!*' as if correcting us. To Alec, or Alexander, he objects in the same manner, & neither replies, comes, nor goes, till we have humoured him by chang-ing the apellation to *Boy.* Thus, when he wants any thing, he
                    Wants   to sit in   Wants   to come to
says '*Mant, Boy, tit mamma's lap.*' '*Mant, Boy, tome papa's arms—*'
                    Milk & water
'Mant, Boy, Mink water.' 'Tis an idiom quite his own.

I told him, one Day, to say I want Milk & Water—he looked very thoughtful, and then said '*I*, Boy—*I*, Mamma,—*I*, papa—*I*, Buff—' as if reflecting upon the general use of *I*, & finding it too indefinite for his comprehension unaided. *Buff* he says for *Puss*, which he cannot yet pronounce.
                                        That's
When he sees a Slop, he cries '*At's a wet!*' & if two, or more,
That's another
'*At's annonner wet!*'

He seemed to have, naturally, an idea of a Centaur, for he would only say '*At's a Man!*' when he saw a Man & Horse, till after he had seen one alight, & then he used the same phraseology

for all Drivers & Carriages, & he now regularly says, as they
coach—   chaise
appear 'At's a Man & totch!—At's a man & tase—At's a man
wheelbarrow.
& Cart—At's a man & webaddy—'

Upon dropping Amelia's Dog, one Day, he tenderly called
fall   fall
out *'don't pall down, Amenie Dog! pall up!'* And to his Father he
again
says, in a Morning, *'Dont lay down, Papa, aden; lay up.'*

As soon as I enter the Room, after any absence, however
go away   again
short, he flies to me, crying *'Don't do eay, mamma, aden!'*

While his poor Father was confined & nursing his foot, in
consequence of the cruel wound from the ax in chopping wood,
he capered up to him, as usual, saying *'Dance, Papa, Dance!'* & I
then recounted to him, as simply as I could, the accident: He
listened to me with his utmost attention, & then, in a voice of
sadness, said *'Poor papa! hurt the wood, & can't Dance!'*

And here, I think, is stuff enough of his first Month's
campaign in the art of Speech. So now for the little April
Fool.—

You will call his Mother one, perhaps, when you hear she
now began teaching him the Alphabet—but it was merely as a
play, and it has proved the amusement he most likes. His dear
Aunt Phillips' Ivory cadeau now came forth, with various
imitations upon Cards, to save the originals, which I love more
than he does. He has taken the utmost delight in playing with
the Letters, placing, bringing, & naming them; but when, upon
a mistake, I call him a little Dunce, he looks quite offended: &
the first time after this affront that he brought me the right
Letter which I had asked for, he exultingly said 'In't a ittle
dunce, now, mamma!' ˡ

In our way, one Morning, to Norbury Park, he had a severe
attack of the stomach. We stopt to fondle & console him, &, as
soon as he felt easy, he looked sorry for my concern, & said
stomach   got   again
'Tomach-ache dot well, aden, mamma.'

Seeing our dearest Mr. Locke stand up, & put on his spectacles, to examine some writing of the rosy Frederick, who was
at home for some holydays, Alec started, & suddenly quitting
his play things, ran to face them both, &, after fixing them

That's
some time, alternately, said, pointing with his Finger *'At's*
that's
Locke,—& at's Boy Locke.'

He fell asleep upon Betty's Lap in our way to our Field, while
we were seated to rest ourselves. Mon^r d'Arblay had not time
to remain with us, & walked on: when the little love awoke, &
had said 'Mamma!—*Bettea!*—' as he calls Betty, he got up, &
looked earnestly around him, & through the nearest Bushes
Boy wants to find
& Trees, & then, returning to me, said *'Mamma,—mant Boy pind
Papa!—'*

I now skip to May.—on the opening of which he had the joy
of presenting a Penny & a Gingerbread Cake to all the Children
of the village, & of little Bookham, & Estwick, who came to our
windows with Garlands. His pleasure was beyond description
great in the office, & in the sight of their little Bows & courtesies.
The two first who came were Boys, & when they had had their
pittance, which he gave them with smiles of delight, he called
Good   come again to-morrow—
out 'Dood by, dear Boys!—tome aden a moddow!' He always
selected the littlest for his first donation, & stopt & hesitated
before he could persuade himself to give at all to any bigger
Children, if they came accompanied by tinies. Ever since, if I
say to him Pray remember the Garland—it brings back all his
first extacy, & he never rests till he has made me recount him
the various adventures of the Morning.

He is now passionately fond of any little Relations made
simple & plain enough for his comprehension, & I can quiet
him from any noise, & amuse him from any naughtiness, &
make him forget any pain, by only promising to tell him a story.
I gave him a brief narrative of the misfortunes of Paul & Mary,
from a little Pocket Book engraving that his papa put into his
hands: & as soon as I had done, he pointed to Paul struggling
Pray come   again   stay
in the Sea, & called out *'Pay tome out, aden, man! don't tay in!*—

He is much entertained with the Drawings hung up in our
parlour, little as he can understand their value; he often ad-
look
dresses them, as imagining they are of our society, & says *'oot*
at me   take me
at ee, Amenie!—tate ee up, Gan'pa!—How do, Narbonne?'

When he is disposed to be whimsical, or naughty, if I fix
                                                      look
him, he waves his hand, to motion me away, crying '*Don't oot*
me
at ee, mamma!—' Though, if I turn aside, obedient, he draws me
                                                     look   me
hastily back, exclaiming '*O mamma! oot at ee, now!*'

When his papa asks for a Kiss, he sometimes refuses,
                            won't kiss   cry
coquetishing, saying, '*no, Boy on't tiss Papa,*—' & adds '*Tye,
papa!*' & when obeyed by his fond Father, he makes a most
                                               that's   cry
grave Face, & with a remonstrative tone, says '*At's bad to tye,
papa!*' & immediately puts forth his little ruby lips to be kissed,
as if to prevent further naughtiness.

After a visit that had much gratified him from our beloved
Friend, I had told him she would soon come again, & he
watched for her continually, running to the window at every
sound of a Carriage; but, after numerous disappointments, he
at length walked off, saying very gravely to himself '*Naughty
Boy, mitty Locke, on't tome back aden.*'

And now, my own Susan, is not this a Letter rather for your
Children than yourself? & yet, does it not remind you of
Norbury's first openings? Your *old bachelor* of that charming
Boy has made me laugh ever since.[2]—but alas—I have not
laughed at a quotation I have received from our Esther!—'tis
from her amie la plus cherie[3]—& cruelly afflictive. If that amie
thinks any *duty* demands the sacrifice so barbarous to herself &
her friends, the latter can but hope such duty may wear a new
aspect—La PAIX *I* am persuaded will change all[4]—& the off-
spring of that amie of Etty will surely be the ⎸ care of Provi-
dence. This is my sincere opinion, as well as consolation. They
are all so worthy their best source—M.d'A. sends you 100000
loves—we join in best Compts. to the Major,—& pray tell my
dear Fanny, Norbury, & Willy, This Letter is almost as much
their's as their Mamma's. I have had good accounts of our
dearest Father—& *not* bad of our Etty—nor of James—Charles

[2] Of the extant Nordianas occurring in SBP's Journals (see *Catalogue*) and of
the copies sometimes taken of them, this one cannot be found.

[3] That is, from SBP, who seems to have written more openly to EBB than to
FBA about her marital troubles. In a letter to FBA of 23 Nov. 1796 (*FB & the
Burneys*, p. 244), SBP gives the hint that Phillips did not read French.

[4] That is to say, no more hard service in times of war in the Marine Corps.

& Charlotte. But my poor Father is dreadfully disturbed by the political career which James now pursues so boldly.[5] I am truly concerned at it. adieu, my most dear Love—tell us always of your Health, & the Climate[6]—you Know my anxiety for both—July 23^d finished.

Heaven bless—bless you! F d A

[*By Mrs. Locke*]

July 24^h 1797 Norbury Park—

Our beloved Fanny has but just sent me her Alexandriana or our precious Sister would sooner have had my scrap of tenderest Thanks for *certain good* altho mixed with apprehensions of lengthened absence which are afflicting for *every* reason — — & yet every line made me love & admire and feel that it is not possible to live any longer separated from such a precious Friend—& I *must* HOPE.—let me say all the *essentials* for I have not space for anything else—I begin with Notre Ange who has had a little sneezing cold owing to the uncertain ungenial weather but who is well today & gone out,—he calls at Book-ham. Our poor Augusta has had many relapses from ye same cause but is quite well & walking out.—the *blight* is compleatly passed & you never saw that *favourite* Child of yours in higher health & spirits nor with a more flourishing appearance—she says she must write a few lines to her own Mrs Phillips—we have had for this week past all ye Boucherett & angerstein families[7]—the latter is gone this morn^g & the former leave us tomorrow & we are to have our Charles his Cecilia & Baby for a week in their way to Goodwood ye D. of Richmond's[8] where all ye family meet.—we shall go for a fortnight probably to Tunbridge.—We have heard of the safe arrival of la bonne Princesse[9]—Alphonse is gone to his Mother[10]—I have just rec^d a letter from my little adriennes mother[11] the most affectionate all their affairs are going on prosperously—she desires to be very affec^{ly} remembered to you.—I trust your sweet Boy is with you at this time—

---

[5] Cf. i, L. 17 n. 11.   [6] The 'Tems' (pseudonym for Phillips).
[7] See i, L. 16 n. 9; iii, L. 150 n. 14.
[8] Cecilia's uncle, Charles Lennox, 3rd Duke of Richmond (ii, L. 60 n. 6).
[9] La princesse d'Hénin.
[10] Alphonse de la Châtre, like so many *émigrés*, took advantage of the easing of strictures against *émigrés* to join his mother, now Mme de Jaucourt (see ii, Intro., p. xvi).
[11] Mme de Chavagnac. See Ll. 201 n. 5, 215 n. 12.

our Fred^c came home for his holidays last Saturday—he is most flourishing & good—God bless you—ever most dear & precious Friend—my Locke found our Fanny is *perfection*—her Dear Partner has a cold but as he had consented to take some St Jamess Powder it was going off rapidly—embrace your dear ones tenderly for me—kind remembrances to ye Major— I cannot bear that your sweet Mickleham dwelling should be prophaned by *such* vulgarity[12]—it looks lovely & is now covered with Honeysuckles—when when shall I once more fold to my heart my own dearest Friend!!

It is believed that peace is near at hand—God grant it! all is quiet now here & I trust it is becoming so with you—Heaven preserve you!

[By Amelia Locke]

I have long foreborne from a discretion I cannot any longer command, filling that paper which can be so much better filled with the assurances of my *unalterable* affection gratitude & *Veneration* for my own dearest Mrs Phillips, & it is her fault the fault of those partial & precious memorials of her goodness to me which every letter ⟨confirms⟩ that I can no longer command it or forbear repeating to her that those feelings of the very earliest & of the very latest with which I shall exist seem to require new force *each day*, for of my Mrs Phillips I never can cease thinking & to think of her must encrease every sentiment of respect & gratitude my heart is capable of. I have only soon to entreat you to tell my darling Husband that he is as much a married Man as ever[13]

ever y^r Am

[12] The Land Tax Assessments (Surrey County Record Office, Kingston upon Thames) show Molesworth Phillips the possessor of a house in Mickleham for the years 1787–1825 inclusive. In the years 1801–11 the house was leased to Thomas Dickins (*c.* 1768–1848) of Vale Lodge, Leatherhead, a wall of the parish church of which bears his monumental inscription and that of his wife. The 'Mrs Dickens', 'occupier' for the years 1796–1800, was probably his mother.

[13] A childish idea or fantasy, attributable to Norbury Phillips, not yet 12 years old.

242   Great Bookham, 27 July 1797

To Doctor Burney

A.L.S. (Diary MSS. vi. 4994–[7], Berg), 27 July 1797
Double sheet 4to   4 pp.   *pmks*   [LEATHER /]HEAD   28 JY 97
wafer
Addressed: Dʳ Burney, / Chelsea College, / Middlesex
Endorsed by CB: answered from / Crewe Hall—Augᵗ —97
Edited by FBA, p. 1 (4994), *annotated and the date retraced*: ⁕ ⁕ July 27—
97 (6)
Edited also by CFBt *and the* Press.

Bookham, July 27—97

My dearest Padre,

a Letter of so many dates is quite delicious to me[1]—it brings
me so close to you from Day to Day, that it seems nearest to
verbal intercourse. *How 'agreeable' I should be* to your keeping one
upon the stocks for me thus in your Journey![2] And how I should
like to receive a Letter from Shrewsbury. ⌐I shall not be *impatient*
enough to press this weekly, but if it should come to pass, what
a joy it will give me!¬—Nevertheless, I am sensible Shrewsbery
will be but a melancholy view now,—but interest does not dwell
alone with merriment, merry as we all like to be; ⌐& Dr.
Johnson once said to me 'No man passes through life without a
desire, in some part of it, to be thought 'a Wag.'¬[3]

⌐Mrs. Rishton's history constantly occupied me yesterday,[4]

242. [1] This was CB's letter (Berg) of successive dates [20], 22–24 July (printed in part
in *DL* v. 330–1; and *Memoirs*, iii. 239–42) telling of his attendance at Mr. Burke's
funeral at Beaconsfield.
   [2] CB had been invited to set out with Mrs. Crewe and Thomas-Louis-César,
marquis de Lambert de Frondeville (1757–1816), President of the Parliament of
Rouen, now an *émigré*, for a leisurely journey by way of Oxford, Blenheim,
Stratford upon Avon, and Birmingham to Shrewsbury, where he revisited the
scenes of his boyhood. Then on to Nantwich and Crewe Hall and from there,
shorter journeys to Liverpool and to Chester, where again he revisited the scenes
of his youth. From Crewe Hall on 2 Aug. CB wrote the travelogue that FBA had
coveted, which, though now missing, she printed in *Memoirs*, iii. 243–9, along with
his letter of 13 Sept. (Berg) describing his peregrinations of Lichfield *c.* 26 Aug.
It was to his exiled daughter Susan, however, that CB sent a long account of the
journey as a whole, one of the most delightful of his letters (composed 26 Oct. and
extant in Barrett, Eg. 3700A, ff. 13–14b).
   [3] FBA had so cited Dr. Johnson (i, L. 24, p. 182). See Johnson's *Life of Denham*.
   [4] In June 1797 Maria had returned to Thornham (L. 222 n.10; iv, L. 269) but
after five or six turbulent weeks of trial, Rishton had again failed to meet the
conditions of reconciliation, that is, to welcome Maria's niece Mary Susanna Allen

that to read, consider, & write, filled up all of my Day my little man allows me from himself.⁋ Your most kind solicitude for him makes me never like to take a Letter in hand to you when his health gives me inquietude—his health alone can do it, for his disposition opens into all our fondest hopes could form, either for our present gratification or future prospects. 'Tis the most enjoyable little Creature, Norbury Phillips excepted, I ever saw at so early an age. ⁋Nor does his health make a serious drawback to his happiness, he is free from complaint & unalterably gay, & active, & we flatter ourselves it is impossible anything can be essentially wrong, but he has entirely lost his appetite—& how he exists we often wonder & are not much comforted by his thirst, which is the opposite extreme. He has frightened us out of all strict regimen for this once, except in withholding from him Butter; but though he now partakes of whatever we can procure, he does not allow as much, in quantity as when he was but a month old. You will not, therefore, be surprised to hear he is thinner & thinner & every little rib, every little bone can be counted & seen, but covered with fine thin skin. His Cheeks, ׀ & his Cheeks alone, still keep their plumpness, & his Eyes—which you may remember were not very glassy, are unaltered. We have tried almost every thing, & tried which we hope is better, *nothing*—he goes out at ⟨least⟩ 2 or 3 miles every Day, sometimes 5 or 6, & walks & is carried by his own dictates of strength & pleasure. We are now to essay the Bark, by order of Mrs. Lock. James's powders succeeded once for his appetite—amazingly, but the attempt I made last night has answered no purpose.

You bid me be minute, my kindest Padre,—& I have not sparingly obeyed. And moreover—if you really would have another Babiana schtoff I (how is it?) Delville⁵ compose one for you to Construe. But then you know you must say yes first, so there I have you, my Lad! as poor Kitty says.

I will not begin upon poor Mrs. R[ishton].⁴ I have written so lately to herself, except to express my warmest wishes she may

(b. 1780) as an inmate of the house (' "*I dont intend she shoud come at all.*" I will not Submit to have that Family forced upon me they are quite disagreeable to me and nothing Shall Alter my determination . . .'). Resisting Rishton's agonized pleas and further promises of reform, Maria had set out for Chelsea College arriving on Tuesday 18 July. These events she had set forth in her letter to FBA of [24 July 1797] (Barrett, Eg. 3697, ff. 252–5b).
⁵ See L. 123 n. 4.

be allowed to repose in the ⟨situation⟩ she had so fervently covetted in right.[n]

I am excessively pleased you go to Mrs. Crewe's. I know no where out of the immediate family that you would be so tenderly watched. As to poor Dickey Coxe[6]—I hope his turn will yet come—for I am for disappointing Nobody—pray mark that!

I was surprised, & almost frightened, though at the same time gratified, to find you assisted in paying the last honours to Mr. Burke. How sincerely I sympathise in all you say of that truly great Man![7] That he was not *perfect* is nothing compared with his immense superiority over almost all those who are merely exempted from his peculiar defects. That he was upright in Heart, even where he acted wrong, I do truly believe: & it is a great pleasure to me that Mr. Locke believes it too, & that he asserted nothing he had not persuaded himself to be true, from Mr. Hastings being the most rapacious of villains, to the King's being incurably insane. He was as generous, as kind, & as liberal in his sentiments, as he was luminous in intellect, & extraordinary ǀ in abilities & eloquence, but though free from all little vanity, high above envy, & glowing with zeal to exalt talents & merit in others, he had, I believe, a consciousness of his own greatness that shut out those occasional & useful self-doubts which keep our judgement in order, by calling our motives & our passions to account. I entreat you to let me know how poor Mrs. Burke supports herself in this most desolate state, & who remains to console her, when Mrs. Crewe will be far off.

Our Cottage is now in the act of being rough cast. Its ever imprudent & *temeraire* Builder made himself very ill t'other Day, by going from the violent heat of extreme hard work in his Garden, to drink out of a fresh drawn pail of Well water, & dash the same over his face! A dreadful head ache ensued,—& two Days confinement, with James's powders, have but just re-instated him. In vain I represent he has no *right* now to make so free with himself—he has such a habit of disdaining all care & precaution, that though he gives me the fairest promises, I find them of no avail. Mr. Angerstein[8] went to see his Field,

---

[6] Richard Cox (i, L. 32 n. 1) of Quarley, Hants, a banker, whom CB visited in summer (Lonsdale, p. 418).

[7] CB's tribute is printed (*DL* v. 331; *Memoirs*, iii. 240).

[8] Probably John Angerstein (*c.* 1774–1858), in a year or two to marry Amelia Locke.

lately, & looked every where for him, having heard he was there—but he was not immediately to be known, while digging with all his might & main, without Coat or Waistcoat, & in his Green leather Cap.

⌐It is so little convenient to me at this time to quit our Hermitage, for the necessary superintendence that keeps M.d'A in his field, & his Son & mama upon the road to ⟨visit⟩ him that, not to make a hasty, & useless journey to Windsor, I wrote to beg an old friend would let me know my chances for the high honor I aspired at of paying my homage before I set out & my answer is the most gratifying imaginable!⁹ assuring me I shall hear *When* & where. Her Majesty will *prefer seeing me*! I have reason to believe it will take place after the Weymouth expedition¹⁰ & that will best suit us, first as ⟨answering⟩ Charlotte's visit—which done with, if possible Greenwich—*but not think of Chelsea* ⌐ because *we never don't.* I could mention that my Windsor answer was written *by order*, & is flattering & sweet in all its manner. My devoirs therefore, when they are paid, will be offered most comfortably.

M. d'Arblay says he has sometimes ⟨superficially⟩ met with M. le president Fronteville¹¹ at Mᵉ la comtesse de Tessé's,¹² & at Mᵉ la comtesse de Sᵗ Priest,¹³ he is a man of beaucoup de caractère & qui a montré beaucoup de fermeté in the assemblée in statements—& he is *fort instruit en tout*, he says. But he has only met him at 2ᵈ persons, without any separate or other acquaintance with him.—He thinks he will add much to the *agrémens* of

⁹ In spite of the permission the Queen had granted for an annual audience (L. 198, p. 184), over a year had now passed since FBA had presented *Camilla*. In consideration of the kindness she had experienced on that occasion (5–6 July 1796), the summons she had received on the death of Miss Schwellenberg (7 Mar. 1796), and apparently a second summons or 'command' (see L. 238), as far as is known still unobeyed, it must have seemed imperative now to make an appearance.
¹⁰ *The Times* (31 July) reported the Royal Family having left Windsor for Weymouth 'yesterday evening about 8 o'clock'. Their return was reported on 18 Sept.   ¹¹ See n. 2 above.
¹² An aunt of Madame de Lafayette, Adrienne-Catherine de Noailles (1741–1814), had married in 1755 René-Mans de Froulay, comte de Tessé (1736–1814). In pre-revolutionary days she had presided over a brilliantly intellectual salon, where apparently M. d'A had met M. le président (n. 2 above).
Early in the revolution Madame de Tessé emigrated to Switzerland but in August 1796 settled at Witmold on Lake Ploën in Holstein, where she was to offer shelter to the Lafayettes on their release from Olmütz on 19 Sept. 1797 (cf. iv, L. 252 n. 2). She was to prove a firm friend to the d'Arblays.
¹³ Constance Guillelmine (de Ludolph) (d. 12 Jan. 1807), who in Sept. 1775 had married at Constantinople the then French Ambassador François-Emmanuel Guignard, comte de Saint Priest (1735–1821).

the journey, as he is extremely literary. Indeed the whole prospect gives me pleasure. I am much touched by the *right* respect so speedily paid to the kind institution of Mr. Burke,[14] as the quick visit to the school of Worthies & commoners offered, & sorry my dearest Father could not be of the party, though perfectly convinced the abstaining was necessary.

I am glad L^y Duncan remembers me still, & has her courts, & does justice to Mr. Burney, & keeps the fancy so in order, with all her original spirit.[15] I am glad too, Fanny was gratified with a day at Chelsea,[16] & that *it was prudent*, & you *liked it*. What say you to the *Seceders?*[17] Mr. Sheridan, his lady and her papa in Law,[18] have all much scandalized our good & pious Mr. Cooke, for, they have never, he says, been at Church, yet, though they have all spent 3 Sundays at Polesdon, but a

[14] Austin Dobson explains (*DL* v. 331 n. 1) that the school at Penn, Bucks., was originally founded ' "for sixty French boys, principally the orphans of Quiberon, and the children of other emigrants who had suffered in the cause" ' and that Burke had taken a great interest in it.

In a codicil to his will, dated 22 Jan. 1797, and printed in *AR* xxxix (1797), 363–4, Burke had recommended the school 'to the kindness of my Lord Chancellor, Lord Loughborough, to his Grace the Duke of Portland, to the Most Honourable the Marquis of Buckingham, to the Right Honourable William Wyndham, and to Dr. Laurence, of the Commons'. He hoped that they would entreat 'the Right Honourable William Pitt to continue the necessary allowances' and that the 'unhappy children' of such 'meritorious parents' should be 'under the more immediate care and direction of Dr. King and Dr. Laurence'.

Accordingly on the day following Burke's funeral, 'the Chancellor, Speaker, Windham, and Mrs Crewe' made plans to visit the school, his Grace the Duke of Portland inviting CB to accompany them. See CB's letter of 20–4 July (Berg).

[15] In a letter of 20–24 July (op. cit.) CB reported having dined last week 'at Lady Polly's, who always inquires after you, and is as hospitable and friendly as ever—'.

[16] In the letter above CB also reported having a visit from his granddaughter 'the dear Fanny from Ld Beverley's . . . "be good I like it, That girl—it is prudent—" '. For her post as governess, see L. 142 n. 3.

[17] Those deserting their seats in the Houses of Parliament. Apparently attracting some attention at the time was an anonymous sixpenny pamphlet *A Letter to the Seceders* that inveighed against those Members of Parliament who 'in a time of imminent danger like the present' absented themselves from the House. The pamphlet, advertised as early as 21 July 1797 in *The Times* as 'this day published', was quoted at length in the 'Monthly Catalogue' of the *Monthly Review*, xxiii (Aug. 1797), 472–4. The chief 'seceder' at this time was Charles James Fox.

[18] In the years 1796–7 Richard Brinsley Sheridan (1751–1816) had acquired at a cost of £12,384 the manors of Polesden Lacey and West Humble and the mansion of Polesden and its lands and pleasure grounds (341 acres) as advertised for sale on 26 July 1796 (see Cecil Price's notes to Sheridan's *Letters*, ii. 44–5).

On 27 Apr. 1795 Sheridan had married as his second wife Hester Jane (1771–1817), a daughter of the Revd. Newton Ogle (L. 132 n. 4). The Dean, formerly described by FB as 'a man of drollery, good humour, and *sociality*' (*ED* ii. 94), and his daughters (living comically in print for their rendering of 'Drink to me only with thine eyes' [*ED* ii. 298]) were old friends of the Burneys, and this may in part account for the heavy obliterating marks to which FBA later subjected the passage.

mile off,—& their predecessors[19] have left them the best Pew in our Church ⟨until they⟩ sell it—he does not publicly admonish them, he is so much offended. Sir Francis Geary gave Mr. Cooke the living. However, the good Rector says often (entrenous) he is sure *nothing is paid*,[20] & he flatters himself the unholy tribe will be sent ere long a *goods off packing*.

May I beg on the next possible opportunity for the ⟨dear⟩ long promised James's & Miss Jardine's letters.⌐

Adieu most dear Sir—⌐*mio Alexander's* ⟨own hand⟩ to you,⌐ & My Love to Sally & Mrs. Rishton—ever most affect¹ʸ

your dutiful F. d'A.

243   Great Bookham, 1 August 1797

To M. d'Arblay

A.L. (Berg), 1 Aug. [17] 97
Double sheet 4to   4 pp.   *pmks*   LEATHER / HEAD   2 AU
2 AU 97   wafer
Addressed: Alexandre d'Arblay Esqr, / At Dr. Burney's, / Chelsea College, / Middlesex.
Edited by FBA, p. 1, *annotated*: (14)
written when our Alex was 3 years old—To his Father then in Town on business.

Bookham,
Augˢᵗ 1ˢᵗ—97

I find I can have no joy that is not yours—I hasten therefore to put aside a certain draw-back I experience to my own present gratification by making it mutual—our little Darling has given me this Morning the only proof I require of his Welldoing, the only one I have sighed for of his improvement, by a return of natural appetite. His Breakfast has had no temptation but for hunger, & yet he has eat of it with *almost* heartiness. Yesterday he would not taste any food till Dinner: & to Day every moment while his little Mouth was at work, I repeated to

---

[19] The former owner of Polesden Lacey, Sir Francis Geary (b. 1710?, see *DNB*) had died on 7 Feb. 1796.
[20] The purchase was effected as a part of the marriage settlement of Sheridan's second wife (above). See National Trust, *Polesden Lacey, Surrey* (1953).

myself—If his Fath[er] did but see it!—However, that Father
will [be] happy such a comfort should have been afforded me
in his absence, which I can't tell how to believe is still within 24
Hours.—The little soul just now calls out *'L'i want papa tome*
                                              give
home, dive Boy a Horse-back!' And now he adds *'L'i want tome
Mama's arms—'* So by, bye, papa.—

⌐──────⌐

So now I am *tome aden,* for I have given him his new Nine pins.
I have spent all the morning that he has not had to himself in
reading 3 News-papers. I think Pichegru[1] disposed to Head the
Moderates against Buonaparte & the Terrorists. My best hope
is that no actual I combat will take place, by seeing that their
forces seem equalising. Were there a great preponderance either
way, I should dread immediate Civil War.

┌I did not understand why you took the printed receipts of
the money in the study unless necessary to be shewn for declaring the dividends—*Athanase* you will say, can you doubt that?
Why no, but the answer only occurred as I had written the
query—

September, I will flatter myself, will be more favourable to
⟨walking⟩ out┐ I only dread your meeting with *Bargains* &
temptations in this season of our parsimony,—& I shudder but
to think of a *Boquinist*[2] till after Michaelmas!—Yet I know you
will keep ⟨helas!⟩ a guard over allurements that you can—&
that nothing will allure you that has not some at least imaginary
allusion to your Athanase or your little one:—so I have only to
pray you would keep in mind they want nothing but *You*—the
one for his *Horseback*, the other for every thing.

┌Give my kindest love to Mrs. Rishton & Sally & tell the
former I shall depend upon another pacquet by you, for which
I am very impatient. And I beg her to write first, if any thing
occurs that demands greater speed—though I shall terribly be

243. [1] Jean-Charles Pichegru (1761–1804), commandant en chef de l'armée du Nord
et des Ardennes (6 Jan. 1794), was the vanquisher of the Netherlands (1794–5).
Elected on 21 Apr. 1797 to the Council of the Five Hundred, he entered into
negotiations with the Royalists. Arrested on 4 Sept. and found guilty of conspiracy,
he was deported to French Guiana, from which he escaped, reaching England in
September 1798. Venturing to return to France in 1804, he was imprisoned and on
5 Apr. 1804 found strangled. See J. R. Hall, *Général Pichegru's Treason* (1915).
  [2] *Un bouquiniste* or second-hand bookseller.

disappointed if your return is delayed beyond Wednesday—⌐
A Letter is come for you from Me. de Monthron,[3] whom I now
trust ⌐ you will see: & pray express for me to her my concern &
mortification in not having the honour of paying my personal
respects to her in England: in France I still indulge my hopes I
shall one Day have the happiness of telling her myself how much
I have admired her constancy & courage of mind, & been
astonished by her noble exertions against calamity & penury,
& been touched by the generous & unrepining spirit with which
she has rejoiced in the felicity of others, even while as severely
as unmeritedly deprived of almost every blessing herself.—My
little play-fellow calls upon me every half line to recover his
Ball, which rolls under ⟨the sofa⟩ twice in a minute upon an
average. And he is now so considerate, that he brings me a stick
                                                      Get
with every request, to aid the extrication, saying '*Dit up*, *Mama*,
—*& help Boy a Ball.*'

I went on with The Italian of Mrs. Radcliffe[4] last night, & it
improved upon me very much. I believe her writings are all
best calculated for lonely hours & depressed spirits. I should
probably have done more justice to Udolpho if I had read it in
one of my solitary intervals. Don't run away again, however,
to give me the trial!—

⌐So now I must go to play at '*Alex Hat's box!*'⌐
How I was vexed for you when I saw the rain this Morning! ⌐

Four o'clock—I have given the little love Bark a 2^d time, & he
has called for some Bread voluntarily. His complexion, this
evening, is much clearer, & moves to its usual bright hue—

1/2 past 5—My little Companion has eat roast lamb with great
delight. Be quite relieved of present fear for him, for I now hope
the Bark can really reinstate him.⌐ Adieu—mon bien aimé!—
what a blank to Day with no post!—

---

[3] See L. 145 n. 3.
[4] *The Italian, or the Confessional of the Black Penitents* (3 vols., 1797), advertised
in the *London Chronicle* (7–10 June 1797) as 'published this day'.

244   Great Bookham, [*pre* 6] August [1797]

To Charles Burney

A.L.S. (McGill), Aug.
Single sheet 4to   2 pp.

Bookham Hermitage,
Augs^t

My dearest Carluci,

In the absence of my Lord & Master, having some *cute* notion I had seen before the hand with the Brighton mark, I ventured to open the same:—& in the same absence, I venture to say *WE* shall most cordially receive our dearest Charles & all whom He will undertake to prepare for our homely fare—trembling only for our Knives & Forks, which having never before been called into Battle by so capital a Regiment, may be foiled by finding their numbers unequal to their assailants. However, I shall leave to *You* all apologies, that being the only part of the adventure I should find disagreeable. I like to be generous mightily.

M. d'Arblay accompanied Mrs. Rishton & Sally, who spent last Sunday at our Hermitage, back to Chelsea, whence he is transacting business essential to our change of dwelling: but I am in daily hope of his return. His little Representative is half devoured by Gnats, but an *agreeable Companion in a lonely house for all that.*

I have this moment received a Letter from Gibraltar, desiring my advice to help forming a selection of Poetry, Novels, & Books of amusement for the Garrison Library there established![1]—It says the existing Catalogue of the present Collection is ordered I me, but not yet arrived. It is signed by the President, Librarian, & Secretary.

I think they had better have addressed a Letter from so military a post to The *Prem^r Adjutant General of the armée du Nord*,[2]

---

244. [1] In 1793 a Garrison Library had been established at Gibraltar by John Drinkwater *later* Bethune (1762–1844), a naval historian and author of *A History of the Siege of Gibraltar, 1779–1783* (1785), which by 1790 had run to four editions (see *DNB* and E. R. Kenyon, *Gibraltar under Moor, Spaniard, and Briton* (1938), p. 71). The reputation of *Evelina* and *Cecilia* as books of interest and entertainment would sufficiently account for this application to FBA, and Bethune may have heard more personally of her through Captain Alexander Jardine and his daughters (i, L. 7 n. 16).   [2] i.e. M. d'A.

than to that fair Dulcenea his sposa. I expect he will open his Eyes a little when I shew him the Date, *Gibraltar Garrison—29ᵗʰ June—97.* before he proceeds to the contents.

I am quite provoked by the continued misbehaviour of your ⟨s⟩kin, but edified by the characteristic severity with which you discipline it. Two blisters again!—which of your Boys can complain of a little wholesome flagelation, seeing this Your real personal taste & practice, even in the joy of retreat & vacation. 'Somebody's skin must be blistered!' I suppose they say to themselves, '& when never a one of Us is at hand, he had rather keep up the custom upon himself, than lack exercise!'—

Seriously, however, I am truly sorry at these repeated attacks, & must hope for a better account on Sunday.—Till when, & After when

My dearest Charles I am thoroughly yours—
F. d'A.

You will distribute for me Love & Compliments properly. I leave to you, You see, all the *proper proprieties.*

245   Great Bookham, 10 August 1797

To Doctor Burney

A.L.S. (Diary MSS. vi. 4998–[5003], Berg), 10 Aug. 1797
Double sheet (8·9 × 7·5″) and single sheet (9·7 × 7·9″) 4to 6 pp. black seal
Addressed: Dʳ Burney.
Endorsed by CB: Augᵗ 1797 Fanny / answered from Crewe / Hall—
Edited by FBA, p. 1 (4998), *annotated and date retraced*: ⁘ ⁘ Augˢᵗ —97 (7) Death of the youngest Brother, & only surviving one of M. d'Arblay. Joigny. Notre oncle Mrs. Crewe Shrewsbury.
Annotated, p. 5 (5002): ⁘ continuation 10 Augˢᵗ —97 (7)

Bookham,
Augst. 10—97

My dearest Father will, I know, be grieved at any grief of M. d'Arblay's,—though he will be glad his own truly interesting Letter should have arrived by the same post.[1] You know,

245. [1] In this letter, dated Crewe Hall, 2 Aug. and received at Great Bookham on 5 Aug. 1797, CB gave the account (requested by FBA) of his journey by way of

I believe, with what cruel impatience & uncertainty my dear Companion has waited for some news of his family, & how terribly his expectations were disappointed, upon a summons to Town some few months since, when the hope of intelligence carried him thither under all the torment of his recently wounded foot, which he could not then put to the Ground: no tydings, however, could he procure,[2] nor has he ever heard from any part of it till last Saturday morning, when two Letters arrived by the same post,[3] with information of the death of his only ⌜Surviving⌝ Brother.[4]

Impossible as it has long been to look back to France without fears amounting even to expectation of horrours, he had never ceased cherishing hopes some favourable term would, in the end, unite him with this last branch of his house: the shock, therefore, has been terribly severe, & has cast a gloom upon his mind & spirits which nothing but his kind anxiety to avoid involving mine in can at present suppress. He is now the last of a family of 17, & not one Relation of his own name now remains but his ǀ own little English son.[5] His Father was the only son of an only son,—which drives all affinity on the paternal side into 4th & 5th kinsmen.

On the Maternal side, however, he has the happiness to hear that an Uncle[6] who is inexpressibly dear to him, who was his Guardian, & best friend through life, still lives, & has been

Shrewsbury to Crewe Hall. Though now missing, the letter, printed in part in *Memoirs*, iii. 242–7, in many passages parallels his letter of 26 Oct. to SBP (op. cit.).

[2] See L. 231.

[3] Probably duplicates sent by Felix Ferdinand (*fl.* 1792–1802), Secretary to the comte de Narbonne, who on a journey by stagecoach to Switzerland made a brief stop at M. d'A's birthplace, Joigny, Auxerre.

[4] François Piochard d'Arblay, Sr de Blécy (L. 122 n. 11). In the Archives départementales d'Auxerre (Q 534) is an 'Inventaire des Effets Appartenant au citoyen d'Arblay capitaine du Second bataillon de la 40e ⟨Demi⟩ brigade, Mort a [Saint] Jean pied de port [Basse Pyrénées] Le 27 pluviose, 3e année républicaine'. Since the active campaign waged against Spain in the Pyrenees in the winter of 1794–5 ended with a treaty signed at Bâle on 12 July 1795, it would seem that the date of death above, that is, 15 Feb. 1795, is correct.

[5] The male line of the Piochard d'Arblay family has been traced from Jean Piochard d'Arblay (1678–1738), lieut. des Dragons, an only son, to his only son Pierre Piochard S^r d'Arblay (1702–61), lieut. col. de l'artillerie, and thus to Alexandre d'Arblay (1754–1818) and his two brothers, Jean-Pierre-Bazille Piochard d'Arblay (1750–78), capt. de l'artillerie, and François Sr de Blécy (1756–95), capt. de l'infantrie. A genealogical table, now being completed by Colonel P. Bertiaux of Joigny, will be shown in vol. vi.

[6] Jean-Baptiste-Gabriel Bazille (1731–1817), whose immediate family is shown in the genealogical table (v). M. d'A's mother Claudine *née* Bazille had died in 1771.

permitted to remain unmolested in his own House, at Joigny: where he is now in perfect health, save from rheumatic attacks, which though painful are not dangerous. A son, too, of this Gentleman, who was placed as a *Commissary de Guerre* by M. d'Arblay, during the period of his belonging to the War Committee, still holds the same situation, which is very lucrative, & which M. d'A. had concluded would have been withdrawn as soon as his own flight from France was known.

He hears, too, that M. de Narbonne is well & safe, & still in Swisserland,[7] where he lives, says the Letter 'très modestement, obscurement, & tranquillement,' with a chosen small society forced into similar retreat. This is consolatory, for the long & unaccountable silence of this his beloved Friend had frequently filled him with the utmost uneasiness.

The little property of which the late Chevalier d'Arblay died l possessed, this same Letter says has been *vendu pour la Nation*, because his next Heir was an *Emigré!*—Though there is a little Niece, M^{dle} Girardin,[8] son of an only Sister, who is in France, & upon whom the succession was settled, if her uncles died without immediate Heirs.

Some little matter, however,—*what* we know not—has been reserved by being *bought* in by this respectable uncle, who sends M. d'Arblay word he has saved him what he may yet live upon, if he can find means to return without personal risk, & who solicits to again see him with urgent fondness; in which he is joined by his Aunt, with as much warmth as if she, also, was his Relation by blood, not alliance. The Letter is written from Swisserland from a person who passed through Joigny, at the request of M. d'Arblay, to enquire the fate of his family, & to make known his own. the commission, though so lately executed, was given before the birth of our little Alec.[9] The Letter adds that no words can express the tender joy of this excellent Uncle & his wife in hearing M. d'Arblay was alive & well.

The late Chevalier, my M. d'A. says, was a Man of the softest manners, & most exalted honour; & he was so Tall & so thin,

7 See L. 184 n. 1 for the comfort of the comte's situation in Switzerland.

8 Apparently Marie-Anne (1785–*pre* 7 Jan. 1794), *daughter* of Jeanne-Emerentienne Piochard d'Arblay (1757–*c*. 1792–3), who had married in 1780 Jean-Nicholas Girardin de Colan [or Colard] (d. *pre* 1794), captain in the *Régiment royal-infanterie*.   9 That is, before December 1794.

he was often nick-named Don Quixote: but he was so completely aristocratic ǀ with regard to the Revolution, at its very commencement, that M. d'A. has heard nothing yet with such unspeakable astonishment as the news that he *'died near Spain* of his wounds from a Battle in which he had fought for the Republic! —— How strange, says M. d'A. is our destiny! that that Republic which *I* quitted, determined to be rather an Hewer of Wood, & Drawer of Water all my life than serve, *he* should die for! —— ' The secret history of this may some day come out, but it is now inexplicable, for the mere fact, without the smallest comment, is all that has reached us. In the period, indeed, in which M. d'A. left France, there were but three steps possible for those who had been bred to arms: Flight, the Guiliotine, or fighting for the Republic. The former this Brother, M. d'A. says, had not energy of character to undertake in the desperate manner in which he risked it himself, friendless & fortuneless, to live in exile as he could: The Guilliotine no one could elect,—& the continuing in the service, though in a cause he detested, was, probably, his hard compulsion. No one was allowed to lay down his arms & retire.

A Gentleman[10] born in the same Town as M. d'A., Joigny, has this Morning found a conductor to bring him to our Hermitage. He confirms the account that all in that little Town has been suffered to remain quiet, his own Relations there still existing undisturbed. M. d'Arblay is gone to accompany him back as far as Ewell. He has been evidently ǀ much relieved by the visit, & the power of talking over, with an old Townsman as well as Countryman, early scenes & connexions. It is a fortunately timed rencounter, & I doubt not but he will return less sad.

This brings me again to my dearest Father's interesting though concise Journal: how I regret *no Townsman* at Shrewsbury could enjoy your patriotic return,[11] & energy of pleasure & pride in displaying its beauties & particularities! How I should have delighted to have seen them with you! Had I not filled my Letter with this prevailing subject, it would have had no other Names than Shrewsbury & Mrs. Crewe; for her kind-

---

[10] Antoine Bourdois (*c.* 1761–1806), son of Edme-Joachim Bourdois, a medical doctor in Joigny. He will appear in iv, Ll. 258, 292, 379, etc.

[11] 'Alas!' wrote CB (*Memoirs*, iii. 243–7), 'not one creature is now alive whom I remember, or who can remember me!' And from 'dearer old Condover . . . all gone for whom I had cared,—or who had cared for me!'

ness in going 40 Miles about to soothe you with this revival of early ideas comes close to my heart. She is, indeed, a friend of ten thousand. How I should like to see your beautiful Quarry[12] —I think your monumental diminuendoing very exactly exemplary, as you say, Swift's Martin Luther, & Jack Calvin.[13] I am glad Crewe Hall is kept up in its original style. I have seen no modern repairs to antique buildings that have not looked like one part of a building picking a quarrel with another. See! says one, my solemn grandeur! see! says the other, my airy elegance!

The Bark, I think, does good to our little Treasure—though his appetite & looks are still fluctuating. Our Cottage, just now, has lost its interest, but I hope we shall re-visit it to-morrow— My companion is not of a nature ¦ to indulge, after the first shock, in a sorrow he cannot have to himself.

Charles & his wife & very good Boy visited us on Sunday, in their way Home from Brighthelmstone, & stayed till past 10 o'clock at Night. He looks well notwithstanding he has a cruel return of his tormenting complaint in the Jaw.

All we can gather of French News is terrific[14]—& M. d'A. who more than ever sighs for peace, that he may yet once more embrace his excellent uncle, is much agitated by the general appearance of menace throughout that devoted nation. I have had no Letter since what I last mentioned from Ireland, & begin, again, to long for news. What a History is poor Mrs. R[ishton]'s![15]—adieu, ever most dear Sir! try to bring me to

[12] At Shrewsbury CB had 'walked in that most beautiful of all public walks, as I still believe, in the world, called the Quarry; formed in verdant and flower-enamelled fields, by the Severn side, with the boldest and most lovely opposite shore imaginable' (*Memoirs*, iii. 243–7).

[13] This allusion is lost with the unprinted part of CB's letter (op. cit.) but may be supplied, conjecturally at least, from parallel passages in his letter of 26 Oct. to SBP. Here he describes 'a little ornamental chapel' which Mrs. Crewe had filled with 'dressed figures of every order of Romish Clergy & religious orders male & female'. The figures, so dressed, may have suggested to CB *A Tale of a Tub*.

[14] With Bonaparte's conquest of Italy, Hoche's victories on the Rhine, coffers filled, and treaties concluded with Prussia and Spain, the Directory had reached a zenith of military power, which, stretching (with previous conquests of Belgium and Holland) from the Channel to the Adriatic, bid fair to subdue England also, if not by invasion, by a blockade of commerce.

Always hopeful of moves to restore the old regime, the d'Arblays were doubtless watching as well the violent internal strife within the Councils culminating in the *coup d'état* of 18 Fructidor ('*The sword is the law*'). Cf. CB to SBP (op. cit.): 'What dreadful tyranny & oppression of all the best inhabitants of Italy!—Of the Cidevant Electorate on the banks of the Rhine!—& what a total bouleversement of Principle all over the Globe, has this infernal Revolution occasioned!'

[15] See L. 222 n. 10; iv, L. 269.

the remembrance of Mrs. Crewe—& indulge me with a *How do*, if possible, dearest Padre, for I shall soon become very impatient to hear how you go on. I beg, also, my best Comp^{ts} to Miss Crewe. Is she as amiable, & as promising to resemble mentally her charming Mother as when I saw her? Adieu, dearest Sir, ever

> most dutifully
> your affect^e F. d'A

A Letter to Day from Charlotte says all are well at Richmond.

246   Great Bookham, 20 August 1797

To Mrs. Phillips

A.L. (Barrett, Eg. 3690, ff. 179–80b), 20 Aug. [17]97
Double sheet 4to   4 pp.   wafer
Addressed: *Ireland* / Mrs. Phillips, / Belcotton, / Drogheda
Edited by FBA *and* CFBt.

> Bookham,
> Augst 20. 97

Our best loved & most precious Friend has now, my ever dearest Susan, brought about a facility for our intercourse that gives me power to write again, contrary to the plan I had adopted, without a new Letter to answer: though it will be almost wholly to say how I long again to hear—again to see the hand that brings me nearest to my beloved—*October* is fast approaching—will it become as kind as it has been afflicting?[1] It is impossible to me to give up hope till the last, yet—how little have I to feed it upon!—

I have much to talk to you about, though I meant but an exhortation for hearing from you:—but now I have pen in hand, I will not be so covetous of ink. I am kept, this time, from uneasiness at your silence by the remembrance you were to have Norbury in July,—& I hope his stay has been prolonged, & I yield unmurmuring to the dear little Boy's possessing all you can spare of you wholly.

246.[1] SBP had set out for Ireland on 17 Oct. 1796.

I know I shall give you—but I cannot help it—sincere concern to hear that my dearest Hermit has suffered the severe blow of losing his only Brother. After a total ignorance of the state, life, or death, of any of his remaining family for nearly 5 years, a Letter is at last arrived.[2] It brings him at once an account of his uncle, his Brother, & M. de Narbonne. It is from Ferdinand. M. d'A. had written to him, by confidential means, to entreat he would endeavour to visit Joigny, & procure information for which he was ardently longing. Ferdinand c^d not comply, nor even write any answer, till some circumstances took him out of France. He then went out of his road, to pass by Joigny; but as he was in a stage Coach, he could procure only a few minutes delay for his good-natured purpose. |

Here he learnt, that M. d'A.'s Brother had been dead these 18 Months! He died of an illness, the consequence of wounds, in the army near Spain. We know nothing else of this melancholy event; but conclude the wounds to have been received in Battle; & the surprise of M. d'A that his Brother the Chev^r should have died *fighting for the Republic* is as great as his grief that he should have died, so soon, at all. He was completely, by education & principle, an aristocrate, as to Government, though in heart & in manners he was gentleness itself. M. d'A. did not think him a character of sufficient energy to brave the difficulties & sufferings of such an exile as he conceived he was banishing himself to; he therefore concealed from him his determination, certain that else his tender affection would have compelled him to run the same risk, though without any of the same resources, mental or corporal, for enduring its consequences. To this it was owing that *my* M. d'A. was not accompanied by him: & now he continually regrets he had not rather induced him to have come. But who must judge by events what decision would have been previously right with any asperity?

Hear, however, the gratitude & justice of these Republicans! —What little was left, still belonging to the late Chev^r d'A. they sold *pour la nation*! says Ferdinand. though he left a niece, his rightful Heir, Mlle Girardin, with numerous Cousins. But they seized | the little property, because his immediate Heir was an *Emigré*. M. d'A. concludes his poor Brother was forced into the service, as the cruel wretches who had the command permitted

---

[2] See L. 245 nn. 3, 4, 5, 6, 7, and the genealogical table vol. v.

no one already in the army to retire. Indeed, at the period which brought me over my Companion for life ⟨service⟩ in France, for officers, had but three points—Flight, serving the Republic, or the Guilliotine.

This fatal intelligence has affected my poor Hermit much more deeply than I had expected. His excessive preference of his elder Brother[3] had deceived me into an opinion his affection for this he has lost was very moderate. However, one delicious consolation reaches him at the same time; his uncle, who is dear to him beyond all words, still lives, & lives unmolested, with his very amiable wife, in his own House at Joigny, & they both heard of the existence of their nephew with a joy that, Ferdinand says, exceeds all description. How readily can I conceive it! They have also, most generously, bought in themselves some little matter—we know not what—belonging to the late Chevalier, which they purchased in the hope they yet might see him, & which, in the *8 Minutes* Ferdinand could spare them, they found time to mention, with an earnest entreaty to see him the instant he could enter France with personal safety. This has infinitely delighted my dear Mate, & is a lasting subject of comfort.

To this is added that M. de N[arbonne] is also safe & well,[4]— & his unbroken silence had created an anxiety the most un- pleasant. To our utter surprise, he is still in Swisserland, & the circumstance which carried Ferd[inand] to France was busi- ness relative to his ⏐ re-entrance, for which his friends are now working. He says *he has written repeatedly to M. d'A.!*—How astonishing!—& Ferdinand adds he *can vouch for his unceasing tender recollections of Northbury Mickleham—& Bookham.* Poor Ferd[inand] desires again & again to be most warmly remem- bered to *you*, & to the Major.—M. de N[arbonne] is still with Me de Laval, he says, mere de M. de Montm[orency]—but has the happiness of the Abbè de Lille[5] added to his society, as well as of M. *Le Breton*,[6] now ⟨commenced⟩ *Garçon Horloger* for subsistence!—These interesting particulars will, I am sure, not seem long to my beloved Susan. Our little love— sole *Heritier du*

---

[3] Jean-Pierre Bazille Piochard d'Arblay (1750–78), see genealogical table v, vol. vi.
[4] See ii, Intro., p. xiv–xv; also L. 184 n. 1.
[5] Jacques Delille (1738–1813), poet and translator of *Paradise Lost* (*Paradise perdu*, 3 vols., 1805).
[6] Referred to by Madame de Staël (23 Jan. 1794) as 'aide-de-camp' to the comte de Narbonne (Solovieff, p. 360 and n. 3).

nom, as he is now called by all M. d'A.'s french friends, begins to revive in appetite. He takes the Bark twice a day, & eats much more equally. our dear Father is in Cheshire, with Mrs. Crewe. Etty & her family at Richmond, where Charlotte & her's are well. Charles gave us a visit, in his way from Brighton, a fortnight ago. He suffers again with his Jaw cruelly. James was here yesterday, to our infinite concern & regret, while we were at Norbury Park, & could not stay. Sally is come till my dear Father's return. M. d'A. is at his field, or would send 20 Loves—Give mine to the Major—& to my dear Fanny & Norbury & Willy—adieu my ever dearest love—write I beg as soon as possibly you can however briefly—*soon* is the first article   God bless.

247   Great Bookham, 17, 29 August 1797

Conjointly with M. d'Arblay
To Mrs. Phillips

A.L.S. (Barrett, Eg. 3690, ff. 175–6b, 177, 178; and Diary MSS. vi. 4952–[5], Berg), 17, 29 Aug. [17]97

Two double sheets 4to   (9·7?×8″), interleaved   8 pp.   From the centre double sheet two cuttings were taken as paste-ons for A.L.S. (Berg, as above), FBA & Frederica Augusta (Schaub) Locke to SBP, 25–27 Nov. 1796

Franked: M Lewis[1] / London Second Sept. 97   *pmk*   FREE 2 SE 97 seal

Addressed: Mrs Phillips / Belcotton / Drogheda / Ireland
Edited by CFBt *and the* Press.

Bookham, Augst 17th
—97

I must not—dare not tell my own beloved Susan the sighs with which I finished her last Letter[2]—& all of its reference which has reached me—If even the printems might be depended upon — — mais—je n'ai q'un Anchor—c'est la paix[3]—et pour mille raisons et mille 'tis my first wish—& all the mille put together would scarcely weigh a grain in the scale that should be put

247. [1] Presumably, Matthew Gregory Lewis (L. 221 n. 9), M.P. (1796–1802).
   [2] This letter is missing.

opposite to the ONE SINGLE expectation which I attach to that epoch.—O what an epoch should it answer my hopes!—I have told you of our Etty's Friend,[3] I think, who writes to her with extreme unreserve upon her affairs—well, this lady has interested us all so much, by Etty's accounts, that she is perpetually in our minds—'tis impossible to conceive any thing more affecting than her situation, or, indeed, more perfect than her conduct in it—I often wish I could let her know what I feel for her, in full extent,—but she has an uncle so odious, & so arbitrary, that I always fear lest any thing I should write should fall into his hands. It gives a cruel constraint—yet, were we without it, what but aggravating her sufferings would be her reading our sentiments of them, & of their inflicter?—alas—Tis a subject upon which, with *every* licence, I could never express what passes within — — —

You speak of our silence, my most dear,—I always fear being unconscionable in writing, knowing how many Letters you must be receiving, all from such distance, & all more expensive than plays[4] or pamphlets—but now, that there is opened a channel which removes this tremendous obstacle, you shall see with what alacrity I shall seize every means of making use of it. I cannot undertake ǀ that my Letters will be all as long as my post folios, but they shall be as frequent as possible, & never short.—I *cannot*, indeed, make them short, but by compulsion, for to write to my dearest Susan gains upon me in every line, & I always feel reluctant to conclude.

I hope it is *now* that dear little Norbury is with you.[5] He is now present to me every Day, in some fancied resemblance of character, & flattering view of future approximation. He is the *model of my wishes* for my little one,—& if I knew, or had ever seen, a little Creature that, *upon the whole*, I thought sweeter, I

---

[3] One thing to tie to. Phillips would return, FBA thought, when the Royal Marines were no longer required for hard service on the seas. For the use of French and the use of the third for the second person with various substitutions for Phillips, and for Susan herself, cf. Ll. 222 and 241 and n. 3.

[4] The postage marked on letters between Belcotton and Bookham totalled 11*d*. A sixpenny pamphlet cost less than a letter travelling that distance.

[5] In December 1796 Norbury had been allowed to spend three weeks at Belcotton (*FB & the Burneys*, pp. 252–8) and was apparently expected for the midsummer holidays.

should not chuse him. It is among my most favourite *Chateaus* that my Alec may make him, by & by, his confidential young Counsellor. The difference of their ages is just of a sort to make such an intercourse desirable, if both are what both have hitherto promised.

I have not *now* time, before this must depart, to go on with the records that you so kindly receive;[6] I can write for the moment much quicker than I can Copy, or recollect what is past.

our dearest Father will probably have written to you from Crewe Hall. I am delighted at his visit there, which seems to have enlivened & done him good.

Aug^{st} 29th I wrote thus much as soon as I had once read, & sent off to the sweetest of Friends, my last dear—but alas sad Letter—Let me however take from it the *great good* of what relates to the excellent Mr. Matu[rin][7] whom I love & respect, & unspeakably should I be grieved if my dear Norbury were to change him, till his arrival in England—an epoch for which the first & dearest prayers of my Heart are daily offered up — — I know how my Susan will submit to all she considers to be right,—but *submit*!—alas—what does not that imply? what of regret & sadness for our disappointments! — — yet we *must*,— & *do* rely upon the Major, if no rational necessity compels an alteration of his intention. Tell him, when you can, we will not be unreasonable, yet cannot give up our Anchor.[8] — —

I have much to tell you now of deep interest from abroad.— Another Letter is received ǀ from the good faithful Ferdinand,[9] who still talks of Mickleham as if such happiness for Bookham & Norbury still existed!—our so long lost, loved & admired & regretted M. de N[arbonne] *still* is in Swiss.—He was preparing to set out, but the new threat of commotion abroad has stopt him. The violent struggle now existing, & contest impending between the moderates & the Jacobins is terrific on one side— & full of the fairest prospects on the other.[10] Taly[rand]—now

---

[6] Alexandrianas, like those included in Ll. 222 and 241.

[7] See Ll. 215 n. 7, 222 n. 13.

[8] In this context perhaps the promise to the Lockes that SBP should return in a year.

[9] This letter is unknown.

[10] Elections in March 1797 had given the moderates (of Royalist sympathies) in France a majority in both Councils, and as a result the strictures against *émigrés* and their relatives were eased or repealed. Fearful of losing control, however, the Jacobin majority of the Directory joined with the Constitutionalists in a struggle with the moderates culminating in the *coup d'état* of 18 Fructidor (4 Sept.).

Minister, is doubtless the Agent & Director of his movements,[11] though his name is never mentioned, nor himself hinted at. Indeed the least suspicion of his interference would risk his place & life. Ferdinand says the return is now postponed for a *month*; his date is Augs[st] 24. & if all continues tranquil till then, the attempt is to be made. God prosper it! I know how you will partake in the anxiety that period will give birth to, & that its *fair* event will be a serious consolation to you. If the attainder is not first taken of,[12] the risk is still frightful, safely as thousand emigrés are now lodged in France.

But now—I call for your congratulations—& how gladly will my generous Susan give them!—for my dearest Partner—he has a Letter, inclosed in the one I mention, from his uncle[13]—that uncle whom he has so sighed to hear of, & whom he loves & venerates with a fondness that has caused his infinitely greatest regret from his exile. This most excellent man writes with a tenderness of joy that his darling nephew is yet in existance that drew from that nephew nearly as many Tears as the fatal tydings of the first intelligence received from his family, though with feelings precisely reversed. He has heard of his Marriage, but not of his Son. *Tu restes seul*, he says, of a family that has made *les delices de ma vie*!—he shews a deep regret for the late Chev. d'A.—but exhorts the survivor to resignation with the most affectionate kindness. He durst not, he says, flatter himself *de nous voir reuni*—though such a day would be the happiest he

---

[11] Talleyrand (ii, Intro., p. xviii), having returned to France in the summer of 1796, became, with the help and machinations of Madame de Staël, Minister of War (July 1797–July 1799). See Herold, pp. 177–80; and *Memoirs of Barras . . .* ed. George Duruy, trans. C. E. Roche (4 vols., 1896), iii. 146–7.

[12] On 28 Aug. 1792 the National Assembly had begun proceedings leading to an '*Acte d'accusation contre Louis de Narbonne, ex-ministre de la Guerre*'. '*De Narbonne a tiré la somme de vingt-huit mille livres de la caisse de la liquidation des anciennes dettes des troupes, et dispose de cette somme, sur le prétexte de différens frais de courses et de dépenses extraordinaires relatives au rassemblement des armées*' (Solovieff, pp. 497–8).

[13] Extant in the Berg Collection, the NYPL, are two more or less identical letters (2 ss. 4tos) written to M. d'A by Jean-Baptiste-Gabriel Bazille (L. 231 n. 3) and dated 8 *juillet*, altered to / *aout* /. The first, Felix Ferdinand had managed on 24 *aout* to send to England, and the second, he sent, as he says, about a week later, i.e. on 1 7bre. On the *verso* of each he wrote a note to M. d'A informing him that with the aid of a banker or businessman, one of the messengers of the ambassadors, or 'quelqu'un d'obligeant à Douvres', it was possible to send letters to Paris. In both notes he gives his own address as 1205, rue de Miroménil, Faubourg St Honoré; and optimistically, with the softening of the sanctions against *émigrés*, he imagined that both the comte de Narbonne and M. d'A could return for the vintage at Joigny.

The loving but almost illegible letter from M. Bazille, both FBA and M. d'A paraphrase in the pages following.

could know,—but his infirmities, & the bad state of things, deprive him of the hope that any change will take place while he yet lives to allow him, with safety, such a *transport of joy*.— Nothing can be more affecting than his expressions, nor more concise, manly, & satisfactory than his relations of the chief circumstances that have passed since their absence, & the present state of all still living of their connexions. And in the end, he says— JE NE CROIS PAS *avoir passé un seul jour sans songer à toi*.—

[*By M. d'Arblay*]

je vous prie de remarquer ce *je ne crois pas* qui vient à la suite du tableau le plus rapide de son bonheur apparent troublé par ses souvenirs et sa façon de penser etc—

[*By Madame d'Arblay*]

How generous, how unlike the Father of M. de Jauc[ourt][14] to forbear thus wholly pressing his return, though so ardently desiring to embrace him! He has lost his youngest son,[15] | whom he says he shall mourn all his remnant Days, in the army. He is evidently profoundly wounded by the Revolution, though he can only speak of it mysteriously & slightly. 3 of the 4 Children which yet live have been married since M. d'A.'s departure, & two of them, with 2 little ones a piece, live under his hospitable roof. He speaks with great depression of his altered habits of life—his relinquishing Paris, Company, & public mixtures, & wrapping himself up in his own family.

My Monima has just said he will write himself—I therefore cut foreign details short.

Have I told you I had a visit from Carlos, with his Sposa & Carlino? He is in remarkably good looks, with regard to a healthy complexion, & clear Eyes, but terribly tormented with the complaint in his jaw. His Son is a most even tempered, well behaved, obliging & excellent Boy, & seems to have as clear & good an understanding as he has an equal & pleasing disposition. Sposa was very gentle, & *well*. They had spent a Month at Brighthelmstone.

[14] How unlike Louis Pierre de Jaucourt, baron d'Huban (1726–1813), who, oblivious to the dangers, had in 1792 pressed his *émigré* son Arnail-François (1757– 1852) to return to France. The hazards and difficulties are reviewed by SBP in a Journal for Nov. 1792 (Berg), wherein she reports a conversation heard at Juniper Hall on the matter.

[15] Pierre Jean Baptiste Edme *dit* de la Mare (1775–Mar. 1796).

Sarah came to us 10 Days ago, & spent a week here. She is become very pleasingly formed in manners, where ever she wishes to oblige, & all her roughnesses & ruggednesses are worn off. I believe the mischief done by her education, & its wants, not *cured*, if *curable*, au fond; but much amended to *all*, & *apparently* done away completely to many. What really rests, is an habit of exclusively consulting *just what she likes best*,—not what would be or prove best for others. She thinks, indeed, but little of any thing except with reference to herself, & that gives her an air, & will give her a character for inconstancy, that is in fact the mere result of seeking her own gratification, alike in meeting or avoiding her connexions. If she *saw* this, she has understanding sufficient to work it out of her: but she weighs nothing sufficiently to dive into her own self. She knows she is a very clever Girl, & she is neither well contented with others, nor happy in herself, but where this is evidently acknowledged. We spen[t] an Evening at Norbury park—she was shown all Mr. William's Pictures & Drawings. I knew her expectations of an attention she had no chance of exciting, & therefore devoted myself to looking them over with her: yet, though Mr. Locke himself led the way to see them, & explained several, & though Amelia addressed [|] her with the utmost sweetness, & Mrs. Locke with perfect good breeding—I could not draw from her *one word* relative to the Evening, or the family, except that *she did not think she had heard Mr. William's voice ONCE.*—she confessed, previously, that she had passed such very disagreeable & dull time[s] at that house, formerly,[16] that she had no desire to repeat the visits. A person so *young*, & with such good parts, that can take no pleasure but in personal distinction—which is all her visits can have wanted, will soon cut all real improvement short, by confining herself to such society alone as elevates *herself*. *There*, she will always make a capital figure, for her conversation is sprightly, & entertaining, & her heart & principles are both good; she has many excellent qualities, & various resources in herself: but she is good enough to make me lament that she is not modest enough to be yet better. —Imagine how we were provoked that our dear James accompanied her, & we

[16] When for instance in the evenings of July–Aug. 1788, SHB, accompanying her mother and CB on a long visit to Mickleham, had accompanied them as well on visits to Norbury Park (SBP's Journals for that summer, Berg).

were at Norbury, where we Breakfasted! & he could not stay Dinner. He was here 3 Hours—yet we missed him entirely. — — I am sure you will be grieved, as I am, to hear what followed his visit—he went hence to Ditton, on a summons to our good Kitty Cooke—it was a second—the first he had obeyed, & seen her, in great danger from a Bowel complaint—the second, he arrived too late.[17] I was quite sad at Heart at this news—as you, I am sure, will be,—& touched most sensibly by her very kind, sweetly kind remembrance, in leaving me the portrait of my ever revered Mr. Crisp, & leaving mine to my Susan. These two donations are equally grateful to me. She has also left you & me 5 G^s each, for mourning,—& the same to James's wife. This is very unexpected indeed—but I am truly glad she felt the conviction of our sincere regard which this mark of her's demonstrates.

I hear good news in general of our Etty, & of her's; & Charlotte & her trio go on well & happily. You will felicitate us de bien bon coeur that our little darling is recovery strength & appetite daily, & that under the direction of our angel Mrs. Locke, who prescribed the Bark, which has had wonderful success. She is herself in perfect health, & looks most beautifully. Augusta is mending, Amelia is well & sweetly amiable & lovely. Adieu, my ever dearest, dearest Susan—God bless & preserve—& restore you to those who sigh for you—Scarce sighing for aught else—

F d'A. |

I am frightened to find I have run on into another sheet, without consciousness. I hope it will not be an indiscretion to occasion any hints [o]f more prudence![18]—Let me now mention that your good Susan's sister is quite well at Swansea, where Betty's sister still resides with her:[19] & let me beg you to

---

[17] Surviving her aunt (L. 224 n. 7) by about seven months, Papilian Catherine Cooke (b. *c.* 1731) had died at Thames-Ditton on 17 Aug. 1797 and was buried on 28 Aug. at Chessington, a wall of the parish church of which bears a tablet commemorating her steadfast qualities.

By the terms of her will (P.C.C. Exeter, 546), she had bequeathed to FBA, SBP, and JB's wife 'the sum of five pounds and five shillings . . . as a small Token of my Affectionate regard for them severally . . . also I give to the said Frances D'Arblay the small painting of my much valued Friend Samuel Crisp Esquire deceased'. There is no mention in the will of a portrait of FB.

[18] Presumably objections usually made by the Major to paying postage.

[19] See L. 222 n. 27.

remember me very kindly to that excellent good Soul. It is an never-ceasing satisfaction to me to think of her at your side, in the many cruel chances run by *every body* of illness. I wish to know if the sprain of her arm is entirely cured. Poor Braissant[20] will, I fear, feel his accident for life; not only from pain, but from some impediment to walking at his ease. How cruel! — — Kitty Cooke, I find, died with *unshaken fortitude,*—James terms it. Indeed if ever any mortal had to look back upon an entirely *guiltless* existence for herself, & *useful* & benevolent one for others, I should think her that mortal. How short has been her term when her long nursing duties were fulfilled!—I know not where she was buried, nor have heard any particulars of her Will but what I have mentioned. Those were written me by our good James, who, I fancy, was present at its opening. The last time I saw the good soul was at Leatherhead Fair, in October— just after I had lost my Susan—I have written to her since, upon her aunt's death, & received from her a most affectionate & characteristic answer. I cannot forget while I live the innumerable kind offices I owed to her upon every visit to once so dear— now so utterly desolate Chesington. — — The whole House, I understand, is now taken by Col. Dalrymple for a Farm.[21]

Kiss my three dears for me, as I trust all 3 are now with you— & give my love to the Major. I shall hope for a whole fol. of traits of my dear Norbury. The *old Bachelor death* diverts us all to this moment.[22] Have you heard Lady Burrel is married to her Son's Tutor, Mr. Clay?[23] I reserve my Windsor excursion annal to the return from Weymouth. It is *comfortably* settled to then take place, as I think I have told you. Otherwise I will next time. adieu, again, most dear—dear Susey!—what a blessing you keep well! & then the Climate is not very ungenial. |

[M. d'Arblay concluded the letter]

Je suis bien sur que ma soeur partage l'extrême bonheur que me fait aprouver une lettre que ma femme lui a transcrite

---

20 Mr. Locke's personal servant (ii, L. 68 n. 50).

21 William Tombes Dalrymple (1736–1832), Lt.-Col. of the Second Regiment of Foot (1778–91), Groom of the Bedchamber to the Duke of Clarence (1792–1814).

22 A lost 'Nordiana'.

23 Sophia Raymond (1750–1802) had married in 1773 William Burrell (1732–96), LL.D. (1760), 2nd Baronet (1788), of Deepdene, Holmwood, and secondly on 23 May 1797 the Revd. William Clay (c. 1766–1836), B.A. 12th Wrangler (1788), M.A. (1791), and tutor presumably to the youngest of Sir William's four sons namely, Percy (1779–1807).

presqu'entiere. Cependant La vérité me force à dire que malgré les talens bien reconnus de la *traductrice*, l'original aurait encore quelqu'interest pour vous si j'avais le tems de vous le copier. Ce n'est pas que cette lettre charmante et extremement courte me demandât beaucoup de tems p^r vous la transcrire, mais c'est que vous en avez dejà la substance—Bien surement aussi vous avez pris part à la pacte que j'ai faite. Elle a rouvert toutes mes playes, et je puis bien dire avec verité que par les malheurs que j'ai eprouvés, j'ai, s'il etait possible, acheté en quelque sorte le sort heureuz dont je jouîs dans mon interieur—Je quitte ce sujet p^r parler encore un instant de mon Oncle que j'espère que vous connaîtrez un jour. Qui sait même si ce n'est pas chez lui que se passera notre prochaine entrevue. Le Major a toujours en l'idée d'aller en France à la Paix. Tres certainement, à moins d'une impossibilité absolue j'y emmene tout mon petit menage passer au moins 6 semaines—Vous voyez donc que le rendez vous que je vous donne pourra fort bien avoir lieu. Ma femme vous mande que cette Lettre de mon Oncle m'a fait verser presqu' autant de larmes, que celle qui annonçait la mort de mon pauvre frère. Qu'allez vous penser de moi, vous Mad^e l'Anglaise, vous l'amie de nos amies de Norbury les quelles ne peuvent s'empêcher de rire de pitié quand elles trouvent dans un livre français quelque heros en larmes—Le fait est pourtant que j'ai lu cette lettre plus de 20 fois (je n'exagère point) sans avoir pu prendre encore assez par moi pour en prononcer d'un ton libre deuz ou trois passages. J'ai donc tout à fait renoncé à les lire à Norbury comme j'en avais d'abord eu l'intention—Je ne vous parle pas aujourd'hui de la maison qui ne faut point, ce qui me donne beaucoup d'inquiètudes : J'ai beaucoup à me plaindre de Mr Ockley[24] sur cet article—Mais tout cela demanderait des details dans les quels la poste qui me presse m'empêche d'entrer. Je suis forcé de garder de même le silence relativement à Lally que je n'ai point vû, mais à qui j'écrirai ces jours cy—Grace au ciel mon oncle ne parait pas regretter d'avoir été par la loi contre les paiens d'emigrés mis hors d'etat de remplir aucun des postes lucratifs de la Republique!! Je lui avais soupçonné un peu d'ambition revolutionnaire : mais il parait que sa tendresse encore plus forte pour moi ne lui a pas même permis un regret ¦ de ce genre. D'un autre coté, j'avais tout lieu de craindre qu'il

[24] Samuel Ockley (L. 122 n. 7), a carpenter.

ne fut en partie ruiné. Mais Je vois avec bonheur que ses enfans ont fait d'excellens mariages,[25] et qu'il mene du coté de la fortune une vie tout au moins confortable. Le seul de ses enfans qui lui reste à pourvoir est commissaire des Guerres en Hollande. C'est une place honorable et lucrative que j'ai été assez heureuz p^r lui faire obtenir peu de tems avant mon depart, précisement le jour même qu'il avait l'âge requis p^r l'occuper. Ce qui me fait surtout un extrême plaisir c'est qu'il la remplit d'une manière tout à fait distinguée; nouvelle, pour moi d'autant plus importante que c'est le seul de mes parens pour qui j'aye rien fait quand j'etais en passe de l'essayer—

Mille et mille complimens, je vous prie au Major que j'aurais bien voulu pouvoir consulter sur une foule de petits renseignemens dans ma petite maison. J'embrasse Fanny et William— VOIRE même aussi the dear Norbury que je voudrais bien revoir dut il me jetter 100 fois mon chapeau dans la *mole*.[26] Nos amis sont à Tunbridge où ils comptent passer une dixaine de jours, aprés quoi j'imagine qu'ils resteront toute l'automne à Norbury

Amen.

[*Page 1 has an interlinear text in pencil, written faintly in the hope perhaps that it might elude the Major but reach Susan's eyes*]

⟨to S⟩ the no hopes she gives of intended return—no time fixed for future expectations all lower our spirits & tho' I still depend on ⟨our⟩ Hostage—& still must look forward to some comfort-⟨ing⟩ intelligence in our next letter

[25] See genealogical table.
[26] The river Mole, which runs between Mickleham and Norbury Park

To Doctor Burney

A.L.S. (Barrett, Eg. 3690, ff. 91–2b), 29 Aug. 1797
Double sheet 4to   4 pp.   *pmks*   LEATHER / HEAD   31 AU 97
31 AU 97   green wafer
Addressed: Dr. Burney / Chelsea College, / Middlesex
Endorsed by CB: Augt 1797
Edited by FBA, p. 1, *annotated*: ⁂   (8)
Letter From notre cher Oncle Bazile & state of France in 1797
Edited also by CFBt.

Bookham—
Augst 29th—97

As I called upon my dearest Father to take part in the sorrow of my dear Mate, I hasten to call for his more chearful sympathy in the joy with which this Morning has opened—it has, indeed, dissolved him almost like grief,—he has just received a Letter from the Uncle he so venerates,[1] so loves beyond all description, —& he has consecrated the whole Day to reading & answering it—which act he is in at present, & will probably be till Midnight.

It has been directed & forwarded by the same confidential person[2] who sent the account I have already transmitted to you. It is written with great caution as to public affairs, though evidently shewing the unhappiness they cause him: but it contains an ample detail, clear, explicit & satisfactory, of their mutual connections—by which it appears that one only '*a peri*' —the term he uses for the Guilliotine.

He laments with anguish the loss of the late Chevalier,[3] though in calling upon M. d'A. with the tenderest exhortation to bear it with resignation. Nothing can be more affecting than the expression of his affection for his only surviving, & always darling Nephew, to whom he has been the most indulgent of Fathers, & the most generous of Friends. ⎮

You are all, he says, that now remain to me of a family that has been '*les delices de ma vie,—comme ton pere, tu restes seul—*' for the Father, as I have mentioned, was an only son: & M. Bazile

248. [1] See L. 247 n. 13.   [2] Felix Ferdinand (L. 245 n. 3).
[3] François Piochard d'Arblay, Sr de Blécy (1756–95).

knows not, as yet, that M. d'A. has here *un petit heritier du nom.* But we fear, by this phrase, the sister's Daughter, Mlle Girardin, is also dead.[4] He forbears to press his Nephew's return, in the present state of affairs, though he fondly says that to meet him again would be the first perfect happiness—but he is very desponding about the times, & declares he has no hopes they will mend while his infirmities will permit him to look forward to such a joy. He is by no means very old,[5] but he is very Gouty, & become so lame he cannot stir out but in a Carriage. He has lost one son in the army, whom he shall mourn, he says, his whole life; & his depression is such, from the *state of things,* that he goes no more to Paris, has dropt all his usual gay habits of mixing with the World, & has no species of satisfaction but in wrapping himself up in the bosom of his own family. He has 3 sons & one Daughter still remaining.

But as M. d'A. himself has been always *at least* as dear to him as even the most favourite amongst his Children, (notwithstanding he is a very fond Father) it is impossible for me to say the gratitude I feel that he restrains himself from soliciting his return at this precarious season. Certainly when Peace comes— if Peace will ever come— | I shall be foremost to promote a meeting so earnestly wished; for the character, & the tenderness of this Uncle excite in me a regard almost such as my Mate experiences for my beloved Father: but still, France seems now on the Eve of so tremendous a civil conflict, that all the Emigrés who have not already ventured thither, now retreat, dismayed & appalled, to wait the unknown event.

M. d'A. is truly sensible of your kind interest in his affairs, & thanks you a thousand times, & with all his Heart: we beg you will also express our gratitude to Mrs. Crewe for her most ready goodness—so characteristic in its zeal,—but he says he is so confident that whatever upon Earth can be done, or devized, to serve him, with safety, will be done, & be devized by his admirable Uncle, that he should think it wrong to take one Step, or even to make one enquiry. The Friend who has contrived this renewed intercourse assures M.d'A. that it is impossible *something* should not be redeemable.

---

[4] Marie-Anne Girardin had died *pre* 7 Jan. 1794 (L. 245 nn. 5, 8).

[5] About 62 years old (see L. 245 n. 6). D'Arblay was not to return to Joigny until December 1801 (see v, L. 461).

⌐How I thank you, dearest sir, for your Album[6]—& how extremely pretty it is, & what a picture it paints of the ingenious goodness & benevolent positiveness of dear Mrs. Crewe! How she rises upon me in every account that comes from her Hand! & her bosom! The Ferme-ornée[7] & the convent school,[8] must both be delightful, & how sweet an idea you give of Crewe Hall by the line that rings through-out it—

'Social joys set their Horses together! — — —'

We should have been most grievously disappointed that you did not come to fetch dear Sarah from our Hermitage, but for the kind word *'postpone my visit'*, & therefore we shall wait with *pleasure*, as well as patience till we can be indulged most conveniently. Sarah will⌐¹ explain how always it will be equally agreeable to us to embrace—since to see you *here* will be best, on account of the summer (as it is called,) & to see you at the new Cottage will be best, on account of our delight to procure it your benediction. ⌐Mrs. Lock means to invite you only not to her place 'till november, as a part of the Family will spend all October at Weymouth.

---

[6] This is the poem that, as CB was to explain to SBP in his letter of 26 Oct. (Barrett, Eg. 3700A, ff. 13–14b), he had written in the White Album at Crewe Hall on his visit there in August of this year. 'I found on the table in my bed-room, a folio MS. with Verses written by almost all the visitors, for more than 20 years past. Among wᶜʰ there are many by Mʳˢ Greville that are very pretty—Ch. Fox Fitzpatric—Mʳ & Mʳˢ Sheridan—the present Master of the Rolls—Mʳˢ Siddons—the late John Sᵗ John Bᵖ of Peterbro'—& many more—this book is entitled the *Album*—and on the first Page is the following Requisition—"All those who divert themselves with reading this book, are desired either to make some poetical addition, or write their names."—And as I did not chuse to set *myself* down an *Ass*, I wrote some *verses*, wᶜʰ I hope to shew you some time or other.'

The fifty-four verses (or lines) that CB composed on this occasion are extant in the copies made by his grandson CPB in a Notebook preserved in the Osborn Collection. FBA had quoted the concluding line of the second stanza:

> For the Bards who want bread,
> Would here be well fed;—
> Here's amusement for all sorts of Weather:—
> On the water,—the Bark,—
> In the house,—in the Park,—
> Social joys set their horses together.—

[7] The *'Ferme-ornée'* was a place of retirement 'fitted up with infinite fancy & good taste', to which Mrs. Crewe retreated 'when the house is crowded wᵗʰ mixt Compʸ', CB explained in his letter of 26 Oct. (op. cit.).

[8] Also reminiscent of the France that Mrs. Crewe knew in 1785–6, accounts of which are to be read in her Journals (BM Add. MSS. 37,926, ff. 19–129), was the charity school, called a 'convent' and taught by an 'abbess' (cf. L. 245 n. 13), where forty girls (presumably Protestants) were instructed in 'needle-work and reading'.

I like the account of M. de Fronteville[9] so much that I hope you will continue the intimacy so pleasantly begun. Mr. Lock likes him much too, from seeing him at the Committee for the Emigrée Ladies—&c—I have had a letter from our beloved Exile. *He too*, I always think, will never return till the Peace— I cannot attribute *retirement* in a character such as MiLord's[10] to *choice*; I always give it to the mere presence of *hard service* which he knows not how to renounce while in the wider & fuller world. I do not think this *resulting* from want of courage, but from new habits of luxury & tyranny, & idleness, & whims that make subordination & regularity & fixed economy intolerable to his spoilt humour. Therefore I expect he will re-appear when he no longer will be wanted, or be liable to being asked *Why he is not with the fleet?* &c

My kind love to Sall[11] ⟨who again⟩ I hope got safe home. I have a Letter for her just arrived from James, which I shall forward. Poor Mrs. R[ishton] is woefully hard tried—but supports her spirits & fights a good fight. I see, now ⟨facing⟩ her an up Hill route. James is [xxxxx ½ *line*] like him and as is ever & ever

dear—dearest sir, affect[y] yours
M. & F.d'A

I took the liberty to beg the first vols of the Critical Review, & Jardine[12] & Beckford,[13] by the cart & I will take great care of whatever comes but have only the 2nd. vol. of Jardine & no Beckford—M.d'A is infinitely obliged for the ⟨print⟩[¶]

---

[9] As he appeared in L. 242 n. 2, and in CB's letters of 2 and 13 Aug. 1797 (op. cit.).

[10] Molesworth Phillips.   [11] SHB.

[12] Alexander Jardine (i, L. 7 n. 16), whose *Letters from Barbary, France, Spain, Portugal* . . . (2 vols., 1788) had run to a second edition in 1790.

[13] Probably William Beckford, whose latest work was *The History of France* (i, L. 17 n. 19).

Conjointly with M. d'Arblay
To Doctor Burney

A.L.S. and A.L. (Diary MSS. vi. 5012–[15], Berg), 25 Sept. [17]97
Double sheet 4to   4 pp.   *pmks*   LEATHER / HEAD   28 SE 97
28 SE 97   black wafer
Addressed: Dʳ Burney, / Chelsea College, / Midlesex
Endorsed by CB: Septʳ 1797
Edited by FBA, p. 1 (5012), *annotated*: ⁖   (9)
French affairs—character & heavenly Disposition of M. d'Arblay. Death
of Kitty Cooke.
Edited also by CFBt *and the* Press.

Bookham,
Septʳ 25—97.

I must not vex my dearest Padre with my vexation—especially
as the ⸢time is now so rushed, & the⸣ season so much further
advanced than when we had regaled our fancies with seeing
him, that many fears for what is still more precious to me than
his sight, his health, would mix with the joy of his presence. ⸢our
house here is very damp,—& though we had planned contriv-
ances & extempores that we think would have secured him from
mischief, the very idea of the possibility would have been a
heart-panic, & therefore I must try, now, to suppose he must
have enough cold to reconcile me to this disappointment which,
I confess, however, to be wholly unexpected.

The mice, however, will joyfully run to the Mountain,though
I cannot say when. All depends upon my summons.[1] Indeed but
for that we should postpone all journeying till Christmas, or the
spring, that we might comfortably establish ourselves in our
own dwelling.

We have hopes of removing the 8ᵗʰ of October; but as we
depend upon circumstances, viz, the weather & the Painters,
we cannot be fixed to any period. The first has been constantly
against us, the latter we are not quite sure when we shall get rid
of. We long inexpressibly to enter in—⸣ ⎮

249. [1] A summons from the Queen in compliance with the request that FBA
had made in July for an audience (see L. 242 nn. 9, 10). The Royal Family had
returned from Weymouth on 18 September.

The return of Ld. M[almesbury][2] has been a terrible stroke to every fond hope of M.d'A. of embracing his venerable Uncle. Not even a line, now, must again pass between them! This last dreadful revolution shook him almost as violently as the loss of his Brother,[3]—but constant exercise & unremitting employment are again, thank Heaven, playing the part of philosophy. Indeed he has the happiest philosophy to join to them, that of always endeavouring to ballance blessings against misfortunes. Many for whom he had a personal regard are involved in this inhuman banishment, though none with whom he was particularly connected. Had the Parisians not all been disarmed in a former epoch, it is universally believed they would have risen in a Mass to defend the Legislators from this unheard of proscription.[4] Such is the report of a poor returned Emigré. But such measures had been taken, that there is little doubt but that military Government will be now finally established!! M.d'A. had been earnestly pressed to go over, & pass les vendanges at Joigny, & try what he could recover from the shipwreck of his family's fortune: but not, thank God! by his *Uncle*! that generous, parental Friend crushes every personal wish while danger hangs upon its indulgence.

M. de Narbonne has never quitted Swisserland.

It is very long since we have heard from our Susey,—I have written twice since, & grow impatient to hear again. ⌐Mrs. Lock has secured ⌐ permission through some agency of addressing all her letters for Susan to Mr. Windham, who undertakes to forward them free himself.[5] I am allowed to partake of this charming licence, by writing under Mrs. Lock's words. This is a very great comfort indeed, as the Major thinks all letters extravagance.[6]

How sorry I am for Sir Walter Farquhar![7] he loved his

---

[2] On 3 July Lord Malmesbury (L. 224 n. 5) had again been sent to France to negotiate a Peace, all hopes of which ended with the *coup d'état* of 18 Fructidor (4 Sept.). On 18 September he returned to England.

[3] By now full details of the *coup d'état* would have reached England. Royalist sympathizers were again worsted and for the *émigrés* there was no hope of a peaceful return to France.

[4] That is, the purge of the Councils and the banishment of Royalist sympathizers to Cayenne in French Guiana and the resumption of further sanctions against the *émigrés*.

[5] The letters sent by the Lockes would normally have been returned to them after SBP's death, and perhaps with them the covers franked by Windham.

[6] Cf. L. 247 n. 18.

[7] Ann Stephenson (d. 22 Sept. 1797), sister of Alexander Stephenson of Barbados

illiterate wife as well as if she had been equal to him in other things as well as in goodness. I am sure he will always lament her.⌐ Dear, kind, deserving Kitty Cooke! I was struck quite at heart with concern at her sudden & unexpected death.[8]—

I pity Mrs. R[ishton] with all my soul. She could have been so happy under your protection![9] And now *two* are unhappy— for those tyrants—who rob others wilfully of all comfort, take what they never enjoy. I question if even a vicious character is as internally wretched as an ill-natured one.

⌐Your little Alex flourishes still, in all but sleep,—he has restless, unquiet nights, & keeps very, very thin. But his appetite is restored & his strength & spirits never have failed.

You say nothing of My poem. I shall long to know if you procure Leisure for a comfortable perusal of it with Dr. Herschel,[10] & whether he joins taste for poetry to his skill in Astronomy & Music.

How peculiarly unlucky for us that we shall be forced to sell out at this low price of stock, to pay our workmen![11] They will have finished in about 2 Days & alas what hope between this & then? We have no further news from Mr. Shirley[12] except one Letter of *fair promises* stated as in comfort to what you saw M.d'A write from Chelsea—M.d'A has promised to come home in time to save the post by making me do with himself—

My kind Love to dear Salkin—
Adieu dearest sir,

your dutiful & most affectionate⌐
F. d'A. |

⌐P.S. I suppose that naughty Mr. Twining[13] is gone back, without a word or a look at us once?⌐

[xxxxx *15 lines by M. d'A relating to the exchange or return of books including* 'the last publication of Count Rumford']

(buried at St. Michael's on 16 Sept. 1774), had married in 1771 Sir Walter Farquhar (*DNB*; and i, L. 23 n. 82). Her obituary (*GM* lxvii. 806) praised her 'gentle unassuming character . . . liberality of sentiment . . . good-natured candour . . . kindness of heart . . . active charity . . . sweetness of disposition'.
   [8] Cf. L. 247 n. 17.
   [9] Further evidence of Rishton's unwillingness to relinquish his marital claims (L. 222 n. 10; iv, L. 269).
   [10] About this time CB visited William Herschel at Slough, to whom he read Books vii and viii of his poem on Astronomy (Lonsdale, pp. 390–1).
   [11] For the disadvantageous sale of stocks, see L. 250 and n. 1.
   [12] See Ll. 193 n. 7, 234 n. 2.
   [13] The Revd. Thomas Twining (L. 133 n. 7) had set out from Colchester on

To Doctor Burney

A.L. (Diary MSS. vi. [5003a–b], Berg), *n.d.*
Originally a double sheet 4to, of which FBA later discarded the second leaf   2 pp.   The first leaf CFBt trimmed at the top and pasted to the single sheet p. 6 [5003] of A.L.S. (Diary MSS. vi. 4998–[5003], Berg) FBA to CB, 10 Aug. 1797
Edited by FBA, p. 1 [5003a], *postdated in error* 25 Sept[r]—97 *and trimmed leaving only part of the annotation*: (10)   out f⟨   ⟩ / Cottage / Wes⟨t⟩ / stea / self / of M. / d'A

How very kind is this, most dear dear sir! & how I lament not instantly to accept what I know my beloved Father would not offer but with his whole kind Heart!—but even while you were writing to save us, the deed was doing!—one of those engaged about our little habitation had petitioned to be paid on Mic[s] Day; the stocks seem little likely to rise, alas, at present,—& therefore yesterday Morning, at 6 o'clock, My indefatgable Builder set off on foot, in search of what stage he could find at Leatherhead, & thence strait to the City, where he arrived at about 1 o'clock, did his business with a broker's help,—sold out, to avoid going again till his final sum total, 200,[1] — ! — ! — & at 3 found a stage again, which he mounted *Airily*, & was set down at Leatherhead by 7, & was with his Hermitess by Eight. In this transaction, I know you will repine for us to hear we lose a clear £40! in the difference from the short time since that

21 June in a chaise drawn by his old horse Jolly, for a tour of ten weeks, the details of which, related in his letters to his brother Richard (BM Add. MSS. 39,934), R. S. Walker has kindly supplied to the editors. Travelling by way of Isleworth, Worcester, and Shrewsbury, Mr. Twining paid a visit of about a month to friends in Llanfwrog, Denbighshire. Returning by way of Bitteswell, Leicestershire, and crossing by Kettering and Cambridge, he reached Colchester on 1 Sept. Though on his setting out he may have visited London from his brother's house in Isleworth, he would have missed it on his return.

250. [1] Somewhere in the obliterated sections of CB's letter of *pmk* 28 SE 97 (Berg) there is doubtless an offer to pay the workmen and so save the d'Arblays the necessity of selling stocks at so disadvantageous a time. The 5 per cents that they had presumably bought in July 1796 at $91\frac{3}{4}$–$90\frac{7}{8}$ (L. 193 n. 3) had fallen steadily in value. On 28 Sept. (see *The Times*, 29 Sept.) 5 per cents were selling between $71\frac{1}{2}$–70 and on an investment of £200 the loss would have been, as FBA says, £40. Had the d'Arblays been able to hold on to their stocks for another year, their loss would not have been so great. During 1798 the 5 per cents fluctuated, rising as high as $84\frac{1}{2}$ in November (*AR* xl (1798), 'Appendix to the Chronicle', 199).

we bought in!—⌐Yet we could not part with less prudently, since there is so little chance of better prospects than even this, & 10 days, when we have heavy claims that must be ⟨h⟩onoured.⌐ I know you will not be *surprised*, as much as *concerned* that our new habitation will very considerably indeed exceed our first intentions & expectations. I suppose it has ever been so, & so ever must be! for we sought as well as determined to keep within bounds; & M.d'A. still thinks he has done it: however, I am more aware of *our tricks upon travellers* than to enter into the same delusion.—

The pleasure, however, he has taken in this edifice is my first joy, for it has constantly shewn me his *Heart* has invariably held to those first feelings which, before our union, determined him upon settling in England.—O if you knew how he has been assailed,—by temptations of every sort that either ambition, or interest, or friendship could dictate to change his plan!—& how his Heart sometimes yearns towards those he yet can love in his native Soil, while his firmness still remains unshaken, nay, not even one moment wavering or hesitating,—you would not wonder I make light of even extravagance in a point that shews him thus fixed to make *THIS OBJECT* a part of whole system of future life.—

What a charming account this of the admirable Herschal.[2]

[2] This account left unobliterated in CB's letter (above) was printed in *DL* v. 344–7.

APPENDIX A

REVIEWS OF *EDWY AND ELGIVA*

PRESERVED in the Burney Collection of Newspapers (BM 885) are about twenty newspapers of 22 and 23 March 1796, apparently gathered in by Charles Burney, Jr. of Greenwich for their reviews of Madame d'Arblay's play *Edwy and Elgiva*, which was produced at Drury Lane on Saturday night 21 March. The Sunday papers of 22 March, *Ayre's Sunday London Gazette*, the *London Recorder, or Sunday Gazette*, the *Observer*, the *Review*, and the *Sunday Reformer, and Universal Register* carried reviews of the play; and on Monday 23 March reviews appeared in *The Times*, *Morning Advertiser*, *Morning Chronicle*, *Morning Herald*, *Morning Post and Fashionable World*, *Telegraph*, *Public Ledger*, *True Briton*, *Evening Mail*, *The Oracle*, *Public Advertiser*, and the *Gazetteer, and New Daily Advertiser*. Missing from the Collection are the *Sun* and the *Star*, which Madame d'Arblay requested her brother James to pick up in London, and the *London Chronicle* (21–4 March). The same review occasionally appeared in more than one paper. Pencilled marks indicate how thoroughly the columns were perused and the nauseous draughts apparently swallowed, with no comment at least from the ebullient Charles, CB remarking that it was but 'one dose of bitter, the more'.

Madame d'Arblay had hoped all along to preserve her anonymity, but apart from the first two Sunday papers above, there is open mention as a matter of course to 'Miss Burney'. 'Expectation has been on tip-toe for a considerable time past, excited by the promised Tragedy . . . from the pen of the *ci-devant* Miss Burney, so well known as the author of two of the most natural, and most interesting Novels in the English language, viz. *Evelina* and *Cecilia*.' And it was this 'expectation' that had crowded the house.

The reviewers had first to recover from their astonishment that the writer of *Evelina* should have risked an 'established reputation' without some proofs of poetical or dramatic talent and secondly from their 'sorrow' that she should have abandoned a 'natural' and 'elegant' style for the 'clouds of words', the 'Declamation, tameness, and torpidity' not to say 'nauseus bombast' of *Edwy*. After some complaint of the neglect of the actors who failed to learn their lines, the more thoughtful and charitable of the reviewers turned to the mirthful reception of the tragedy, regretting that some friend of the author should not have expunged passages, which, lending themselves to low and vulgar associations, caused tittering or bursts of laughter. Such was the phrase ' "Bring in the Bishop!" ' which, though uttered by Edwy (Kemble) 'in a voice of tragic command', suggested quite '*another* Bishop, and hot wine and roasted oranges delighted the "mind's eye" of many a jolly son of Bacchus present'. Dunstan, when in the council room, raised a laugh by some ejaculation about the roof falling. So also did Sigibert, who, rushing on the stage 'open mouthed, and out of breath', on being questioned by the King as to what brought him, answered, ' "Nothing!" ' And finally laughter 'inconceivable' rose at the 'dying words of Mrs Siddons' herself when at a solemn juncture in one of the closing scenes Elgiva was brought in mortally wounded, and a countryman, asked if there was no place of shelter near, effectively punctured the solemnity of death by his reply, ' "Yes, and close by, on t'other side of the hedge" '.

'The language of the Play can boast nothing of Poetry, and is often inelegantly familiar, or ridiculously absurd', the reviewers complained, and it was apparently the sudden juxtaposition of the two styles that so often brought the house down. The blemishes were removable, it was thought (and are so removed in the revised manuscripts of the play); but notwithstanding the mirth that the piece afforded, it was found that an ungrateful majority of voices would not permit of its repetition. There was applause, therefore, when Mr. Kemble came forth to say that ' "the piece is withdrawn for alterations" '—an applause that would not have been less had he stopped at the first four words, "the piece is withdrawn".

APPENDIX B

REVIEWS OF *CAMILLA*

In a letter (Bodleian) of 3 August 1796 CB had worriedly recounted to CB Jr. how on a business call at Paternoster-row, 'when Camilla was mentioned, R[obinson] was frank enough to tell me, that "there was but one opinion about it—Mme d'Arblay was determined to fill 5 Volumes—& had done it in such a manner as w^d do her no credit— He had seen the critical reviewers that morning, & they did not like it—They had said that the book w^d be praised in the M[onthly] Review by Dr Charles B.—& that's all the praise it w^d get".' CB, by his own testimony, then bounced a little, asserting that if the reviewers abused it they would disgrace themselves, but fearing Godwin, Chalmers, and others, he went on to propose to son Charles that he (Charles) review the novel for the *Monthly Review*. 'The work if it has fair play must do credit, not only to Fanny, but to us all—I never felt so zealous for the defence of any of her writings; but I see nothing I can do in the present Case, except to put you, James, & T. Payne on your guard.— . . . Griff[iths] . . . whose family is reading & full of the book, is perfectly well disposed— . . . If you give him a hint before it is put into other hands, [he] will, I dare say gladly accept your offer.' And since, whether or not CB Jr. should review the novel, the *Critical Review* will give him the credit for it, 'it w^d be a worthy action that you will long think of with pleasure, to preserve and augment the fame of such a Sister & such a work. . . . *I* w^d not recommend to you Such a task, if not stimulated by the peculiar intrinsic merit of the work.'

CB Jr. and/or Griffiths, perhaps, thought better of the suggestion and gave the review to William Enfield (1741–97), though, according to B. C. Nangle, *Monthly Review, Second Series* 1790–1815: *Indexes of Contributors and Articles* (Oxford, 1955), p. 99, Griffiths contributed the closing paragraphs of the review.

As events were to prove the *Critical Review* treated *Camilla* more leniently than did the *Monthly* (see L. 211 n. 1).